GUIDE TO GREATER LONDON
Hotels, pubs and restaurants

GUIDE TO
GREATER LONDON

Hotels, pubs and restaurants

Consumers' Association of Great Britain

Consumers Union
Mount Vernon, New York

GUIDE TO GREATER LONDON: Hotels, Pubs and Restaurants is a Consumer Reports Book published by Consumers Union, the nonprofit organization that publishes *Consumer Reports*, the monthly magazine of test reports, product Ratings, and buying guidance. Established in 1936, Consumers Union is chartered under the Not-For-Profit Corporation Law of the State of New York.

The purposes of Consumers Union, as stated in its charter, are to provide consumers with information and counsel on consumer goods and services, to give information on all matters relating to the expenditure of the family income, and to initiate and to cooperate with individual and group efforts seeking to create and maintain decent living standards.

Consumers Union derives its income solely from the sale of *Consumer Reports* and other publications. In addition, expenses of occasional public service efforts may be met, in part, by nonrestrictive, noncommercial contributions, grants, and fees. Consumers Union accepts no advertising or product samples and is not beholden in any way to any commercial interest. Its Ratings and reports are solely for the use of the readers of its publications. Neither the Ratings nor the reports nor any Consumers Union publications, including this book, may be used in advertising or for any commercial purpose. Consumers Union will take all steps open to it to prevent such uses of its material, its name, or the name of *Consumer Reports*.

Copyright © 1987 Consumers Union of the United States, Inc.
          Mount Vernon, New York 10553
          and Consumers' Association Ltd, London, United Kingdom

Material taken from *The Good Hotel Guide* copyright © 1986 Hilary Rubinstein Books Limited (published in the United States as *Europe's Wonderful Little Hotels and Inns* by St Martin's Press, Inc., New York)

Material taken from *The Good Pub Guide* copyright © 1986 Alisdair Aird and Consumers' Association Ltd, London

Maps copyright © 1987 Wm. Collins Sons & Co Ltd, Glasgow, United Kingdom

All rights reserved, including the right of reproduction in whole or in part in any form.

Library of Congress Cataloging-In-Publication Data

Guide to Greater London.

   Includes index.
   1. Hotels, taverns, etc.—England—London Region—
Directories. 2. Restaurants, lunch rooms, etc.—England
—London Region—Directories. I. Consumers' Association
(Great Britain)
TX910.G7G84 1987   647'.9442101   87-591
ISBN 0-89043-083-7

First printing, April 1987

Text designed by Fox + Partners, Bath, England
Typeset in the United Kingdom by
Rowland Phototypesetting Ltd, Bury St Edmunds,
Suffolk, England
Manufactured in the United States of America

Contents

Introduction	7
How to use this Guide	10
London	13
Trips out of London:	167
Brighton, Cambridge, Canterbury, Oxford, Windsor and Eton	
General Section	213
Licensing information	215
Real ale	216
Pub games	217
Glossary	218
Gazetteer of places in London	220
Maps	223
Report forms	234

Introduction

The *Guide to Greater London* and its companion volume *Guide to Scotland and the Lake District* are compilations extracted mainly from four of the annual guidebooks published by Consumers' Association in London, also publishers of *Which?* magazine. The oldest of the four, *The Good Food Guide*, was first fallen on by eager British palates recovering from a dozen years of food rationing during and after World War II. *The Good Hotel Guide*, now ten years old, began as another crusade against mediocrity at a time when more and more people were travelling at home and abroad and starting to rebel at the shoddy standards they found to exist on a widespread scale.

The Good Pub Guide did not appear until 1983 but it too made a timely entrance. At that time, many British pubs were having to choose which way to go: either adhere to the traditional pub virtues of decent beer, food, comfortable surroundings and a welcoming atmosphere, or be tastelessly modernised, usually by a fairly cynical big brewery chain caring more about profits than quality. The younger *Budget Good Food Guide* appealed to the growing numbers of people who wanted to eat out more often but who didn't have the wherewithal to indulge in expensive meals with any frequency. A few entries, mainly in London, have been borrowed from a fifth guide published by Consumers' Association: *Which? Wine Guide* concentrates on British wine merchants and their products but also contains a section on the best wine bars in Britain.

The lifeline of all the *Guides* is an extensive network of reporters, usually ordinary members of the public who commit to paper their impressions of a meal eaten or a hotel stayed at, and send their report to the appropriate Editor. By sifting and assessing the many thousands of reports received, each Editor draws up a shortlist of places to include and sends an anonymous inspector to eat or stay at the establishment. If the go-ahead is given by the inspector, a questionnaire is sent to the proprietor to fill in, so that basic information – opening hours, credit cards accepted, etc. – is accurately conveyed in each *Guide*. No cash changes hands at any point; there is no advertising; no one is rewarded for writing to us; establishments do not pay for their entries; the Editors and their staff accept no free hospitality.

For those who aren't familiar with these books, the following is each Editor's comments on the driving forces behind their publication, and what the reader can expect to glean from them.

INTRODUCTION

The Good Food Guide (Editor: Drew Smith)

'The restaurants listed in the *Guide* provide a shop window for the foods being cultivated in this country, the way they are handled, and the way they are being cooked. Some of the restaurants are expensive and luxurious, others more humble, the meals less ambitious. All serve good food. All offer value for money in their own ways; there is no other context in which to make judgements. A restaurant in a castle does not necessarily rate higher than one in a crofter's cottage, nor is a restaurant considered better if it has more waiters per table than another. Similarly, a restaurant serving lobster and caviare is not entitled automatically to a higher grading than somewhere that serves herring and boiled potatoes. The *Guide* is complete in the sense that we have tried to give coverage to most areas and have covered different cuisines. We have deliberately tried to include as broad a range of cooking as possible. In the end, good food is about variety and choice.

'While food in Britain has improved dramatically in some areas in the last ten years, this still remains a book of exceptions. But there is a real gleam of hope. Our national cooking has reasserted itself. A new mood is evident. For the first time since the end of rationing, British cooks are producing British dishes that bear comparison to the major cuisines. The new style of cooking has an identity of its own. It partakes of regionality and the menu tends to follow the market from day to day, according to the seasonal availability of supplies and the quality of the produce. There is a tendency to revive the heart of British cooking in the relishes – jams, jellies, chutneys, stuffings, spices – to lend vivid contrasts. Vegetables are used abundantly, puddings have come back into their own, and the traditional cheeseboard now supports a new generation of farmhouse cheesemakers.

'We do not claim to have invented this modern British cooking, only to be recording it. It is what is sometimes called market cookery and has a different expression in different countries – most obviously California cuisine in America – but that should not detract from the fact that here in Britain it has its own proud colours.'

The Budget Good Food Guide (Editor: Drew Smith)

'The places listed in this *Guide* offer an enormous variety of foods and styles: there are cafés and tea shops, pubs and pizza houses, Chinese restaurants, fish and chip shops, and country house hotels. But they all have one thing in common: they are inexpensive.

'The people who run them may not be saints, but they don't play tricks or deceive their customers. Most of them will have contact with the best local suppliers – the butchers, the bakers, the chutney makers – but will also make a good deal in their own kitchens. They keep prices low by not overstretching themselves, by ensuring that there are not too many cooks to spoil the broth, by working long hours, and by settling for clean, simple, modest surroundings. Simplicity, value for money, fresh food, and that mysterious ingredient – atmosphere – are the key qualities that distinguish the eating places in this book.'

The Good Pub Guide (Editor: Alistair Aird)

'To be included in the *Guide*, a pub must have some special quality that would make non-locals enjoy visiting it. What often marks it out for special attention is good value food (and that might mean anything from a well-made sandwich, with good fresh ingredients at a low price, to imaginative cooking outclassing most restaurants in the area). Maybe the drinks are out of the ordinary (pubs with several hundred whiskies, with remarkable wine lists, with home-made country wines or good beer or cider made on the premises, with a wide range of well-kept real ales or bottled beers from all over the world). Perhaps there's a special appeal about it as a place to stay, with good bedrooms

INTRODUCTION

and obliging service. Maybe it's the building itself (from centuries-old parts of monasteries to extravagant Victorian gin-palaces), or its surroundings (lovely countryside, attractive waterside, an extensive well-kept garden), or what's in it (charming furnishings, extraordinary collections of bric-a-brac).

'Above all, though, what makes a good pub is its atmosphere – you should be able to feel at home there, and feel not just that *you're* glad you've come but that *they're* glad you've come. It follows from this that a great many ordinary local pubs, perfectly good in their own right, don't earn a place in the book. What makes them attractive to their regular customers (an almost clubby chumminess) may even make non-locals feel rather out of place.

'Another important point is that there's not necessarily any link between charm and luxury. A basic unspoilt tavern in a woodland village, with hard seats and a flagstone floor, may be worth travelling miles to find, while a de luxe pub-restaurant may not be worth crossing the street for. Landlords can't buy the *Good Pub* accolade by spending thousands on thickly padded banquettes, soft music, and luxuriously shrimpy sauces for their steaks – they can only win it by having a genuinely personal concern for both their customers and their pub.'

The Good Hotel Guide (Editor: Hilary Rubinstein)

'If there is a single reason for publishing this *Guide*, it is in the hope that it can help the committed individual hotelier to survive and flourish against the formidable opposition of the big battalions, with all their resources and economies of scale which they are able to deploy. We loathe the safe, boring, homogenised hotel that insulates its guests from their environment. We treasure the personal and idiosyncratic establishment that is waging a fight against entropy.

'Individualism – individual character and a personal concern for the welfare of guests – continues to be central to the *Guide*'s process of selection. And as so many departments of our lives become increasingly standardised and packaged, the pleasure to be had from hotels that don't altogether conform to the conventional norms becomes proportionately greater. It is no accident that almost all the hotels in this book are run by their owners. Bad hotels can be personally bad or impersonally bad. Good hotels can never be faceless.'

All the *Guides* have always relied on reports sent by members of the public and will continue to do so, in particular valuing the comments of overseas visitors, who are often better equipped to give an impartial commentary. If you would like to contribute to the venture, which will in turn benefit any future editions of this compilation, please send your reports to Dept. SD, Association for Consumer Research, 14 Buckingham Street, London, WC2N 6DS, United Kingdom. All letters will be acknowledged.

How to use this Guide

FINDING YOUR WAY ROUND

All the entries for restaurants, pubs and hotels are arranged alphabetically within areas of London which are listed on page 13. If you want to stay in Knightsbridge, for instance, the list will tell you that the Knightsbridge section begins on page 90. The same goes for finding good eating places not too far from your hotel. If you want to explore further afield, turn to the map section at the end of the book. The columns down the sides of the maps will direct you to the page where each entry is to be found.

SYMBOLS

At the head of each entry appear symbols to denote restaurant: ✗, hotel: 🏨, pub: 🍺, wine bar: 🍷, and tea shop: ☕. They are listed in order of importance at each place: for example ✗ 🏨 ☕ means that the restaurant is the main reason for a visit, though you may well strike lucky with accommodations too, especially if the entry contains a description of the hotel facilities; and tea (available to non-residents) is likely to be good, too, because the kitchen is competent on other fronts. 🍺 ✗ 🏨 is another frequent combination, particularly out of London. The ✗ may be an unknown quantity and we often merely state that a separate restaurant exists. Usually you will eat better and more cheaply in the bar. Somewhere with the ☕ symbol only is likely to be a tea shop, a pleasant café concentrating on tea and coffee, cakes and light snacks from mid-morning until 5 o'clock or so in the afternoon. Tea shops are not usually licensed to sell alcohol.

MEAL PRICES

The *Guides* in their British covers give quite detailed prices but we thought that it would be more helpful here to give broad price ranges. So: £ = meal for about £5 per head; ££ = meal for about £12; £££ = meal for about £20; ££££ = meal for £30 or more (per head). Pubs will almost invariably sport the single pound sign, and many of the 'Budget' places, too – cafés, tea shops, wine bars. Where a range of prices is given, eg £–£££, this means that some meals available at the place, say a snack lunch or afternoon tea, will cost about £5, although you should expect to part with over £20 for a full dinner with wine. Reading the entry should make this clear. Where a restaurant supplies a set meal (with a price quoted in the text) you will need to add on several pounds to cover wine and possibly service (see below). Value Added Tax at 15 per cent is already included in quoted prices.

ACCOMMODATIONS PRICES

The £ symbol at the top of an entry refers only to meal prices. The cost of accommodations is given below the entry. The price quoted is for one person for bed and full breakfast. Where there are two prices, the first is for one person sharing a double room, the second (higher) price is for one person in a single

HOW TO USE THIS GUIDE

room, with a bathroom if applicable. We always state whether rooms with a private bathroom are available if we have that information. When booking accommodations, make clear your requirements for such facilities (and if you prefer a bath [tub] or shower), and differentiate between a double room (with one double bed) and a twin-bedded room. Double beds are usually smaller than Americans and Canadians are used to (4 foot 6 inches or 5 foot wide). Note: please don't rely on the prices given – you should always check when booking. If you are planning to stay for two or more nights it would be worth asking if reduced rates are offered, particularly if you are travelling off-season or mid-week. 'D, B&B' is the cost of the evening meal, bed and breakfast.

PUBS

British licensing laws are contrary and confusing – see page 215 for an explanation of **pub opening and closing hours**. **Pub games**, found in country pubs more often than in city ones, are of interest, particularly to overseas visitors. A description of many of the games mentioned in entries is to be found on page 217. The words **real ale** occur frequently in these pages – see page 216 for more information on how real ale is made and served. Other drinks worth investigating are **whiskies** in Scotland, or **bottled beers** if the pub happens to have a fine collection, or **cider** (mainly in the west and south-west of England). Wine is increasingly popular as a pub drink but is still usually not worth the asking. In pub entries we try to give an idea of the availability of food, which may not be over the whole period that the pub is open, especially later on in the evening. **Children** under 14 are usually allowed into at least some part of most pubs listed in this *Guide*, but not into wine bars. 'Children welcome' means that the landlord is happy for children to enter any part of his pub. Under-18s must be accompanied by an adult. No children under 16 may drink alcohol; the only alcohol permitted to 16-to-18-year-olds is cider.

LOCATIONS, RESERVATIONS, CREDIT CARDS AND TIPPING

Each entry gives the address of the establishment and some help with locating the place if it is remote or otherwise difficult to find. **Telephone numbers** are supplied for places where you need to make table or room reservations. **Credit cards** ('cards') accepted are listed if the place is the sort where it would be appropriate to pay for a meal in this way; you are unlikely to be able to pay for a pub snack or other meal under about £5 by credit card. We also give an indication of any **service charge** of which we're aware. If the menu or bill clearly states that service is 10 or 12½ per cent, you are obliged to pay it unless you found the service exceptionally wanting. If, on the other hand, the menu or bill states 'Service not included' or 'Service optional', only the niceties of convention oblige you to pay a similar sum. You would not need to add on an amount for service if you had queued up at a counter, of course.

HOW TO USE THIS GUIDE

OTHER DETAILS

Entries cover details about the availability of **vegetarian dishes,** how welcome **children** are, perhaps with age or time limits, whether **music** is played (hated by some, liked or not minded by others), and any **smoking restrictions** or **dress requirements.** We supply information about **wheelchair access** only when we are sure about it, which tends to be in restaurants and hotels. Many pubs may also be accessible to wheelchairs. The entrance to the establishment should be free of steps and at least 33 inches wide, and the passages at least 4 feet across.

GLOSSARY

Many of the dishes mentioned in the entries, from trotters and black pudding to Scotch eggs and bubble and squeak, are explained in the Glossary on page 218.

LONDON
DISTRICT BY DISTRICT

Barnes 15
Battersea and Clapham 16
Bayswater 20
Belgravia 21
Bloomsbury 26
Camden 27
Chelsea 29
Chiswick 34
The City 35
Covent Garden 46
Dulwich 54
Earl's Court 56
East End 58
Euston 61
Fulham 62
Greenwich 67
Hammersmith and Shepherd's Bush 68
Hampstead and Highgate 70
Holborn 78
Islington 80

Kensington 84
Kilburn and Maida Vale 88
Knightsbridge 90
Lambeth 96
Marble Arch 97
Marylebone 99
Mayfair 104
North Kensington 117
Pimlico 120
Richmond 121
St James's 124
St John's Wood 128
Soho 130
South Bank 149
South Kensington 151
Southwark 156
Tottenham Court Road 158
Wandsworth 162
Westminster 164
Wimbledon 165

BARNES

BARNES

Barnaby's Map 1 ✶

39B High Street, SW13 *Telephone* 01-878 4750   £££

After six years the Harrys are well set up in this little bistro. The menu's inclination is towards the more classical French dishes from different regions – the pea soup from St Germain; trout marseillaise with a wine, cream and saffron sauce; choucroute strasbourgeoise; omelette normande. The menu offers plenty of choice, with around ten dishes at each course. Fish, for instance monk with a sauce of butter and shallots, has been reliably good. House wine is £5.99. Children are welcome and there is access for wheelchairs.

Open Mon to Sat, exc Mon L and Sat L **Closed** Christmas and Easter, 3 weeks Sept **Meals** 12.30 to 1.30, 7 to 10.15 **Cards** Access, Amex, Diners, Visa **Service** Inc **BR station** Barnes Bridge

Bulls Head Map 1 🍺

373 Lonsdale Road, SW13 *Telephone* 01-876 5241   £

This well-run and comfortable riverside pub is very popular for the top-class modern jazz groups every evening, and weekend lunchtime big band sessions (practice on Saturday, concert on Sunday). Though admission to the well-equipped music room is £2 to £3, the sound is perfectly clear – if not authentically loud – in the adjoining lounge bar. This is well-carpeted and comfortably furnished with solid seats upholstered in a sort of candlewick material. Alcoves open off the main area around the efficient island servery, which has well-kept Youngs Bitter and Special on handpump, reasonably priced for London. Bar lunches include soup with crusty bread, sandwiches, filled French bread, hot roast meat sandwiches, a pasta dish of the day, home-baked pies, and at lunchtime a carvery of home-roasted joints; darts, fruit machine and space game in the public bar. Across the road, you can sit on the flood wall by the Thames. Nearby parking may be difficult.

Open 11 to 3, 5.30 to 11 **BR station** Barnes Bridge

Sonny's Map 1 ✶
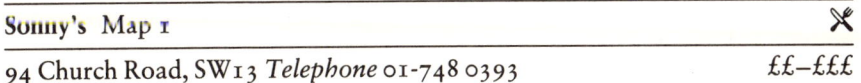

94 Church Road, SW13 *Telephone* 01-748 0393   ££–£££

The frontage is out of the office furniture suppliers school of design – grey micro-blinds and battleship grey paintwork in a row of well-established antique shops. Inside is all designer decor: white and black and the same grey, the only warmth coming from the wall lights. The menu has been tailored, too – by Sue Miles, who has been the Svengali behind the opening of a series of restaurants over the last few years. The formula is fresh ingredients, with starters and sweets that can mostly be pre-prepared, leaving the kitchen time to concentrate on the main dishes. Although in many ways the menu shows the inclinations of modern British cooking, its real loyalty is to be reassuringly cosmopolitan. Merguez

LONDON

sausages are cleverly served with tabouleh, for instance. The pissaladière is excellent. Main courses are done simply – navarin of lamb, brill, and sea-bass left to glory in a simple sauce of butter and chervil. The kitchen is confident enough not to offer cream with its exemplary summer pudding. Lunch is a set meal (£7.95). The wine list is short and sweet, mixing good European choices with some sensational Australian. House claret is £6.50. Children are welcome. There's music and air-conditioning, and access for wheelchairs.

Open All week **Meals** 12.30 to 2.30 (3 Sun), 7.30 to 11 **Cards** Access, Visa **BR station** Barnes Bridge

BATTERSEA AND CLAPHAM

L'Arlequin Map 1

123 Queenstown Road, SW8 *Telephone* 01-622 0555   £££–££££

This part of London is now very much on the up, but it is doubtful even so whether the neighbours can afford to eat here very often. The entrance is unremarkable. A tiny vestibule camouflages the restaurant from what was, at least when the place opened, a rough area. Mme Delteil sits in a small, boxed-in pulpit overseeing the bevy of young French waiters, but helps out as and when necessary. Dishes come out of the tiny kitchen on trays, are put on a trestle stand, then finally brought to the table. The menu has, sensibly, been shortened and raises expectations (vegetarians need have no worries, though). The style is modern French with a few imports. Some of the dishes are first-class, for instance pigeon, carved and arranged around the plate on a sticky, brown stock reduction subtly flavoured with anise. Fish usually features on the list of daily specials: fennel ravioli with langoustine or scallops; skate wing with tomato sauce; fricassée of monk-fish with fresh noodles. The marquise au chocolat is superb. Lunch is a set meal at £12.50, dinner a more expensive *carte*, with a minimum charge of £22. The short wine list has some expensive clarets and Burgundies and a few oddities, such as a Vendange Tardive 1964 at £26, but mercifully both the Muscadet and the Vacqueyras – virtually the only bottles under £10 – are good partners for the food. They expect men to wear a jacket and tie. Access for wheelchairs.

Open Mon to Sat, exc Mon L and Sat L **Closed** 1 week in winter, 3 weeks Aug **Meals** 12.30 to 2, 7.30 to 11 **Cards** Access, Diners, Visa **Service** Inc **BR station** Battersea Park/Queenstown Road

La Bouffe Map 1

13 Battersea Rise, SW11 *Telephone* 01-228 3384   £

Small bistro in a street of shops and restaurants. The tables are close together and covered with white paper cloths. In the evening the excellent practice continues of having just three fixed-price menus (the cheapest around £7, most expensive £13, both excluding service and drinks). The food is fresh and cooked to order French country-style: tongue and tomato salad, rabbit with mustard sauce, strawberry soufflé. Lunch offers a short, daily changing à la carte, plus a set meal for £5.

Open 12.30 to 2.30, 7.30 to 11 **Closed** Sat L; Sun **BR station** Clapham Junction

Butters Map 1

54–56 Clapham High Street, SW4 *Telephone* 01-720 0425   £

Extraordinary Guyanese restaurant – the only one in England. Although basically informal, a meal here has more of a sense of occasion than at most ethnic high-street restaurants. Regular customers seem to dress up more and there is often live music at weekends – jazz, Brazilian or a steel band. The menu shows a strange mix of influences: prawn cocktail, egg mimosa, tomato soup, coq au vin and steaks are all there, but so are Caribbean Indian dishes such as pepperpot, and Chinese Guyanese dishes such as the richly aromatic bora pork. Accompaniments range from cassava and yellow plantain to cook-up rice and green banana. Licensed.

Open 6pm to midnight **Closed** Sun and Mon **Underground** Clapham Common

Chez Nico Map 1

129 Queenstown Road, SW8 *Telephone* 01-720 6960   £££–££££

For several years one of the most innovative chefs in the country, Nico Ladenis, held sway here before moving out of town, leaving his pupil, Philip Britten, in charge. Britten is a fine chef in his own right, but the prices charged here invite comparisons with the best kitchens in London. Here the money is spent on caviare garnishes, foie gras, cheese at '£4.85 for one', and a plethora of young waitresses dressed in white blouses, black skirts and stockings with short hair-do's who swarm. You are hardly on the seat before you have a roll and butter, the menu, the offer of a drink, the drink, a plate of fishy terrine and salad and the order taken. The whole thing is a little manic. With all this stacked against him, not least living in the Ladenis shadow, Britten has fought back in the best way possible – on the plate. The sorcerer's apprentice is quite capable of matching his master in some respects. His terrines, such as sole or sweetbreads with wild mushrooms, or else duck mousseline with a butter sauce flavoured with ceps, are excellent. The pastry work is accomplished and prevalent on a menu that offers a surprisingly large choice. A tiny tartlet is used to hold a cream sauce of chives as a garnish to turbot with a langoustine sauce. As if to re-affirm the Francophile nature of the proceedings, vegetables have been a weak point, but the sweets combine contrasting textures with intense flavours, as with the armagnac parfait or the tarte au citron. Lunch is a set meal (£14.50), dinner a *carte* that will work out easily double that. The wine list runs to fifty virtually exclusively French bottles, strong on clarets and also, helpfully, in half-bottles. The house Sauvignon at £9 sets the tone. Children are said to be welcome. Access for wheelchairs.

Open Mon to Sat, exc Mon L and Sat L **Meals** 12 to 2, 7.30 to 10.45 **Cards** None accepted **Service** Inc **BR station** Battersea Park/Queenstown Road

LONDON

Just Williams Map 1

6 Battersea Rise, SW11 *Telephone* 01-228 9980   £–££

One of Battersea's more endearing spots, with a patio for summer evenings, Just Williams has an impressive, thoughtfully compiled wine list. As well as basic house red and white, there are five others at £4.95/95p, including Côtes du Rhône Villages 1983 and Muscadet sur Lie 1984, Rémy Pannier. Further afield, and still excellent value for money, are Bulgarian Sakar Mountain Cabernet 1978 (£5.65), Portuguese Camarate 1980 da Fonseca (£5.25) and a Portuguese Branco 1983 João Pires (a dry Muscat, £5). Add to those a dozen impressive clarets and the same number of Burgundies (many in useful half-bottles), and you will understand the temptations. Try the François Paquet trio of Beaujolais (Morgon, Les Rigottes 1983, £7.50) or Ch de Lascombes Rosé 1982 (£6.95). Good bistro cooking – more adventurous in the adjacent restaurant, Pollyanna's (see opposite).

Open Mon to Sat 12 to 3, 5.30 to 11 (Sat 6.30 to 11), Sun 7 to 10.30 **Closed** Sun L, Chr, Easter Day **Cards** Access, Amex, Visa **BR station** Clapham Junction

Leek's Fish Bar Map 1

23 Lavender Hill, SW11 *Telephone* 01-228 9460   £

Up-market fish and chip bistro and take-away. Not quite in the Seashell league (see under Marylebone) but a welcome addition to the South London cheap-eating scene. Clever frying and good ingredients make the standard range of cod, haddock and so on, worth a couple of miles' drive. Chips are good but the mushy peas too highly seasoned with lemon juice. Good home-made fish soup, fishcakes and dishes of the day such as steamed brill and trout with ginger butter and new potatoes. The microwave is much in evidence but seems not to harm the traditional British puddings, such as spotted dick.

Open 11.30 to 2.30, 5 to 10.30 **Closed** Sun; 1 week at Christmas **BR station** Clapham Junction

Olde Windmill Map 1

Clapham Common South Side, SW4 *Telephone* 01-673 4578   £

The front room in this large Victorian inn, with its fancy plaster ceiling, is dominated by the substantial and heavily manned bar counter – even so, it can be difficult to reach on fine evenings, as it then seems to serve not just the pub but half the Common too. The spacious and domed main room has clusters of

---

Taxi tips: London taxi drivers are famous for their wide knowledge of their city and for their courtesy. But note that they can refuse to take you to your destination if it is after midnight, your destination is more than seven miles from the centre of London, you have more luggage than they deem necessary, or if you are not in a fit state to travel. If you wish, you can ask your hotel to ring one up for you.

orange leatherette seats, sofas and small armchairs around elegant black tables, and big prints of Dutch windmill pictures on the flowery black and brown wallpaper. Meals and snacks (not on Sundays) include ploughman's, macaroni cheese, cottage pie, chilli con carne or ham salad, clam fries, curry and rice and lunchtime grills from the efficient food counter in this inner room; well-kept Youngs Bitter, Special and John's London Lager on handpump, quite cheap; fruit machines. There are picnic tables in courtyards at each end, one with a colonnaded end shelter and tubs of shrubs.

Open 11 to 3, 5.30 to 11 **Accommodations** B&B £12.50 to £20 (all rooms have shower) **Underground** Clapham Common/Clapham South

Pollyanna's Map 1

2 Battersea Rise, SW11 *Telephone* 01-228 0316   ££–£££

Looks and feels more like a neighbourhood bistro than a serious restaurant, but the food is fashionable, imaginative and British. Three fillets of meat – one of beef, one of pork, one of veal served with a mushroom mousse – and terrines of sole, scallop and salmon, are typical successes. The menu is remarkably extensive, and the dining-room is deceptively large, too, and gets lively, especially towards the end of the week. It is in the bringing together of the best ingredients in the daily market and combining them that the menu reflects the current renaissance in British cooking – for instance, prawns with an orange and mint dressing; for instance, fillets of red mullet and sea-bass served with an aubergine mousse; for instance, the array of vegetables on large oval platters which come with main courses, such as broccoli with hollandaise, red cabbage with raisins, and boiled fennel; for instance, treacle tart to finish on the good-value (£8.95) Sunday lunch menu (though normally sweets rely on the more *nouvelle cuisine* style of iced soufflés, creams and sorbets). We have here also one of the best collections of wine south of the river. Not only are claret and Burgundy well represented – eight vintages of Ch Gruaud-Larose, for instance – but careful selection, including a few English bottlings, keeps prices reasonable: there is not much over £30 in two decades. The choice under £10 is limited but sound: Domaine de Gaillat 1981, Beaujolais 1983 from the Villages, and Alsace from Louis Gisselbrecht. Vegetarian meals; children's helpings. Bistro music.

Open Mon to Sat, D only, and Sun L **Meals** 1 to 3, 7 to 12 **Cards** Access, Amex, Visa **Service** 10% **BR station** Clapham Junction

La Preferita Map 1

163 Lavender Hill, SW11 *Telephone* 01-223 1046   ££–£££

Bustling, smart little trattoria. There is a choice of seven pasta dishes, and other main courses have been reliable, from grilled lamb cutlets to veal with aubergines and cheese. A small herb garden at the back is used by the kitchen, and the vinegars and oils are of good quality. Children's helpings.

Open Mon to Sat **Meals** 12.30 to 3, 7 to 11.30 **Cards** Access, Amex, Diners, Visa **Service** 12½% **BR station** Clapham Junction

LONDON

Tea Time Map 1

The Pavement, SW4 *Telephone* 01-622 4944   £

The essence of the place is pure, classic camp, from the background music of *Kitten on the Keys*, big band and Marilyn Monroe, to the original 1930s and 1940s china and cutlery: a stylish pastiche of tea-rooms from films such as *Brief Encounter* and *Mrs Miniver*. At the front, a glass-fronted counter sells cakes and chocolates to take away; beyond is the seating area where you can drink 20 types of tea and eat from a stunning range of tea-time treats: Marmite toast, banana and grated chocolate sandwich, croissant, scrambled egg and smoked salmon toasted sandwiches and many a sticky fancy. Irresistible.

Open 9.30am (10am Sun) to 7pm **Closed** 1 week at Christmas **Underground** Clapham Common

BAYSWATER

Central Park Map 2

Queensborough Terrace, W2 *Telephone* 01-229 2424   ££

Large, modern hotel with smallish but well-designed and impeccably maintained rooms (all with bath) just off Bayswater Road and with views of Kensington Gardens from most of the rooms. Its friendly staff, quietness, moderate prices and proximity (by Central Line tube) to the West End are considerable advantages.

Open (Restaurant) 12 to 2, 5 to 10 **Cards** Amex, Visa **Accommodations** 287 rooms (all with bath) B&B £30 to £45 **Underground** Queensway

Diwana Bhel Poori Map 2

50 Westbourne Grove, W2 *Telephone* 01-221 0721   £

Functional, often crowded, Indian vegetarian restaurant. Snacks include puris, chaats, iddly and dahi vada. Slightly more substantial are the dosais. There are dishes of the day, and three thalis. The most luxurious of these is the Annapurna which comprises dhal, rice, two vegetables, farsan (a savoury dish), pappadum, raita, shrikhand, pickle, a sweet, and three chapatis or four puris – all for £3.50. Salt or sweet lassi are good to drink with this. Finish with spiced tea. The menus are the same at the two sister addresses in Drummond Street, NW1 (see under Euston).

Open Noon to 3, 6 to 11 (noon to 11 Sat & Sun) **Closed** Mon; Christmas Day **Underground** Bayswater/Royal Oak

---

✗ = *restaurant*
🏨 = *hotel*
🍺 = *pub*
♀ = *wine bar*
☕ = *tea shop*

BELGRAVIA

Hung Toa Map 2

54 Queensway, W2 *Telephone* 01-727 6017   ££

The roast meats hanging in the window are perhaps the finest in London and as good as those found in Hong Kong. Here are crispy roast pork, brilliant roast ducks, spare ribs, white or soya chicken, and char sui. Combine one of them with a rice or noodle dish to make one of the best cheap lunches in London. The rest of the long Cantonese menu is solid without dazzling in quite the same way. House wine is £6 or bring your own (corkage charge £1). Air-conditioning.

Open All week **Meals** Noon to 11 **Cards** None accepted **Service** 10% **Underground** Queensway/Bayswater

Kalamaras Map 2

76–78 Inverness Mews, W2 *Telephone* 01-727 9122   ££

A walk round the cavernous basement of Stelios Platonos' long-standing Greek restaurant is an odyssey through rooms of different hues. Waitresses recite the menu rather faster than a cruise round the Greek isles and are quick to bring stuffed vine leaves and sausage to start. This is the most ambitious of the London tavernas but suckling pig is a fixture and familiar dishes, such as moussaka, are excellent, as is the roast lamb. Vegetarian possibilities. Children's helpings. There is no pressure on customers to leave. Eighteen Greek wines are mostly priced around £6. Music, air-conditioning and access for wheelchairs. **NB** This is Mega-Kalamaras, right at the end of the Mews. Micro-Kalamaras, which you pass on the way, is also good fun but unlicensed so bring your own wine.

Open Mon to Sat, D only **Meals** 6.30 to 12 **Cards** Access, Amex, Diners, Visa **Underground** Bayswater/Queensway

Maharajah Map 2

50 Queensway, W2 *Telephone* 01-727 1135   ££

An Indian restaurant in the old style, with flock wallpaper and richly sauced curries. Tandoori specialities include duck and lobster, or there are generous helpings of chicken dhansak, methi gosht and the like, and some vegetarian choices. Music, air-conditioning, access for wheelchairs. Children's helpings.

Open All week **Meals** 12 to 3.30, 4.45 to 11.45 **Cards** Access, Amex, Carte Blanche, Diners, Visa **Underground** Queensway/Bayswater

BELGRAVIA

Antelope Map 3

Eaton Terrace, SW1   £

This pretty and pleasantly old-fashioned pub, not far from Sloane Square, has an almost villagey atmosphere, with settles – old and modern – in the front part and

21

LONDON

plenty of standing room around the central bar servery; the side room houses the fruit machine. Food is served from a counter in the smartly tiled back area and includes generous helpings of ploughman's, pâté or creamy taramosalata with granary bread, quiche, and hot dishes such as shepherd's pie; there is an upstairs wine bar. Meals and snacks not available on Saturday evenings or Sundays. Well-kept Benskins and Ind Coope Burton on handpump. It gets lively in the evening. There are a couple of long seats outside in the quiet street.

Open 11 to 3, 5.30 to 11 **Underground** Sloane Square

Ciboure Map 2

21 Eccleston Street, SW1 *Telephone* 01-730 2505   £££

The name is taken from a small town outside St-Jean de Luz. The dining-room looks crisp and white and mirrors give it a feeling of space. Richard Price cooks a thoroughly modern French menu of half a dozen starters and main courses (lunch from £14, dinner from £18). Portions are small and precise: rabbit terrine with pistachios and cherries, red mullet fillets with a rosemary cream, roast duck with a lemon compote. Some sauces lack brio, but the presentation is consistently artistic. Vegetarian dishes, too. The short wine list is cleverly chosen and backed by some senior clarets. House Rhône is £6.30. Despite the air-conditioning, cigar- and pipe-smoking is unwelcome. Access for wheelchairs.

Open Mon to Sat, exc Sat L **Meals** 12 to 2.30, 7 to 11.30 **Cards** Access, Amex, Diners, Visa **Service** Inc **Underground** Victoria

Como Lario Map 3

22 Holbein Place, SW1 *Telephone* 01-730 2954   £–££

Agreeable Italian restaurant handy for a leisurely meal after a trip to the cinema or the Royal Court nearby, with last orders at 11.30pm and no evident pressure on you to leave, even well after midnight. The atmosphere is good; the decor reminiscent of a small Roman trattoria. Eat the seafood arrabbiata if it's on. Decent espresso coffee.

Open 12.15 to 2.30, 6.45 to 11.30 **Closed** Sun; public hols **Underground** Sloane Square

Eatons Map 3

49 Elizabeth Street, SW1 *Telephone* 01-730 0074   £££

A useful bolt-hole in Belgravia. The menu has a very permanent feel about it these days, but is supplemented weekly by half a dozen market-inspired dishes. Cream and wine predominate in the sauces. The plainer dishes are best: lamb noisettes and kidney; veal escalope. The wine list is also sound and conservative. Children are welcome. Music. Wheelchair access.

Open Mon to Fri **Closed** Public hols **Meals** 12 to 2, 7 to 11.15 **Cards** Access, Amex, Diners, Visa **Underground** Victoria/Sloane Square

BELGRAVIA

Ebury Court Map 2

26 Ebury Street, SW1 *Telephone* 01-730 8147   £££

'Amazing to find a Cheltenham Ladies' College lady and retired barrister running a small hotel, but it produces just the sort of delightful atmosphere one would expect. They care about people being comfortable, about their staff, about their food (since the owners eat right there in the restaurant with the guests they would note any sag in the standards). A sort of country house in London. Yes, the rooms *are* small and simple and the bathroom often distant, and there is not a great deal of cupboard space often, and it certainly has no polished professional hotel feeling about it. It just feels like somebody's loved, lived-in house in which you are a most cherished guest. Which hotel could aspire to more?'

Diana and Romer Topham's remarkable hotel, housed in several adjoining terraced houses on either side of No 26, for almost half a century has been offering hospitality to visitors to the capital. This year, as usual, there have been murmurs of discontent, somewhat more vocal than previously, as well as compliments: poor housekeeping, surly reception, a mattress that has seen better days, a room that could do with a fresh lick of paint, faulty electrics. The ayes still have it – but we think that a major investment in refurbishment is now somewhat overdue. Early supper can be served from 6.30pm for theatre-goers. No under-fives in the restaurant.

Open All year **Cards** Access, Visa **Accommodations** 39 rooms, 14 with bath or shower. B&B £27 to £36 **Underground** Victoria

Ebury Wine Bar Map 3

139 Ebury Street, SW1 *Telephone* 01-730 5447   ££

A refuge from Victoria Coach Station is this bustling, bare-floored, air-conditioned wine bar. It fills up, and tables are shared. The food is basic, fresh, home cooked and changes with the markets. Steaks are a feature, and the plats du jour are adventurous – for instance, fricassée of sole and mussels in saffron sauce. There are good wines, too, and a Cruover machine allows twenty of the better ones to be tasted by the glass, such as Gisselbrecht's lovely Pinot d'Alsace 1983, Muscadet, Domaine de la Sénéchalière 1984 and Chardonnay di Appiano, Alto Adige 1984. House champagne is from Boizel. Children are welcome.

Open All week **Closed** 25 and 26 Dec **Meals** 12.15 to 2.45, 6 to 10.30 (7 to 10 Sun) **Cards** Access, Amex, Diners, Visa **Underground** Victoria

Gavvers Map 3

61–63 Lower Sloane Street, SW1 *Telephone* 01-730 5983   £££

Quality is more apparent than quantity in the corner building that housed Le Gavroche in its first incarnation (see under Mayfair). It is a good place to start to discover the Roux brothers' empire. For value it is pipped by the exceptional Le

LONDON

Mazarin (Pimlico), nevertheless the all-inclusive dinners (£18.75) and the wines are still a match for most other London French restaurants. For instance, the foie gras salad, the chicken with shallots, and the excellent fish, served skin side up for identification. The Roux chocolate truffle cake is the best in London. The menu changes quarterly but is supplemented by dishes of the day; vegetarian meals by arrangement. Service is young and Gallic and the atmosphere generated at the tightly packed tables is that of a swish bistro. The inclusive wines are well chosen. Air-conditioning. Access for wheelchairs.

Open Mon to Sat, D only **Meals** 7 to 11 **Cards** Amex, Diners **Service** Inc **Underground** Sloane Square

The Goring Hotel Map 2

15 Beeston Place, SW1 *Telephone* 01-834 8211   ££–£££

This distinguished traditional hotel lies within a stone's throw of Buckingham Palace – or at least of its gardens: 'It has the solidly decent old-fashioned feeling of quality that such hotels used to have before so many became run down. The staff are delightful: they show you to your room and look really interested in whether or not you like it. Although everywhere has been painted and refurbished they have not put prices up to a ridiculous figure.' George Goring, the owner, explains endearingly: 'My life and that of my father and grandfather before me has been dedicated to ensuring the absolute tranquillity and comfort of all guests who visit the Goring Hotel (our Family Home). I prefer to operate one personally-managed hotel of style and excellence than to own an empire. My aim is that future generations of Gorings will always inherit an establishment of greater merit than the last. I sleep in every bedroom myself in order to ensure that they are as comfortable as they look. César Ritz built The Ritz, Claridge built Claridge's, Mr Brown built Browns. These famous hoteliers have sadly passed on, but there will always be a Mr Goring at the Goring to welcome you and to make you feel "at home from home".' No word on the meals (lunch £14, dinner £16).

Open All year **Cards** Access, Amex, Diners, Visa **Accommodations** 90 rooms, all with bath and shower, some with air-conditioning. B&B £60 to £80 **Underground** Victoria

Mijanou Map 3

143 Ebury Street, SW1 *Telephone* 01-730 4099   ££££

While other restaurants follow trends, Mijanou just follows its own nose, not pigeon-holing comfortably into any recognisable style. The decor leads the way: a red room upstairs for smokers, with a view of the kitchen; beige flock downstairs with assorted prints and pictures. Ingredients – salmon, kidneys, fillet of lamb – are good and obvious skill turns them into bright dishes: fresh scallops and shrimps sit on top of the thinnest green ribbon pasta with tiny dice of peppers and mushrooms, lubricated with a delicate, creamy sauce; a frozen bombe of white, dark and green minty chocolate is served in a clear caramel sauce with brittle meringue on top. The flavours don't always balance, though; sometimes the menu gives the impression that ingredients have been thrown

BELGRAVIA

together just to see what happens – sprigs of redcurrant and segments of lime, for example, have done little to improve a perfectly good piece of salmon. But taken as a piece, the restaurant is sound, with good service from the genial Mr Blech, and a classy, if expensive, list of mostly French wines, strong on good claret vintages.

Open Mon to Fri **Meals** 12.30 to 2.30, 7.30 to 10 **Cards** Not accepted **Underground** Victoria

Santini Map 2

29 Ebury Street, SW1 *Telephone* 01-730 4094 and 8275   £££–££££

Here's a rarity in London these days, a good regional Italian restaurant. The dining-room is fresh and airy and the menu loyal to Venice. At least a third of the customers are Italian, which is another pointer to the quality. Risotto can be made to order with a twenty-five minute wait, in season there is game served with polenta, and, also in season, Gino Santin does a variation on carpaccio, scalding thin slices of fillet steak for two minutes and topping them with the sharp-tasting leaf of the ruccola he grows in his garden. Fish is the main line, though, and the sea-bass has been particularly impressive. Pasta is made on the premises. Service is generous and accommodating. The wine list features many of the best names of Italian wines but no other details. Wheelchair access; children's helpings.

Open All week, exc Sat L and Sun L **Closed** Public hols **Meals** 12.30 to 2.30, 7 to 11.30 **Cards** Access, Amex, Diners, Visa **Service** 12% **Underground** Victoria

Wilbraham Hotel Map 3

1 Wilbraham Place, SW1 *Telephone* 01-730 8296   ££

An old-fashioned Belgravian hotel in a quiet side street off Sloane Street. Once three Victorian terraced houses, the conversion has retained the gracious staircases, panelled walls and archways of the original structure. Prices are reasonable for this location, rooms, even the smaller ones, are elegantly furnished with good lights, a porter carries your luggage up in a tiny wooden lift. Breakfasts are served in bedrooms. 'The hotel is old-fashioned in the nicest sort of way; the rooms are decorated with taste and comfort; and the amenities such as early morning tea and beds turned back in the evening are of the kind I thought had vanished from small reasonably priced hotels in London. The staff were helpful and friendly.'

Open All year. Buttery closed Sun and public holidays **Cards** None accepted **Accommodations** 52 rooms, 36 with bath and shower. B&B from about £30 to £40 **Underground** Sloane Square

---

It is always advisable to bring a supply of British money and coins with you for tips, fares, etc. on your initial arrival, especially since there are frequently long queues (lines) at airport exchange booths. American Express cards are convenient for the larger cities, but traveller's cheques are probably the safest way to carry the bulk of your cash.

25

LONDON

BLOOMSBURY

Lamb Map 4

94 Lamb's Conduit Street, WC1   £

Well-kept and friendly, this cosy pub has cut-glass swivelling 'snob screens' all the way around the U-shaped bar counter, lots of sepia photographs on ochre panelling of 1890s actresses and traditional cast-iron-framed tables with neat brass rails around the rim. Good bar food includes a wide range of snacks such as filled rolls, sandwiches, pastries, ploughman's and salads, as well as lunchtime hot dishes such as home-made cottage pie or steak and kidney pies, and daily specials. Meals served at lunchtime except Sunday; snacks during weekday lunchtimes only. Youngs Bitters and Special on handpump; good service. There are slatted wooden seats in a little courtyard (no children allowed here), beyond the quiet room which is down a couple of steps at the back.

Open 11 to 3, 5.30 to 11 **Underground** Holborn/Russell Square

Museum Tavern Map 4

Museum Street, WC1   £

On a corner, opposite the British Museum, this friendly old-fashioned Bloomsbury pub is decorated to emphasise its links with the days of Virginia Woolf – and even Karl Marx is fondly supposed to have had the odd glass here. There are old-fashioned high-backed benches around the traditional cast-iron pub tables, old advertising mirrors between the wooden pillars behind the bar and gas lamps above the tables outside. Good bar food includes sandwiches, ploughman's with a choice of cheeses, and a changing choice of five main dishes such as shepherd's pie, steak and kidney pie, stuffed peppers and chilli con carne; mini grills in the evening. Children are allowed in the eating area. A good choice of real ales on handpump might include Greene King IPA and Abbot, Brakspears, Everards, Ruddles County, and Websters Yorkshire, and there is a wide range of wines by the glass; fruit machine, maybe piped music. Afternoon cream teas are served from 3.45 to 5pm (not Sunday).

Open 11 to 3, 5.30 to 11 **Underground** Tottenham Court Road/Holborn

North Sea Map 2

7–8 Leigh Street, WC1 *Telephone* 01-387 5892   £

One of the best fish and chip restaurants and take-aways in London: bright, functional, homely and well run. Some say it is better even than the Seashell (see under Marylebone), and there are excellent reports of the 'revolutionary' prawn

---

Telephone numbers may not be given for those places where you do not need to make table or room reservations.

cocktail, grilled sardines and seafood platter. The fish is delivered daily and can be fried in egg and matzo meal, deep fried in batter, or grilled. The chips are thick and crisp. Home-made trifle to finish. Licensed. A typical three-course meal with a half-carafe of house wine will set you back about £9.

Open Noon to 2.30, 5.30 to 10.30 **Closed** Sun **Underground** Russell Square/King's Cross

CAMDEN

The Bengal Lancer Map 2

253 Kentish Town Road, NW5 *Telephone* 01-485 6688   £–££

This cool, comfortable restaurant exudes an air of old colonial style with photographs of Indian army officers on the walls, and a profusion of cane and greenery. Meat or vegetarian thalis are good alternatives to the individual dishes, which include tikkas, sheek kebabs and chicken chaat along with all manner of curries. House French £5. Wheelchair access; music; children's helpings.

Open All week **Meals** 12 to 3, 6 to 12 (12.30 Thur, Fri and Sat) **Cards** Access, Amex, Diners, Visa **Underground** Kentish Town

Le Bistroquet Map 2

273–275 Camden High Street, NW1
Telephone 01-267 4895/485 9607   £–££

Situated between Camden Lock and Camden Town tube station, this brasserie has extended into its courtyard. The menu has remained much the same for the last two years: warm salads, cold poached salmon, entrecôte steak and cod Mornay are the style. The floating island is excellent. Standards fluctuate but are usually buoyed up by the quality of the ingredients. The bar area at the front offers a range of light meals along the lines of spicy merguez sausages, salade niçoise and steak sandwich. House Rhône is £4.95. Music; wheelchair access; children's helpings.

Open All week **Meals** 12 to 3, 7 to 11.30 (11 Sun) **Cards** Access, Amex, Visa (restaurant meals only) **Service** 12½% **Underground** Camden Town

La Bougie Map 2

7 Murray Street, NW1 *Telephone* 01-485 6400   ££

The candles – one on each table – have dripped so much wax that it is hardly credible that this little quasi-bistro has only been open since December 1985. Its

---

£ = *meal can be had for about £5*
££ = *meal can be had for about £12*
£££ = *meal can be had for about £20*
££££ = *meal can be had for about £30*

LONDON

chief virtue is its cheapness – main courses are all £3.75, or £5 with vegetables. The menu is imaginative and quite over the top in places, but the ingredients hold it on course. Parsley soup, veal with lime and red-pepper sauce, and venison in green-pepper sauce have all been good. Vegetarian choices. Children are welcome. House wine is £4.50. Wheelchair access; music.

Open All week, exc Sat L **Meals** 12 to 3, 7 to 11.30 **Cards** None accepted **Service** 10% **Underground** Camden Town

Daphne Map 2 ✕

83 Bayham Street, NW1 *Telephone* 01-267 7322 ££

A noisy, bustling café in a terraced house, serving some of the best-value Greek/Cypriot food in town. The stuccoed walls are hung with Mediterranean-style murals and pencil drawings, and there are candles and green checked cloths on the tables as well as bowls of olives with coriander and garlic. All rather romantic. The menu has sharp, well-rounded avgolemono, tsatsiki, good afelia and chicken shashlik, and the meze is a lot of food for just over £5. Fish specials have been outstanding: fresh cuttlefish in a wine and saffron sauce, perfectly grilled halibut with delicate green and red pepper sauce. The kitchen excels with roast potatoes, though vegetables have often been soggy. Baklava is home made and Greek coffee comes with nutty Turkish delight. House Beaujolais is £5.90. Wheelchair access; music.

Open Mon to Sat **Meals** 12 to 3, 6 to 12 **Card** Access **Underground** Camden Town/Mornington Crescent

Mustoe Bistro Map 2 ✕

73 Regents Park Road, NW1 *Telephone* 01-586 0901 £–££

Noisy, cheerful, long-established bistro with wooden floors and tables. Mr Morgan cooks, his wife and others serve. Seafood salad is more salad than seafood but comes in a light dressing, aïoli salad is very garlicky. Good main courses include lamb Shrewsbury and beef casserole in sour cream sauce. Vegetables are fine and simple – crisp broccoli, buttered beetroot – and the chips are excellent. There are always vegetarian choices and for Sunday lunch there are two roasts at £2.50 each. Simple wine list.

Open 6.30pm to 11.15pm (1 to 3, 6.30 to 10.45 Sun) **Closed** Mon L to Sat L; Christmas and Easter **Underground** Camden Town/Chalk Farm

Nontas Map 2 ✕

16 Camden High Street, NW1 *Telephone* 01-387 4579 ££

The meze at £5.70 in this smarter than average, family-run Greek/Cypriot taverna encompasses most of the menu. Highlights are the hummus, the stuffed vine leaves, the spicy sausages and the moussaka. The charcoal-grilled steaks at £4.70 underline the good value of this friendly restaurant. The dish of the day may be something out of the ordinary, such as marinated chicken and Jerusalem

CHELSEA

artichokes cooked in red wine, or tavas – lamb baked with potatoes, onions and marrow. House Ulysses is £4.45. Wheelchair access; music.

Open Mon to Sat **Meals** 12 to 2.45, 6 to 11.30 **Cards** Access, Amex, Diners **Underground** Camden Town/Mornington Crescent

Le Petit Prince   Map 2

5 Holmes Road, NW5   *Telephone* 01-267 0752   £–££

This is one of the best places in town for an authentic couscous, and it also serves kebabs, merguez, boulettes and special dishes such as braised rabbit with brandy and red wine. It's loud, boisterous and brightens up a dingy part of the city. It sometimes closes at lunchtime if there's no great demand, so it's best to telephone first.

Open 12.30 to 2.30, 7 to 11.30 (11.45 Fri) **Closed** Sat L, Sun L and Mon L; Christmas Day and Boxing Day; public hols **Underground** Kentish Town

Yerakina   Map 2

10 Kentish Town Road, NW1   *Telephone* 01-485 5743   ££

'Meze is Greek cuisine at its finest . . . ideal for those who have the time,' explains the menu of this Cypriot taverna by Camden Town Underground station. Inside are Mediterranean white-plastered textured walls, and to one side there is the edge of a red-tiled roof slanting into the dining area as if there were a villa next door. The colours are of the sea, with blue tablecloths, and of the hills, with flowers on each table. The meze runs to nearly thirty dishes, each snack-size, freshly made, blending into a satisfying whole. It comes in waves – squid salad with coriander, octopus in white vinegar, half a cold quail, again in vinegar, char-grilled haloumi cheese, and then four fish dishes, and then the stews, and finally a refreshing Greek salad. There is a slight imbalance of protein which would be erased by more rice or vegetable dishes, but otherwise this is a persuasive illustration of the breadth of the cooking. With coffee come grapes, figs, Turkish delight, mixed raisins and candied peel. The house Rotonda at £4.50 is one of the better cheap Greek reds; otherwise there is ouzo, Metaxas brandy or retsina. Music and air-conditioning. Children and the wheelchair-bound are welcome.

Open Mon to Sat **Meals** 12 to 3, 6 to 12 **Cards** Access, Diners, Visa **Service** 10% **Underground** Camden Town

CHELSEA

Cross Keys   Map 2

Lawrence Street, SW3   £

This friendly Victorian pub is a popular and lively meeting place in the evenings; at lunchtime, though, it's much more relaxing, and the good-value food includes sandwiches and home-made hot dishes prepared by the Thai chef, such as

29

LONDON

home-made fisherman's pie, crispy fried pancakes and lamb curry. Snacks are not available on Sundays. Children are allowed in the eating area. Well-kept Courage Best and Directors on handpump; good mulled wine and a cheery open fire in winter. Service is quick and efficient. The decor is old-fashioned, with high ceilings, military prints on the dark green walls, a walk-round island serving counter and an open fire in winter. Shove-ha'penny, dominoes, cribbage and fruit machine. There are tables in a pretty little sunny back courtyard planted with creepers and tubs of brightly coloured flowers.

Open 11 to 3, 5.30 to 11 Underground South Kensington/Sloane Square (quite a long way from both)

Front Page Map 3	🍺
35 Old Church Street, SW3 *Telephone* 01-352 2908	£

Done up carefully to evoke the back-to-basics mood that has caught on elsewhere, this light and airy Watneys pub has a relaxed and chatty atmosphere. The bar servery is nearly an island (in a sea of wood-strip floor) and around the panelled walls are heavy wooden tables, pews and benches, with an open fire in one cosy area. There are big navy ceiling fans and huge windows with heavy navy curtains; lighting is virtually confined to brass picture-lights above small Edwardian monochrome pictures. Big blackboards at either end of the pub list the good-value and nicely presented food: avocado, blue cheese or curry dip with crudités, egg and bacon, pork and liver terrine with cranberries, avocado, Mozzarella and tomato salad, pasta of the day, steak sandwich, devilled kidneys, bacon and chicken liver salad, scrambled egg and smoked salmon, home-made fishcakes or smoked salmon mousse, melon, langoustines and prawn salad and rump steaks. Children may go into the eating area. Combes, Ruddles County and Websters Yorkshire on handpump; fruit machine, piped music. Big copper gas lamps hang outside the pub, above pretty hanging baskets.

Open 11 to 3, 5.30 to 11 Underground South Kensington

Habitat Café Map 3	☕ ✕
208 King's Road, SW3 *Telephone* 01-351 1211	£

Light, airy room on the high-ceilinged first floor of the popular store. The range of snacks includes quiche, pies, salads and soup, and there are pastries, biscuits and cakes, too.

Open 10am (9.30am Sat) to 5pm (6pm Wed) Closed Sun; Christmas Day, Boxing Day and 1 Jan Underground Sloane Square/South Kensington

Henry J Bean's Map 3	🍺
195–197 King's Road, SW3	£

A pub for the homesick. The decor in this popular and well-run Watneys pub is late 1950s American, though the music is late 1970s: the main part is decorated

CHELSEA

with an interesting collection of old enamel advertising placards, photographs of Hollywood movie stars, snow shoes and old skis. There are good solid wooden tables with high stools – spaced well apart – on the polished wood-strip floor, and up some low steps is a railed-off carpeted area with pale plum button-back banquettes and more tables. The long bar counter is manned by neat slicked-hair barmen, backed by tall mirrored shelves housing an excellent collection of whiskies. An interesting range of beers (no real ales) includes several Americans, and you can have them served by the jug, as well as with slugs of this and that, in small or outsize glasses; there are American as well as good French house wines, and of course they do cocktails. You order food from the barman, and the till transmits the order to a grill area: a video screen shows your number when it's ready. The food includes deep-fried potato skins with sour cream, hot dog or saucy chicken wings, salads, chilli con carne, barbecued spare ribs and burgers. Children are allowed in the dining-room. A cream-tiled area with bentwood chairs opens through tall glass French windows into a really big crazy-paved back courtyard, with sturdy seats and tables under plane and lime trees among well tended green pergolas and old streetlamps, and a central fountain playing around a tall flame.

Open 11.30 to 3, 5.30 to 11 **Closed** 25 Dec, 1 Jan **Underground** South Kensington

Monkeys Map 3

1 Cale Street, Chelsea Green, SW3 *Telephone* 01-352 4711   ££–£££

With more the moodiness of an orang-utan than the cheerfulness of a chimpanzee, Monkeys straddles bistro and restaurant. There is no name on the front, just a few bounced cheques displayed in the window. Mirrors and round tables give a feeling of France, though the atmosphere is rather like that of a snug. The menu (lunch from £8, dinner from £15) is a sensible formula of steaks and salmon augmented by daily specials. In autumn there is an especially fine selection of game – snipe, woodcock and grouse, for instance. The plain fish dishes, such as turbot, have been executed with élan. The wine list is short but interesting. Children's helpings.

Open All week, exc Sun D **Closed** Aug **Meals** 12.30 to 2.30 (1.15 to 3 Sun), 7.30 to 11 **Cards** None accepted **Underground** South Kensington

Pasta Connection Map 3

25–27 Elystan Street, SW3 *Telephone* 01-584 5248   £–££

Small, informal Italian restaurant with garden-style furniture and a stripped wooden floor. Good tagliatelle with tomato sauce, plus more expensive choices such as excellent seabass lightly cooked in butter and garlic. The service is helpful and there are nice little touches – glasses of iced water brought automatically to the table, for example. A good place for a casual meal.

Open 12.30 to 2.30, 7 to 11.15 **Closed** Sat L; Sun; public hols **Underground** Sloane Square

LONDON

Le Suquet Map 3   ✗

104 Draycott Avenue, SW3 *Telephone* 01-581 1785   £££

Good fish restaurants are rare enough but Le Suquet has proved its worth over the last thirteen years. It is a favourite of the six restaurants in which Pierre Martin has a hand, and was the second to open, after La Croisette (see Fulham). The menu here is à la carte. It features fine oysters, both French and English, shellfish, either on massive platters or else sauced, in pastry cases, and fillets of white fish in wine sauces. There are suggestions that the vegetables have improved. Single recommendations extend from the fish soup and the salmon feuilleté, to sea-bass with a beurre blanc, and tarte Tatin. The waiters are like an artillery unit, loading and reloading tables in the cramped dining-room where not one millimetre of space has been wasted; even so wheelchairs can be accommodated. Only the paintings of Cannes give a sense of open air and sunshine. The wine list stays mainly in the Loire.

Open All week **Closed** 1 week at Christmas **Meals** 12.30 to 2.30, 7.30 to 11.30 **Cards** Amex, Diners **Underground** South Kensington/Sloane Square

Tante Claire Map 3   ✗

68–69 Royal Hospital Road, SW3   £££–££££
Telephone 01-352 6045 and 351 0227

More space, more light, more comfort, more joy: the expansion of the dining-room of one of London's premier restaurants has been an unmitigated success. The colours are of a summer's day – yellows, creams, mustards, blues. Tables are set with fine glass, heavy cutlery and very white linen. The spectacular desserts have tended to mirror the symmetry of the design: grapefruit mille-feuille, five ways with chocolate, and three mousses, one of chocolate, one of coffee, one of white chocolate, served in wafer-thin pastry cups sitting in a coffee sauce . . . It is the subtlety of the saucing that distinguishes M. Koffmann as one of the finest French chefs of his generation. He has moved on from his days under the Roux Brothers' wing and developed his own style (it is now his own restaurant financially as well). The menu, be it for the good-value set lunch (£17) or the tantalising *carte*, has as one of its trade marks a fondness for fish, notably scallops – in a ragoût with oysters and truffles – and red mullet – roasted with cumin and tomatoes and a cake made with its livers. Also, there is a healthy *bourgeois* liking for roast pigeon, for pigs' trotters with wild mushrooms and an apple mousseline, and for offal. The expansion has resulted in a certain amount of delegation, which is seen in more failures

---

Theatre tips: most theatres begin at around 7.30 pm. You'll have to plan an early dinner, or a later one after the show. Some theatres have buffets, so you can get a drink and snack between the acts. If you arrive late, you will not be seated until the next interval (intermission). The levels of a British theatre tend to be called (from ground level upwards): the stalls, the circle or dress circle, the upper circle and the balcony.

CHELSEA

than before, though these have become noticeably fewer. The triumph of the year has without doubt been the sweets. The service has established a brisk, relaxed routine and is able to raise the atmosphere a notch, as if to say that this is not an everyday place. The wine list opens with some interesting French country wines from Savoie and the Camargue, the latter being sensibly priced at under £7, although it is not a rapacious list anyway. There are strong sections of Burgundy and *cru* claret which make it expensive, but there are also carefully selected wines from Alsace at just over £10, and the Loire is taken seriously too. This is a jacket and tie sort of place. Wheelchairs present no problems. There is a minimum charge of £25 at dinner.

Open Mon to Fri **Meals** 12.30 to 2, 7 to 11 **Cards** Amex, Diners **Service** Inc **Underground** Sloane Square

Waltons Map 3

121 Walton Street, SW3 *Telephone* 01-584 0204   £££–££££

The marigolds and grey wallpaper and drapes act as a protective cocoon from the outside world. The staff, too, have perhaps been locked up amid all this decor for so long that they have forgotten why they were there in the first place. 'It is a bit like those chaps who build cathedrals out of matchsticks – sounds great, and in a way it is, but in the end all you have got is a lot of matchsticks.' The menu is ordinary and decent for this price-level, but it is designed to reassure rather than arouse. Sometimes the kitchen worthily takes very simple things, like obviously fresh snails or fresh peas, and serves them just so, but, equally, if we wanted to carp we might say that sauces are meek or that the lamb – served off the bone, naturally – was carelessly cooked at one meal. The set meals at lunchtime (£11) and after ten (£17.50) are considerably better value than the *carte*, which is as expensive as anything in London. The wine list has some excellent clarets, though not many half-bottles, and the sommelier gives sound advice. House wine starts at £7.50. Air-conditioning. People in wheelchairs and children are welcome.

Open All week **Closed** Public hols **Meals** 12.30 to 2.30 (2 Sun), 7.30 to 11.30 (10.30 Sun) **Cards** Access, Amex, Diners, Visa **Service** 15% **Underground** South Kensington

Zen Map 3

Chelsea Cloisters, Sloane Avenue, SW3 *Telephone* 01-589 1781   ££–££££

This is the premier new wave, third-generation Chinese restaurant. Lawrence Leung's menus and lush decor have been the seminal influence on Chinese restaurants. The decor is in the shape of square slabs of mirror cut into the ceiling, chairs with pin-stripe upholstery, a fountain, windows of black with patterned glass. On the table there are turquoise candleholders with lit wicks in oil, red-rimmed teapots, heavy cutlery and flowers. The atmosphere is effervescent. The food does not really deserve to be judged alongside that at other Chinese restaurants. It is like the building it is in, Chelsea Cloisters, where the flats are being renovated – small portions for large amounts of money. Compared to a French restaurant, though, it is not costly, and the menu is a

LONDON

tantalising collection of glittering prizes from one of the greatest cuisines of the world – minced quail wrapped in iceberg lettuce; the cold pork dressed in garlic and chilli oil rivalled only by the Dragon Gate (Soho); classically simple poached squid served with two sauces, one of hoisin and the other of chilli and soy. On the nights that the kitchen is not sparkling there is always the chilli oil ... and even the brilliant Gewürztraminer 1983 from Traber at £9.50 can deal with that. There is a minimum charge of £8 at dinner. Access for wheelchairs; music; air-conditioning. Children and vegetarians welcome.

Open All week **Closed** 25 to 27 Dec **Meals** 12 to 2.30, 6 to 11.30 (noon to 11.30 Sat and Sun) **Cards** Access, Amex, Diners, Visa **Service** 15% **Underground** South Kensington/Sloane Square

CHISWICK

Bulls Head Map 1

Strand-on-the-Green, W4 £

There's a pleasant and relaxed atmosphere at this riverside Watneys pub, with its little rooms rambling through black-panelled alcoves and up and down steps, and the traditional furnishings include benches built in to the simple panelling and so forth. Small windows look past attractively planted hanging flower baskets to the river just beyond the narrow towpath (where you can take your Combes, Ruddles County or Websters Yorkshire, well kept on handpump); it's not too crowded even on fine evenings, except perhaps at weekends. A separate lunchtime food bar serves reasonably priced ploughman's, chicken curry, lasagne, moussaka, chilli con carne, shepherd's pie, steak and mushroom pie and salads (main dishes around £2.75). A games-room at the back has darts and a fruit machine. Children may go into the eating area and games-room. The original building here, then an inn, served as Cromwell's HQ several times during the Civil War, and it was here that Moll Cutpurse overheard Cromwell talking to Fairfax about the troops' pay money coming by horse from Hounslow, and got her gang to capture the moneybags.

Open 11 to 3, 5.30 to 11 **BR station** Kew Bridge

Christian's Map 1

1 Station Parade, Burlington Lane, W4 £££
Telephone 01-995 0382 and 0208

Christian Gustin has expanded his one-man operation and taken in a helper. Fish supplies have also improved and there are now English cheeses. The herb garden in the back has come into production. All this translates into a short, changing *carte* in the modern style – goats'-cheese soufflé, cucumber and mint soup, braised marinated lamb with juniper, bacon and chives. Most of the cooking is last-minute and the pace is unhurried. The short wine list has been sensibly assembled and is not expensive. Music; access for wheelchairs.

Open Tue to Sat, exc Sat L **Meals** 12.30 to 2, 7.30 to 10.15 **Cards** Not accepted **Service** 10% **BR station** Chiswick

THE CITY

La Dordogne Map 1

5 Devonshire Road, W4 *Telephone* 01-747 1836

£££

The bustle and charm of this bohemian dining-room are a big boon in the neighbourhood. Since the restaurant opened the menu has moved up from the bistro style to take in the likes of foie gras. This has put the prices up and the value down. The kitchen's strengths are seen in the robust dishes: monkfish, for instance, rather than brill; fillet of beef with béarnaise and aubergines; char-grilled brochet of chicken with prunes and garlic and a strong orange and ginger sauce. The wine list is more faithful to the Dordogne than the food, having five wines from Cahors. House Bergerac is £5.70. Music; wheelchair access; children welcome.

Open Mon to Sat, exc Sat L **Meals** 12 to 2.30, 7 to 11 (12 Fri, Sat) **Cards** Access, Amex, Diners, Visa **Underground** Turnham Green

THE CITY

Balls Brothers Map 6

2/3 Old Change Court, St Paul's Churchyard, EC4
Telephone 01-248 8697
5/6 Carey Lane, EC2 *Telephone* 01-606 4787
6/8 Cheapside, EC2 *Telephone* 01-248 2708
42 Threadneedle Street, EC2 *Telephone* 01-628 3850
142 Strand, WC2 *Telephone* 01-836 0156
Bucklersbury House, Cannon Street, EC4
Telephone 01-248 7557
Gows Restaurant, 81 Old Broad Street, EC2
Telephone 01-628 0530
Great Eastern Hotel, Liverpool Street, EC2
Telephone 01-626 7919
Laurence Pountney Hill, EC2 *Telephone* 01-283 2947
Moor House, London Wall, EC2 *Telephone* 01-628 3944
St Mary at Hill, EC3 *Telephone* 01-626 0321

£

Balls Brothers wine bars stick to the successful formula of offering their own good wines at reasonable prices in rather staid, mostly City, surroundings. The most attractive are probably the clubby Edwardian bar in the Great Eastern Hotel, the atmospheric two-floor bar in Threadneedle Street, and the St Paul's Churchyard bar with outside tables. Ten routine wines by the glass are pepped up by special offers: perhaps the delicious Muscadet Fief de la Brie 1985 and Ch du Grand Moulas 1985, Côtes du Rhône. Bordeaux range from La Tour Michèle to Ch Camensac 1976. The lack of producers' names makes it difficult

London buses are big and red, have top decks, and are a great way to get to know the city. The conductor collects fares as he comes through the bus; prices are according to your destination.

LONDON

to evaluate, for example, Mercurey 1980, Alsace Riesling 1984 and Ockfener Bockstein Spätlese 1983. Try, perhaps, some of the less usual wines: Chilean Concha Y Toro Cabernet Sauvignon 1982, Torres or Californian Zinfandel 1980, Parducci. Note, too, the bargain champagnes (Joseph Perrier, £12.50) and fine range of sherries, ports and Madeiras. Rather dull sandwiches and salads, plus hot dishes in most branches.

Open Mon to Fri 11 to 3, 5 to 8 **Closed** Sat, Sun, public holidays **Cards** Access, Amex, Diners, Visa

Black Friar   Map 6

174 Queen Victoria Street, EC4   £

Go prepared to search out the detail at this pub. The back inner room is the best, with every inch of its walls and arched ceiling full of inlaid Florentine marble, bronze reliefs of jolly monks, slender marble pillars, glittering mosaics, intricate nursery-rhyme scenes and so forth. In the front room, see if you can spot the opium-smoking hints modelled into the fireplace. Well-kept Adnams, Bass, Charles Wells Eagle and Morrells on handpump. All food is home cooked, including sandwiches, big filled rolls (some of which may still be available in the evening), shepherd's pie, lasagne or moussaka, beef and ale pie, scampi in a basket, lamb curry and plaice. Meals only served at weekday lunchtimes; snacks also available at Saturday lunchtime. There's a wide forecourt by the approach to Blackfriars Bridge.

Open 11.30 to 3, 5.30 to 9.30 **Closed** Sat evening and Sun **Underground** Blackfriars

Bleeding Heart   Map 6

4 Bleeding Heart Yard, EC1 (between Hatton Garden and Saffron Hill)   £
Telephone 01-242 8238/2056

The yard itself features in *Little Dorrit* and the more expensive restaurant has a collection of Dickensian prints and first editions. The heart referred to is that of Lady Elizabeth Hatton, which is supposed to have been found the morning after her murder here still pumping blood on to the cobblestones. As might be expected, her ghost is said to haunt the place. (A St Valentine's Day menu included a graphic red pepper salad and steak with tomato béarnaise.) Cheap eaters should head for the wine bar (or terrace in summer) for French-style dishes such as pork rillettes, black pudding, steak in baguette and apple tart.

Open 11 to 2.30, 5.30 to midnight **Closed** Sat and Sun (exc in summer); public hols **Underground** Chancery Lane/Farringdon

Bow Wine Vaults   Map 6

10 Bow Churchyard, EC4 *Telephone* 01-248 1121   £

This address near Cheapside houses wine merchant, cellars, restaurant, private dining rooms and two wine bars. It is deservedly popular, for though there may be few bargains, there are few boring bottles either. (Check the blackboard for

THE CITY

special offers.) By the glass, consider Vin de Pays de Coteaux de Salavès Blanc; Châteauneuf-du-Pape, Ch de Beaucastel 1980; and Paul Jaboulet's Crozes Hermitage, the red 1982 and Mule Blanche 1984. Once into the main list, possibilities are endless: a trio of Lucien Tempé Alsace 1983s; Waldracher Krone Riesling Spätlese 1979 Peter Scherf, several vintages of Marc Brédif Vouvray (from 1981 at £8.30 to 1947 at £36.60); Languedoc Mas de Daumas Gassac Rosé 1984 (£7.95) or Rouge 1982 (£8.65); delicious Fronsac, Ch de la Rivière 1979 and 1980, each £10.55; and so much more . . . The house Private Cuvée Rosé Champagne (£13) is no damp squib. Food in various styles, depending on where you find a perch.

Open Mon to Fri 11.30 to 3, 5 to 7 **Closed** Sat, Sun, public holidays **Cards** Access, Diners, Visa **Underground** Mansion House

Café Rouge Map 2

2c Cherry Tree Walk, Whitecross Street, EC1   £££
Telephone 01-588 0710

Outside is modern precinct urbanity. The smells of the stocks mingle with the clatter of the trolleys from the nearby supermarket. It is on the borders of the Barbican, with its concert- and theatre-goers, the City, and the last of the council tenements of what was once a very poor area. The fire-engine-red plant-boxes form a square flank to fend off the outside world. Café Rouge is very rouge, lipstick-red on the doors, with iron grilles on her windows to protect her chastity. As a building it is not dissimilar to the original Quat' Saisons in Oxford. As a menu it is sharp, French, and à la mode (set meals £12.95, plus a *carte*). Courgette flowers are stuffed with salmon mousse, while the still-attached vegetable is fanned out in hollandaise sauce. Steak with a sauce of no fewer than four kinds of peppercorns is predictably potent, while lamb is cooked in a light pastry with a wrapping of laver-bread; vegetarian choices. Sauces tend to be well-reduced stocks. Cheeses come from Androuët in Paris, and the ices and sorbets make refreshing finishes. White and dark chocolate are served with coffee. The wine list has many country wines worth exploring, though the house Domaine de l'Echanson white at £5.95 is first-class. Access for wheelchairs; music.

Open Mon to Sat, exc Sat L **Closed** 1 week Christmas, public hols **Meals** 12 to 2.30, 6 to 11.30 **Cards** Access, Amex, Diners, Visa **Service** 12½% **Underground** Barbican

Café St Pierre Map 2

29 Clerkenwell Green, EC1 *Telephone* 01-251 6606   ££

This cheerful café/brasserie boasts a splendid wine list of interesting wines carefully described, even to the date when each wine was last tasted by the selection panel. There are few bargains, though top quality, whether you stick to the blackboard wines by the glass, the house wines (described as Mâcon-style and Rhône-style) or explore the 20-page list. France dominates: for example, Clos Ste-Hune Riesling 1979, Trimbach (£15); Ch Potensac 1979 (£20); Gigondas 1983, Vidal-Fleury (£15). Non-French attractions include Italian

LONDON

Tignanello 1979 (£15); Zinfandel 1979, Ch Montelena (£15); and New Zealand Fumé Blanc 1985, Matua Valley (£14). Access for wheelchairs.

Open Mon to Fri 7.30 to 11 **Closed** Sat, Sun, public hols, Chr Day to New Year's Day **Cards** Access, Amex, Diners, Visa **Underground** Farringdon

---

Le Champenois Map 6	✗
Cutlers Gardens Arcade, 10 Devonshire Square, EC2 *Telephone* 01-283 7888	£££–££££

Wear a black suit or you may feel out of place. This is the rich end of town. Le Champenois is difficult to find, in the depths of a new precinct that has been added on to the more historic Devonshire Square. Its pedigree is thoroughbred – both owners and chef come from Magno's Brasserie in Covent Garden (see entry). This is no brasserie, but a sleek, air-conditioned basement with low ceilings, fat pillars, tubular chairs, waiters with designer haircuts operating out of a black central dais. Spotlights pick out the white of the tablecloths. The pastel mural of kitchen utensils around two walls is subdued by all this elegance, like a view outside, as if from one age to another. The champagne bar itself runs down one side – a glass is £3.25 – and the tables down the other are divided by a sofa. The menu changes daily (£12.95). It is a colourful rendition of modern French cooking which does not stint on its ingredients. A salad starter in June comprised asparagus tips on a bed of ratatouille (which included peppers) surrounded by crayfish tails in a deep, almost metallic-tasting crustacean sauce. Equally intriguing were roast sweetbreads with a spinach sauce flavoured with foie gras. It is a wide-ranging menu that sensibly is not above serving grilled sea-bream or pan-fried sirloin steak with onions. There has been a great renaissance, at last, in the City for food, and this can be counted among the leaders, though at these prices so it should be. Small points like a good white wine brought to the table warm, and the tell-tale grey of an avocado that has been pre-prepared. It is a rich man's wine list – the wine of the month, a sensible policy, for instance, is likely to cost about £16, but there is good Beaujolais from Georges Duboeuf from the fine 1985s at around £10 and house Blanc de Blancs is £6.25.

Open Mon to Fri, L only **Meals** 11.30 to 2.30 **Cards** Access, Amex, Diners, Visa **Service** Inc (set L); otherwise 12½% **Underground** Liverpool Street

---

Corney & Barrow Map 6	✗ ♀
44 Cannon Street, EC4 *Telephone* 01-248 1700	£–££££

Corney & Barrow appear to have researched their bullish restaurant expansion with the precision of a stock market coup. This outlet is aimed at the younger end of the market, as befits this end of the City, traditionally the home of furriers and insurers. Upstairs is a shop and wine bar, with videobox tunes at night, serving less expensive snacks; downstairs an air-conditioned salmon-pink dining-room with a crew of attentive waiters in black and white. The menu is cosmopolitan, tailored to the needs of international business – chilled cucumber soup, asparagus with a pimento mayonnaise, red bream with vegetables au

THE CITY

gratin, grilled shark steak with hot chilli sauce. There are imaginative puddings, taking in the California-style fruit kebab or a Francophile version of summer pudding. The wine list is twenty pages long and the advice from the sommelier steers downwards in price towards some unusual bottles. The Moorgate and Cannon Street branches have the same excellent range with some brilliant wines. There is a bit under £10 in the usual places, Loire, Beaujolais, and one or two (literally) in Italy and Spain, but the overall emphasis seems to be on expense account drinking. At this branch breakfasts are served from 7am.

Open Mon to Fri, L only **Meals** 11.30 to 3 **Cards** Access, Amex, Diners, Visa **Service** 12½%
Underground Cannon Street

Corney & Barrow Map 6	
118 Moorgate, EC2 *Telephone* 01-628 2898	£–££££

From this air-conditioned Hollywood-style basement done out in chrome, black, reds and show-business-style down-lighting the wine merchants Corney & Barrow have launched a great drive for good food in the City. Snack lunchers, drinkers and serious lunchers mingle in the basement so the atmosphere is, as the French would say, *mouvementé* and by 1 o'clock there is a fair amount of noise. Robin Stewart has taken over the kitchen and there has been a noticeable improvement in the food, though the service can bend under the strain at peak hours. This is a shame, because the food is delicate and needs careful handling in the dining-room. The *nouvelle* influence is stronger here than at the other branches (see above and below) and more use is made of particular ingredients, such as unusual fungi or walnut oil. Fine examples of a persuasive style have been terrine of salmon and turbot in a semi-set jelly with French parsley, basil, tomato and chopped hard-boiled egg, served with a side salad as a starter, and sole fillets with oyster mushrooms in a white wine sauce. The cheeseboard has flags for easy identification and usually sports some twenty specimens in good condition, most of them French. Sweets have been excellent (noticeably better than at the Cannon Street branch), and French-inspired in their leaning to chocolate, banana mousses and pastries. Another difference in this parent branch has been that it appears to have attracted more women and more non-City people. There is a minimum charge of £20 in the restaurant proper. The wine list is what you might expect, subtly different from the other branches, running to two hundred bottles and stronger in claret than red Burgundy, with good representations from other areas of France. Even if you're only having a light snack, it's worth asking to see the main list, where, apart from everything else, are 15 useful half-bottles.

Open Mon to Sat **Meals** 11.30 to 3 **Cards** Access, Amex, Diners, Visa **Service** 12½%
Underground Moorgate

Corney & Barrow Map 6	
109 Old Broad Street, EC2 *Telephone* 01-638 9308 and 920 9560	££££

This is hard-core City – the Bank of England, the Stock Exchange, Bendick's mints, Church's shoes. The restaurant in the air-conditioned basement reflects

39

LONDON

this and is noticeably different from the other two Corney & Barrow restaurants. Note that this hasn't got a wine bar, either. First, the decor is old school, redolent of the English country house, full of old oil paintings, mahogany and marble. The food comes on patterned Limoges porcelain. The menu is an altogether more ambitious proposition. It is more continental, richer, less fashionable, shorter. François Schmitt has a more distinctive style, relying on cream but evoking stronger, more Middle European flavours, albeit with subtlety – for instance, potato pancakes, horseradish, pike, cherry vinegar. Smoked oysters are used to garnish soup. One excellent starter comprised an oval feuilleté with pearl onions and a cream sauce flavoured with orange and garnished with tomato. Grilled venison is served with a port sauce with strips of celeriac and a small pile of fresh spätzli noodles, some green, some red, some white. The petits fours and the sweets match. No pipes to be smoked in the dining-room; music. Just look what's happened to the wine prices. Dom Pérignon 1978 at Moorgate is £50; here it is £68. Ch Pétrus 1976 at Moorgate is £160; here £200. And so on.

Open Mon to Fri, L only **Meals** 12 to 2.30 **Cards** Access, Amex, Diners, Visa **Service** 15%
Underground Liverpool Street

Davys of London Map 6 (mostly)   ♀

Arch 9 Arch 9, Old Seacoal Lane, EC4 *Telephone* 01-248 8991   £
Bishop of Norwich 91–93 Moorgate, EC2 *Telephone* 01-920 0857
Bishop's Parlour 91–93 Moorgate, EC2 *Telephone* 01-588 2581
Boot & Flogger 10–20 Redcross Way, SE1 (Map 2) *Telephone* 01-407 1184
Bottlescrue 53–60 Holborn Viaduct, EC1 *Telephone* 01-248 2157
Bung Hole 57 High Holborn, WC1 *Telephone* 01-242 4318
Burgundy Bens 102/108 Clerkenwell Road, EC1 (Map 2)
Telephone 01-251 3783
Champagne Charlies 325 Essex Road, Islington N1 (Map 2)
Telephone 01-226 4078
Chopper Lump 10C Hanover Square, W1 (Map 4) *Telephone* 01-499 7569
City Boot 7 Moorfields High Walk, EC2 *Telephone* 01-588 4766
City Flogger 120 Fenchurch Street, EC3 *Telephone* 01-623 3251
City FOB Lower Thames Street, EC3 *Telephone* 01-621 0619
City Pipe Foster Lane, EC2 *Telephone* 01-606 2110
City Vaults 2 St Martins-le-Grand, EC1 *Telephone* 01-606 8721
Colonel Jaspers 161 Greenwich High Road, SE10 (Map 1)
Telephone 01-853 0585
Colonel Jaspers 190 City Road, EC1 (Map 2) *Telephone* 01-608 0925
The Cooperage 48–50 Tooley Street, SE1 *Telephone* 01-403 5775
Crusting Pipe 27 The Market, Covent Garden, WC2 (Map 5)
Telephone 01-836 1415
Davy's Wine Vaults 161 Greenwich High Road, SE10 (Map 1)
Telephone 01-858 7204

---

*See the back of the Guide for ideas for day trips out of London:
Brighton, Cambridge, Canterbury, Oxford, and Windsor and Eton.*

THE CITY

Grape Shots 2/3 Artillery Passage, E1 *Telephone* 01-247 8215
Gyngle Boy 27 Spring Street, W2 (Map 2) *Telephone* 01-723 3351
Lees Bag 4 Great Portland Street, W1 (Map 4) *Telephone* 01-636 5287
Mother Bunch's Seacoal Lane, EC4 *Telephone* 01-236 5317
The Pulpit 63 Worship Street, EC2 (Map 2) *Telephone* 01-377 1574
Segar & Snuff Parlour 27A The Market, Covent Garden, WC2 (Map 5) *Telephone* 01-836 8345
Skinkers 42 Tooley Street, SE1 *Telephone* 01-407 9189
The Spittoon 15–17 Long Lane, EC1 *Telephone* 01-726 8858
Tappit-Hen 5 William IV Street, WC2 (Map 4) *Telephone* 01-836 9839
Tapster 3 Brewers Green, Buckingham Gate, SW1 (Map 2) *Telephone* 01-222 0561
Udder Place Wine Rooms Russia Court, Russia Row, 1–6 Milk Street, EC2 *Telephone* 01-600 2165
The Vineyard International House, St Katherine's Way, E1 (Map 2) *Telephone* 01-480 6680
Wine Shop 151 Borough High Street, SE1 (Map 2) *Telephone* 01-407 1484

There are probably fifty Davys wine bars by now, most in the City, the rest in other parts of London and (a few) in the country. In pleasingly eccentric locations – railway arches are popular – they ooze atmosphere with casks, candles and sawdusty floors. John Davy is an astute and active wine merchant so look out for special offers on the blackboard. The basic list offers a reliable three dozen bins, eight of them by the glass: French 'Ordnary' No 1 red or white; fresh and delicious hock and Bordeaux Sauvignon 1985, claret and Rioja. By the bottle, choose perhaps from the Gisselbrecht Pinot Blanc d'Alsace 1984 (£5.35), Beaujolais St Amour Domaine de Billards 1985 (£7.25) and Davys Graves (bottled at Ch Millet, £8.25). The Boot and Flogger, where Davy himself is to be found, has a breathtaking list of fine claret, Burgundy and port, all of which can be summoned to one of the other bars on 24 hours' notice: a run of Ch Latour from 1881 to 1971 (£150 to £40), Ch Margaux 1957 (£48), a magnum of Ch Calon-Ségur 1962 (£65), Louis Latour Romanée-St-Vivant or Volnay 1971 (each £45), Warre's 1963 vintage port (£45), or – low for price if not quality – Ch La Mission-Haut-Brion 1976 (£20). The blackboard often yields other fine ports, and the 'ordnary' is very drinkable at £1.25. The English-sounding food often tastes less interesting than it sounds.

Open Weekdays 11 to 3, 5.30 to 8 **Closed** Sat, Sun, public holidays **NB** Hours may vary from branch to branch

Fox and Anchor Map 6

115 Charterhouse Street, EC1 *Telephone* 01-253 4838

This pub, right by Smithfield meat market and frequented by the meat porters, has established itself as a good place for enormous, reasonably priced breakfasts. The complete version comes piled with bacon, eggs, sausage, beans, tomatoes, mushrooms, fried bread and black pudding (though you

LONDON

can order less if you want). With a couple of cups of coffee, the bill should not be much more than £6. Licensed to sell alcohol from first thing in the morning.

Open 6am to 3pm **Closed** Sat and Sun; Christmas; last week Aug **Underground** Barbican

Ginnan Map 6

5 Cathedral Place, EC4 *Telephone* 01-236 4120 and 5150   £–£££

The Ginnan is virtually two restaurants in one. At lunchtime, when the set meals are £3 and £5.80, it is a packed café offering extraordinarily good value where Japanese businessmen eat at an extraordinary pace. Tables can be turned round in fifteen minutes. In the evening the pace slows down and some very fine classic Japanese cooking is on offer. There are two set meals in the evening (from £15), plus some daily dishes written in Japanese that are worth pursuing. For instance, there has been eel wrapped in seaweed, tuna with fermented beans, and beef with lemon sauce. There is a wide range of Japanese drinks, too. Air-conditioning and music.

Open Mon to Sat, exc Sat D **Closed** Public hols **Meals** 12 to 2.30, 6 to 10 **Cards** Access, Amex, Diners, Visa **Underground** St Paul's

The Greenhouse Map 6

16–17 Royal Exchange, EC3 *Telephone* 01-236 7077   ££

The City's smallest, most elegant – and most crowded – wine bar, run by wine merchants Green's, welcomes the Big Bang in style with a range of fine Champagnes: Floquet Brut Réserve; Krug 1979 (£48). There are few other wines by the glass – try Sancerre Clos du Roi 1984 Domaine Reverdy-Ducroux (£1.80) unless you fancy the good house sherries, Madeiras and port (Superior Old Tawny, £2.20). Freshly squeezed orange juice is £1.50 alone, £2.70 as part of a buck's fizz. There are appropriately elegant smoked salmon sandwiches and quails' eggs to nibble.

Open Mon to Fri 11.30 to 3, 5 to 8 **Closed** Sat, Sun, public holidays **Cards** None accepted **Underground** Bank

Hana Guruma Map 6

49 Bow Lane, EC4 *Telephone* 01-236 6451   £££–££££

This has a good reputation in the Japanese community, though the cooking seems to verge on the safe side. The atmosphere and style are geared towards Japanese in London and the menu features most of the main styles of cooking. Yakitori dishes include dried fish flown in from Japan. Standards are consistent; the tofu and eel dishes are particularly interesting. Regulars have their own bottles of whisky put aside. Wheelchair access; music and air-conditioning. Like most Japanese restaurants in this country, Hana Guruma offers sushi.

Other London restaurants offering an unusually diverse sushi selection are:

THE CITY

Matano, 25–27 Brewer Street, W1 (01-734 1859); **Defune**, 61 Blandford Street, W1 (01-935 8311); and **Sakura**, 9 Hanover Street, W1 (01-629 2961).

Open Mon to Fri **Closed** 25 Dec and 1st week Jan **Meals** 12 to 2.30, 6 to 11 **Cards** Access, Amex, Diners, Visa **Underground** Mansion House

Museum of London Restaurant Map 6

150 London Wall, EC2 *Telephone* 01-726 4446

One of the new wave of fine museum cafés run by Milburns. The bare concrete interior is made stylish with standing lamps and light wooden furniture and there is a terrace outside for warm weather. All the food is prepared on the premises from ingredients bought in every day. The self-service arrangement offers everything from a cup of tea and a croissant to a three-course meal with wine. Mushroom soup, cold roast beef salad, apple and peach tart and cheeses have all been good.

Open 10am (noon Sun) to 5pm **Underground** Barbican/St Paul's

Olde Cheshire Cheese Map 6

Wine Office Court; off 145 Fleet Street, EC4
Telephone 01-353 6170/4388

The small rooms in this interesting and unpretentious pub, up and down stairs, have sawdust on bare boards, bare wooden benches built in to the walls, and on the ground floor high beams, crackly old black varnish, Victorian paintings on the dark brown walls, and a big open fire in winter; the vaulted cellars survived the Great Fire of London (1666). Congreve, Pope, Voltaire, Thackeray, Dickens, Conan Doyle, Yeats and perhaps Dr Johnson used to eat and drink here, and the bustling mixture of tourists, lawyers and journalists, squeezing up and down the panelled stairway or spilling out into the narrow courtyard, somehow suits it very well. Real ales include a well-kept Marstons Pedigree tapped from the cask; snacks like filled rolls (the steak, kidney, mushroom and game pie – £4.50 – in the busy little upstairs restaurant is something of an institution). Children are welcome.

Open 11.30 to 3, 5 to 9 **Closed** Sat, Sun and public hols **Underground** Blackfriars

Old Mitre Map 6

Ely Place, EC1; there's also an entrance beside 8 Hatton Garden

This carefully rebuilt Taylor-Walkers pub, with its quaint façade, carries the same name of an earlier inn built here in 1547 to serve the people working in the palace of the Bishop of Ely, who actually administered the law here. In theory, the police still have to get permission to enter the court, and only recent fire regulations have ended the tradition of the beadle locking up the entrance gates

For an explanation of licensing laws in London, see page 215.

LONDON

with the cry of 'Past ten o'clock and all's well'. The dark-panelled small rooms have antique settles, jugs hanging from the beams and big vases of flowers. Perhaps because of the way this cottage is so discreetly tucked away from the big-building City bustle, it has a pleasantly countrified atmosphere. Bar snacks include Scotch eggs and pork pies, pork sausages, ham or cheese rolls, and a good selection of plain or toasted sandwiches such as ham, salmon and cucumber or egg mayonnaise, turkey and roast beef; there is also French bread with Cheddar cheese or Camembert; well-kept Friary Meux and Ind Coope Burton on handpump, reasonably priced for the area. There are some seats with pot plants and jasmine in the narrow yard between the pub and St Ethelreda's church.

Open 11 to 3, 5.30 to 11 **Closed** Sat, Sun and public hols **Underground** Chancery Lane

Old Wine Shades Map 6

6 Martin Lane, EC4   £

The interior of this pub looks much as it did in Victorian times, with antique tables and old-fashioned high-backed settles, old prints, subdued lighting and dignified alcoves; the heavy black beams and dark panelling conjure up the days before the Great Fire of 1666 and, indeed, this building is one of the very few in the City to have escaped it. It's a lively place at lunchtime, quieter in the evening, and they keep a good range of wines; bar lunches include sandwiches, jacket potato filled with cheese, various pies and quiche, pâté and French bread with a choice of seven cheeses. They insist on collar, tie, jacket and trousers for men, and no jeans or jump-suits for women.

Open 11.30 to 3, 5 to 8 **Closed** Sat, Sun and public hols **Underground** Monument

The Pavilion Map 6

Finsbury Circus Garden, Finsbury Circus, EC2   ££
Telephone 01-628 8224

Pale green walls, air-conditioning and a good view of the bowling-green (this used to be the clubhouse) distinguish the Pavilion from other City dives. David Gilmour's wines are interestingly chosen and so enticingly annotated that you want to sample the lot. Even the blackboard tempts with Hidalgo sherries, Rutherford & Miles Madeiras (splendid with the fruit cake) and Taylor's ports, as well as eight table wines: Humbrecht's Muscat d'Alsace 1983 (£1.75); Ch La Terrasse 1981 (£1.60); house French white or hock (£1.35). Thereafter range through excellent examples from classic regions (Brédif's Sparkling Vouvray, £9; St-Aubin Les Frionnes 1984, Hubert Lamy, £10.80; fine Bordeaux and Burgundies) as well as California Merlot 1981, Firestone (£8.20) and a 'racy, light, dry' Greek, Gentilini 1984 (£13.50). Service is hard-pressed but charming; there is a basement restaurant, and continental breakfast is served from 7.45am to 8.30am, to advance order.

Open Mon to Fri 7.45 to 8.30, 11.30 to 3, 5 to 8 **Closed** Sat, Sun and public hols
Cards Access, Amex, Visa **Underground** Moorgate/Liverpool Street

THE CITY

Le Poulbot Map 6

45 Cheapside, EC2 *Telephone* 01-236 4379   ££–££££

The queues upstairs are a good recommendation for the inexpensive brasserie here, called Le Poulbot Pub, while the basement is the (air-conditioned) executive suite, where the bill will be twice as much, or more. Rowley Leigh cooks a weekly changing menu (£24.50) with a choice of half a dozen dishes. The ingredients come via the Roux network and the style is that potently sauced, slightly rich mix of classic and modern that is peculiar to the brothers. Mr Leigh is a faithful disciple, conjuring up lobster minestrone, turbot with lentils, and sweetbreads with noodles and onions. The sauces lead meals like banners at the front of a procession: cream and shrimps with quenelles, rosemary with red mullet, tarragon with lamb, wild strawberry with poached peach. At the foot of the menu are sensible, if expensive, suggestions of wines to drink. The service has French as its first language. At inspection it was nice to see the sommelier's duties being carried out by a woman, for a change. Men should, of course, wear a jacket and tie, this being the City.

Open Mon to Fri, L only **Closed** Public hols and 1 week at Christmas **Meals** 12 to 3 **Cards** Access, Amex, Carte Blanche, Diners, Visa **Service** Inc **Underground** Mansion House/St Paul's

Punters Map 6

5 Abchurch Yard, Abchurch Lane, EC4 *Telephone* 01-623 2355   £–££

Caroline Mack's cellar bar is deservedly popular, for her interest shows in both the carefully chosen wines and the advice she offers when asked. French house wines and a few others are available by the glass, but the interest lies in the main list: an excellent Entre-Deux-Mers, Ch Thieuley 1984 (£6.95), Trimbach's delicious Pinot Blanc 1983 (£6.45), a Premières Côtes de Blaye, Ch Grolet 1976 (£7.75), the organic Côtes de Ventoux, La Vieille Ferme 1983 (£5.55/£2.95 half) and the good Spanish Raïmat Abadía Reserva 1981 (£5.60). House champagne comes in magnum for celebrations (£23) and there are many fine ports by the glass (including two vintage ones decanted daily). Freshly cooked snacks and full restaurant meals.

Open Mon to Fri 11.30 to 3, 5 to 8 **Closed** Sat, Sun and public hols **Cards** Access, Amex, Diners, Visa **Underground** Bank/Cannon Street

Reynier at Fleet Lane Map 6

29 Fleet Lane, Old Bailey, EC1 *Telephone* 01-236 0552   £

On the analogy of a 'restaurant with rooms', this is a 'wine shop with tables'. You choose – with sound advice – from the 700 or so items on the impressive Eldridge Pope/Reynier list at off-sales prices, and then go down to the clubbily stylish cellar bar to enjoy your find along with pâtés, cheeses, fruit and coffee (£5). The list, with its strong French bias, is worth leisurely study. Note particularly the generous number of halves: chosen almost at random, the house champagne (£4.57); Muscat les Amandiers 1983 Dopff & Irion (£2.83); Ch

LONDON

Feytit-Clinet 1982 (£4.83); and the Chairman's delicious late-bottled port (£2.83). Full bottles range from Colombard Vin de Pays de Côtes de Gascogne (£5.47) through fine Australians and Californians and superb Bordeaux – even Ch Lafite 1975 (£103.50). Beware City cigars, a hazard in the tiny cellar.

Open Mon to Fri 11.30 to 3, 5 to 7.30 **Closed** Sat, Sun and public hols **Cards** Access, Visa **Underground** St Paul's/Blackfriars

COVENT GARDEN

Ajimura Map 5

51–53 Shelton Street, WC2 *Telephone* 01-240 0178   ££

As Japanese food, with its fresh flavours, artful presentation and nutritional soundness, gets more popular in the capital, old-stagers such as this restaurant finally come into their own. The moon-shaped sushi bar holds about 15 people for its constructions of raw fish, sheet seaweed and vinegared rice, or there is a dining-area with varnished pine tables. Clear soups, tuna sushi, and fried pork and salmon – both served with rice – make a good introduction to the cuisine. Beautifully carved fruit to finish. Saké to drink. Any confusion that arises from the waiters' English is more than made up for in profuse apologies.

Open Noon to 3, 6 to 11 (10.30 Sun) **Closed** Sat L and Sun L; 24 Dec to 3 Jan **Underground** Covent Garden

Boulestin Map 5

1A Henrietta Street, WC2 *Telephone* 01-836 7061   £££–££££

Boulestin is like a great football club. It may not be top of the league, but its reputation is constant. Of all the dining-rooms of London it is among the most impressive – orange-brown marbled wallpaper, a couple of Greek-style columns, original oils, chandeliers with decorative segments that look like the arched body of a scorpion. The menu, written in over-the-top French, is basically French and relies on fashionable luxuries for impact – scallop tartare with snails' eggs, magret of goose with prunes and armagnac, chicken with crab and Sauternes. Boulestin is in the super-financial stratosphere, and the less expensive set lunch (£15) does not seem to be of the quality of the *carte* (minimum £25 at dinner). But typical of successes are the hot slices of foie gras on a faint quenelle of duck with some potent wild mushrooms in an excellent pastry cup and a sauce made of reduced stock. Cheeses come from Androuët in Paris, waiters are everywhere, and the wines are mostly from Burgundy and Bordeaux. The last are by no means cheap, but they are from good vintages, ready for drinking – clarets from 1961, 1966 and 1970, nothing later than 1979 in 1986, for a *bourgeois* choice half-bottle of Ch La Gurgue 1979 at £8, and the Burgundy section especially is from good shippers.

Open Mon to Sat, exc Sat L **Closed** 3 weeks Aug, 1 week at Christmas **Meals** 12.30 to 2.30, 7.30 to 11.15 **Cards** Access, Amex, Diners, Visa **Service** 15% **Underground** Covent Garden

COVENT GARDEN

Le Café du Jardin Map 5

28 Wellington Street, WC2 *Telephone* 01-836 8769 and 8760   ££–£££

Staff used not to be surprised by complaints in this busy brasserie, but standards have levelled out considerably recently. The food is prepared with care and the menu is artfully constructed to give the kitchen time to concentrate on the main dishes, which are in the *routier* tradition of chicken with a champagne sauce made with stock and flour, or onglet (blade steak) with a confit of onions. Vegetables are charged separately but have been worth it; sweets rely heavily on fruit and cheese. House wine is £5.45. Other bottles appear to be overpriced, but as there are no details on the wine list it is hard to be certain. Vegetarian meals; children's helpings; wheelchair access, music; air-conditioning. They offer a pre-theatre menu at £6.45.

Open Mon to Sat, exc Sat L **Meals** 12 to 2.30, 6 to 11.30 **Cards** Access, Amex, Diners, Visa **Service** 10% **Underground** Covent Garden

Café Pelican Map 5

45 St Martin's Lane, WC2 *Telephone* 01-379 0309   £–£££

On the same scale as some of the large famous Parisian brasseries, such as La Coupole on boulevard Montparnasse: the single, long room has white linen, cane chairs and there are some pavement tables. There is a wide range on the menu, from saucisson sec, sliced thinly into a large, crisp baguette roll, accompanied by a little pot of gherkins and onions, to thick fish soup, a creamy rouille and crisp croûtons. The entrecôte frites is reliable, but there are more ambitious formal dishes, including lobster or a very rich mousse of bitter chocolate. You can have anything from a snack, to a set meal (£12.95) or anything off the *carte*. If standards lapse it is because the turnover is four hundred covers a day, which is a feat in itself. The Pelican opens early and closes late, making it doubly useful in the area. House wine is £5.50. Vegetarian meals; children's helpings; wheelchair access; music; air-conditioning.

Open All week **Meals** 11am to 2am **Cards** Access, Amex, Diners, Visa **Underground** Leicester Square

Calabash Map 5

38 King Street, WC2 *Telephone* 01-836 1976   £–££

African restaurant serving dishes from Egypt, Uganda, the Ivory Coast, Zaïre and Nigeria. Set at the back end of a basement with a separate bar in front, it is a long, narrow, relaxed room with sofas round the walls and ethnic tablecloths and pictures; everything else is of the cafeteria style. Délice de Calabash to start

---

We give information about wheelchair access only when we are sure about it, which tends to be in restaurants and hotels. Many pubs may also be accessible to wheelchairs.

LONDON

is avocado with black-eyed beans in a vinegary dressing with a heap of grated coconut and a garnish of onion slivers. Main courses have been variable: kuku wa kupaka, from the East African coast, is tender, wet-cooked chicken in a thin, translucent coconut cream; moambe, from Zaïre, is coarse stewing beef in spinach and palm oil gravy. Service is informal. Don't go if you're in a hurry.

Open Noon to 3, 6 to 10.30 **Closed** Sun **Underground** Covent Garden

Charing Cross Hotel Map 4

Strand, WC2 *Telephone* 01-839 7282   ££

Thought by some to be much the best of the London railway hotels built by the Victorians, this one actually sits astride the station. It would be a good choice for an avid theatre- or opera-goer, being at most fifteen minutes' walk from the majority of the theatres, including the National Theatre complex the other side of the river across Hungerford foot bridge. Rooms are practical, comfortable and painted in pastel colour schemes. Trafalgar Square is so close that with a periscope Lord Nelson and his armada of pigeons could almost peer down from their column into the rooms at the front. The Carvery offers a set meal at £9.50.

Open (Restaurant) 7 to 10, 12 to 3, 5.30 to 11 **Closed** 3–4 days at Christmas **Cards** Access, Amex, Diners, Visa **Accommodations** 218 rooms, all with bath and shower. B&B £25 to £43 **Underground** Charing Cross

La Corée Map 4

56 St Giles High Street, WC2 *Telephone* 01-836 7235   £–£££

Not much English is spoken at this little Korean restaurant in the shadow of Centre Point. The food is beautifully presented, and the corner-stones of the cooking are handled with unusual skill – potent kim-chee, fine bulgogi, good pickles and fried meat dumplings. It is unpretentious and welcoming. Barley tea is free. Children welcome; wheelchair access; music.

Open Mon to Sat **Meals** 12 to 2.45, 6 to 10.15 **Cards** Access, Amex, Diners, Visa **Service** 10% **Underground** Tottenham Court Road

Cranks Map 5

17 Great Newport Street, WC2 *Telephone* 01-836 5226   £–££

See the Soho section for the main Cranks entry.

Open 8am (10 Sat) to 7.30pm **Closed** Sun; public hols **Underground** Leicester Square

Diana's Diner Map 5

39 Endell Street, WC2 *Telephone* 01-240 0272   £

Small and steamy café serving cheap, huge portions of fish and chips, pie and chips, home-made burgers, omelettes and fry-ups. The meat is from Smithfield,

COVENT GARDEN

the fish from Billingsgate, the vegetables from Spitalfields: all good, honest, gutsy stuff. Unlicensed.

Open 8.30am to 7pm (9am to 2pm Sat) **Closed** Sat D; Sun; 1 week at Christmas **Underground** Covent Garden

Fielding Hotel Map 5

4 Broad Court, Bow Street, WC2 *Telephone* 01-836 8305

A small modest hotel in a quiet pedestrian alley across the yard from Bow Street Magistrates' Court and within 100 yards of the Royal Opera House. 'A super situation. The hotel is unpretentious and not suitable for those who find stairs difficult or who suffer from claustrophobia. The first time our room was small but adequate, with good roomy furniture but not much circulating space. The second time I was on my own and had a single "suite" which turned out to be a very ingenious use of space. A little sitting-room, then down a steep flight of stairs to the bed and the bathroom. It was rather fun, and newly decorated. Between the two visits a few more coats of paint had been deposited on the stairways to good effect. There is a little bar with a talkative mynah bird and efficient but minimal staff. Both times I had breakfast in Covent Garden. For the right sort of visitor it is such a delightful situation that its limitations are totally acceptable.' No children under twelve. No restaurant.

Open All year except Christmas **Cards** Access, Amex, Diners, Visa **Accommodations** 26 rooms (24 with shower) – 5 rooms on ground floor. B&B £17.50 to £35 **Underground** Covent Garden

Food for Thought Map 5

31 Neal Street, WC2 *Telephone* 01-836 0239

There is room to sit in the basement of this vegetarian food bar, but not much. The cooking is continuous so the menu changes twice a day, rolling through casseroles, bakes, quiches, and salads (the choice gets a bit limited around tea-time). The smells fill the room. Chilled apple juice comes in mugs when the glasses run out. Unlicensed, but bring your own: no corkage charged. There is a takeaway counter upstairs, which at peak times is the sensible course of action. Children are welcome but not smokers.

Open Mon to Fri **Closed** 2 weeks at Christmas **Meals** 12 to 8 **Underground** Covent Garden

Gordon's Wine Bar Map 4

47 Villiers Street, WC2 *Telephone* 01-930 1408

A real piece of old London, with real drips off the real cavernous brickwork ceiling, real cobwebs, real old headlines framed into posters, real old ports, Madeiras and sherries behind the bar, and real food for which real queues form. The cooking has one eye on London for its pies – notably good pork – and one on the Mediterranean for pissaladière or mussels provençale. It is earthy fare, and can be as simple as a parsnip bake. Rarely is it the same. The back-up is half a dozen imaginative salads plus good cheeses. Wines aren't up to much apart

49

LONDON

from the fortified ones. Gordon's claims to be the oldest wine bar in the country. When it's fine the tables outside by the old Thames watergate are popular.

Open Mon to Fri **Meals** 12.15 to 2.45, 5.45 to 8 **Cards** None accepted **Service** Inc **Underground** Charing Cross/Embankment

---

Inigo Jones Map 5

14 Garrick Street, WC2 *Telephone* 01-836 6456 and 3223   ££££

This has never been a place to go to if you worry about money. The cooking aspires to the first division in Europe – and some of it is there. Paul Gayler runs with the fashions and he offers a vegetarian menu, a *bourgeois* dish of the day, and an affordable set lunch and pre-theatre menu (£14.75) as well as a scandalously pricey *carte* that owes a lot to his mentor, Anton Mosimann at the Dorchester. He has his own trademarks. As a stylist he is perhaps the most accomplished in Britain today. Dishes, especially the sweets, look like works of art. But they are also characterful in conception and execution – for instance, brill with a sauce flavoured with sea-urchins; lambs' sweetbreads and kidneys served with tiny squares of pastry in a sauce of port and redcurrant jelly; ravioli with mussel and oyster sauce; cabbage broth with creamed Roquefort spiced with cumin. The vegetables are like toys. At its worst it is designer food, but at its best it is stunning. The sauces can be either vibrant or, occasionally, a bit dull. Passion-fruit mousse is three mounds topped with kiwi and strawberry, and strawberry sauce with an ace of spades pattern repeated three times on the sauce. The decor matches: downstairs is pink carpets, rough red brick walls, crisp white cloths, large glasses, black marbled plates; the place is air-conditioned. Service is attentive and the trimmings are of a very fine restaurant indeed – a choice of fresh breads, of which the black is a favourite, and a choice of butters. The wine list is unrepentantly French in content and price, with the merest nod to Germany. A tenner will not buy much more than one of the twenty-five half-bottles, but there are some solid buys for solid wallets, such as Ch Caronne Ste-Gemme 1979 at £18.50. The 1983 vintage from Alsace is well represented – Beyer's Riesling Les Ecaillers is £14.30 – and Henri Maire wines from the Jura add interest.

Open Mon to Sat, exc Sat L **Meals** 12 to 2.30, 5.30 to 11.30 **Cards** Access, Amex, Diners, Visa **Service** 15% **Underground** Leicester Square

---

Joe Allen Map 5

13 Exeter Street, WC2 *Telephone* 01-836 0651   ££–£££

Not as sharp as it was, but on its night the homesick can still feel as if they're in New York. Splendid burgers, real chips, fine black bean soup, excellent ribs and great salads are the things in this cavernous basement (hardly marked from the pavement outside). Minus points are the smoky atmosphere and (if you're famous) the autograph hunter.

Open Noon to 1am (midnight Sun) **Cards** None accepted **Underground** Covent Garden/Charing Cross

COVENT GARDEN

Lamb & Flag Map 5

Rose Street, WC2   £

A Dickensian pub with a fine choice of well-kept cheeses, this is so handy for Covent Garden that it does get very crowded. But somehow – perhaps because it's hidden away up its own alley – it seems to escape being dominated by the somewhat brash Covent Garden atmosphere that has pervaded so many pubs around here. The back room is much as it was when Dickens described the Middle Temple lawyers who frequented it when he was working in nearby Catherine Street – a low ceiling, high-backed black settles and an open fire. Other bar food includes ham and pâtés served with hot or French bread, and lunchtime hot dishes (served weekdays only) such as pasty, mash and beans, steak and kidney pie, salt beef or chilli con carne. Children are allowed during lunchtime only. Well-kept Courage Best and Directors on handpump under light blanket pressure. Darts in the small front public bar. Dryden was nearly beaten to death by hired thugs in the courtyard outside.

Open 11 to 3, 5.30 to 11 **Closed** 25 and 26 Dec, evening of 31 Dec and 1 Jan **Underground** Leicester Square/Covent Garden

Magno's Brasserie Map 5

65A Long Acre, WC2 *Telephone* 01-836 6077   ££–£££

The bistro ambience is compiled by bentwood cane chairs, wooden wine racks, tables close together and a sensibly short menu. Sauces are particularly fine – vinaigrette for kidneys, fennel for plaice, leek for monkfish. The cooking straddles both modern and traditional: fish is as equally well achieved as, say, the calf's liver glazed with honey and offset by plain braised endive. The menu has got slightly more expensive to take on board a few more luxuries such as wild mushrooms and foie gras. But the mundane impress too: tomato soup, poached cod with tarragon sauce, and rich chocolate mousse. If you go for the set dinner at £8.45, £8.45 is what you end up paying since it includes wine and service. The relatively small but perfectly formed wine list takes white seriously from Jura, Loire, Alsace, Burgundy, Australia and California – and reds even more so: Dujac and Tollot-Beaut Burgundies; Ch Rayas and Jaboulet Rhônes; Ch de Pez 1979 among the clarets; and a misclassified but first-rate 1983 Ch Bellevue-la-Forêt from Côtes du Fronton at £6.75. For the most part, all that's left from a £10 note is the rustle.

Open Mon to Sat, exc Sat L **Closed** 24 Dec to 2 Jan **Meals** 12 to 2.30, 6 to 11.30 **Cards** Access, Amex, Diners, Visa **Service** 12½% (à la carte only) **Underground** Covent Garden

Mon Plaisir Map 5

21 Monmouth Street, WC2 *Telephone* 01-836 7243 and 240 3757   ££–£££

This old favourite has been spruced up without being messed about, and the food is competent and well presented. The pleasures are somewhat old-fashioned, but the dining-room bustles as a neighbourhood restaurant

51

LONDON

should, with tables close together. It is a useful source for omelettes, sole, steak with thin chips, and coq au vin. Vegetables are an extra charge. The set lunch is £8.75, the set dinner £18. Alsace wines stay under £10, Burgundy is the strong suit, but there is also St Emilion, Ch La Picherie, at £13. Children's helpings; wheelchair access; music.

Open Mon to Sat, exc Sat L **Meals** 12 to 2.15, 6 to 11.15 **Cards** None accepted **Service** 12.5% **Underground** Leicester Square

---

Neal Street Restaurant   Map 5

26 Neal Street, WC2 *Telephone* 01-836 8368   ££££

The Neal Street Restaurant is rather English, in the sense that it is reserved about its virtues. It veers towards the expensive but the return visit rate is high because it consistently does well what other restaurants do badly. The menu is modern, offering a genuine choice and quite a lot of it – from foie gras served on radicchio, to duck breast with mango, to fine crème brûlée. White truffles in the autumn and wild mushrooms through the year – the twin enthusiasms of manager and Svengali Antonio Carluccio – are specialities. As with the modern British cooking (this is really more European) there is no over-embellishment but a precision of ideas, whether the result is steak and kidney pie or smoked eel with scrambled egg. The paintings are by Hockney and the clarets are predominantly *crus classés*, though there are less expensive Beaujolais. The quartet of house wines at £6.50 are eminently drinkable. Wheelchair access; air-conditioning.

Open Mon to Fri **Closed** Christmas to New Year **Meals** 12.30 to 2.30, 7.30 to 11 **Cards** Access, Amex, Diners, Visa **Service** 15% **Underground** Covent Garden

---

Neal's Yard Bakery & Tea Room   Map 5

6 Neal's Yard, WC2 *Telephone* 01-836 5199   £

Set up as a bakery and wholefood co-operative in 1978, Neal's Yard has bloomed into a thriving centre for real food. Some say their wholemeal bread, made from organically grown cereal ground in their own mill, is the best in London, but that is just the start. There's also a dairy shop selling one of the finest selection of cheeses in the land, an organic fruit and vegetable shop, a general wholefood store, an apothecary and a therapy centre. Above the bakery is the tea room, serving all kinds of bread, pizzas, quiches and pasties, plus sugarless cakes. Across the way is a little stand-up bar selling soups, salads and freshly squeezed juices. At the entrance to the yard is a charming water clock which activates metallic gardeners to lift their watering cans on the hour.

Open 10.30 to 8 (5 Wed, 4.30 Sat) **Closed** Sun; public hols; 1 week Christmas to New Year **Underground** Covent Garden

---

We give details of service charges where we know what these are; otherwise, you should expect to add 10–15% to the total of your bill unless the menu or bill states that service is included.

COVENT GARDEN

Orso Map 5

27 Wellington Street, WC2 *Telephone* 01-240 5269   £££

This is a sleek, new-wave Italian restaurant, related to the nearby Joe Allen (see above), with a menu that offers a wide range of properly done dishes without pretensions. It is just as easy to eat a light, inexpensive meal as to push out the gondola. The decor is sharp, with ceramic tiles, mirrors and black and white photographs, and the staff, in white aprons, are largely well informed. The menu takes in pizzas which are among the best in town, but there is also a subtlety to the cooking. Baby squid, for instance, are stuffed with herbs and char-grilled, and, in classic Genoa style, cold breast of veal is stuffed with artichoke, boiled egg and herbs and served with a combustive pesto sauce. The extras are of a classy restaurant – the painted plates, the proper espresso coffee, the variety of leaves in the salads. The wine list is exclusively Italian with some unusual bottles, albeit starting with Valpolicella at £7.50. Children are welcome.

Open All week **Closed** 25 and 26 Dec **Meals** Noon to 11.45 **Cards** None accepted **Underground** Covent Garden/Charing Cross

Punch & Judy Map 5

The Market, WC2   £

Right in the middle of the Covent Garden pedestrian complex – which is full of interesting shops, craft stalls, covered open-air cafés and impromptu street entertainment – the rambling bare brick cellar bar of this pub is a popular meeting place: stand on the flagstones in the main section, sit in the relative peace of a series of barrel-vaulted bays at the back, or at the front with a view of the pub's courtyard below the galleries of shops. The relatively small – and sometimes quieter – upstairs bar has a balcony overlooking the spacious piazza where acrobats, mimers, tumblers, jugglers or musicians are usually performing. Fruit machine, space game and good piped pop music. Bar food (lunchtime only) includes ploughman's, salads with quiche, crusty pie and cold meats, and hot food (in the cellar and lunchtime only) such as filled baked potato, lamb curry, steak and kidney pie, liver and bacon or beef carbonnade. Children are allowed in the eating area. Courage Best and Directors on handpump.

Open 11.30 to 3, 5.30 to 10.45 **Underground** Covent Garden

Savoy Hotel Map 5

Strand, WC2 *Telephone* 01-836 4343   £–££££

The Savoy, well placed for theatres and the opera, is a one-hundred-year-old London institution. Bits of it have stayed behind in certain years – for instance, the Thames Foyer in the '20s, the cocktail bar in the '30s. Afternoon tea in the former would be an inexpensive treat, in ornate marble Art Deco trompe l'oeil surroundings with a pianist tinkling away in his gazebo. For £6.25 a formally attired waiter will bring delicate sandwiches and light scones or a savoury snack

LONDON

or whatever you desire. The air-conditioned Grill Room is a character among hotel dining-rooms, serving excellent smoked salmon in particular. There is always a very English dish according to the day of the week – Friday's is steak and kidney pie. The River Room is pink, elegant and also very English with its potted shrimps, and haddock in a cream sauce. The staff throughout the hotel are thoughtful and professional. Most of the rooms are entirely comfortable, especially those overlooking the river, and if some are a little down at heel, you may be compensated by a bathroom with original fittings.

Open (Thames Foyer) 10am to midnight; (Grill Room) 12.30 to 2, 6 to 11.15; (River Room) 12.30 to 2.30, 7.30 to 11.30 (Sun 7 to 10.30) **Cards** Access, Amex, Diners, Visa **Accommodations** B&B £70 to £115 **Underground** Charing Cross

Unicorn Café Bar Map 5

Arts Theatre Basement, Great Newport Street, WC2
Telephone 01-240 3787

£

The café-bar is down some steps into the children's theatre – a large basement decorated in primary colours. Service is canteen-style, the cooking vegetarian and the choice varied. As well as quiches there are leek-stuffed potatoes, stuffed aubergines, vegetable kebabs and guacamole. Chocolate brownies with walnuts or puréed mangoes with fresh cream for pudding. Plenty of herb teas and wines too. Loud music.

Open 10am to 11pm (5pm Sun) **Closed** Christmas Day and Boxing Day; most public hols **Underground** Leicester Square

DULWICH

L'Auberge Map 1

44 Forest Hill Road, SE22 *Telephone* 01-299 2211   ££–£££

Sami Youssef's attractive green dining-room in this long row of featureless shops is often full to bursting. The fixed dinner menu (£12.95) offers a good variety of imaginative and interesting dishes – aiguillettes de foie de veau, feuilleté de coquilles St Jacques au currie, navarin of lamb à la menthe, all of which have been good. The Sunday lunch (£5.95) is one of the bargains of South London and begins about 1.30pm; Mr Youssef will dish up children's helpings at this meal. The wine list keeps the accent on value for money with good choices under £10. Music; wheelchair access.

Open Tue to Sat D, plus Sun L **Closed** Last 2 weeks Aug **Meals** 12 to 2.30, 7 to 10.30 **Cards** Access, Visa **Service** 10% **BR station** Honor Oak Park

Dewaniam Map 1

133–135 Stanstead Road, SE23 *Telephone* 01-291 4778   £££

Next door is a take-away with the same name but less to offer. The restaurant menu is more adventurous than the flock wallpaper and dim lighting suggest. As

DULWICH

well as a standard selection of tandoori dishes, dhansaks and birianis, there are poultry and game specialities using pheasant, partridge, quail, goose, duck, venison and hare. Gallasi is venison marinated in olive oil, yoghurt, red wine and vinegar, then lightly spiced and cooked with almonds, pistachio nuts and sultanas. Pheasant is cooked and served in a kahrai with a sauce of cream, almonds, fresh coriander, garlic and ginger. The menu appears to run right through the year irrespective of seasons. To finish, there have been good Indian sweetmeats as well as glorious fresh mangoes. Children are welcome. Music; air-conditioning. Prices, sadly, are in the West End league.

Open All week **Meals** 12.15 to 2.15, 5.30 to 11.45 **Cards** Access, Amex, Diners, Visa
BR station Forest Hill

Luigi's Map 1

129 Gipsy Hill, SE19 *Telephone* 01-670 1843 and 1396   £££

A fancy frontage hides the crisp lines and colours inside, which is packed with tables. Gazpacho is garlicky, skewered marinated chicken is fragrant and spicy, and calf's liver is consistently good. The kitchen is as free with oil and butter on the vegetables as the waiters are with pepper. Sweets may look better than they taste, but service is spot on. Wines are not cheap, but the house wine is made by Luigi Palgharame's family and is £6.90. Wheelchair access.

Open Mon to Sat, exc Sat L **Meals** 12 to 3, 6 to 11.30 **Cards** Access, Amex, Diners, Visa
BR station Gipsy Hill

Phoenix & Firkin

5 Windsor Walk, SE5   £

You will find other branches of David Bruce's Firkin chain dotted around these pages. (A firkin is a small cask.) There are a great many virtues in his pubs – simple basic furnishings, beer brewed on the premises, and a relaxed easy-going atmosphere which readily embraces quite a mixed clientele (mostly young, casually dressed). This pub shows that atmosphere, but it's in another class for architecture. Its remarkable renovation shows what can be done by a small local society determined to rescue a worthwhile building. In this case it was the Camberwell Society which spent over three years drumming up support and money for the ambitious project that eventually turned a roofless fire ruin of a railway station into one of London's most unusual pubs. Besides a good deal of money raised locally, British Rail, the Historic Buildings Council and the Greater London Council contributed substantially towards the £300,000 cost of restoring the building's fabric. It's a palatial Victorian building spanning the railway cutting – you feel it throb when trains pass underneath. David Bruce has been responsible for the inside – the pub part. The bar is a vast lofty pavilion, with a huge double-faced station clock, originally from Llandudno Junction, hanging by chains from the incredibly high ceiling, and two rows of arched windows in one tall bare brick wall. There's a bar counter made from a single mahogany tree, solid wooden furniture on the stripped wooden floor, paintings of steam trains, old seaside posters, Bovril advertisements, old-fashioned station

55

LONDON

name signs, plants and big revolving fans. At one end there's a gallery with similar furnishings reached by a spiral staircase, and at the other arches lead into a room with a big model train running backwards and forwards along the gantry above the bar and food servery. Food includes big filled baps, portions of pie, bread with a selection of cheeses, salads and a daily hot dish. The beers include Phoenix, Rail and Dogbolter, as well as Greenalls Bitter, Huntsman Dorchester on handpump under light top pressure. Piped music. Outside there are some tables and chairs with parasols, and the steps that follow the slope of the road are a popular place to sit.

Open 11 to 3, 5.30 to 11 **BR station** Denmark Hill

EARL'S COURT

Baalbek Map 2

18 Hogarth Place, SW5 *Telephone* 01-373 7199   £

Down a little alley off Earl's Court Road is this tiny Lebanese restaurant with geometric flock wallpaper and tables close together. The food is freshly prepared with great care by the owner: there is a range of 20 starters, such as tabbouleh, ful medames, and fried aubergine with yoghurt, before grills and half a dozen stews, from couscous to okra with lamb. Vegetarians have their own menu. Licensed, but you are welcome to bring your own wine, with no corkage charged.

Open Noon to 11pm **Closed** Sun **Underground** Earl's Court

Bahn Thai Map 2

35A Marloes Road, W8 *Telephone* 01-937 9960   £££

A much-loved basement Thai restaurant which has initiated many people into the enchantments of the cuisine. The menu's seductions are many – steamboat soup, served in a silver tureen, contains prawns, crab-meat, clams, mussels, chunks of fish, squid and smelt and tastes marvellous. Equally wondrous is the hot and spicy tom yum soup. The food is authentically spicy and the chillies run like bush fires through meals. Chicken curry with lime leaves draws much enthusiasm. To finish, the ice-creams – notably coconut and sometimes the expensive and pungent durian too – help cool off. The cover charge (75p) covers the free prawns, orchids and hot towels. The wine list has been supplemented with Sauvignon and Gewürztraminer, which can handle the food; otherwise there is Thai beer. Air-conditioning; no cigars or pipes; music. Vegetarian meals and children's helpings.

Open Mon to Sat **Closed** Christmas, 2 weeks in summer **Meals** 12 to 2.15, 6 to 11.15 **Cards** Access, Amex, Visa **Underground** Earl's Court/High Street Kensington

---

If you are planning a trip to Scotland and the Lake District, there is another Guide in this series to those areas.

EARL'S COURT

Lou Pescadou Map 2

241 Old Brompton Road, SW5 *Telephone* 01-370 1057   £££

No bookings are taken at this 'bar de la mer' on the site of Earl's Court's legendary West Indian restaurant, Toddy's. It is part of the Croisette (Fulham)/Suquet (Chelsea)/Quai St Pierre (below) chain of French fish restaurants – less expensive, more relaxed, with a menu that takes in a few pastas, pizzas and perhaps a meat plat du jour such as pork with lentils. Otherwise, the decor is on the same lines – fishing nets, old coral, waiters in matelot shirts, fragile bamboo chairs. The chief glory is the fish delivered by van three times a week from Brittany because London cannot provide. Spectacular plateaux de fruits de mer are made up on request – mussels, two kinds of oysters, crab, whelks, winkles, even sea urchins in season. The cidre bouché at £1.50 a flagon makes a change from Muscadet or Gros Plant. Sorbets are the pick of the sweets. Wheelchair access; music. Children are welcome. The waiters wait rather than serve.

Open Mon to Sat **Meals** 12 to 3, 7 to 12 **Cards** Access, Amex, Diners, Visa **Underground** Earl's Court/West Brompton

Le Quai St Pierre Map 2

7 Stratford Road, W8 *Telephone* 01-937 6388   £££–££££

Part of the same chain as Lou Pescadou et al (see above) and run on the same lines: fresh fish, including live lobsters; brusque, laconic waiters; and the feeling of being on the sea-front at Cannes. The shellfish platter is enormous and quite a bargain for £11; sauced and pastry dishes can be more variable. House wine is £7.30 a bottle. Children are welcome. Access for wheelchairs; music.

Open Mon to Sat, exc Mon L **Closed** 2 weeks Christmas **Meals** 12.30 to 2.30, 7 to 11.30 **Cards** Amex, Diners **Underground** High Street Kensington/Earl's Court

Tiger Lee Map 2

251 Old Brompton Road, SW5 *Telephone* 01-370 2323 and 5970   ££££

On booking a table the man at the other end may ask which company you represent. This gives an indication of the prices in this smart Chinese restaurant that specialises in fish. The olive walls and leather banquettes are reflected in the green jackets of the waiters who fill the small room. Usually there are half a dozen to serve a dozen tables. It is a restaurant in which some dishes stand out as being conspicuously better than others. Pigeon, at £12 each, are marinated, lacquered, deep-fried then served with the head still on and split into six, with roasted salt and Worcester sauce. Equally impressive are the deep-fried crispy chicken (the Cantonese equivalent of Peking duck), lobster stir-fried with ginger and spring onions, and, for eel aficionados, eel served with garlic, ginger and pork. Other dishes are not of the same calibre and garnishing is rampant. The wines are expensive. There is a useful section of Alsace, supplied by Zind-Humbrecht, which complements the food well, but prices, alas, are well

LONDON

into double figures. House white is £8.80. No-smoking area, plus air-conditioning. Access for wheelchairs.

Open All week, D only **Closed** Christmas **Meals** 6 to 11 **Cards** Amex, Diners, Visa **Service** 15% **Underground** Earl's Court/West Brompton

EAST END

Angel Map 2

Bermondsey Wall East, SE16 *Telephone* 01-237 3608 £

It's from this waterside pub in Rotherhithe that you see Tower Bridge looking just as it does in picture books, and in the other direction the exceptional river views take in the Pool of London – usually there's something interesting moving on the water, though of course it's no longer nearly so busy these days. Inside, the pub is open-plan and comfortably furnished, with captain's chairs around the tables by the river windows. Bar food includes giant sausages and French bread, Cheddar ploughman's, home-cooked ham and salad, various pies with salad and at lunchtime a hot dish of the day such as steak and mushroom pie or chilli con carne; snacks are not available on Saturday evenings; there is also a separate restaurant. Well-kept Courage Best and Directors on handpump.

Open 12 to 3, 5.30 to 11 **Underground** Rotherhithe

Bloom's Map 2

90 Whitechapel High Street, E1 *Telephone* 01-247 6001 £–££

That everyone says Bloom's is not as good as when Morrie was alive is perhaps predictable. Thirty-five years after opening this is still the best place in London to eat kosher cooking without any frills. The salt beef is always mentioned but there are other things to eat, which we now start to think are, if anything, better – the boiled gefilte fish look less appetising than the fried but are delicious, the cold borshch is reliably excellent but so, too, are the other soups, such as kneidlach. Boiled fowl leg is just about everything the name suggests it won't be – succulent and full of flavour. The latkes and the strudel do not show the lightness of touch that they might, but we live in hope. The original Mr Bloom used to play a very up-front role and current staff carry on the tradition and the banter. 'I have to give him good service. He is my father-in-law.' Lemon tea is the regular drink or there is Cabernet Sauvignon and Chenin Blanc 1982 from 'Carmel, the land of the Bible' at £5.90. Vegetarian meals and children's helpings. Wheelchair access; air-conditioning.

Open Sun to Fri, exc Fri D **Meals** 11.30 to 9.30 (3 Fri) **Cards** Access, Visa **Underground** Aldgate East/Aldgate

---

Pubs described in this Guide are pleasant places to have a drink, and many offer the added bonus of good bar snacks. Some pubs also have a separate restaurant which we may not have described.

EAST END

F Cooke Map 2

41 Kingsland High Street, E8 *Telephone* 01-254,2878   £

The Buckingham Palace of eel and pie shops and an institution in its own right. The interior has been marvellously preserved, with marble-topped tables, sawdust on the floor, huge mirrors on the walls and everywhere pale green, blue and white tiles; there's also a monastic stained glass window in one of the doors and a mosaic at the door proclaiming that the firm was established in 1862. Eels come in masses from Billingsgate and are dealt with on the chopping blocks at the front of the shop. They end up jellied or stewed and served with good mash and thin parsley liquor. Steak and kidney pies are popular too, and connoisseurs always turn them upside down before eating them. Take-away. Unlicensed.

Open 10 to 10 (6 Tue and Wed, 8 Mon and Thur) **Closed** Sun; public hols **BR station** Dalston Junction

Good Friends Map 1

139–141 Salmon Lane, E14 *Telephone* 01-987 5541 and 5498   ££–£££

Now the best of the Friends restaurants, which were the first places really to give Cantonese cooking a good name in London after the War. Billingsgate market around the corner obviously helps by supplying the finest raw materials that are essential to a serious Cantonese restaurant. Look also for the soups and the bean-curd dishes. The decor is running down, but at peak times booking is necessary well in advance. House wine is £3.95. Music; access for wheelchairs. Children are welcome.

Open All week **Meals** 12 to 3, 5 to 11.30 **Cards** Access, Amex, Diners, Visa **Service** 10% **Underground** Stepney Green/Mile End **BR station** (nearer than underground) Stepney East

Grapes Map 1

76 Narrow Street, E14 *Telephone* 01-987 4396   £

The glass-roofed back balcony in this friendly little pub in Limehouse, close to the opening of Regent's Canal, is one of the most sheltered places for a riverside drink; as it's off the tourist track, it has a quieter and more genuine atmosphere than many other river pubs. There are lots of prints, often of actors, on the partly panelled walls of the long narrow bar. Bar food includes sandwiches, ploughman's or pâté, Irish stew, prawn curry and fish and seafood pie. Meals and snacks are not served in the evening during weekends; meals also not available on Monday evenings. Well-kept Ind Coope Burton and Friary Meux and Taylor-Walker Bitter on handpump. Dickens used the pub as the basis of his 'Six Jolly Fellowship Porters' in *Our Mutual Friend* on the strength of its grim reputation for losing its best customers to the anatomists: when they were insensibly drunk, people would row them out into the Thames, tip them in, then fish them out as drowned and sell them as raw material for anatomy experiments.

Open 11 to 2.30, 5 to 11 **BR station** Stepney East

59

LONDON

Hollands Map 1

9 Exmouth Street, E1 £

The present landlord's great grandfather opened this friendly little Stepney pub early in Queen Victoria's reign and it has hardly changed since then. The decorations are all original and lovingly tended; the heavy bar counter in the main bar has etched and cut-glass snob screens (allowing a certain privacy in former times), and on the walls are antique mirrors, *Vanity Fair* pictures, Victorian cartoons and photographs. A clutter of trumpets, glass and brass ornaments hang from the ochre-painted and panelled ceiling – dimly lit with fairy lights strung along the cornice. The lounge bar, on two levels and separated from the main bar by an arched doorway and heavy velvet curtains, has panelled and velveteen-cushioned bench seats, a red tiled floor, old sepia photographs, brass pots hanging from the ceiling and a big Victorian fireplace with large china ornaments on the mantelpiece. Bar food includes sandwiches, baked potatoes, ploughman's, pâté, hot flans with salad and hot specials in winter such as home-made soup or shepherd's pie; snacks are available at lunchtimes but served at weekends only with advanced warning. Fremlins on handpump; darts, cribbage.

Open 11 to 2.30, 5 to 11 **Underground** Shadwell

Mayflower Map 1

117 Rotherhithe Street, SE16 *Telephone* 01-237 4088 £

This carefully restored eighteenth-century pub takes its name in honour of the Pilgrim Fathers' ship which sailed from here in 1611: one side room has a set of pictures showing the way it would have been built, and there's a model of the *Mayflower*. The rather dark old-fashioned main bar has black ceiling beams, dark panelled walls, latticed windows, and high-backed winged settles and wheelback chairs around its tables. Meals and snacks are available on weekdays; meals only served at Sunday lunchtimes. There is also a separate restaurant upstairs which is open only in the evenings. Well-kept Bass and Charringtons IPA on handpump; fruit machine. The wooden jetty outside feels very close to the Thames of days gone by, with its heavy piles plunging down into the water, converted high old warehouse buildings on either side and lighters swinging on their moorings.

Open 11 to 3, 5.30 to 11 **Underground** Rotherhithe

Prince of Orange Map 1

118 Lower Road, SE16 £

There are different jazz acts and styles every night and weekend lunchtimes at this popular pub, East London's premier jazz spot. There's a central stage at one end of the large L-shaped open-plan bar, with orange plastic chairs and wooden kitchen ones set around the low dark wooden tables below it; the ceiling and walls are decorated with posters of forthcoming acts, some neon signs and photographs of various groups. Two small rooms – you can stand at the bar in one, or eat at tables in another – have walls completely covered with old photographs including some old 1930s jazz sessions at Abbey Road Studios. Food is simple but good and includes toasted sandwiches, pizzas, and chilli con carne or burgers. Trumans on handpump. It's a cheerful place for listening to music.

Open 11 to 3, 5.30 to 12 **Underground** Rotherhithe

Tower Thistle Hotel   Map 2

St Katharine's Way, E1 *Telephone* 01-481 2575   £–£££

This vast, white, modern hotel complex is right by two of London's most famous landmarks – Tower Bridge, which lifts up whenever a major vessel needs to pass up river, and the Tower of London itself, home of beefeaters, ravens, the Crown jewels and a superabundance of English history. The London World Trade Centre is also next door. St Katharine's Dock is a busy marina with plenty of amenities including interesting shops – it was one of the first focuses in the exciting Docklands redevelopment project. Many of the air-conditioned, comfortable, even lavish rooms overlook the Thames, but the price for all this history on the doorstep seems to be a certain impersonal quality. However, the hotel would be a good choice, particularly for someone travelling on business, with all its amenities – laundry service, 24-hour room service, opulent riverside bar, three restaurants (including a carvery and the 'Picnic Basket') – as well as its proximity to the City.

Open (Princes Room restaurant) 12.30 to 2.30, 7 to 10.30 (01-488 3580); (Carvery) 12.15 to 2.30, 6.15 to 10 (01-488 4600); (Picnic Basket) 7.30am to 12pm **Cards** Access, Amex, Diners, Visa **Accommodations** B&B £43 to £85 **Underground** Tower Hill

EUSTON

Diwana Bhel Poori   Map 2

114 Drummond Street, NW1 *Telephone* 01-388 4867   £

Tiny Indian vegetarian restaurant in Jayant Patel's chain of four (the most recently opened is in Paris). Preferred by many travellers for a last meal in London to anything available at Euston Station, and quite rightly so. Unlicensed, but there are juices and mango milkshake to drink; alternatively, take your own wine (no corkage charge).

Open 10 to 10 **Closed** Mon; Christmas Day **Underground** Euston/Euston Square/Warren Street

Diwana Bhel Poori   Map 2

121 Drummond Street, NW1 *Telephone* 01-387 5556   £

Brighter than its sister across the road, but with the same range of Indian vegetarian dishes from Gujerat, Bombay's Chowpaty beach, and the south. For

61

LONDON

a full meal at rock-bottom prices, the thalis are difficult to beat. Unlicensed but no corkage charge.

Open Noon to midnight **Closed** Christmas Day **Underground** Euston/Euston Square/Warren Street

Ravi Shankar (Bhel Poori House) Map 2

133–135 Drummond Street, NW1 *Telephone* 01-388 6458

And the third on the busy scene of London's Little Madras. Thalis are great value: just over £3 buys rice, three puris or chapatis, dhal, vegetable curries and gulab jamun. Drink creamy lassi or freshly squeezed juices, or wine if you want alcohol. It's light, airy and relaxed, although the waiters often seem becalmed in a state of trance.

Open Noon to 11 **Underground** Euston/Euston Square/Warren Street

FULHAM

Blakes Hotel Map 3

33 Roland Gardens, SW7 *Telephone* 01-370 6701

£–££££

Since we fell in love with Anouska Hempel's sleek basement restaurant our affair has been passionate, tempestuous, exhilarating, at times frustrating. But it has now settled into a comfortable contentment. James Robins has shown a sure hand on the stove and persuaded us that the menu is not just a capricious, eclectic choice of dishes from across the globe, but something of substance, reflecting a multi-national city in the late 1980s. His version of Szechuan duck is superb – the breast cut through, the skin crisp, the leg to one side garnished with a pile of spring onions, served on a black plate. The waiter draws a line along one rim with roasted salt and pepper. The expense translates into the finest quality ingredients – the fattest langoustines figure in a salad of lamb's lettuce and diced bacon, the rack of lamb served with a rosemary sauce is impeccable. The ravioli is home made and served with a sauce that is just strained tomatoes with coriander. The staff, dressed in black to match the monochromatic decor which is broken only by explosions of flowers and the colours of the traditional Thai costumes in boxes on the walls, are young and accomplished. The wine list is sensibly concise but does not have much under £10. The house white is, alas, Gros Plant at £9.50 but the red, at the same price, is a stunning Spanish Cabernet Sauvignon, Raïmat Abadía. Children's helpings and light snacks. No pipes to be smoked in the dining-room; air-conditioning; music. Bedroom decor is similarly cool, with lots of mirrors, brass bedsteads, white everywhere. Some rooms are in the annexe over the road. The hotel has a sauna; afternoon teas served to non-residents.

Open All week **Closed** 25 and 26 Dec **Meals** 12.30 to 2.30, 7.30 to 11.30 **Cards** Access, Amex, Diners, Visa **Service** 15% **Accommodations** 58 rooms, all with bath/shower. B&B £67.50 to £92. Baby facilities **Underground** South Kensington/Gloucester Road

FULHAM

Busabong Map 3 ✗

331 Fulham Road, SW10 *Telephone* 01-352 4742   £

The mother of many other Thai restaurants, and still exceptional value. Downstairs is more expensive and regularly features Thai boxing and dancing, but the upstairs Marokot room is for fast food Thai-style. Choose from the curries on the hot plate or order satay, dim-sum or meaty spare ribs from the main menu. Take-aways too.

Open 12.30 to midnight (10.30pm Sun) **Closed** Christmas Day to 29 Dec **Underground** West Brompton

Chanterelle Map 3 ✗

119 Old Brompton Road, SW7 *Telephone* 01-373 5522 and 7390   ££–£££

One of the early bistros, and an old standby: panelled, friendly, with set-price menus (lunch £7, dinner £11). Good-value dishes – such as roulade of spinach stuffed with smoked salmon; pork fillets with oyster mushrooms and madeira sauce, served with carrot and parsnip purée; fish pie; brains sautéed in breadcrumbs; and raspberry shortcake – go on impressing. After 10pm there is a bargain two-course supper menu, at £7.50, of what has not gone earlier. Standards can be a bit patchy, as can the service. But the two dozen wines, like the food, have been carefully selected. House French is £4.95. Children are welcome. Access for wheelchairs.

Open All week **Closed** 4 days at Christmas **Meals** 12 to 2.30, 7 to 11.30 **Cards** Access, Amex, Diners, Visa **Underground** South Kensington/Gloucester Road

Chelsea Pasta Bar Map 3 ✗

313 Fulham Road, SW10 *Telephone* 01-352 6912   £

The first of this small chain of pasta bars. The queues get hectic before and after the main films at the ABC across the road. Standards are patchy but rarely poor.

Open Noon to 3, 6.15 to midnight (noon to midnight Sat and Sun) **Closed** Christmas Day and Boxing Day **Underground** West Brompton

La Croisette Map 2 ✗

168 Ifield Road, SW10 *Telephone* 01-373 3694   ££££

From this basement a dozen years ago Pierre Martin began his conquest of West London on the simple principle that he would serve fresh fish while every other restaurant was moving towards frozen. Not satisfied with what he could find at Billingsgate, he bought a van. Three times a week it went to Brittany to pick up shellfish. The dining-room was decorated to look like the South of France – and

---

If you have to cancel a reservation for a bedroom or table, please telephone to warn the proprietor. A small place will suffer if you don't.

63

LONDON

the pressure on the table space is the same as it is on the sea-front at Cannes. There is something Heath Robinson about the way so much food can be arranged on such small table surfaces. The menu is fixed rigidly at a set price (£20), from a glass of Kir, through the massive platters covered with crustaceans or more delicate pastry cases filled with fish and surrounded by cream and wine sauces. The waiters equip you with all the necessaries for the evening, which can take them quite a long time. The only extra item on the bill, apart from service, is the house wine at £7.30. The formula has since produced Le Suquet (Chelsea), Le Quai St Pierre and the new Lou Pescadou (Earl's Court) and L'Olivier, the meat branch (see below) – all of an equal standard. Music; children are welcome.

Open Tue to Sun, exc Tue L **Closed** 2 weeks at Christmas **Meals** 12.30 to 2.30, 7.30 to 11.30 **Cards** Amex, Diners **Service** 15% **Underground** West Brompton

Ferret & Firkin Map 1

Lots Road, SW10   £

This gives a good idea of David Bruce's small chain of pubs brewing their own beer on the premises (others listed include the Frog and Firkin in North Kensington and the Phoenix and Firkin in Dulwich – a firkin is a small beer cask). It's an old pub with unsealed bare floorboards and furnishings well-made from good wood. The main wall is curved, with tall airy windows, and sturdy seats form booths around tables along it, leaving plenty of standing room in front of the long bar counter – which is itself curved to match the front wall. Fittings such as the slowly circulating colonial-style ceiling fans and punning advertisements for the beers put an old-fashioned streak in the atmosphere, but the main ingredient is the relaxed feeling you get from the easy-going crowd of customers – most youngish but otherwise a very mixed bag indeed. The beers include ones named along the lines of the pub (here, Ferret, Stoat, an occasionally brewed much lighter Weasel Water or superstrong Balloonatic), plus always a strong Dogbolter, and usually a Bruce's. With twenty-four hours' notice you can collect a bulk supply. There are also two or three guest beers from other breweries. Bar food includes home-made giant sausages, heftily filled giant meat and salad rolls, quiche, Stilton ploughman's and hot dishes. There's usually a pianist on duty in the evening, and there are seats out on the pavement.

Open 11 to 3, 5.30 to 11 **Underground** Fulham Broadway (quite a walk)

Gastronome One Map 1

311–313 New King's Road, SW6 *Telephone* 01-731 6381   ££–£££

Like the rest of the tail end of Fulham, this olive green basement has shown distinct signs of being on the way up. In the kitchen Thierry Aubugeau has directed the menu to a sensible exposition of modern French style. There are some very good things to eat indeed. The home-made ravioli filled with morels and set on a deep beurre blanc have been sublime. The snails in a feuilleté are of good quality. Typical of the cooking is perhaps salmon baked in the oven under a fierce heat on coarse salt so it is slightly dry and served with a light champagne

FULHAM

sauce, some braised chicory, and kidney-bean-shaped puff pastry. Vegetables have been excellent. The rather baroque presentations reach a climax with the sweets, such as nougat glacé avec son coulis. The wine list rather snottily lists the Loire, the Rhône and the Alsace under *vins régionaux*, but the clarets are of good pedigree and therefore not cheap. The five house wines are £7, but half a bottle is included in the fixed price. Lunch is £12.50 to £16.50, dinner £16.50 to £18.50; whichever price you pick, that is what you will end up paying – no extras. No under-sevens; no-smoking area; access for wheelchairs; music.

Open Mon to Sat, exc Sat L **Meals** 12 to 2, 7 to 11.30 **Cards** Access, Amex, Diners, Visa **Service Inc Underground** Parson's Green

---

Hiders Map 1

755 Fulham Road, SW6 *Telephone* 01-736 2331   ££–£££

There is a lot of decor here: a heavy velvet curtain cloaks the doorway, and beyond is revealed a spacious dining-room with gilt-framed mirrors and thickly folded drapes lit by sparkling chandeliers. Canapés are served swiftly. The set menu (from £11.50) provides good value and commendably includes vegetables and coffee. Dishes are fashionable and currently modern French: vegetable soup with wild mushrooms and a dash of brandy, pork with green peppers, and breast of pigeon. Some are quite classy. Two sets of scrambled eggs, one with chives and one with curry, are put back in their shells and served as a starter. As a main course monkfish has been served with a purée of aubergine and a Burgundy sauce. Vegetables are presented on crescent-shaped dishes – neat portions of lyonnaise potatoes, leeks and puréed swede. The sweets tend towards mousses and ices. The wine list is sensibly short, with twenty-five well-known brand labels listed. A few more cocktails would help. The clarets are at their best over £10 – Ch Millet 1978 £15.50, Ch Cissac 1979 £16.25. House wine is £5.50. Children are welcome. Access for wheelchairs.

Open Mon to Sat, exc Sat L **Closed** 2 weeks Aug, public hols **Meals** 12.30 to 2.30, 7.30 to 11.30 **Cards** Access, Amex, Visa **Underground** Parsons Green

---

L'Hippocampe Map 1

131A Munster Road, SW6 *Telephone* 01-736 5588 and 4711   ££–£££

There is no name on the door, just a series of blue neon waves to signify that this is both French and a fish restaurant. The inside is built around a bar and a long corridor by the kitchen. There is more blue inside. The cooking features some creative dishes, such as very fine cold red mullet terrine with leeks and a sauce of anchovies, and poached brill on a mustard and cream sauce with whole white pickling onions. Salmon is wrapped in ravioli and served with a lobster sauce. Vegetables, like the prints on the wall, are sparse. Sweets, as with much of the cooking, seem to fluctuate to the exceptional – the chocolate marquise, for instance. Lunch is a set meal (from £4.50). House Muscadet is £5.20. Children's helpings; music; access for wheelchairs.

Open Mon to Sat, exc Sat L **Meals** 12.30 to 2.30, 7.30 to 11 **Cards** Access, Amex, Visa **Service** 10% **Underground** Parsons Green

65

LONDON

Hungry Horse Map 3

196 Fulham Road, SW10 *Telephone* 01-352 7757/8081   £–££

Bistro-style basement with pine tables in alcoves. The food is filling, stodgy English grub: roast beef and Yorkshire pudding, steak, kidney and mushroom pie, jugged hare, salmon fishcakes with spinach, treacle tart, summer pudding. Wide-ranging wine list. Handy for the nearby cinemas.

Open 12.30 to 2.30 (3 Sun) 6.30 to midnight **Closed** Sat L **Underground** South Kensington

L'Olivier Map 2

116 Finborough Road, SW10 *Telephone* 01-370 4183   £££–££££

The meat wing of Pierre Martin's expanding fish empire, which began with La Croisette on the other side of the road (see above). The basement tables are packed tightly together and, as with the other restaurants in the chain, there is an excellent-value set meal (lunch £15, dinner £20), in this case charcuterie, soup, and a meat of the day. Offal, for example sweetbreads in pastry or veal tongue with a ravigote sauce, is excellent, as are the steaks. House wine is from Provence and £7.30. There is a cover charge of £1.50 (only on the *carte*).

Open Mon to Sat, exc Mon L **Closed** 2 weeks at Christmas **Meals** 12.30 to 2.30, 7.30 to 11.30 **Cards** Access, Amex, Diners, Visa **Underground** West Brompton

Villa Estense Map 1

642 King's Road, SW6 *Telephone* 01-731 4247   £

The inside of this pasta and pizza place is cool, white and green, with a clattery tiled floor and well-spaced tables set with fresh flowers. There are about 20 fresh pastas and the same number of pizzas on the menu, plus a few standard dishes, such as pollo sorpresa and piccata limone. The tortellini with ricotta and fresh basil turns out to be three fat parcels of tender, resilient pasta with a well-judged filling and a puddle of fine garlicky tomato sauce. Pizzas have a proper thin dough base with generous toppings. Salads are crisp and fresh. Good coffee, too. Taped music. There is a children's disco downstairs at Sunday lunchtime.

Open 12.30 to 2.30, 7 to 11.30 **Closed** Sun; public hols **Underground** Fulham Broadway

Wine Gallery Map 3

49 Hollywood Road, SW10 *Telephone* 01-352 7572   £

The value for money equation in the comparison between the wine bar and the parent restaurant (Brinkleys) next door comes out very much in the wine bar's credit. They have the same kitchen, the same supplies, and, if the dishes in the wine bar are not quite so polished, they are nevertheless imaginative and served in elegant, if often crowded, surroundings. Typical are carrot and ginger soup, timbale of scallops with lobster sauce, massive plates of sticky spare ribs; monkfish goujons with tartare sauce. Nothing is over £4, much is under £2, and

GREENWICH

a canny choice of wines running around the world is firmly pegged in the £5 to £6 bracket.

Open All week **Meals** 12 to 3.30, 6.30 to 11.30 **Underground** Gloucester Road

GREENWICH

Crowders Map 1

Greenwich Theatre, 13 Nevada Street, SE10   £
Telephone 01-858 1318

An excellent spot for a snack before or after the theatre – provided you don't mind the crush. The good, honest food centres on a buffet with cold honey-roast gammon, beef, salads and home-made turkey pie. There are also hot and cold dishes of the day.

Open Noon to 12.30, 6 to 11 **Closed** Sun; Christmas and public hols **BR station** Greenwich

Mandalay Map 1

100 Greenwich South Street, SE10 *Telephone* 01-691 0443   ££–£££

This husband-and-wife-run restaurant is open only on Wednesdays to Saturdays, but is the only place to eat Burmese in Britain. The dishes are authentic and the menu helpfully structured and explained. Meals comprise either a single centrepiece such as pungent mohinga – rice noodles in a fish-based soup – or combinations of dishes, which would normally include a curry, rice, and a soup plus one of the vegetable side dishes. Particularly good are pet-to, marinated minced pork, deep-fried in wun-tun and served with a sauce of chilli and soy, and also chicken nun-nun-bin curry, a fillet cooked with tomatoes, onions, ginger, garlic and coriander. Puddings are less good. Mango ice-cream is adequate, but faluda, a kind of Burmese knickerbocker glory, may not taste quite as wondrous as it looks. The short wine list has some good wines in the £6 region, but the Gewürztraminer 1984 at £7.50 may be the only match for the subtle, colourful flavours. Music. Children are welcome.

Open Wed to Sat, D only **Meals** 7.30 (7 Fri and Sat) to 10.30 **Cards** Access, Visa **BR station** Greenwich

Le Papillon Map 1

57 Greenwich Church Street, SE10 *Telephone* 01-858 2668   ££–££££

Well named: a pretty restaurant with a menu that flutters around according to market. It is by the Cutty Sark, where parking is difficult. The decor is dark wooden panels, red flock wallpaper and red velvet banquettes. The butterflies are prints. Lunch is a set meal (from £4.95), dinner £18.50, or there is a *carte*. The traditional strengths of British cookery, such as game and ribs of beef, are

---

If you cannot honour a restaurant booking, always telephone to cancel.

LONDON

strong suits, though the mood is French. Notably good have been scallops, tomatoes and mushrooms, and the noisettes of lamb and venison with garlic and a fine madeira sauce. Pastry remains a problem. Not so the wines, which are a joy, spread through all the major French regions with representation at most money-levels – late 1970s clarets, good Loires and Alsace wines catch the eye. Children are welcome; music; access for wheelchairs; air-conditioning.

Open All week, exc Sat L and Sun D **Meals** 12.15 to 2.30, 6.45 to 10.30 **Cards** Access, Amex, Diners, Visa **BR station** Greenwich

---

Treasure of China Map 1	✕
10 Nelson Road, SE10 *Telephone* 01-858 9884	££–£££

The extensive menu draws on the cooking of many regions and includes some spectacular dishes from Mongolia. Some of the more familiar fare, however, is more impressive, such as aromatic duck, seaweed with grated scallops, and a very good hot-and-sour soup. Specialities include steamed sea-bass with ginger and spring onions, crispy Peking duck in a pancake, and hollowed-out pineapple filled with prawns in a sweet sauce and pineapple and lychees. The decor is primarily black and gold with a nod to oriental modernism; music and air-conditioning. Service is friendly and helpful. House wine is Soave at £5.50. No children under four.

Open Mon to Sat **Closed** 25 and 26 Dec **Meals** 12 to 2.30, 6 to 11.30 **Cards** Access, Amex, Diners, Visa **Service** 10% **BR station** Greenwich

---

HAMMERSMITH AND SHEPHERD'S BUSH

Albertine Map 1	♀ ✕
1 Wood Lane, W12 *Telephone* 01-743 9593	£

A cheerfully bustling place by Shepherd's Bush – plenty of BBC fall-out for company – with imaginative home-cooked food (at least two vegetarian dishes every day) and an exceptional wine list chosen from first-class suppliers. There are over 90 wines (helpfully annotated), with a dozen by the glass and even more by the half-bottle: Chanut house wines (£4.50/85p); Côtes de Gascogne, Domaine de Rieux 1984 (£4.70/90p); Rioja Berberana Carta de Plata 1982 (£5.10/95p); Mondavi Fumé Blanc 1983 (£5.40 half); Ch Méaume 1983 (£3.85 half). Otherwise choose from Gisselbrecht Alsace, Chanut Beaujolais, distinguished clarets and Burgundies (Ch Cissac 1979, £8.60; Gevrey-Chambertin 1982, Armand Rousseau, £12.30), and various sensibly priced French country wines (Côtes de Provence Rosé 1984, Les Maîtres Vignerons St-Tropez, £5.30). Outside France, the German wines are routine, but Italians, Australians and Californians are interesting, and they have the attractive English Woodhay 1984 (£5.85), to say nothing of good sparklers, and Taylor's Port by the glass. Wheelchair access.

Open Mon to Fri 11 to 3, 5.30 to 11 **Closed** Sat, Sun, public hols **Cards** Access, Amex, Diners **Underground** Shepherd's Bush

HAMMERSMITH AND SHEPHERD'S BUSH

Aziz Map 1

116 King Street, W6 *Telephone* 01-748 1826   ££–£££

The Aziz is reliable and reasonably priced. Curries and tandooris are the main lines. Confirmation of individual dishes ranges from chicken tikka to tarka dhal and prawns with spinach. The moghlai specialities for four people at £30 require twenty-four hours' notice and a deposit. Service is attentive, down to stocking Anadin for headaches, though mathematics are not a strong point. Lassi comes in a jug. Music; access for wheelchairs.

Open Mon to Sat **Closed** 25 and 26 Dec **Meals** 12 to 2.15, 6 to 11.45 **Cards** Amex, Diners, Visa **Service** 10% **Underground** Ravenscourt Park/Stamford Brook

Bombay Inn Map 1

177 King Street, W6 *Telephone* 01-748 1156   £

For budget eating the Bombay Inn wins over local Indian competition by providing above-average tandoori staples at below-average prices. The room is low, long and dark, service is obliging and the cooking shows some flair. All the meat on the menu is sheep. The dhansaks, tandoori chicken dishes, onion bhajis and fresh vegetables are all good. Licensed.

Open Noon to 2.30, 6 to midnight **Closed** Christmas Day and Boxing Day **Underground** Ravenscourt Park/Stamford Brook

La Copita Map 1

Askew Road, W12 *Telephone* 01-749 9365   £

Informal wine bar, similar to many in Spain, serving an impressive list of Spanish wines, fine tapas, and two main-course dishes that change daily. There is no mystique to tapas, they are just snacks to eat along with the booze: marinated mini-kebabs, anchovy fillets, chorizo (spicy sausage), tortilla, olives, deep-fried squid rings, meatballs in saffron and sherry sauce, cuttlefish in wine sauce. Main dishes might be beef casserole with nutmeg, and red beans with rice and tomato salad. Puddings include chocolate and brandy mousse and 'adults only' trifle. There is live music on Tuesdays and sometimes live flamenco – ring for details.

Open 6.30pm to 11pm **Closed** Sun; public hols **Underground** Stamford Brook

Dove Map 1

19 Upper Mall, W6   £

This intimate seventeenth-century riverside pub is best at lunchtime when it's quiet, relaxed and less likely to be crowded. The beamed main bar has black wood panelling, red leatherette cushioned built-in wall settles and stools around dimpled copper tables, and old framed advertisements, photographs of the pub and a manuscript of 'Rule, Britannia' on the walls: James Thomson, who wrote

LONDON

it, is said to have written the final part of his less well known 'The Seasons' in an upper room here, dying of a fever he had caught on a trip from here to Kew in bad weather. There's a tiny front snug. The upper room is light and airy, with a wood-strip floor, beams, cushioned wall benches, stools and small farmhouse chairs around heavy rustic wooden tables, Dickensian characters and river scene pictures on the walls, an open brick fireplace with a coal-effect gas fire and a big, clean and efficiently served glass food cabinet: taramosalata and pitta bread or home-made quiche, ploughman's, sausage and beans, salads and hot lunchtime specials such as cauliflower cheese, home-made shepherd's pie, chicken pie and lamb curry or pork Stroganoff; well-kept Fullers London Pride and ESB on handpump. From here, big windows open out on to the newly renovated smallish terrace. Part, with the original grapevine and other plants and a continuation of the wood-strip floor, is covered. Steps lead down to the main flagstoned area, which has lots of teak tables and white metal and teak chairs looking over the lowered river wall directly out on the Thames reach just above Hammersmith Bridge, and across to the playing fields on the far side. If this pub is really crowded you may find more room a short stroll up the river at the Old Ship.

Open 11 to 3, 5.30 to 11 **Underground** Ravenscourt Park

Shireen Tandoori Map 1

270 Uxbridge Road, W12 *Telephone* 01-743 6857 and 749 5927   ££

The food at this well-groomed restaurant is distinctive, and the short menu has a few unexpected items. There are votes for the masala aubergine with spiced yoghurt and the murgh Hyderabadi – chicken with yoghurt and tamarind, cooked with browned onions and saffron. Onion bhajias are light and ungreasy; tikkas are well prepared and parathas worth trying. The home-made ice-cream is good too. The house red is called Pot du Diner and costs £4.70 a bottle. Children's helpings; wheelchair access; music.

Open All week **Closed** 25 and 26 Dec **Meals** 12 to 3, 6 to 11.30 **Cards** Access, Amex, Diners, Visa **Service** 10% **Underground** Shepherd's Bush

---

HAMPSTEAD AND HIGHGATE

Akasaka Map 1

10A Golders Green Road, NW11 *Telephone* 01-455 0676   ££–£££

An unpretentious Japanese restaurant (north of Hampstead in Golders Green) in a spacious room in a Victorian building. In front of the sushi bar are five high stools, and there are matt-black tables divided from each other by bamboo screens. Sushi is the main speciality and has been fresh and skilfully handled. The set meals (lunch from £5, dinner from £10.50) and dishes such as simmered aubergine

---

Safety tip: the British drive on the left hand side of the road, so be very careful crossing busy streets. Look first to your right before stepping off the kerb.

HAMPSTEAD AND HIGHGATE

and grilled clams are more than competent and not overpriced. A range of whisky can be bought by the bottle and kept over until another visit. Music.

Open Tue to Sun D, and Sat L and Sun L **Meals** 12 to 2.30, 6 to 10.30 **Cards** Amex, Visa **Underground** Golders Green

Bambaya Map 1

1 Park Road, N8 *Telephone* 01-348 5609   ££–£££

Actually in Crouch End, but a pleasant walk along Shepherds Hill from Highgate underground (the shell of Alexandra Palace can be seen on the left; television programmes were first transmitted from here in the 1930s). The restaurant's frontage on a bend declares proudly that this is 'African, Caribbean, Black American cooking'. The inside is split into two levels with tile friezes to one side and abstract Ghanaian prints to the other. It is spacious, relaxed. The staff are experts at guiding customers around a menu that takes in much traditional cooking from Africa to America, with some innovative touches. There are four sections – starters, vegetarian, fish and side dishes. The cooking can be very hot, as in the soups of coconut and fish or again in the West African fish stew, which is a degree hotter than the Caribbean version. But the cooking is broader than just heat, and takes in freshly baked corn bread, a large plate of aubergines diced and mixed with pungent dried shrimps, king prawns in coconut milk, and, of course, rice and peas. The hot fruit sweets are recommended, as is the Jamaican rum chocolate cake. The wine list is long on cocktails and non-alcholic fruit juices. Children are appreciated. Music; access for wheelchairs.

Open All week, D only **Meals** 6.30 to 11 (10.30 Sun) **Cards** Access, Visa **Service** 10% **Underground** Highgate

Bayleaf Tandoori Map 1

2 North Hill, N6 *Telephone* 01-340 1719 and 0245   ££

The music may be restrained but the food is lively in this smart Indian restaurant run by a workers' co-operative. Although the menu looks and reads like a clone of Lal Qila (see the Tottenham Court Road section) there have been a few recent additions: a new speciality is ruhi jhol, described as a large Indian river fish, marinated and cooked in small pieces with herbs; while sweets now include gajar-ka-halva, made with carrots, pistachios, almonds, milk and sugar cane, as well as payesh, prepared from Basmati rice, coconut, sultanas and almonds. There is praise for char-grilled king prawns masala, lamb pasanda, and chicken makhani – superbly tender meat in a sauce pointed up with fenugreek. Both the sag and the mushroom bhaji are fresh and well made; rice and breads are good, too. Service can be over-attentive. To drink there are exotic cocktails, a choice of lagers and a minimal selection of wines. House French is £4.50. Children's helpings. Access for wheelchairs.

Open All week **Meals** 12 to 2.15, 6 to 11.15 **Cards** Access, Amex, Diners, Visa **Service** 10% **Underground** Highgate

LONDON

Il Cavaliere Map 1 ✕

14 North End Road, NW11 *Telephone* 01-455 3849 ££–£££

The menu is not going to win the Nobel Prize for innovation, but Pietro Matraxia does the shopping and cooking himself. He does well what a lot of other Italian trattorias do badly – pasta, veal, trout with pepper, zabaglione. Other sweets, and the vegetables, can be less good. House Merlot or Tocai is £4.95. Children's helpings; music; access for wheelchairs.

Open Tue to Sun **Closed** 2 weeks July to Aug **Meals** 12 to 3, 6 to 11.30 **Cards** Access, Amex, Diners, Visa **Service** 10% **Underground** Golders Green

Flask Map 1

77 Highgate West Hill, N6 *Telephone* 01-340 3969 £

Outside this extended old inn there are sturdy wooden tables by the flowering cherry trees, with one or two protected by a wood-pillared porch decorated with hanging baskets of geraniums and petunias. Inside, the original, lower part is not much changed since its 1767 rebuilding: small, partly panelled rooms with a high-backed carved settle, little wooden armchairs, copper jugs hanging from the beams, an open fire, and a sash-windowed bar counter – so that you have to stoop below the sashes to see the barman. This was where one of Hogarth's rowdy friends clobbered a regular with his tankard, and Hogarth himself nearly got clobbered back for sketching the result. Some steps lead up to the more spacious tile-floored extension, which has Windsor chairs, low settles, and tables for the food: bread and cheese, sandwiches, big sausages, filled rolls, salad, quiche or vegetarian pie, and (except Sunday) shepherd's pie; Taylor-Walkers and Ind Coope Burton on handpump. It gets very busy in the evenings and at weekends. There's a separate lunchtime restaurant; children allowed in here but not the rest of the pub.

Open 11 to 3, 5.30 to 11 **Underground** Archway/Highgate

Fleet Tandoori Map 2 ✕

104 Fleet Road, NW3 *Telephone* 01-485 6402 ££

This local curry-house is a bit spartan but has good tandoori chicken, boti kebab and chicken dhansak. Sweets include home-made yoghurt, for which the milk is heavily reduced before the culture is added. Some say the service is helpful and excellent, others disagree. House wine is £4 a bottle, lassi £1.20 a glass. Children's helpings. Access for wheelchairs.

Open All week **Meals** 12 to 2.30, 5.30 to 11 (11.30 Fri, Sat, noon to 11 Sun) **Cards** Access, Amex, Diners, Visa **Service** 10% **Underground** Belsize Park

---

Food can be obtained at nearly all the pubs listed in the Guide but may not be available throughout opening hours, especially in the evening.

HAMPSTEAD AND HIGHGATE

Green Cottage II Map 2

122A Finchley Road, NW3 *Telephone* 01-794 3833   ££–£££

The only restaurant in Britain, as far as we know, to serve only Chinese vegetarian cooking. The decor is modern, almost stark, and if the bill is on the expensive side it is because the ingredients are not cheap – bean curd skin, dried mushrooms, and so on. The main substitutes for meat are wheat gluten – an assortment of deep-fried and boiled pieces in different colours and flavours, ranging from red to brown, and from sweet-and-sour to curry, meant to simulate roast pork, abalone and chicken, is served as a rather chewy starter – and bean curd, which is braised with black mushrooms and green vegetables. A house speciality is deep-fried, breadcrumbed bean curd skin, which is rather good. Tea is jasmine. Children are welcome. Music; wheelchair access; air-conditioning.

Open All week, exc Tue **Meals** 12 to 3, 6 to 11.30 **Cards** Access, Amex, Diners **Service** 10% **Underground** Finchley Road

Holly Bush Map 2

Holly Mount, NW3   £

In a corner of Hampstead Village, the front of this modernised but old-fashioned pub has hardly changed during the last quarter-century: real gas lamps (which have been there for seventy years), a dark and sagging ceiling, brown and cream panelled walls (which are decorated with old advertisements and a few hanging plates), and cosy bays formed by partly glazed partitions. The back room has an intimate atmosphere with subdued electric lighting, an embossed red ceiling, panelled and etched-glass alcoves, and ochre-painted brick walls covered with small prints and plates. This part's named after the painter George Romney: the present tavern was built in 1802 on the site of his stables. In between the two bars, home-cooked food is served, including toasted sandwiches and a selection of hot and cold daily dishes; evening basket meals and a traditional Sunday lunch. No food available at Monday lunchtime. Well-kept Benskins and Ind Coope Burton on handpump, with draught cider; fruit machine, space game. Children may go into the coffee room which is adjacent to the bar. Live music is played on Mondays, Wednesdays and Thursdays. There are seats on the pavement by the quiet cul-de-sac. There is very little parking nearby.

Open 11 to 3, 5.30 to 11 **Underground** Hampstead

Laurent Map 2

428 Finchley Road, NW2 *Telephone* 01-794 3603   £–££

One of a handful of restaurants in London to specialise in couscous, the North African dish of dry, savoury semolina topped with vegetable and/or lamb casserole and served with hot harissa sauce. The Royale version here keeps the protein count up by also including spicy sausage and a lamb chop. Start with a

73

LONDON

good example of brique à l'oeuf – a thin sheet of crisp pancake deep-fried with an egg inside. Moroccan wines. Turkish coffee.

Open Noon to 2, 6 to 11 **Closed** Sun D; last 2 weeks Aug **Underground** Golders Green

Marine Ices Map 2

8 Haverstock Hill, NW3 *Telephone* 01-485 3132   £

As well as the thriving ice-cream part of the business there is an eat-in pizza/pasta café worth checking out. The interior is divided into sections with a black and white marble-effect floor, and embossed white paper on the walls. Some tables are exclusively for the consumption of ice-cream – some simply laid with straw mats and salt and pepper. There are fresh-tasting pastas, such as linguine alla carbonara, tortellini bolognese, spaghetti napolitana and ravioli aurora, and a list of well-topped pizzas, including one with tuna and clams. The daily special might be chicken escalope with mushroom and wine sauce.

Open 11 to 11 (plus 11 to 6 Sun for ice-cream only) **Closed** Christmas Day D and Boxing Day **Underground** Belsize Park

Mediterranean Kebab House Map 2

265 Finchley Road, NW3 *Telephone* 01-794 9981   £

Turkish restaurant that stays open late to pick up the custom from the nightclubs. Hummus, cacik, lamb and baklava have all been good and the Turkish coffee comes with delights, which are exactly that. Service is well organised and the value for money high. A pianist plays from about 9 o'clock.

Open 7pm to 5am **Closed** Mon; Christmas Day and 1 Jan **Underground** Finchley Road

Molnars Map 2

144 Finchley Road, NW3 *Telephone* 01-794 9942   ££–£££

One offshoot of the Gay Hussar (see Soho) is this rustic restaurant full of colourful woven cloths and stable-like wooden partitions between tables. The menu is heroically Hungarian. Especially recommended are the soups – bean, pea, and a hangover soup that appears as a special some days comprising cabbage and sausage – the smoked goose with scholet (brown beans, barley and spices baked for twenty-four hours), and duck in red wine, though it can be on the fatty side. To finish, there are fine pancakes or sour cheesecake. The cooking is a little erratic but not overpriced. Saturday and Sunday lunches are set meals (£7). House Hungarian is £5. Access for wheelchairs; music; children's helpings.

Open Tue to Sun, exc Sun D **Meals** 12.30 to 2.30, 6.30 to 11.30 **Card** Visa **Service** 10% **Underground** Finchley Road

---

Bangers and mash, anyone? Gammon? Now and again, the typical British menu may be a bit of a puzzler to Americans. Please consult the Glossary on page 218 for an alphabetical listing of unusual food items.

HAMPSTEAD AND HIGHGATE

M'sieur Frog's Bistro Map 1

36 Hornsey High Street, N8 *Telephone* 01-340 2116   ££–£££

The frogs are everywhere: wooden ones, soft toys, etc. They must like the romantic dimness of this bistro, and have a good command of French to understand the menu. The cooking is more than convincing – rich parfait of chicken livers; fine moules marinière; powerful carbonnade de boeuf; rabbit with prunes. Vegetables come on side plates and have included pungent garlic potatoes. There is a generosity about the food – plenty of different lettuces in the salad, unlimited coffee – but the extras, including bread at 50p, can push the bill up, though it is hardly expensive by London standards. House claret is £4.75, otherwise there are some interesting wines, mostly under £10; also French cider at £3. Children's helpings; vegetarian meals. Access for wheelchairs.

Open Tue to Sat, D only **Closed** 1 week at Christmas, 3 weeks Aug to Sept **Meals** 6.30 to 11 **Cards** Access, Visa **Service** 10% **Underground** Turnpike Lane **BR station** Hornsey

Olde White Bear Map 2

Well Road, NW3   £

This three-roomed pub has recently had a careful neo-Victorian refurbishment. The main room, dimly lit, has a tiled gas-effect log fire with a heavy wooden over-mantel and two big tasseled armed chairs in front of it, a mix of wooden stools, cushioned captain's chairs and a big farmhouse chair around the tables, a flowery sofa surrounded by the excrescences of an ornate Edwardian sideboard, and lots of Victorian prints and cartoons on the walls. A small central room – also dimly lit – has Lloyd Loom furniture, dried flower arrangements and signed photographs of actors and playwrights. The brighter end room has cushioned machine-tapestried ornate pews, marble-topped tables, a very worn butcher's table, dark brown paisley curtains and a food cabinet serving sandwiches, ploughman's, salads (such as quiche, ham or salami), leek and potato bake, shepherd's pie, spicy lamb bake or cold curried chicken and steak and kidney pie or good moules marinière. Well-kept Ind Coope Burton and Taylor-Walker Bitter on handpump; house wine is served by small, medium or large glass, and there's a good choice of over a dozen others, including good Australian wine and chateau-bottled clarets; also twenty-two malt whiskies. Loud piped pop music on our evening visit, maybe quieter classical at lunchtime. Friendly service and a chatty, relaxed atmosphere. Children are welcome.

Open 11 to 3, 5.30 to 11 **Underground** Hampstead

Peachey's Map 2

205 Haverstock Hill, NW3 *Telephone* 01-435 6744   ££–£££

The walls are covered with pictures and paraphernalia in this bar-cum-restaurant beside the Screen on the Hill cinema. The cooking is French with a few inventions such as a variation on steak tartare – cannibale – or its fish equivalent. Duck comes with a clear lime sauce, garnished with pineapple and

LONDON

peppercorns. Vegetables are plentiful, the cheeseboard well kept. There's a set lunch or dinner at £8.95. The wine list has some astounding bargains, such as Ch Talbot 1970 at £26, which is below the shelf price of some off-licences. Music; wheelchair access. Vegetarian meals and children's helpings.

Open Mon to Sat, exc Sat L **Meals** 12 to 2.30, 7 to 11.30 **Cards** Amex, Diners, Visa **Service** 12½% **Underground** Belsize Park

Quincy's Map 2

675 Finchley Road, NW2 *Telephone* 01-794 8499   ££–£££

A sophisticated bistro in an unlikely no-man's-land. The quirky interior, with its painted cement walls and tacky bric-à-brac, would not necessarily lead one to expect this standard of cooking. The atmosphere is the jolly side of noisy. Soups are impressive – Scotch broth, smoked fish, tomato and carrot – as are other starters of duck galantine with redcurrant sauce, and vegetable and veal terrine with tomato coulis. Fish is treated with some style, as in plump mussels served hot on a celeriac salad, and quenelles of halibut and crab with saffron. We are assured of the freshness of the dill in the gravlax. The eclecticism and invention continues through main courses of veal in artichoke sauce, lamb with onion, and ten-day-hung pheasant with pomegranate. There are many votes for the rich chocolate-pot dessert, iced marc de champagne soufflé, and a steamed apple suet pudding with calvados cream. Dinner costs £13.75, Sunday lunch from £8.50. House wine is £6 a bottle. Children's helpings; wheelchair access; music; air-conditioning.

Open Tue to Sun D and Sun L **Meals** 12 to 2, 7.30 to 10.30 (9.30 Sun) **Cards** Access, Visa **Underground** Golders Green

Sandringham Hotel Map 2

3 Holford Road, NW3 *Telephone* 01-435 1569

For 32 years this modest, friendly B&B has been run by the Dreyer family at their large Victorian house in a quiet street on the edge of Hampstead Heath. It is a friendly place, has lots of flowers and plants around, offers good coffee for breakfast, and its prices are exceedingly reasonable. A typical report from a grateful American visitor: 'Our warm welcome, from the enchanting lady of the house, was wonderfully soothing after being up all night. There is no lift, and if you have much baggage (as we did), be prepared to carry it! We walked up four flights of stairs to an airy, medium-sized room, clean and well-appointed. Breakfast is served in a large room overlooking a lovely garden. Service was prompt and gracious and the food was good. The hotel could not have been more delightful.' No restaurant.

Open All year **Cards** None accepted **Accommodations** 15 rooms, 4 with bath. B&B £16 to £18 **Underground** Hampstead

---

Symbols to denote hotel, pub, restaurant, tea shop and wine bar are given in order of importance at the establishment.

HAMPSTEAD AND HIGHGATE

Spaniards Map 1

Spaniards Lane, NW3   £

Built in 1585, this popular old pub has genuine antique winged settles, open fires, snug little alcoves in the low-ceilinged oak-panelled rooms and some nice touches like barmen in hunting pink and candle-shaped lamps in pink shades. It's a lively, busy place in the evenings, full of regular customers. The home-cooked good-value food that changes daily includes giant sausages, filled rolls, quiche, ploughman's pie, macaroni milanese, chicken provençale and lamb kebabs; in cool weather they make hot toddies. Charringtons beer. Fruit machine. During the 1780 Gordon Riots the innkeeper cunningly gave so many free drinks to the mob on its way to burn down Lord Mansfield's Kenwood House that by the time the Horse Guards got here the rioters were lying drunk and incapable on the floor. The attractive sheltered garden has slatted wooden tables and chairs on a crazy-paved terrace, which opens on to a flagstoned walk around a small lawn, with roses, a side arbour of wistaria and clematis, and an aviary.

Open 11 to 3, 5.30 to 11 **Underground** Hampstead (quite a walk)

Swiss Cottage Hotel Map 2

4 Adamson Road, NW3 *Telephone* 01-722 2281   ££

A conversion of four Victorian terraced houses in a quiet residential street, yet close to underground and bus services and thus within 15 minutes of the West End. A medium-priced and medium-sized alternative to the big flashy city hotel, and also a hotel of genuine character – mostly ornate Edwardian and Victorian in its style, but carried out with panache. Even its shortcomings tend to be looked on as endearing: fairly exiguous single rooms, volatile plumbing, slow whimsical room service. 'It is primarily a hotel for psychoanalysts and do-it-yourself enthusiasts. One should still bring along Rawlplugs, Araldite, plumbing repair kit and some spare light bulbs. But if one's mind is lingering on pre-war Vienna or Zurich, one may feel very much at home amongst the slightly continental furnishings, the Oriental rugs and antiques. The hotel is uniquely individual and friendly – every room is different – very much an hotel to make one's *pied-à-terre* in Hampstead. There is also the allure of their delightful small paved garden with its honeymoon cottage. Sometimes there are flowers or fruit in your room – sometimes not. The dining-room has once again become chaotic and infuriating, after a rather more settled phase. We still forage around the dining room picking up packets of butter, marmalade, or the odd spoon so that we can get on with our breakfast. But overall this hotel is to me absolutely uniquely warm, charming and welcoming, and we shall continue to return to it again and again. If it has its personal peculiarities, so I suppose do we.' The restaurant is open at lunch and dinner (£7.50 and £12).

Open All year **Cards** Access, Amex, Diners, Visa **Accommodations** 69 rooms, 42 with bath, 23 with shower. B&B £22.50 to £36 **Underground** Swiss Cottage

LONDON

Wakaba Map 2 ✖

31 College Crescent, NW3 *Telephone* 01-722 3854   £££

This easy-paced, relaxing Japanese restaurant has a feeling of a smart café – small melamine tables packed close together, and a very plain decor of white walls, a few inexpensive pictures, and black beams painted across the ceiling. When it fills it can get stuffy, but before that happens there are well-prepared dishes from most major aspects of the cuisine. It is a good place to begin on Japanese food. There is a mixed starter of up to eight morsels served on a wooden platter, which illustrates the subtle contrasts important in Japan – for instance, mild sweet pickled ginger, fried prawn, and marinated tofu. Fish for the sushi or sashimi is supremely fresh, the meats for the yakitori and teriyaki are of good quality, the soups are delicate and fragrant and the batter for the tempura is, as it should be, lumpy, lacy and light. To finish, drink green tea; wines are ordinary. Music. Children's helpings and vegetarian meals.

Open Tue to Sun, D only **Meals** 6 to 11 **Cards** Access, Amex, Diners, Visa **Service** 10% **Underground** Swiss Cottage/Finchley Road

Zaki's Map 1 ✖

634 Finchley Road, NW11 *Telephone* 01-458 2012 and 9273   £££

This is a modern Jewish restaurant. The cooking is of the Middle East, not Russia, and in that divided area at least cooking provides one unifying factor. All the food is prepared on the premises, including hummus, tahini, and baklava; peanuts are roasted and turnips pickled. A meze will encompass much of the intriguing first courses, such as stuffed vine leaves, kubeba shamia, and fish croquettes. Dishes of the day have taken in all points on the compass from Persia for a kebab of beef served with a spicy rice, to Greece for braised chicken with onions, garlic, wine and tomatoes. Roast veal, though, remains a stalwart main course. The service is friendly and the Hebrew/Mediterranean music is an exotic enhancement. House wine is £4.50. Children's helpings at lunchtime only. Access for wheelchairs.

Open All week, exc Sat L, Fri L in winter, Sat D in summer **Closed** Jewish hols **Meals** 12 to 2.30, 6 to 11 **Cards** Access, Amex, Diners, Visa **Service** 10% **Underground** Golders Green

HOLBORN

Chez Gerard Map 6 ✖

119–120 Chancery Lane, WC2 *Telephone* 01-405 0290   £££

The service is diabolical, but there is very little wrong with the food in this quasi-French chain (see also in the Mayfair and Tottenham Court Road

---

See the back of the Guide for ideas for day trips out of London: Brighton, Cambridge, Canterbury, Oxford, and Windsor and Eton.

sections). The formula is entrecôte et frites with cold starters and sweets – and good cheeses. Extras put the bill up. House Rhône is £5.50, but Beaujolais is the most considered section of the list. Music. Children's helpings.

Open Mon to Fri, breakfast and L only **Meals** 8 to 5.30 **Card** Access **Service** 10% **Underground** Chancery Lane

Cittie of York Map 6	
22 High Holborn, WC1	£

This pub may be found by looking out for its big black and gold clock. The main hall has the longest bar counter in Britain, with vast thousand-gallon wine vats (empty since prudently drained at the start of the Second World War) above the gantry, and a cat-walk running along the top of them. The raftered roof is extraordinarily high, with big bulbous lights hanging from it, and below a line of high windows is a long row of intimate old-fashioned and ornately carved cubicles with heavy wooden armchairs and other seats. A particular thing to search out is the big stove – uniquely triangular, with grates on all three sides. The pub gets packed at lunchtime and early evening, particularly with lawyers and judges. A smaller, more comfortable but less atmospheric wood-panelled room has lots of little prints of York and attractive brass lights. There's a lunchtime food counter in the main hall, with more in the downstairs cellar bar snacks (not available on Saturday evenings or Sundays): sausage and beans, ploughman's, chilli con carne, grilled trout, chicken in mushroom sauce or old brewery beef pie, corned beef bake, salads, scampi, salmon steak and fillet steak; well-kept Sam Smiths OB and Museum on handpump; fruit machines, darts. The ceiling of the entrance hall has medieval-style painted panels and plaster York roses.

Open 11 to 3.30, 5.30 to 11 **Closed** Sun **Underground** Holborn

Porte de la Cité Map 4	
65 Theobald's Road, WC1 *Telephone* 01-242 1154	£££

The navy blue decor matches the business suits that frequent this lunch-time-only French restaurant (though it opens by arrangement for private dinner parties), related to Au Bois St Jean (see St John's Wood). The menu (from £14) concentrates on mousses and pâtés to start, as well as gimmicks, such as deep-fried cheese kebabs with mustard sauce, before good-quality meats fashionably carved – duck breast is fanned out on the plate and is sauced, equally fashionably, with raspberry vinegar. Wines are imported direct from France and start at £5.75.

Open Mon to Fri L only **Closed** Public hols **Meals** 12 to 2.30 **Cards** Access, Amex, Diners, Visa **Service** Inc **Underground** Holborn

---

Most pubs in this book sell wine by the glass as well as beer. We mention wines only if they are better than average.

LONDON

Princess Louise Map 4

208 High Holborn, WC1   £

Though it's well-kept and lively, the real reasons for including this spacious two-floor pub is the good range of real ales and elaborate Victorian decor (improved by the recent renovations) such as etched and gilt mirrors, brightly coloured and fruity-shaped tiles and a high, deeply moulded, crimson and gold plaster ceiling. There are always nine well-kept beers on handpump including Adnams, Brakspears, Darleys Thorne, Greene King IPA and Abbott, Lorimers, Sam Smiths, Vaux Bitter and Samson, and Wards. Downstairs, the open-plan room has an enormous island bar stretching down the middle flanked by green plush seats and banquettes. Food, from a separate serving counter, includes sandwiches, home-made pie, lasagne and salads; no food on Saturday evenings or Sundays. Upstairs they have a wider range of food and several wines by the glass, including champagne. It can get very busy at lunchtime. Jazz is played on Saturday and Sunday evenings.

Open 11 to 3, 5.30 to 11 **Underground** Holborn/Chancery Lane

ISLINGTON

Anna's Place Map 2

90 Mildmay Park, N1 *Telephone* 01-249 9379   £££

Tables in this Swedish café now have to be booked about two days in advance. Anna Hegarty is still very much the presence, having a word for everyone. 'It should be called beef Greta, but I call it Strindberg, as everyone knows that morose Swede.' The dining-room is no more than the downstairs of a converted house with a bar, flashy cash register, and a bright-red Aga, now used as a plate-warmer. There are tables in the garden for hot evenings. The menu, on a blackboard, is built around the old favourites, such as gravlax – still excellent – and roast duck with a sauce of gin and juniper. Clever ideas include trout covered with a tapénade and goats' cheese and warmed under the grill. There are some subtleties, too, such as fennel seeds in the sweet bread rolls. The wine list is not as perfunctory as might seem at a glance. House wine is £4.95. Music; wheelchair access. Vegetarian meals and children's helpings.

Open Tue to Sat **Closed** 1 week Christmas, 1 week Easter, Aug **Meals** 12.30 to 2.30, 7.15 to 10.15 **Cards** None accepted **Service** 10% **Underground** Highbury and Islington (quite a walk) **BR station** Dalston Junction

Compton Arms Map 2

4 Compton Avenue, off Canonbury Lane, N1   £

Hidden away up a mews, this villagey little pub has small and cheerful rooms with low ceilings and little local pictures on the walls; it's simply furnished with wood and leatherette, and the really friendly service extends to free snacks at Sunday lunchtimes. Cheap freshly cooked food includes sandwiches,

ISLINGTON

ploughman's, burgers, sausages, garlic mushrooms and dishes of the day. Meals are available at lunchtime only (not Sunday); snacks weekdays and Saturday lunchtime. The unusual range of well-kept real ales includes Adnams Southwold and Extra, Arkells, Greene King Abbot, Sam Smiths OB and guest beers such as James Paine; dominoes, cribbage, chess. A quiet little crazy-paved back terrace has benches around cask tables under a big sycamore tree.

Open 11 to 3, 5.30 to 11 **Underground** Highbury and Islington

George IV Map 2

60 Copenhagen Street, N1

A real curiosity this – a neatly run Lancashire pub here in North London, with masses of old photographs of Burnley, Blackburn, and of the brewery which supplies its well-kept ale; even the ploughman's comes with a good northern-sized helping of Lancashire cheese. There's a lot of stripped woodwork and pine furniture, a Victorian tiled fireplace, soft pinkish lighting and a good chatty atmosphere; a smaller room has French windows opening on to a trellised patio with white metal and wooden garden furniture. The larger part of the bar (where on our visit a cheerful darts match was being held) is on two levels. Bar food (lunchtime, not Sunday) includes sandwiches and omelettes; a new kitchen is due to supply soup, home-made steak and kidney pie, chilli con carne, curry, fish and steaks. Thwaites Bitter and Mild on handpump; dominoes, cribbage, fruit machine and country and western piped music on our visit; friendly landlord. There's a park beside the pub and an adventure playground for children.

Open 11.30 to 3, 6 to 11 **Underground** King's Cross/Angel

Hodja Nasreddin Map 2

53 Newington Green Road, N1 *Telephone* 01-226 7757

An inexpensive Turkish restaurant with salami in hot spicy sauce among more familiar starters of dolma, imam bayildi and borek. Main courses consist of kebabs, minced doner, and chops, with some steak and chicken dishes, and salads, and baklava and kadayif to finish. Villa Doluca and Buzbag are on the short wine list. Children's helpings, but no under-fours. Music; access for wheelchairs.

Open All week **Meals** Noon to 2.30 am **Cards** Access, Amex, Diners, Visa **Underground** Highbury and Islington (quite a walk) **BR station** Canonbury

Island Queen Map 2

Noel Road, N1 *Telephone* 01-226 0307

Close to Camden Passage antiques area, this popular and extraordinarily decorated pub has monstrous caricatures above the bar of *Alice in Wonderland* characters; there are big mirrors with simulated green palms and jungle

81

LONDON

vegetation stuck over them, and an open coal fire in cool weather, but otherwise furnishings are simple. There's a good choice of freshly made and often unusual food, such as ploughman's, carrot, orange and ginger soup or chicken liver and brandy pâté, filled baked potato, burger, grilled tandoori prawns or vegetable gratin, tagliatelle with blue cheese and spinach sauce, shepherd's pie, leeks and ham in cheese sauce, prawn, spinach and potato curry, and chicken and cashew stir-fry or beef and broccoli in oyster sauce; puddings. On weekday lunchtimes it's very quiet and spacious, with its airy big windows, but at weekend lunchtimes it's packed with trendily dishevelled regular customers – often with children or grandchildren; snacks are available only at lunchtimes from Mondays to Saturdays; the restaurant is open on Thursday, Friday and Saturday evenings. In the evenings, when the juke box with its good nostalgic collection of 1960s and 1970s records is turned up, it can get quite lively. Well-kept Bass, Charrington IPA and (very reasonably priced for London) Springfield on handpump; pool in a back room, and two space games. There are tables in front of the creeper-covered pub, by the quiet street.

Open 11 to 3, 5.30 to 11 **Underground** Angel

Jacques Wine Bar Map 2

130 Blackstock Road, Highbury Vale, N4 *Telephone* 01-359 3410   ££

In the wine bar tradition, this acts as a repository for Victorian junk. It also has small wooden tables and chairs, and the dogs may get a bit much, but the food, and the prices, are up to restaurant standard. Grilled goats' cheese comes on a croûton with salad leaves; chicken livers turn up in a pâté with a relish of onion marmalade, or pink and hot with sherry vinegar. Duck breast with cherries is better than the pigeon, and vegetables are up to the mark. A fine pudding is a charlotte of rummy white cake around a light chocolate mousse with custard. Forty wines are as French as the patron and his staff and from good sources. Mark-ups are not greedy, and there is a wine of the week. Children are welcome. Access for wheelchairs; music.

Open Tue to Sun, exc Tue L **Closed** 1 week at Christmas, 1 week Aug **Meals** 12 to 2.30, 7 to 10.30 **Cards** Access, Diners **Underground** Arsenal/Finsbury Park

---

Lakorn Thai Map 2

197–199 Rosebery Avenue, EC1 *Telephone* 01-837 5048   ££

The name is the Thai for a female dancer, parodying this restaurant's former guise as an Italian restaurant named The Ballerina. It is in the modern mould – light and airy, informal, extremely clean, and the food delicate. The menu

---

The London subway, called the underground or tube, is the best in the world – clean, fast, efficiently laid out and exceptionally well signposted. A ticket may be purchased at a ticket office at tube stations or, if you have the correct change, at a machine in the station. Hold on to your ticket until the end of your journey, when it will be collected at the exit. You won't be bored waiting for your train – the platform advertisements are usually many, varied, literate and fun to read.

ISLINGTON

flavours extend through lemon grass, chilli, galanga, coconut, and hot-and-sour. The separate sections on the menu reflect the way of eating, which is helpful. The staff provide explanations, which lead into fine potent soups, such as the chicken, galanga, and coconut (always a favourite), paw-paw salad, chicken and noodles, and even a variation on tempura. There's a set lunch (from £7). Ten wines around £5. Music; access for wheelchairs. Children are welcome.

Open All week, exc Sat L **Meals** 12 to 3, 6 to 11.30 **Cards** Access, Amex, Visa **Service** 10% **Underground** Angel

---

Minogues Map 2

8 Theberton Street, N1 *Telephone* 01-354 5220

£££

An Irish restaurant in the heart of Islington, in among the estate agents. The glass door is engraved in old pub fashion; the dining-room is simple, decorated in contemporary colours. The swing doors at the back lead straight into the kitchen. The menu for the set dinner (£13.50) is on a blackboard and is heroically patriotic, featuring Irish stew, beef in Guinness, and plenty of salmon dishes. Potatoes are done in four ways – mashed, sauté, new, or as potato-cakes – and, often as not, arrive on the main course plate as well. The bread alone is almost worth a visit. Sometimes the cooking has been a bit careless, which is a pity, because at others it has been excellent. Game is a feature in season, the cheeseboard will often have brilliant Gubbeen, and the Queen of Puddings is fine. House Burgundy is £5.90, or else there is bottled Guinness. Children's helpings. Music.

Open Tue to Sat, D only **Closed** 2 weeks at Christmas **Meals** 7 to 11 **Cards** Access, Amex, Diners, Visa **Underground** Angel

---

M'sieur Frog Map 2

31A Essex Road, N1 *Telephone* 01-226 3495

£££

The lily pond is as active as ever. After twelve years the mood on the menu lately is classical French. Trends towards the bistro and also towards *nouvelle cuisine* have been over-ruled by potage crème Dubarry and filet de sole au vermouth. At least the Frog is a brasserie, and it is the robust dishes at which it excels – mussel soup with saffron; the duck breast with elderberry sauce; the navarin printanier; the ragoût of mushrooms. The staff hold their own even when the place is crowded. There are good wines, but the house claret or Sauvignon at £4.75 are fitting. Access for wheelchairs. Children's helpings.

Open Mon to Sat, D only **Closed** 1 week at Christmas, 3 weeks Aug **Meals** 7 to 11.30 **Cards** Access, Visa **Service** 10% **Underground** Angel

---

Shish Mahal Map 2

113 Holloway Road, N7 *Telephone* 01-607 4595

££

Probably the best of the Indian restaurants between Highbury Corner and the Holloway Odeon. Variations on chicken, meat, prawn and lobster include

83

LONDON

sweet-and-sour with lentils, medium-hot with egg, and hot with a touch of lemon. There are tandoori and karahi dishes, and good Bombay potatoes in yoghurt and tomato, with kulfi to follow. Draught or Kingfisher lager to drink. Music. Vegetarian meals; children's helpings; take-away service.

Open All week **Meals** 12 to 3, 6 to 12 (1 Fri, Sat) **Cards** Access, Amex, Diners, Visa **Underground** Highbury and Islington

Upper Street Fish Shop Map 2

324 Upper Street, N1 *Telephone* 01-359 1401   £

Olga Conway presides over this Islington institution with a good humour that makes her as indispensable as the salt and vinegar. She gives out bowls of chips to queues or directs you to the pub next door for a pint until a table is free. She will even chill white wine in the fridge and provide tumblers and a corkscrew. Excellent fresh fish is cooked in ground-nut oil, and the chips are crisp and ungreasy. The poached halibut and jam roly-poly are legendary, and there might be seasonal extravagances such as fresh salmon and summer pudding. There's a minimum charge of £3.50. Air-conditioning; wheelchair access; children's helpings.

Open Mon to Sat, exc Mon L **Closed** Public hols, Christmas **Meals** 11.30 to 2, 5.30 to 10 **Cards** None accepted **Underground** Angel

KENSINGTON

The Ark Map 2

122 Palace Gardens Terrace, W8 *Telephone* 01-229 4024   ££

For the best part of twenty-four years, this cramped, stuffy bistro has been a favourite. Often it gets more votes than far more accomplished places. The value for money is good, most of what is cooked is fresh, and perhaps above all it has a style – an Elizabeth David version of a French country restaurant – that is both revered and increasingly hard to find. The name is becoming appropriate: the escargot vol-au-vent go two by two. Anything that needs skill or judgement is unreliable. It is at its best for the simple things such as the rack of lamb, artichoke vinaigrette, or grilled pork with herbs. The bread, house wine and vegetables (al dente) are good. Best to book, as it gets very busy. Wheelchair access; children's helpings.

Open All week, exc Sun L **Meals** 12 to 3, 6.30 to 11.15 **Cards** Access, Amex, Visa **Underground** Notting Hill Gate/High Street Kensington

Clarke's Map 2

124 Kensington Church Street, W8 *Telephone* 01-221 9225   ££–£££

There is no choice on the menu at night (£17), but the quality of Sally Clarke's ingredients and some imaginative combinations can make brilliantly successful meals. One such comprised confit of wild duck with lettuce, lamb cutlets with

KENSINGTON

potato-cake and provençale vegetables, mature farmhouse Cheddar served with radishes and bread, ginger ice-cream, and excellent chocolate truffles to finish with the coffee. On another night, quiche of leek and shallot with sun-dried tomatoes, pine-nuts and prosciutto, fresh tuna with herbs, a salad of deep-fried onion rings and lettuce, and Hilary Charnley's Exmoor cheese. The charcoal grill is often used for vegetables, for example leeks marinated first in oil and basil. But the style is not really Californian, where Sally trained, but her own. As she puts it: 'Lots of char-grilling, lots of very good olive oil, herbs from the South of France, and, in summer, lots of English fruits, salads and vegetables.' She too can claim to be part of the British renaissance in cooking. Many have been enthralled by her support for traditional English cheeses. Service is young. There is a limited choice on the menu at lunchtime (from £9.50), when Sally herself cooks. The wine list up-dates itself four times a year, and shows the same accuracy as the cooking. The Californian section has expanded. Among the clarets is Ch Clarke 1979 at £22. House Côtes du Ventoux is £6. Access for wheelchairs. Children are welcome.

Open Mon to Fri **Closed** Christmas, Easter, 2 weeks in summer **Meals** 12.30 to 2, 7.30 to 11 **Cards** Access, Visa **Service** Inc **Underground** Notting Hill Gate

---

Geales Fish Restaurant   Map 2

2 Farmer Street, W8 *Telephone* 01-727 7969   ££

Cottagey turn-of-the-century building converted into a two-storey fish and chip restaurant. The Geale family have been here since 1919. The fish is fresh from Grimsby and fried in beef dripping. The menu changes daily, according to what's available, but haddock leads the popularity stakes along with shark when it's on. House Champagne comes at £11.75 a full bottle, or £6.75 a half. With main courses at around £4 to £5, you may find the bill here considerably more than that in your local chippie.

Open Noon to 3, 6 to 11.30 (11 Sat) **Closed** Sun, Mon; 2 weeks Christmas; last 3 weeks Aug **Underground** Notting Hill Gate

---

Launceston Place   Map 3

1A Launceston Place, W8 *Telephone* 01-937 6912   ££–£££

'Our aim is to provide fresh seasonal food, simply prepared, at affordable prices.' That will do nicely, thank you. The elegance of both the surrounding streets and also the dark fascia belie the fact that Nick Smallwood's and Simon Slater's new restaurant is not expensive, especially at lunchtime or before 8 o'clock when the set meals (from £7.50) operate. The two dining-rooms are handsome and manage to achieve what is so often said but so rarely true, namely that the feeling is of dining at home – a rather Victorian gentrified home, perhaps, thanks to the elaborately framed mirrors, the oil paintings and the height of the ceilings. The atmosphere generated is akin to a wedding reception – if extra tables have been brought in you may find yourself sitting among the other side's family. The menu is new British cooking and shows no qualms at serving things like asparagus and lobster plain if that is what is best. The

LONDON

supplies are excellent and have featured thickly sliced smoked lamb with a little pot of herb mayonnaise as a relish to the side. There is cooking, though, too, as in calf's liver with an orange sauce, brill wrapped in a lettuce leaf, poached and served with a sharp vinaigrette, and strawberry tart. The cheeseboard features the best of the new generation of English hard cheeses, such as Swaledale. Even when the kitchen gets itself into trouble, it manages to bail itself out – for instance, a rather dry compacted egg filling to wholemeal pastry tart is saved by the generosity of the salad bed, including tiny green beans as well as lettuce in a sharp dressing, and the contrast of dry and wet works well. One of the great strengths of having a kitchen loyal to the market is that it is able to do such things. It is also faithful to some old-fashioned dishes such as roast beef, steak and kidney in Yorkshire pudding, brandy-snaps with clotted cream, and apple and rhubarb crumble. The wine list has been skilfully assembled. It is not overlong, but it is able to feature no fewer than four dessert wines by the glass, including sometimes 1976 Auslese and Barsac. House wine is claret, naturally – fifty per cent Cabernet, fifty per cent Merlot and £6.95. Air-conditioning; no pipes in the dining-room. Access for wheelchairs. Children's helpings at lunchtime only.

Open All week, exc Sun D **Meals** 12.30 to 2.30, 7 to 11.30 **Cards** Access, Visa **Underground** Gloucester Road

---

London Tara Hotel Map 2

Scarsdale Place, Wright's Lane, W8 *Telephone* 01-937 7211 £–£££

Bright, modern, many-storeyed hotel off Kensington High Street, very handy for the tube just round the corner and only a few minutes' walk from Kensington Gardens. Public rooms are more than spacious and attractively decorated. Well-organised, not too cramped bedrooms all have good bathrooms. The hotel has an all-day coffee shop. Wheelchair access.

Open (Restaurant) 6.30 to 1.30; (coffee shop) 7am to 11pm **Cards** Access, Amex, Diners, Visa **Accommodations** 830 rooms, all with bath B&B £33 to £54 (breakfast extra) **Underground** High Street Kensington

---

Malabar Map 2

27 Uxbridge Street, W8 *Telephone* 01-727 8800 ££–£££

Jo Chalmers and Anil Bist specialise in a version of Indian home cooking, offering quite a few dishes that are outside the range of most Indian restaurants. Chicken wings are grilled and served with yoghurt and spices; venison is marinated in tamarind; king prawns are skewered with onion and ginger and served with lemon sauce. Vegetables take in sliced green bananas with ginger; pumpkin fried with herbs; and kachumber (an Indian salad). On Fridays there is a fish curry that might be mullet, eel, trout, or pomfret; self-service buffet lunches are available on Sundays; there's also a set lunch or dinner for two at £18. Drink lassi or Kingfisher beer. Children are welcome.

Open All week **Closed** 1 week Aug **Meals** 12 to 3, 6 to 11.30 **Cards** Access, Visa **Service** 12½% **Underground** Notting Hill Gate

KENSINGTON

Michel Map 2

343 Kensington High Street, W8 *Telephone* 01-603 3613   ££–££££

This French restaurant has been here for four years, but has started to hum since the arrival of Gerard Mosiniak in the kitchen. It is not a formula restaurant. Interesting materials translate on the plate into subtle flavours that have some affinity with the other ingredients: for instance, beef is sliced off a piece of fillet cooked whole, fanned out on a plate with a deep brown sauce flavoured with cardamom and to one side a little pastry tart filled with red onion purée. That is a dish straight out of modern British cooking, though the Frenchness of this menu is irreproachable – fish soup of red mullet served with rouille and croûtons. There is an eye for the unusual in steamed sea-bass served on seaweed with some Lapsang Souchong tea as a sauce. The cheeses have been impressive, and to finish there is coffee parfait with rum and coffee sauce. A small, good list of French wines concentrates on fresh young bottles that do not cost too much. Music; air-conditioning. Vegetarian meals; children's helpings.

Open All week **Closed** Public hols **Meals** 12 to 2.30, 7 to 11 **Cards** Access, Amex, Diners, Visa **Service** 15% **Underground** Kensington Olympia/Earl's Court/High Street Kensington

Phoenicia Map 2

11–13 Abingdon Road, W8 *Telephone* 01-937 0120   ££–£££

This long-standing family-run Lebanese restaurant has provided a bridge for many people between Europe and the Middle East. The menu offers a good all-round mix of the cuisine, being strongest in the starters, which range from hummus to sautéed lambs' brains in black butter. Main courses centre on charcoal grills. The meze at £8.50 a head for four people includes fifteen dishes; the set dinner is from £12.95. Sweets can be illuminating, going rather further than just baklava. To drink there is arak, Ch Musar or mint tea. Vegetarian meals and children's helpings. Music and air-conditioning.

Open All week **Meals** Noon to midnight **Cards** Access, Amex, Diners, Visa **Service** Inc (set meals); 15% à la carte **Underground** High Street Kensington

Steamboat Charley's Map 2

205 Kensington Church Street, W8 *Telephone* 01-727 3184   £

Up-market fish and chip restaurant with life-on-the-ocean-wave decor of life-size mounted fish and crustacea. Above the woodblock floor covered with sawdust, and pine and plaster walls, the chippie theme extends to a newspaper-lined ceiling. The short menu includes kedgeree, fish pie, crab cakes, New England clam chowder, whitebait and skate, with chocolate mousse to follow. A great place to take the younger members of the family.

Open 6pm (noon Sun) to 11.30pm **Underground** Notting Hill Gate

---

We always say if we know whether bedrooms have private bath or shower.

LONDON

209 Map 2 ✖

209 Kensington High Street, W8 *Telephone* 01-937 2260 £

Calm, informal basement restaurant with a straightforward Thai menu. A single dish, such as beef with chillies, plus rice and tea, is the best way to eat for under £5. Vegetarian meals and take-aways available.

Open Noon to 3, 6 to 10.30 **Underground** High Street Kensington

Windsor Castle Map 2 🍺

114 Campden Hill Road, W8 £

Delightfully old-fashioned, this well-kept and friendly pub has a series of little rooms with dark panelling and wooden partitions, sturdy built-in elm benches, time-smoked ceilings and soft lighting; there's even a snug little pre-war-style dining-room opening off the bar – and no fruit machines or piped music. Bar food includes cheese and biscuits or French bread, a good choice of sandwiches (including a chip butty or grilled bacon), toasted sandwiches (grilled gammon or mini steak), pâté, cod or plaice, ham or beef with chips, salads such as hot or cold quiche or smoked salmon, bacon, egg and black pudding, scampi, eight-ounce rump steak and home-made fruit pie; no snacks on Sunday evenings; well-kept Charringtons IPA on handpump, reasonably priced by London standards. A special summer feature is the big tree-shaded back terrace which has lots of sturdy teak seats and tables on flagstones, knee-high stone walls (eminently sittable-on) dividing them, high ivy-covered sheltering walls, and soft shade from a sweeping low-branched plane tree, a lime and a flowering cherry. A bar counter serves the terrace directly, as does a separate food stall. Note that, unusually, no children are allowed there. Usually fairly quiet at lunchtime, the pub is often packed in the evenings.

Open 11 to 3, 5.30 to 11 **Underground** Notting Hill Gate/Holland Park

KILBURN AND MAIDA VALE

L'Aventure Map 2 ✖

3 Blenheim Terrace, NW8 *Telephone* 01-624 6232 £££

A good, no-fuss little French restaurant with a modern menu that puts the accent on fish. In summer, the doors of the dining-room are opened to give a view of the terrace, but in winter the old prints, tapestry, dried flowers, and pine long-case clock evoke their own bourgeois warmth. The menu (£10.50) offers four or five choices at each course. Rack of lamb is brought whole to the table, carved and spread out on the plate with baked cloves of southern French garlic. Equally familiar favourites, such as magret of canard, and salmon with sorrel, are well executed; vegetarian meals can be ordered. There are thoughtful touches throughout: wholemeal raisin bread, good coffee, and well-tended cheeses. A skilful hand with pastry in the kitchen has turned out fine raspberry tarts. The service is professional without being fawning. The

KILBURN AND MAIDA VALE

thirty bottles are well spread in terms of regions and price. House Burgundy is £6.25. No cigars or pipes; music; access for wheelchairs. Children are welcome.

Open All week, exc Sat L **Meals** 12.30 to 2.30, 7 to 11 **Cards** Amex, Visa **Service** 10% **Underground** Maida Vale/St John's Wood

Colonnade Hotel Map 2

2 Warrington Crescent, W9 *Telephone* 01-289 2167   ££

Elegant Georgian hotel with a handsome garden at the front. People like the place for a good mixture of modern amenities and traditional comforts. Four-poster beds in seven of the individually decorated bedrooms will attract many; nicely kept bathrooms others (some rooms have only a shower, though). An evening meal at about £9 is available. Weekday laundry service.

Open (Dining-room) **Cards** Access, Amex, Diners, Visa **Accommodations** 54 rooms, all with bath or shower. B&B £23 to £35.50 **Underground** Warwick Avenue

Crockers Map 2

24 Aberdeen Place, NW8   £

The main room of this imposing Victorian gin-palace has the most elaborately moulded ceiling of any pub we have seen in London; also a sweeping marble bar counter, marble pillars supporting arches inlaid with bronze reliefs, and a vast pillared marble fireplace with a log-effect gas fire. A row of great arched and glazed mahogany doors opens into a similarly ornate but more spacious room. Darts, bar billiards, dominoes, fruit machine and space game are in a less opulent room; also piped music; occasional pianist. The good range of well-kept real ales on handpump includes Bass, Brakspears, Darleys Thorne, Godsons, Greene King Abbot, Vaux Bitter and Samson and Wards. Bar food at lunchtime includes cold meals and various home-made dishes; in the evening they do grills such as burgers and rump steaks. Children are allowed in eating area. The pub's Victorian nickname – Crocker's Folly – came after its builder miscalculated where the entrance to Marylebone Station would be; he built it hoping to cash in on floods of customers from the new railway – missing them by half a mile or so.

Open 11 to 3, 5.30 to 11 **Underground** Warwick Avenue

Dalat Map 2

11 Willesden Lane, NW6 *Telephone* 01-624 8521   £–££

An inexpensive Vietnamese café-cum-restaurant with close-packed tables and a long menu. Chicken, pork and beef are given similar treatment – with mushrooms, or mixed vegetables, or bamboo shoots and Chinese mushrooms, or caramel – and no main dish is much above £2. Chicken sautéed with caramel is a must. There are good spring rolls, very busy special crispy noodles with vegetables, meat and seafood, and grilled sliced pork on a stick. Some dishes

LONDON

may be oily, some under-flavoured, but the kitchen uses good ingredients and everything is fresh. Drink lager. Music.

Open All week, exc Mon L **Meals** 12 to 2.30, 6 to 10.45 **Cards** Access, Diners **Underground** Kilburn/Kilburn Park

The Lantern Map 2

23 Malvern Road, NW6 *Telephone* 01-624 1796   ££

Peter Ilic is now better known for his new restaurant, Just Around the Corner in West Hampstead (not in this *Guide*), where the customer decides how much to pay. This is his original bistro, where it is quite hard to spend £10, which means that it is packed most of the time. The cooking is an extraordinary amalgam of styles – moules marinière, deep-fried Emmental, lamb with kiwi fruit, venison with banana. Sometimes it surpasses itself with light profiteroles with rich hot chocolate sauce garnished with almond flakes. House French is £4.60. Music. Children's helpings.

Open All week **Meals** 12 to 3, 7 to 11.45 (11 Sun) **Cards** None accepted **Service** 10% **Underground** Queens Park

Red Sea Map 2

51 Kilburn High Road, NW6 *Telephone* 01-624 5289   ££

This is one of very few Ethiopian restaurants in London. The bread, engera, is the centrepiece. A foot square, thin and spongy, it comes with all the meat and vegetable dishes, and takes the place of fork and spoon to pick up spiced beef, fish, chicken or lamb, lentils, vegetables and cracked barley (kinche). Yoghurt, tomato, garlic and pepper are used a lot. You eat with your fingers, so hot towels are brought at the start. Drink beer or water. Music; wheelchair access. Children are welcome.

Open All week, D only **Meals** 6.30 to 11.30 **Cards** Access, Visa **Service** Inc **Underground** Kilburn Park

KNIGHTSBRIDGE

Berkeley Hotel Map 3

Wilton Place, SW1 *Telephone* 01-235 6000   £££–££££

Very comfortable, very discreet and very elegant, and a bastion of formal English hotelkeeping. Everything glides here – and you pay for it. The foyer is flowery and really rather intimate with a log fire burning and nothing so brash as a reception desk. Other rooms are also thoroughly impeccable, just like the

---

Prices for accommodations normally include cooked English or Scottish breakfast, Value Added Tax (currently 15%) and any inclusive service charge that we know of.

KNIGHTSBRIDGE

formal staff. All the rooms, especially the suites, are in keeping with the place, and very quiet for Knightsbridge. The Restaurant and Buttery are both stylish and competent.

Open (Restaurant) 12.30 to 2.15, 6.45 to 10.45 (Sun 7 to 10.15); (Buttery) 12.30 to 2.45, 7.30 to 11.15 (Sat 7 to 11.15) **Closed** (Restaurant) Sat; (Buttery) Sun, public hols, Aug **Cards** Access, Amex, Diners, Visa **Accommodations** 160 rooms (all with bath). B&B £75 to £150 **Underground** Knightsbridge

Capital Hotel Map 3

Basil Street, SW3 *Telephone* 01-589 5171   £££–££££

The Capital is a thoroughly modern, privately owned, medium-sized (by central city standards) establishment with, as a special selling feature, a distinguished restaurant, one of only five hotels in the capital to earn a *Michelin* rosette. 'Splendid designer Nina Campbell at work here, has made all harmonious, has a great gift for combining interesting furniture, prints etc. Lavish bathrooms, marble, amazingly well equipped. Marvellous loos downstairs, quite the most glamorous I have seen in London. Food delicious, well presented, finishing with immense silver tray of hand-made chocolates. Pleasant friendly service.'

Open All year **Cards** Access, Amex, Diners, Visa **Accommodations** 56 rooms, all with bath and shower. B&B £65 to £105.50 **Underground** Knightsbridge

L'Express Map 3

16 Sloane Street, SW1 *Telephone* 01-235 9869   £

Fashionable café in the basement of a fancy modern furniture store offering salads such as palm heart and Roquefort, club sandwiches, all-day continental breakfast and good, strong coffee.

Open 9.30 to 6 **Closed** Sun, Christmas Day and Boxing Day **Underground** Sloane Square

General Trading Company Map 3

Sloane Street, SW1 *Telephone* 01-730 0411   £

Go through the shop (where both the Princess of Wales and the Duchess of York had wedding lists) to reach this unfussy eating place run by the Justin de Blank team. The blackboard menus might include delicate borshch, ratatouille and Chinese dry-fried beef as well as salads, cheeses and sweets. You can have a full meal or just one course – with or without wine. Queues at lunchtime, but service is quick and friendly.

Open 9 to 6 (7 Thur, 2 Sat) **Closed** Sun; public hols; Christmas Eve to 1 Jan **Underground** Sloane Square

---

We give information about wheelchair access only when we are sure about it, which tends to be in restaurants and hotels. Many pubs may also be accessible to wheelchairs.

LONDON

Grenadier Map 3   🍴 ✕

Wilton Row, SW1 *Telephone* 01-235 3074   £

When searching for this pub the turning off Wilton Crescent may look prohibitive, but the barrier and watchman are there to keep out cars; walk straight past – this tucked-away little pub is just around the corner. The cramped front bar is a lively place, crowded with a wide variety of customers. Besides the well-kept Ruddles County, Combes (Watneys London brew) and Stag and Websters Yorkshire on handpump from the rare pewter-topped bar counter, the licensee or Tom, the very long-standing head barman, will shake you a most special Bloody Mary; in fact on Sunday mornings the food counter is turned into a Bloody Mary manufactory (see if you can help them beat their current record – as we went to press it had crept up to 163). A corner snack counter serves very reasonably priced lunchtime food (not available at weekends) such as French bread and cheese, sandwiches, quiche, ploughman's or pâté and steak and kidney pie; in the evenings bar food is limited to giant sausages. There is an intimate candlelit restaurant to which children are permitted. The pub is proud of its connection with Wellington, whose officers used to use it as their mess and had their horses stabled nearby; there's a grand painting of the Duke of Wellington presiding over a military banquet after Waterloo, prints of guardsmen through the ages and several weapons and powder horns.

Open 11 to 3, 5.30 to 11 **Closed** 25 and 26 Dec **Underground** Hyde Park Corner

Holiday Inn (Chelsea) Map 3   🏨 ✕

17 Sloane Street, SW1 *Telephone* 01-235 4377   £££

In our scheme of things this should be the Holiday Inn (Knightsbridge), being near neighbours of Harrods and Harvey Nichols. It's typical of the chain – in other words, well designed, attractive and luxurious, with pleasant and efficient staff, and a number of useful amenities, ranging from a hairdressing and beauty salon to a comfortable lounge by the magnificent, be-chandeliered, marble foyer. Bedrooms are small and bathrooms smaller but well equipped. The major attraction apart from its location is the hotel's swimming-pool which can be indoor or outdoor as the weather and season dictate.

Meals (Restaurant) 7 to 10 **Cards** Access, Amex, Diners, Visa **Accommodations** 206 rooms, all with bath. B&B £52 to £93 + breakfast (£4 to £6.75) **Underground** Knightsbridge

L'Hôtel Map 3   🏨 ✕

28 Basil Street, SW3 *Telephone* 01-589 6286   ££

A centrally located bed-and-breakfast hotel owned by the Levins, who also own the neighbouring Capital (see above); Margaret Levin has been responsible for the decor, rustic in style, with French pine furniture and fabric wall coverings. One reader reports a comprehensively disappointing experience: small uncomfortable room, poor electrics, no morning hot water, staff not particularly friendly. A rare bad patch? The following is more typical: 'The hotel is remarkable in that it provides a very personal big city experience. The young staff are relaxed, cheerful and chatty, but unfailingly professional under pressure. The Métro wine bar in the basement is a gem (see below). Breakfasts are served there – fresh orange juice, warm rolls and croissants and so-so coffee. All in all, a superb London base – moderate prices, a choice of unpretentiously excellent food or haute cuisine available at the Capital next door, pleasant and efficient staff.' No room service.

Open All year **Card** Amex **Accommodations** 12 rooms, all with bath and shower. B&B £40 to £80 **Underground** Knightsbridge

The Knightsbridge Hotel   Map 3

10 Beaufort Gardens, SW3 *Telephone* 01-589 9271

'A comfortable, cheery little hotel at the lower end of the price scale, one of a row of similar houses on a quiet tree-lined street a few minutes' walk past Harrods from Knightsbridge underground. On checking in, you are given a room key and a front-door key, and from then on you come and go as though it were your own home. The atmosphere is bright, pleasant and casual. My room was a bit small, but functional. I paid extra for a room with shower, but the public bathroom was so clean and inviting that next time I will take the cheaper room without private facilities. What was special about the Knightsbridge was the complete absence of the dreary run-down atmosphere so often encountered in lower-priced hotels. Obviously, at these prices this is not a place of great charm or style, but for those who would rather give their money to Harrods than to a hotel, it's a nice place to return to after an exhausting day running around the city.' No restaurant.

Open All year **Cards** Amex, Visa **Accommodations** 20 rooms, 9 with bath, 4 with shower. B&B £17 to £32.50 **Underground** Knightsbridge

Knightsbridge Green Hotel   Map 3

159 Knightsbridge, SW1 *Telephone* 01-584 6274

A small family-run hotel close to Harrods and Hyde Park, unusual in having mostly suites, each with a bath; there are five single rooms, but only one has its own bath, and two have showers with WCs. It is a hotel of some character and the rates are reasonable. 'Stepping into your "suite" feels a bit like entering the young Hubert Gregg's bachelor flat in a 1950s film; I was surprised not to have an immediate telephone call from Kay Kendall. There is a lot of cream paintwork – everywhere – and my bedroom had a vast cream vanity unit with gilt handles and a matching fitted wardrobe. There was a little sitting room with a sofa, standard lamp, dining table and chairs and a couple of Braque still lifes; the colour television seemed a bit *de trop*. The Knightsbridge Green Hotel is idiosyncratic, unfashionable, original and very comfortable. A delicious breakfast of scrambled eggs arrived hot on time with hot milk for the coffee. The waitress and receptionist were charming; I could have stayed for a week.'

Apparently, a £300,000 programme of renovation – installing

LONDON

double-glazing, new central heating and refurnishing is about to take place. Will the hotel ever be the same again? (No restaurant.)

Open All year (except 5 days at Christmas) **Cards** Access, Amex, Visa **Accommodations** 17 rooms, all suites with bath, all singles with shower. B&B £22.50 to £36 + breakfast **Underground** Knightsbridge

Maroush II   Map 3

38 Beauchamp Place, SW3 *Telephone* 01-581 5434   ££–£££

Under Beauchamp Place is a menagerie of restaurants that has spread out in the cavernous cellars like a gastronomic underworld. Here there is even a fountain and a gold fish-pond beneath street level. For westerners it is one of the most accessible of London's Lebanese restaurants, mostly due to the waiters' enthusiasm for the food. Each table is set with generous bowls of lettuce, peppers, olives and carrots, all absolutely fresh. The meze runs to over forty items. The olive oil brings out the flavour of the ful medames and also counteracts the vicious heat of the sujuk sausages. More familiar items, such as hummus and the aubergine dishes, are executed with élan. Eating in the European style with wine is expensive, but a leisurely parade of starters with coffee to finish need not bankrupt; upstairs is an inexpensive meze bar. Children's helpings. Air-conditioning; music.

Open All week **Meals** Noon to 5am **Cards** Access, Amex, Diners, Visa **Underground** Knightsbridge

Le Métro   Map 3

28 Basil Street, SW3 *Telephone* 01-589 6286   ££

Hidden away, almost literally, around the corner from Harrods is an elegant, air-conditioned basement wine bar under l'Hotel (see above), equipped with a Cruover machine for drinking expensive vintages by the glass. The fashionable modern French menu features such dishes as lamb with Dijon mustard, chicken sautéed in madeira, casseroles and warm salads. The wine list would shame many a restaurant, and is a peer among wine bars. For instance, there are no fewer than five red wines from the Loire and seven different producers listed in Alsace. Unfortunately, the bar is usually too crowded for serious tasting. Children's helpings at lunchtime only. Note that Sunday morning is alcohol-free breakfast time.

Open All week, exc Sat D and Sun D **Closed** Public hols **Meals** 12 to 2.30, 5.30 to 10 (Sun 8am to 11am) **Card** Amex **Underground** Knightsbridge

Nag's Head   Map 3

53 Kinnerton Street, SW1   £

Attractively placed in a quiet mews, this tiny pub has a little old-fashioned front area with a low ceiling, panelling, and an old cooking range with a wood-effect gas fire; a narrow passage leads down steps to an even smaller back bar with comfortable seats. Benskins and Ind Coope Burton on handpump. Food includes a three-course Sunday roast for £4.50 (no meals on Sunday evenings; snacks not available at all on Sunday). Children are allowed in the eating area. It can get crowded in the evening.

Open 11 to 3, 5.30 to 11 **Underground** Knightsbridge/Hyde Park Corner

Ports Map 3

11 Beauchamp Place, SW3 *Telephone* 01-581 3837   ££–£££

Another restaurant in the cavernous underworld beneath Beauchamp Place – Russians, Italians, Portuguese, Chinese, English and Arabs cook à gogo separated by barely the breadth of a brick. There is so much excavation going on it is a wonder the whole block does not collapse in on itself. Half the Portuguese restaurants in England are found here, and this one is the smartest – all lemons and creams and decorative tiles, and the sweets displayed by the bar. The short menu (lunch from £6.50, dinner £15) manages a compromise not often found in Portugal itself, between traditional dishes and an almost *nouvelle cuisine* eye for presentation. Of course, fish is its main business and rather more subtle than the mandatory grilled sardines. Smoked marlin with lemon and rosewater, prawns piri piri, and three ways with bacalhau have been successes. Typical of the effort at presentation is the char-grilled squid arranged in a circle on a plate of cream, fish stock and lemon sauce. More regional dishes are the marinated pork with clams, the cabbage soup, and also that other powerhouse of Portuguese cuisine, the sweets – rice pudding served cold, warm custard tarts, and egg rolls in syrup. The thirty-three wines are drawn from all over Portugal and are not to be discounted. Portuguese wines are rarely as consistent as, say, French wines, but they are often a match for the very best. Try, for instance, Bairrada from Mealhada, a town famed throughout Portugal for its suckling pig, or the house white from Ribatejo, Serradayres 1981 at £5.30. Music; air-conditioning.

Open Mon to Sat **Closed** Christmas, Easter, and public hols **Meals** 12.15 to 2.30, 7 to 11.30
Cards Access, Amex, Diners, Visa **Service** 12½% **Underground** Knightsbridge

Salloos Map 3

62 Kinnerton Street, SW1 *Telephone* 01-235 4444   £££

Features of this white room are the fretwork at the windows and the way the ceiling is built up of ornate ridges. The short menu takes in Pakistani as well as north Indian specialities and there are some interesting, unusual dishes: chicken taimuri is marinated chicken deep-fried in a batter made from flour, milk, eggs, onions and tomatoes; aloo zeera is potato cooked with nine different spices. Tandoori dishes are outstanding, particularly the lamb chops, which are crisp and spicy on the outside, pink within. To start there is almond soup and to finish there is rich kulfi. The wine list is better than average. Children are welcome.

Open All week **Closed** Public hols **Meals** 12 to 2.30, 7 to 11.30 **Cards** Access, Amex, Carte Blanche, Diners, Visa **Underground** Knightsbridge

LONDON

San Lorenzo Map 3   ✗

22 Beauchamp Place, SW3 *Telephone* 01-584 1074   ££££

The razzmatazz basement, looking like a subterranean greenhouse with a sliding roof, cheers up enormously when full. The service does not always understand much English, but the food is above average for London Italian – carefully cooked veal with competent sauces, carpaccio smothered in a strong mustard mayonnaise, three ways with bresaola, raw-fish salad with fruity olive oil, and cold poached salmon trout. The regional dishes are predictably rather better than the international ones. Vegetables are a bit of an afterthought. The house wine is from Sardinia and costs £7.50. Children's helpings.

Open Mon to Sat **Meals** 12.30 to 3, 7.30 to 11.30 **Cards** None accepted **Underground** Knightsbridge

Wolfe's Map 3   ✗

25 Basil Street, SW3 *Telephone* 01-589 8444   £–££

Claims to be London's only luxury hamburger restaurant (along with its brother on Park Lane – see Mayfair). It's certainly comfortable and serves a wide range of decent burgers with various toppings. Stick to those, and you needn't exceed the minimum charge of £5 by much.

Open 11.30am to midnight **Closed** Christmas Day and Boxing Day **Underground** Knightsbridge

---

LAMBETH

Rebato's Map 1   ♀ ✗

169 South Lambeth Road, SW8 *Telephone* 01-735 6388   ££

This Spanish wine bar and restaurant is well used in this tract of south London which is neglected as far as good food is concerned. The front half is a tapas bar with high stools and low coffee tables. At the back is a restaurant set with thick linen cloths and serving good-value set meals (£9.25). It is very Spanish in that all the staff are male, a guitarist plays some evenings, and there is no hurry about anything. Tortillas, kidneys in a boozy sherry sauce, seared chicken livers, and octopus browned in a lethal chilli oil have all been excellent, and occasionally there are elvers again fried in hot oil. The bacalhau has disappointed, though, lacking the silkiness found in Spain or Portugal. House Torres is £4.95. Children are welcome. Access for wheelchairs.

Open Mon to Sat, exc Sat L **Meals** 12 to 2.30, 7 to 11.15 **Cards** Access, Amex, Diners, Visa **Underground** Vauxhall

---

£ = *meal can be had for about £5*
££ = *meal can be had for about £12*
£££ = *meal can be had for about £20*
££££ = *meal can be had for about £30*

96

MARBLE ARCH

Le Chef Map 2

41 Connaught Street, W2 *Telephone* 01-262 5945   ££–£££

While most of this part of London is now notable for its Middle-Eastern restaurants, Alan King carries on with his artichaut vinaigrette and jambon au porto, defiantly keeping alive the cause of the French bistro. The set menu at night (£17) runs to six courses, including fish – for instance skate with black butter – a salad and a cheese course. (The set lunch is £14.) Vegetarian meals and children's helpings. House wine is £4.30. Access for wheelchairs; music.

Open Mon to Sat, exc Sat L **Closed** Mid-Aug to mid-Sept **Meals** 12.30 to 2.30, 7 to 11.30 (11 Sat) **Cards** Access, Visa **Service** Inc **Underground** Marble Arch

Cumberland Hotel Map 2

Marble Arch, W1 *Telephone* 01-262 1234   ££–£££

A huge Trust House Forte hotel, many of its comfortable, modern bedrooms looking out over the bustle of the Oxford Street shops (particularly handy if you are a Marks & Spencer freak). The hotel has a sauna and a coffee shop (10.30am to 1.30pm) as well as several bars away from the busy reception/boutiques area on the ground floor. The Restaurant features game in season, and roast meats and other traditional English fare are options in the Carvery (£9.95).

Open (Restaurant) 12.30 to 2.30, 6.30 to 10.30; (Carvery) 5 to 10 (6 to 10 Sun) **Cards** Access, Amex, Diners, Visa **Accommodations** 897 rooms, all with bath and shower. B&B £43 to £68 + breakfast (£5.95) **Underground** Marble Arch

Al Diwan Map 2

61–69 Edgware Road, W2 *Telephone* 01-724 1161   £££

The decor is extraordinary: the dining-room is split in two by a mirrored wall, a band of Arab musicians plays at the bar, and a ball of psychedelic lights revolves on the ceiling, its colours glinting over the modern crystal chandeliers. The menu contains a lot of familiar Middle Eastern dishes as well as a few Gulf specialities. Raw vegetables and olives are brought to the table before excellent montabal (smooth aubergine purée); hummus piled with strips of fried lamb; falafel with chickpea sauce; and little minced lamb pasties, together with pitta bread and a plate of salted vegetables. The main dish of the day might be savoury, tomato-based lamb and okra stew. Grilled meats are well handled and the Basmati rice is first-rate. There is a set menu at £12. Orange juice is fresh, and Turkish coffee is flavoured with cardamom. Air-conditioning; access for wheelchairs. Children's helpings.

Open All week **Meals** Noon to 11.30 **Cards** Access, Amex, Diners, Visa **Service** 15% **Underground** Marble Arch

LONDON

Holiday Inn (Marble Arch) Map 2

134 George Street, W1 *Telephone* 01-723 1277   £££

Right in the West End, near all the Oxford Street shops, and offering the usual Holiday Inn package, but with larger rooms than sometimes. All the extras that the chain has become known for – individual heating controls in bedrooms, trouser presses, good modern bathrooms – are there, plus some very comfortable public rooms, a sauna and indoor swimming-pool; the brasserie is open all day, the Bibliothèque Restaurant just in the evening.

Open (Restaurant) 7 to midnight **Cards** Access, Amex, Diners, Visa **Accommodations** 241 rooms, all with bath and shower. B&B £60 to £100 + breakfast (£7.85) **Underground** Marble Arch

Knoodles Map 2

30 Connaught Street, W2 *Telephone* 01-262 9623   ££–£££

Small, but the tables are not greedy on space and there is a feeling of roominess, helped by the beige decor and the pleasant staff. Reliable are tagliatelle with cream and green peppercorns, and the black pepper pasta with stir-fried vegetables. House special is Swiss roll filled with spinach and ricotta and served with tomato sauce. Coffee is standard Cona. Children's helpings. Music.

Open Mon to Sat **Meals** 12 to 3, 6.30 to 10.45 **Cards** Access, Amex, Diners, Visa **Service** 12½% **Underground** Marble Arch

Maroush Map 2

21 Edgware Road, W2 *Telephone* 01-723 0773   ££–£££

From this deeply Arab restaurant on a ground floor near Marble Arch a small empire has built up of four restaurants. Further down the road is Ranoush Juice and newest of all is Les Fruits de Mer, a fish restaurant, in Seymour Street. The quality of the thirty-nine starters is outstanding. The place is not expensive, unless you drink alcohol, and it is open until the small hours. Music and air-conditioning. Children's helpings.

Open All week **Meals** Noon to 4.30am **Cards** Access, Amex, Diners, Visa **Service** 15% **Underground** Marble Arch

Montcalm Hotel Map 2

Great Cumberland Place, W1 *Telephone* 01-402 4288   £££–££££

Plush and peaceful medium-sized hotel in an elegant Georgian crescent just round the corner from Marble Arch and the shops of Oxford Street. Inside, the colour scheme of the public rooms is chocolate and coffee; quiet bedrooms are

---

The £ symbols at the head of entries refer to the approximate cost of meals. For prices of accommodations see the bottom of entries.

MARYLEBONE

pretty, intimate even, but fully equipped and thoroughly comfortable, especially the luxurious Studio rooms. Laundry and valeting service. Friendly staff.

Open (Restaurant) 12.30 to 2.30, 7 to 11 **Cards** Access, Amex, Diners, Visa **Accommodations** 116 rooms, all with bath and shower. B&B £69 to £115 **Underground** Marble Arch

MARYLEBONE

Boos Map 2

1 Glentworth Street, NW1 *Telephone* 01-935 3827   £

The Roses' new cellar is more spacious and airy than their previous tiny bar, but equally popular. The impressive and modestly priced wine list launches off with fine aperitifs, including Palo Cortado (£1.20) and Chambéry (£1). The few wines by the glass include Willm's Pinot Blanc 1983, Marqués de Cáceres Rioja 1981 and a delicious Crémant de Bourgogne Rosé, all at reasonable prices. Among the useful halves is Côtes du Rhône Cuvée Personnelle 1980, Pascal (£5.95/£3.20 half). The Roses' French explorations pay off in some interesting finds: Ch Fortia Châteauneuf-du-Pape Blanc 1984 (£11.50), Condrieu Ch du Rozay 1985 Multier (£18.50), and Ch Monbousquet 1978 (£11.95), to say nothing of eight excellent Alsace wines. Gestures outside France are few but worthy: for example, Australian Orlando Chardonnay 1985 (£6.95) and Pio Cesare Vino da Tavola 1984 (£6.95) and Barolo 1981 (£12.50). Good home-made food.

Open Mon to Fri 11.30 to 3, 5 to 8 **Closed** Sat, Sun, public hols, 3 weeks Sept, 2 weeks Chr **Cards** Access, Amex, Diners **Underground** Baker Street

Don Pepe Map 2

99 Frampton Street, NW8 *Telephone* 01-262 3834   £££

Rather north of Marylebone, and tucked up a side street towards Maida Vale is this Spanish restaurant/tapas bar and delicatessen. The sausages and the ham are the genuine article. More unusual dishes are Galician octopus or tripe with a spicy sauce; otherwise quantity is a virtue of the main course. The Riojas are imported directly. There's a £1.25 cover charge at dinner. Music. Children are welcome.

Open All week **Meals** 12 to 2.30 (2 Sun), 7 to 12.15 (11 Sun) **Cards** Access, Amex, Diners, Visa **Underground** Edgware Road

Durrants Hotel Map 4

George Street, W1 *Telephone* 01-935 8131   ££-£££

A traditional, well-bred and relatively inexpensive hotel, encased in a late eighteenth-century shell, with boxes of geraniums all along the front. Close by is Marylebone High Street – 'probably the last civilised and unspoilt shopping area in central London, with none of the self-conscious trendiness of Hampstead, seedy looniness of King's Road or expensive ultra-chic of Bond

LONDON

Street'. As for the hotel, the food seems to have improved though somewhat patchily, and there is now a pleasant ground-floor Breakfast Room in place of the subterranean room. Some bedrooms have been refurbished with great success. There have been improvements in many of the bathrooms, too. Some of the staff receive warm compliments for their civility, others the reverse. The general impression is of a management trying hard but failing to achieve any consistent performance. Rooms vary in size: it's worth discussing accommodations in detail to get what you want.

Open All year. Restaurant closed Christmas Day **Cards** Access, Amex, Diners, Visa **Accommodations** 97 rooms, 85 with bath and shower. B&B £25 to £75 + breakfast **Underground** Marble Arch

George Map 4

55 Great Portland Street, W1   £

Popular with BBC regulars, this solid place – embellished with heavy mahogany panelling, etched windows, deeply engraved mirrors and equestrian prints – has a good choice of well-kept real ales on handpump: Adnams, Eldridge Pope Royal Oak, Felinfoel Double Dragon, Greene King IPA and Abbot and Charles Wells Bombardier and a monthly guest ale. There are comfortable green plush high chairs at the bar, and captain's chairs around traditional cast-iron-framed tables. Bar food includes sandwiches, ploughman's, salads and at lunchtime hot meals such as three-egg omelette, home-made steak pie, gammon or scampi.

Open 11 to 3, 5.30 to 11 **Underground** Great Portland Street/Oxford Circus

Green Leaves Map 2

77 York Street, W1 *Telephone* 01-262 8164   ££–££££

Unusual among Chinese restaurants in that Mr Tao is a chef/patron. The long menu centres on Peking and Szechuan but we have eaten here a lot and conclude that the starters are far and away the best dishes – Shanghai dumplings, deep-fried flower rolls, sesame toasts, spicy hot spare ribs, pickled cabbage, and hot-and-sour soup. For main course we have a single recommendation, for Szechuan aromatic and crispy duck, in which the bones are so crisp they become edible. This is accompanied by home-made mandarin pancakes. Some of the sweetness of other dishes is typical of Taiwan, where Mr Tao originates. The house wine is £4.80. There are set meals at £9.50. Music and air-conditioning.

Open Mon to Sat, exc Sat L **Meals** 12 to 2.30, 6 to 11 **Cards** Access, Amex, Diners, Visa **Service** 10% **Underground** Marylebone/Baker Street

Langan's Bistro Map 4

26 Devonshire Street, W1 *Telephone* 01-935 4531   ££–£££

The outrageous Peter Langan is proprietor of this bistro, Odins (not in the *Guide*), the Bar & Grill and the Brasserie (see under Mayfair). The Bistro seems to have been suffering from an inferiority complex, but despite the competition,

MARYLEBONE

it carries on; Mark Sage is in the kitchen, the parasols are still upside down on the ceiling, and the black leather seal is over the door. It is what its name implies: the brown paper tablecloths give the impression of a place in which to relax and enjoy the short, interesting menu. Good dishes have been chicken livers in port; avocado and melon salad with lime sauce; and brill with shellfish and mussel sauce. Sorbets are beautiful, the coffee excellent. The 75p cover charge includes some rather sparse crudités. The wine list is the expensive sting in the tail – best to stay on the house wine. Vegetarians and children are welcome. Access for wheelchairs.

Open Mon to Sat, exc Sat L **Meals** 12.30 to 2.30, 7 to 11.30 **Card** Amex **Service** 10% **Underground** Regents Park/Baker Street

---

Masako Map 4

6–8 St Christopher's Place, W1 *Telephone* 01-935 1579   £££–££££

For the last twenty years this uncluttered Japanese restaurant has provided a reliable launching-pad for westerners to explore the cooking, yet has, at the same time, kept its quota of Japanese business. The Fuji dinner of appetiser, clear soup, grilled chicken or raw fish, tempura, sukiyaki and dessert is the way in. Sashimi and sushi are expertly handled, the miso soup impressive. Meats may not be quite so good – an authentic failing, at least. Lunches are relaxed, dinners more polished. To drink there is saké, tea, or whisky. No children under ten. Music and air-conditioning.

Open Mon to Sat **Meals** 12 to 2, 6 to 10 **Cards** Access, Amex, Diners, Visa **Service** 15% **Underground** Bond Street

---

Le Muscadet Map 2

25 Paddington Street, W1 *Telephone* 01-935 2883   £££

Good bistros are an endangered species these days. Even the decor here feels like provincial France – the carpet creeps up the bar, which is stocked with eaux-de-vie and armagnac, tapestries hang from the box-like side walls, and the tables are solid. The bread is excellent, as are the cheeses. The menu is on the blackboard, *bien sûr* – suprême de canard au poivre vert, carré d'agneau, and boudin noir have all been eaten and approved. The sauce with the prawns 'tasted as if it had been made from beautiful fish stock or the leftover bouillabaisse, and the butter had anchovy in it which gave it even more fishiness'. The choucroute garnie, mind, is a bit of a lazy English version, as if the kitchen feels more comfortable with the southern dishes. Service is, well, French . . . and the wine list is abbreviated. Music; air-conditioning; wheelchair access. No children under twelve.

Open Mon to Sat, exc Sat L **Meals** 12.30 to 3, 7.15 to 11 (10 Sat) **Cards** Access, Visa **Underground** Baker Street

---

See page 216 for an explanation of 'real ale' and the terminology associated with the subject.

Nanten Yakitori Bar Map 4

6 Blandford Street, W1 *Telephone* 01-935 6319   ££–£££

In other countries Japanese food can be cheap and fast. Only in London does it seem to affiliate itself mainly to French-style pretensions and prices for what is usually middle-of-the-road cooking. The Yakitori bar redresses the balance somewhat. This is more of an eating-house than a restaurant with a sweeping bar-counter in front of the rough-and-ready grill and steaming pans. Grilling is the speciality, for example asparagus wrapped in bacon with a dab of mustard dip, or skewers of mushrooms, chicken gizzard, ox heart. Two skewers make up a portion. Two kinds of saké. You can bring your own wine but will be charged half its value as corkage. Music; access for wheelchairs.

Open Mon to Sat, exc Sat L **Meals** 12 to 2, 6 to 10 **Cards** Access, Amex, Diners, Visa **Underground** Marble Arch/Baker Street

Reuben's Map 4

20A Baker Street, W1 *Telephone* 01-935 5945   £

Kosher restaurant and food bar which is handy for a quick meal. A quarter-pound of salt beef with a latke costs around £2 to take away and the quality is excellent. The menu also includes other Jewish favourites such as chopped liver and gefilte fish.

Open Noon to 3, 5 to 10 (noon to 10 Sun) **Closed** Fri D; Sat; Jewish hols; 10 days Apr **Underground** Marble Arch/Baker Street

St George's Hotel Map 4

Langham Place, W1 *Telephone* 01-580 0111   £

The non-stop lift in the far corner of the lobby whisks you up to the spacious modern fourteenth-floor lounge, with great picture windows looking westwards over and far beyond London. It's by no means a pub, this stylish and comfortable skyscraper bar (part of the Trust House Forte group), but it's a relaxing place for a drink with small armchairs well spaced between the white marble walls. Uniformed and warmly friendly bar staff mix cocktails, bring your drinks to your low gilt and marble table, and make sure that your dishes of free nuts and little biscuits are always topped up. If you get there early enough they may give you little freshly grilled cocktail sausages wrapped in bacon, too. There's usually a pianist at the grand piano (not Sunday), and always plenty of room. They don't expect you to pay until you leave: given the surroundings and service, you obviously can't expect normal pub prices, though a bottled beer, say, shouldn't cost you more than about £1 here. Bar food includes sandwiches, toasted chicken and cheese sandwich, open fish or cold meat sandwich, steak sandwich, Parma ham and melon salad, beef Stroganoff or spiced seafood and dressed crab. Children are welcome.

Open 10.30 to 3, 5.30 to 11 **Accommodations** B&B (all rooms have bath or shower) £37 to £47 (much cheaper weekend rates) **Underground** Oxford Circus

MARYLEBONE

Seashell Map 2 �

49–51 Lisson Grove, NW1 *Telephone* 01-723 8703   ££

The take-away is still at the front, but steps at the side lead to a two-floor restaurant linked by a spiral staircase. The decor is all varnished wood, glass partitions etched with scenes of Old Billingsgate, framed pictures, waitress service... The Seashell's re-incarnation, twenty years after it first opened, has put it into a different league. Only Harry Ramsden's at Guiseley, near Bradford in Yorkshire, could claim to match it for character, if not for food. The fish is fresh, freshly fried, and it is usually pretty big too – plaice tends to cover the plates so the chips have to be brought in side dishes. Chips are cut thick. Vinegar is in elegant little vases. The menu encompasses salmon, halibut, hot cod's roe, and skate, fried or grilled or in matzo meal. The list of ten wines is sensibly chosen, from house champagne at £12.50 to house white at £3.50. If you bring your own, £1.50 corkage will be charged. Tea, though, is 25p. Children are welcome, of course.

Open Tue to Sat **Closed** Christmas to New Year **Meals** 12 to 2, 5.15 to 10.30 **Cards** Access, Visa **Underground** Marylebone

Topkapi Map 4 ✗

25 Marylebone High Street, W1 *Telephone* 01-486 1872 and 935 3188   ££

The Eastern atmosphere comes from the brass plates on the walls, the Turkish lamps and the music. This is the best regarded of London's Turkish restaurants among the Turkish community. The ingredients, mostly via the Stoke Newington importers for oils, pulses and spices, are of good quality, and dishes are freshly prepared each day. Service is authentically haphazard. The dish of olives, radishes, and so on, may appear, unusually, between the first and second courses. Stuffed aubergines, taramosalata, stuffed vine leaves and delicious muska böreği – fried pastry triangles filled with soft cheese, eggs and herbs – precede shish kebab or kuzu firin – minced lamb with vine leaves, peppers and rice, served with warm pitta bread. Ten Turkish wines range from £6 to £7. Children's helpings. Access for wheelchairs.

Open All week **Meals** Noon to midnight **Cards** Access, Amex, Diners, Visa **Service** 10% **Underground** Baker Street

Woodlands Map 4 ✗

77 Marylebone Lane, W1 *Telephone* 01-486 3862   ££–£££

One of a chain of three restaurants with widely contrasting decor, ranging from stylish modernity here in Marylebone Lane to cool, classical pale pink in Panton Street (see the Soho section). (The third is out in Wembley, not covered in this *Guide*.) The menus are the same and the standards are almost on a par with the other main Gujerati places in London. The southern Indian vegetarian repertoire takes in dosas, iddlies, samosas, bhajis and vadors, which are subtly and distinctively spiced. Breads and rice are first-rate and there are three

LONDON

good-value thalis, including a cut-price express version for a quick snack. Lassi comes salt or sweet. Service is keen and polite. Air-conditioning; access for wheelchairs.

Open All week **Meals** 12 to 3, 6 to 10.30 **Cards** Access, Amex, Diners, Visa **Service** 12½%
Underground Bond Street

MAYFAIR

L'Autre Map 4

5B Shepherd Street, W1 *Telephone* 01-499 4680   £

A relaxed and friendly spot in Shepherd Market, with the bonuses of outside tables and elegantly thin tulip glasses. The wines, mainly from Michael Druitt and Berkmann, include a decent dozen available by the glass: for example, Siglo red and white Rioja (£5.50/£1.20). Since the short list has now been computerised, it could surely include essential producers' names and avoid alternative vintages: three of the five clarets are listed as '1982/1983'. The several Georges Duboeuf wines include Morgon 1984/1985 (£8.50); among the Pierre Ponnelle Burgundies is Crozes-Hermitage Blanc 1983 (£6.95); and the Léon Beyer Alsace wines include Pinot Blanc 1983/1984 (£6.50). Varied and imaginative food, usually including some vegetarian items.

Open 12 to 3, 5.30 to 11.30 **Closed** Sat L, Sun, most public hols **Cards** Access, Visa
Underground Green Park/Hyde Park Corner

Brown's Hotel Map 4

Dover Street, W1 *Telephone* 01-493 6020   £££

In the heart of one of London's most elegant areas is this hotel regarded by its faithful as the quintessence of the old style of English hotel-keeping. It was founded by Lord Byron's manservant, and such adjectives as 'discreet', 'immaculate', 'courteous', 'peaceful' and 'charming' all spring to mind to describe its virtues. The very varied bedrooms are kept in tip-top repair: most people will probably prefer the ones furnished with antiques to those assigned a more modern feel. Bathrooms are uniformly well equipped, and one of the most cherished aspects is a quiet writing room. Even if you fail to make a room reservation at short notice, such is the popularity of the hotel, afternoon tea taken between 3 and 6 in the comfortable, flowery, panelled lounge, a drink in the tailored St George's Bar or lunch or dinner (£22 and £23 and English, of course) would be a good way to imbibe some of the place's old-fashioned charms.

Open (Restaurant) 12.15 to 2.30, 6 to 10 (01-499 6122) **Cards** Access, Amex, Diners, Visa
Accommodations 130 rooms, all with bath/shower. B&B £62.50 to £105 **Underground** Green Park

---

We give details of service charges where we know what these are; otherwise, you should expect to add 10–15% to the total of your bill unless the menu or bill states that service is included.

MAYFAIR

Bunch of Grapes   Map 4
Shepherd Market, W1   £

Bang in the bustle of Shepherd Market, this very busy pub has a cosy and relaxed little alcove at the back; the main area has a traditional-style decor of old photographs and prints, stuffed fish, a grandfather clock and elaborate net curtains in its tall windows. Besides food that includes shepherd's pie, beef salad or smoked salmon salad, upstairs you can get yourself an unlimited amount of hot and cold dishes such as cold roast beef, turkey, ham, tongue and unusual salads. Meals are served at weekday lunchtimes; snacks available at lunchtime every day of the week. Children are allowed in the restaurant. Well-kept Arkells, Brakspears, Wethereds and Whitbreads on handpump; fruit machine, juke box, maybe piped pop music.

Open 11 to 3, 5.30 to 11 **Closed** 25 and 26 Dec **Underground** Hyde Park Corner/Green Park

Champagne Exchange   Map 4
17C Curzon Street, W1 *Telephone* 01-493 4490   ££–££££

Lunch on a 100 gram plate of beluga caviare washed down with a bottle of Dom Pérignon 1978 would, with service, top £170. It is not essential to invest so much to eat and drink in this elegant, air-conditioned room, played to by a pianist. The menu is designed as a series of delicacies to go with the champagnes. Hence baked potatoes come with sevruga or keta caviare, there are platters of smoked fish that include sturgeon and halibut, or else plates of meats, including Parma ham, coppa and bresaola. Eighteen champagne houses feature on the wine list and there is a choice from half a dozen by the glass. It is a top-hole place for a fling.

Open All week, exc Sat L and Sun L **Meals** 11.30 to 3.30, 5.30 to 12 (7 to 11 Sun) **Cards** Access, Amex, Diners, Visa **Service** 12½% **Underground** Green Park

Chez Gerard   Map 4
31 Dover Street, W1 *Telephone* 01-499 8171   £££

The service is diabolical, but there is very little wrong with the food in this quasi-French chain. The formula is entrecôte et frites with cold starters and sweets – and good cheeses. The Dover Street branch is thought to win by a clear head over the other two (see under Holborn and Tottenham Court Road). Extras put the bill up. House Rhône is £5.50 but Beaujolais is the most considered section of the list. Children's helpings. Music.

Open Mon to Sat **Meals** 12 to 2.45, 7 to 11.30 **Cards** Access, Visa **Service** 10% **Underground** Green Park

---

Restaurant hints: sweets are candy and a sweet is dessert (often a pudding unless otherwise specified). If you want your drink straight up, ask for it neat. Out of London ask for ice if you want a drink on the rocks (but you won't always get it). At the end of the meal, ask for the bill, not the check.

LONDON

Claridge's Map 4

Brook Street, W1 *Telephone* 01-629 8860   ££–££££

Claridge's is one of the few London hotels that has sought to keep (and achieved) the high standards of traditional British hotel-keeping – impeccable service, discretion, good taste – while introducing the best of modern amenities. Nothing so vulgar as a bar – drinks are brought by waiters in tailcoats while an orchestra plays. Room service is equally good. Many bedrooms are still done out in their original '30s guise of Art Deco, the bathrooms keeping their old-fashioned baths. The hotel's main Restaurant is opulent, the more informal Causerie very inviting, with help-yourself smorgasbord and some light hot dishes.

Open (Restaurant) 12.30 to 3, 7 to 11; (Causerie) 12 to 3, 6 to 11 (Sun 7 to 11) **Closed** (Causerie) Sat and some public hols **Cards** Access, Amex, Diners, Visa **Accommodations** 205 rooms, all with bath and shower. B&B £75 to £140 **Underground** Bond Street

Connaught Hotel Map 4

Carlos Place, W1 *Telephone* 01-499 7070   ££££

The Connaught resists changes in fashions and still provides a good example of the kind of grand-hotel food that has dominated British catering for a century and more. It attempts to do no more, so comparisons with modern, French-style restaurants are unfair and irrelevant. This is where to eat foie gras, consommé, quenelles, the famous croustade d'oeufs de caille Maintenon, or potatoes cooked eight different ways. The sauces smell of history – beurre Nantais, piccata de veau forestière, sauce pudeur with turbot terrine and lobster sauce. That said, the Troisgros recipe for salmon has made an appearance. Of course, the ingredients are excellent and the onus is on the diner to construct his or her own level of complexity from a huge choice. The same goes for the wines. The list starts with Frascati at £10.50 and accelerates through Burgundies for between £30 and £40, to three-figure clarets from top, pre-1978 vintages. No children under six. No pipes. Access for wheelchairs; air-conditioning. Afternoon teas are served.

Open (Restaurant) All week; (Grill Room) Mon to Fri **Closed** (Grill Room) Sat, Sun, public hols **Meals** 12.30 to 2, 6 to 10.15 **Card** Access **Service** 15% **Accommodations** 90 rooms, all with bath and shower. Rooms for disabled. B&B £97 to £145 **Underground** Bond Street/Green Park

Country Life Map 4

123 Regent Street, W1 (entrance 1 Heddon Street)   £
Telephone 01-434 2922

This leafy basement offers some of the best vegetarian food and best value in the West End. The self-service vegetarian buffet has 'all you care to eat' with plastic cutlery and paper plates for £3.50, but individual dishes are much cheaper. There are imaginative soups, a vast array of salads, breads and spreads, hot dishes, such as oat burgers and vegetable pie, and highly rated puddings, not to mention unlimited helpings of fresh fruit salad. Children are charged half-price. No animal products on the menu, no alcohol on the premises, no smoking.

Open Mon to Fri, L only **Closed** Public hols **Meals** 11.30 to 2.30 (3 Fri) **Cards** None accepted **Underground** Piccadilly Circus

Dorchester Hotel Map 4

(1) Grill Room (2) Terrace Restaurant Park Lane, W1A 2HJ ££££
Telephone 01-629 8888

The Grill Room is less expensive and less romantic than the Terrace and has a menu that is by and large British served in distinctly Spanish surroundings. Most renowned are the chicken liver pâté and the bread-and-butter pudding. Centre stage are the roasts of the day, but the menu also holds some recipes – for instance for duck – that are robustly convincing. It is an extraordinary achievement by Mr Mosimann to have a kitchen produce on the same night what are three virtually completely different styles of cooking. In the Terrace, where the mood is set by a dance band, the portions are like gems cut by a jeweller. The descriptions give away the laborious preparations behind the scenes – a pâté of lambs' tongues on a lentil base with tiny tomatoes; beef consommé with marrow; guinea-fowl with cabbage stuffed under the skin served with wild mushrooms and chicory. On Valentine's Day the sweet was a heart-shaped passion-fruit mousse. At their best the menus, be they *cuisine naturelle* or *cuisine nouvelle*, rival anything in London, and yet . . . as is often the case with hotels, standards are frustratingly unbalanced from one night to the next. Wine, alas, is not the Dorchester's strength. There are good bottles, but there is a feeling that this is because the list is extensive rather than because of design. House wine is £10.50. No children under nine; access for wheelchairs; afternoon teas.

Open (Grill Room) All week; (Terrace) Mon to Sat, D only **Meals** (Grill Room) 12.30 to 3 (2.30 Sun), 6.30 to 11 (10.30 Sun); (Terrace) 6.30 to 11.30 **Cards** Access, Amex, Diners, Visa **Service** Inc **Accommodations** 280 rooms, all with bath/shower. Rooms for disabled. B&B £140 to £190 **Underground** Hyde Park Corner

Le Gavroche Map 4

43 Upper Brook Street, W1 *Telephone* 01-408 0881 ££££

The Queen Mother *mange ici*. Or, more precisely, a team from the kitchens goes to Clarence House for her. Albert Roux's vision of a great restaurant is of its catering to the aristocracy, to the rich, and also to those who love food and who want to feel rich and aristocratic. The ambitions are simply greater than in any other restaurant in Britain. Service is *ancien régime* in its discipline. The menus still bear the stamp of the bourgeois – pigeon fermier has succulent flesh surrounded by a scatter of tiny vegetables, the little white onions lightly pickled, the carrots lightly steamed. Poached chicken sits on a bed of spinach, on which is a bed of marinated turnips, and all around are shredded vegetables and noodles – and tiny mussels. It is gutsy food in which powerful sauces play off against centrepieces. Little boats of extra sauce are offered more in the English

LONDON

style of gravy than the French style of sauces. Of course there are the luxuries, such as the caviare in baked potatoes, and the foie gras, on the menu of the day in a little tartlet surrounded by salsify and slivers of truffle, or else cooked in a serviette and kept in its aspic *à l'ancienne*. The famous soufflé suissesse is typical of the allegiance to cooking with eggs and cream, which can make meals very rich. Colours come into play, too – green asparagus in a creamy cheese sauce, a deep red Bandol sauce with redder salmon and pinker langoustines. Also worth a mention are warm salads such as courgettes and foie gras; the classic from the Roux brothers' book, the boudin Joceline; brilliant apricot soufflé which the waiter slits across the top before pouring in an aromatic apricot sauce; the tarte tatin. The cheeses are encyclopaedic. Huge baskets of Roux chocolates now come with the coffee and petits fours. Lunch is lower key and cheaper (£19.50 as opposed to £35). (There is a minimum charge of £30.) The wine list is more remarkable for its breadth than its accuracy in individual regions – halves are a clumsy gathering, but even so there is ample to drink. There are half-bottles under £10, and the *cru* Beaujolais would not cause the same financial damage as one of the runs of vintages in the great clarets, which reach such heights as Ch Cheval Blanc 1961 at £450. The sommelier gives sound advice. No children under eight. They require men to wear a jacket and tie. No pipes in the dining-room.

Open Mon to Fri **Closed** 23 Dec to 2 Jan **Meals** 12 to 2, 7 to 11 **Cards** Access, Amex, Carte Blanche, Diners, Visa **Service** Inc **Underground** Marble Arch

The Greenhouse Map 4

27A Hay's Mews, W1 *Telephone* 01-499 3331   £££

Hay's Mews, a T-shape, is one of Mayfair's secrets. The Greenhouse is reached under a long awning. The inside is smart: fans rotate above the throng of suited lunchers. The decor is deliberate – a railing pattern is drawn on the window-panes, there are oils of country scenes and waters or prints of country walks, panels are cream and walls and pillars white. The napery is white and crisp, plates are Wedgwood, the chairs carved wood, the service is sharp and friendly. The menu is attractive, wide-ranging and essentially English, or at least English favourites such as shrimp bisque and roast rack of lamb with rosemary. Fish has been excellent, as in a mix of langoustines, scallops and mussels with root vegetables in a superior shellfish and cream sauce. Also recommended have been the pan-fried venison with red and white cabbage and smoked goose breast salad with gooseberry chutney. Rösti potatoes need ordering separately. To finish, the menu enters the realms of syllabub, rice pudding with jam, vanilla ice-cream with fudge sauce and chopped walnuts, and steamed currant and raisin sponge with custard. It is perhaps rather more cosmopolitan than other examples of new English cooking, although large parts of the menu have moved along that road. Service can be slow for a business lunch. A dozen wines span Blanc de Blancs at £5.55 to house Champagne at £17.50. Children are welcome.

Open Mon to Sat, exc Sat L **Meals** 12 to 2.30, 7 (7.30 Sat) to 11 **Cards** Access, Amex, Carte Blanche, Diners, Visa **Underground** Green Park

MAYFAIR

Al Hamra Map 4 ✘

31–33 Shepherd Market, W1 *Telephone* 01-493 1954 and 6934 £££

This is a great place, not expensive, in the style of a high-class French restaurant with, frankly, sensational food, and the waiters do their utmost to ensure that any cultural barriers are quickly crossed. A massive chandelier is inset into the ceiling; the windows on three sides and a plant-lined mirror on the fourth give blotches of light. The tables are set with crisp white linen and with a basket of raw vegetables – broad beans, cos lettuce, radishes, cucumber, spring onions. A plate of black and green olives comes with the menu. It needs stressing that this is a menu of quaint sophistication drawing on a great cuisine largely unknown in this country. There is no equivalent Greek or Turkish or Arab near this menu, and it is unlikely that there are many restaurants as good as this in the Middle East itself. By way of a start there are forty-three cold hors d'oeuvre mostly around £2. These include – forget the Arab names for the moment – purée of chickpeas with sesame oil and lemon juice; baked aubergine, its flesh the colour of Devon cream; French beans cooked in olive oil, tomatoes, onions and garlic; and fried lambs' kidneys. The cuisine takes the aubergine in particular to sublime pastures. To go with the starters are freshly baked warm pitta bread puffed up in the shape of little turtles. The main course relies heavily on the charcoal grill. Bite-sized pieces of marinated chicken are grilled and dressed in yoghurt; shish and lamb kebabs are accompanied, as in the Middle East, with paper-thin onion slices and flat-leaf parsley. An alternative to these are the specials of the day; these lose in translation – stuffed lamb is in fact baked with cinnamon, pine kernels, and toasted and brown rice, and is served with a huge bowl of yoghurt. The sweets too are revelations – pistachio-stuffed shortcake balls; kataif stuffed with salt-less white cheese. They are an acquired taste, but by this stage in the meal you should have the confidence to explore. Coffee is cardamom. The wine is a dead loss and expensive. Children's helpings. Access for wheelchairs; air-conditioning; music.

Open All week **Closed** 25 Dec and 1 Jan **Meals** Noon to midnight **Cards** Access, Amex, Diners, Visa **Service** 10% **Underground** Hyde Park Corner/Green Park

Hard Rock Café Map 4 ✘

150 Old Park Lane, W1 *Telephone* 01-692 0382 ££

The most famous queue in London – even in the rain, even in mid-afternoon certainly late at night, it snakes out into Mayfair. The cult for Hard Rock T-shirts has swelled numbers. Inside, the formula stays the same – a rock 'n' roll

---

The British railway system is exceptionally good, with modern, clean and fast trains. For long trips, first class is preferable to second class for privacy and comfort. If you do not buy your tickets in advance, allow at least 30 minutes to get them at the station. London has many termini serving different parts of the United Kingdom – Charing Cross, Paddington, St Pancras, Liverpool Street, King's Cross, Euston, Waterloo, Victoria, Marylebone and others – so make sure you know where your train leaves from.

LONDON

vision of the greatest roadside café of all: loud music rooted largely in the late '60s, Americana from juke-box to baseball emblems, practised, maternal waitresses, excellent char-grilled burgers, steaks, club sandwiches, enormous salads, and sweets off a soda fountain. Children welcome; vegetarians catered for; access for wheelchairs. The formula for working out how long the wait will be is: a hundred seats mostly divided into twos and fours and the average party stays forty minutes...

Open All week **Meals** Noon to 12.30am (1am Fri and Sat) **Credit cards** None accepted **Service** 10% **Underground** Hyde Park Corner

Hilton Hotel Map 4

Park Lane, W1 *Telephone* 01-493 8000   £££–££££

The Hilton chandeliers hang over the wide spiral staircase leading up to the first floor, while another plant-like construction dangles from the tall ceiling over the British Harvest restaurant. None of them is particularly in keeping with the sentiments of the dining-room, which has been laudably dedicated to the cause of British cooking. Unfortunately, the results, in the manner of big hotels, have been unpredictable, swaying from the out-and-out excellent to the mundane. The menu is a persuasive document on the merits of British cooking – fine hot beef tea, ribs of beef, venison with a sauce of sloe gin, lamb chops wrapped in bacon and served with an intense demi-glace, and summer pudding. Other features illustrate how much thought and enthusiasm have gone in to this dining-room – four loaves of different breads are brought round to start and sliced to order, while at the end of meals the trolley of unpasteurised English cheeses is perhaps the finest in London. But the place needs a day-to-day guiding hand to make it less erratic. The second restaurant in the hotel is on the rooftop and has spectacular views over London. There, the lunchtime buffet is better value than the evening meals. Wines in both restaurants are grossly overpriced ... to the point that the management is able to assure us that the English wines have all been reduced from £13 to £9 – hardly bargains, even so. Children's helpings. Music; air-conditioning; access for wheelchairs. Afternoon teas.

Open All week **Meals** 12 to 2.45, 6 to 10.30 **Cards** Access, Amex, Carte Blanche, Diners, Visa **Accommodations** 503 rooms, all with bath/shower. Rooms for disabled. B&B £144 to £167. Baby facilities **Underground** Hyde Park Corner

Ho-Ho Map 4

29 Maddox Street, W1 *Telephone* 01-493 1228   ££–£££

A note on the menu says that 'Chinese cuisine is famed for its vegetable cookery'. If that is the case then it certainly has not reached London, where on a good night the limit of most restaurants is just a few sticks of choy sim. Despite the long, inter-regional menu the restaurant's reputation is vested in a mere six dishes, of which one is the not-so-original stir-fried bean sprouts. But quibble not. This is a smart second-generation Chinese restaurant out of the orbit of Chinatown and yet producing dishes of similar standard. The set menus (lunch £8.50, dinner from £11) feature Peking, Szechuan and Nonya cooking, three

MAYFAIR

ways with duck with the impressive steamboat making four. But individual fish dishes show the subtlety of the cooking – fried squid with snow peas, and sliced sole in wine sauce with wood-ear lichens. Service is proficient, and the wine list has a pair of Alsace wines from Willy Gisselbrecht, both gold medal winners and both 1983s – Pinot Blanc at £6.50 and Gewürztraminer at £8.50. Both complement the food well. Wheelchair access; music; air-conditioning. Children are welcome.

Open Mon to Sat **Meals** 12 to 2.30, 6 to 10.45 **Cards** Access, Amex, Diners, Visa **Service** 12½% **Underground** Oxford Circus

Holiday Inn (Mayfair) Map 4

Berkeley Street, W1 *Telephone* 01-493 8282   £££

Probably the most luxurious of the four Holiday Inns in London and further blessed by its location right in the middle of Mayfair, this elegant member of the group would be a good central London base. Bedrooms are comfortable and efficiently organised with lots of extras as well as double-glazing, air-conditioning and individually controlled room heating. The Berkeley Room restaurant offers an international menu.

Open (Restaurant) 7 to 2.30, 3 to 5, 5 to 11 **Cards** Access, Amex, Diners, Visa **Accommodations** 190 rooms, all with bath. B&B £52.50 to £93 + breakfast (£4 to £6) **Underground** Green Park

Ikeda Map 4

30 Brook Street, W1 *Telephone* 01-499 7145 and 629 2730   £££–££££

The cuisine here is rather different from the other big London Japanese restaurants, although the atmosphere is markedly Japanese, and the menu repays efforts at exploration. The cooking is really country-style, with less emphasis on presentation and more on flavours, some of which – such as the vinegared crab as a starter, or the aubergines split in half and spread with miso – are stunning. Other styles, like the sushi or yakitori, are competently done. Each day there are ten to fifteen specials, but look also to the side dishes such as raw beef with daikon. Short, dark blue curtains hang from the ceiling – another example of the national ingenuity for packing an awful lot into a small space. Plum wine, saké or tea to drink. No children under ten. Access for wheelchairs; air-conditioning; music.

Open Mon to Fri **Meals** 12.30 to 2.30, 6.30 to 10.30 **Cards** Access, Amex, Diners, Visa **Service** 15% **Underground** Bond Street

Inter-Continental Hotel Map 3

1 Hamilton Place, W1 *Telephone* 01-409 3131   ££££

The most international of Park Lane's grand hotels. It claims to have the highest occupancy of any. The building is brash and modern and the atmosphere is heavy with that anaesthetising airport-departure-lounge spirit. The restaurant,

LONDON

Le Soufflé, is loud with reds and chromes. Cut-glass bowls are filled with water and have single, floating roses. The menu is an extraordinarily long list of extravagant and indulgent combinations of the most expensive ingredients. Through all this ostentation Peter Kromberg's kitchen is capable of producing genuine *haute cuisine* of a level that is only found in the very best dining-rooms of Europe. For instance, a pair of gratiné oysters arrive unannounced as an appetiser. There has also been immaculate wild-mushroom soup containing a huge, home-made ravioli filled with minced pigeon and garnished with morels. Freshly made pasta is a favourite device, appearing as a pile of spaghetti with braised monkfish in an intense red-wine sauce, with bone-marrow cooked in a salt crust. Calf's kidney is cooked in a salt crust which is broken by the waiter at the table and the meat sliced neatly round some diced vegetables. The soufflés are, predictably, very fine and varied and rise almost twice the height of their dishes. Much energy is directed into such creations. Yet, as is seemingly the trouble with all hotel dining-rooms, consistency is missing and one dish is as likely to be average as the next might be spectacular. The cheeseboard has sometimes been an affront. The drinks trolley would be more impressive if it had tracked down more single-maker alcohols. They require men to wear a jacket and tie; air-conditioning; wheelchair access; no-smoking area; children's helpings. Afternoon teas.

Open All week, exc Sat L **Meals** 12.30 to 3, 7 to 11.30 **Cards** Access, Amex, Diners, Visa **Accommodations** 500 rooms, all with bath/shower. Rooms for disabled. B&B £141 to £173 **Underground** Hyde Park Corner

---

Justin de Blank   Map 4

54 Duke Street, W1 *Telephone* 01-629 3174   ££

Quite a jam builds up at this self-service restaurant run by young staff on behalf of Justin de Blank. The blackboard menu has included terrine of chicken with tomato mayonnaise, cucumber and mint soup served hot or cold depending on the weather, and fresh and inventive salads – jacket potatoes with cream and peppers, smoked ham and mushrooms. Sweets are notably good – wine trifle, and lemon fudge tart. Coffee is excellent, but the cups are not generous. Children's helpings.

Open Mon to Sat, exc Sat D **Closed** Public hols **Meals** 8.30 (9 Sat) to 3.30, 4.30 to 9 **Cards** None accepted **Underground** Bond Street

---

Kitchen Yakitori   Map 4

12 Lancashire Court, New Bond Street, W1 *Telephone* 01-629 9984   £–££

The set meals dispel the myth that Japanese food is inevitably expensive. Written in black in Japanese characters on the red lantern that hangs from the awning are the words *unagi* (grilled eel) and *yakitori* (grilled chicken kebab). At the pine food-bar in the basement the emphasis is on the simpler cooking techniques. Set meals are excellent value, bringing generous portions (lunch from £3.80, dinner from £8.50). Over and above clear soups, grilled fish and tempura are such delicacies as eel livers and steamed savoury custards. Service is relaxed and there is no pressure to leave. Japanese tea is free. Music; air-conditioning.

Open Mon to Sat, exc Sat D **Closed** Public hols **Meals** 12 to 3, 6 to 9.30 **Cards** None accepted **Service** 10% **Underground** Bond Street

Korea House Map 4

10 Lancashire Court, New Bond Street, W1
Telephone 01-493 1340 and 491 4761

£££

A formal Korean restaurant catering for businessmen and people from the nearby embassy. Upstairs is a snazzy bar, downstairs is the dining-room, with bright pink walls, spotlights in the ceiling and pretty white crockery on the tables. The long menu reads adventurously and dishes are clearly explained in English. Reliably good are the fermented kim-chee, fresh fish-cakes with soy and spring onion dip, and the bulgogi – rare beef seasoned with sesame, soy and sugar, and cooked at the table on a flat iron pan. Rice is above average and the hot barley tea topped up on request. Large portions, high prices and well-mannered service. Air-conditioning; music; children's helpings.

Open Mon to Sat **Meals** 12 to 3, 6 to 11 **Cards** Access, Amex, Diners, Visa **Service** 12½% **Underground** Bond Street

Ladbroke Curzon Hotel Map 4

2 Stanhope Row, Park Lane, W1 *Telephone* 01-493 7222

£££

Modern, comfortable and quietly elegant small hotel in the shadow of the boys in the big league on Park Lane, but quieter, possibly, and less expensive. Rooms are on the smallish side, attractively decorated with quite a lot of pine; marble bathrooms, on the other hand, are spacious; both are well equipped, even with a safe. Public rooms are attractive and there's a cosy oriental-style cocktail bar. The hotel is just round the corner from one of London's nicest and most popular cinemas, the Curzon, which is usually showing a rather arty film.

Open (Restaurant) 12 to 3 (room service menu), 6 to 10 **Cards** Access, Amex, Diners, Visa **Accommodations** 71 rooms, all with bath or shower. B&B £47.50 to £78.50 **Underground** Hyde Park Corner/Green Park

Langan's Bar & Grill Map 4

7 Down Street, W1 *Telephone* 01-491 0990

£££

The first of what Peter Langan plans to be a chain of restaurants is not quite the National Gallery that his original restaurant Odins is (not in this *Guide*); nevertheless it houses an impressive selection of large paintings. From the bar a portrait of Mr Langan himself stares back. Many other portraits are signed. The mahogany windows with small panes give plenty of light. The menu takes its text from the Brasserie (see below), offering some thirty-two dishes and perhaps sixteen wines served by young staff in neat black uniforms. The chef is David Bickford; he was at Langan's Bistro before. Trout quenelles with a herb sauce

LONDON

are at one end of the spectrum, grilled fish at the other. The menu changes, but the fixtures, such as good béarnaise sauce, the oil for the salad dressings, and even the butter, lend it the clothes of a very classy restaurant. The house wine starts at £6.50 – this is Mayfair, after all.

Open Mon to Sat exc Sat L **Meals** 12.30 to 2.45, 6 to 12 **Cards** Access, Amex, Visa **Service** 12½% **Underground** Hyde Park Corner

---

Langan's Brasserie Map 4	🍴
Stratton Street, W1 *Telephone* 01-493 6437	£££

Some people get very boring, saying the food at Langan's is no good. Bilge. The point about Langan's is that the place really does live up to its awesome reputation. The atmosphere crackles, it is packed every night and the wonder is that the whole operation does not cave in on itself. Amid all the bustle, the kitchen manages (nine times out of ten) to cook successfully a massively long, daily changing menu, and the waiters manage to get it to the table with a modicum of respect. Although a direct descendant of the big Paris brasseries in style, this is modern British cooking. Cannily, Richard Shepherd does not gild the lily, and it is this that makes the menu feel and taste British. The calf's liver arrives as quarter-inch slices, seared, criss-crossed and served unadorned, or else, on another night, with a little basil and onion sauce mixed with the meat juice. Fish, despite the hectic atmosphere, gets to the table in trim – deep-fried skate wings with tartare sauce; salmon hollandaise. What happens at Langan's night after night is real cooking, and quite a lot of it. It straddles definitions and is loyal only to the market; on one table there may be bubble and squeak, at another, mousseline de coquilles St Jacques. Pastry does not seem to take the strain quite as well as other things, for instance traditional puds such as rice pudding and crumble. It is a champagne lover's wine list. Access for wheelchairs; children's helpings; music; air-conditioning.

Open Mon to Sat, exc Sat L **Meals** 12.30 to 2.45, 7 to 11.45 (8 to 12.45 Sat) **Cards** Access, Amex, Diners, Visa **Service** 12½% **Underground** Green Park

---

Miyama Map 4	🍴
38 Clarges Street, W1 *Telephone* 01-499 2443	£££–££££

This restaurant produced one of the finest *Good Food Guide* inspection meals in London last year. It is in the international zone off Piccadilly, not far from the anomaly of the Lebanese Tourist Office. It is high-tech Japan in an old London street: a bar at the entrance, a complex of white box cubby-holes stacked high with whisky, Chivas Regal being the favoured drink of most businessmen at the moment, waitresses in breast-flattening kimonos, who have enthusiasm if not quite a command of English. The decor is akin to a coffee shop in Tokyo – marble floors, British Home Stores-style pot-plants, abstract 3D square linear drawings. Downstairs are the private rooms; upstairs is more accessible. The delicacy, precision and the balance of the cooking impress. Three oblong lozenges of tofu, spread with miso paste, are served on a single plate, each one skewered on a tiny wooden tuning-fork. On another plate, this time a deep

MAYFAIR

square bowl, an avocado is sliced through and arranged chameleon-like in the centre, while piled in the corner is a heap of daikon topped with salmon eggs. Again, tucked up in the corner of a small bowl is the shell of a scallop, out of which come tumbling a dozen tiny queens, their corals arranged underneath. The difference between Japanese and Western cooking techniques is crucial. In Japan, an entire meal might consist of a whole fish cooked in eight different ways. So here there is teriyaki served on a blue plate – the pink flesh, marinated in soy, saké and mirin, curled over to reveal the searing marks of the grill. Its garnish is a turnip cut into a chrysanthemum shape, and in the very centre a little fleck of red, perhaps pepper, indicates a bud. Salmon tepenaki (cooked on a hot flat iron surface) arrives as five triangles of fillet arranged like slices of a half-eaten cake offset against a wedge of lemon. Similarly, aubergine is deep-fried or else appears in a style of ragoût. To finish, the ice-creams are excellent, including the green tea one, which is in fact made from the more expensive Macha used for the tea ceremony rather than the Ocha that is served in the restaurant. Music; air-conditioning; wheelchair access. Children are welcome.

Open Mon to Sat, exc Sat L **Meals** 12.30 to 2.30, 6.30 to 10.30 **Cards** Access, Amex, Diners, Visa **Service** 15% **Underground** Green Park

Ninety Park Lane, Grosvenor House Map 4

90 Park Lane, W1 *Telephone* 01-499 6363   ££–££££

Rocco Forte, probably the most powerful man in British catering, wanted somewhere he could have a decent lunch. In exasperation he went finally to Louis Outhier of l'Oasis at La Napoule in the South of France for guidance, and over the last two and a half years the interchange between the kitchen there and Ninety Park Lane has been like the exchange of spies on the Berlin bridge. THF has come off rather better. The dining-room is long and palatial, the sofas deep, the sweets table four or five tiers high, the waiters well versed. A pianist plays. Make no mistake, fine dishes are to be eaten here, and not just foie gras. The care and attention to detail extends to main courses, such as wild salmon with sliced mushrooms and diced tomato with a light beurre blanc flavoured with tarragon. Of all the big London hotels, this has had the most alive and challenging menu, albeit at a price. The wine list is extensive and reflects current auction prices. It favours first-growth clarets and also runs of great vintages with more than twenty 1966s in the heady stratosphere between £26 and £125. House wine is £14 and £15 for the white and red respectively. A much cheaper part of the hotel is a self-service buffet, Pasta Vino e Fantasia (open 12.30 to

---

Going out to dinner? Hotel and restaurant dining, especially outside London, is usually conducted at a pleasantly civilised pace. Upon entering the restaurant, you and your party are invited to sit in the lounge and order drinks while you study the menu. Your food order is then taken and, after a suitable interval, you are ushered to your table. Coffee (and tea) after the meal can also be taken in the lounge. This dining ritual lends a leisurely touch to eating out and is especially pleasant if you have several in your party.

LONDON

2.30, 7.30 to 11, closed Saturday lunch and Sunday). Specialities are home-made involtini di ricotta, and tortelloni papalina. The hotel offers a swimming-pool and sauna.

Open Mon to Sat, exc Sat L **Meals** 12.30 to 2.30, 7.30 to 10.45 **Cards** Access, Amex, Carte Blanche, Diners, Visa **Service** Inc **Accommodations** 460 rooms, all with bath/shower. Rooms for disabled. B&B £128 to £196. Deposit required. Baby facilities **Underground** Marble Arch/Hyde Park Corner

One Two Three Map 4

27 Davies Street, W1 *Telephone* 01-409 0750   ££–££££

This is an unpretentious, yet at the same time high-class, Japanese restaurant. It is possible to eat excellent set meals (lunch from £7.50, dinner from £18.50) and also explore some of the more intriguing avenues of the cooking. Where a few years ago the prices would have been regarded as expensive, now, compared to meals in French restaurants or in the big hotels, they are very competitive. Dishes arrive beautifully presented, service is first-class and the cooking is precise. Each year the superb belly-pork simmered in saké and also the picturesque soups are mentioned. Pickled vegetables are crisp and the sashimi excellent. No children under ten. Music; air-conditioning.

Open Mon to Fri **Meals** 12 to 2.30, 6.30 to 10.30 **Cards** Access, Amex, Diners, Visa **Service** 15% **Underground** Bond Street

Red Lion Map 4

Waverton Street, W1 *Telephone* 01-499 1307   £

At the end of a quiet cul-de-sac, this Mayfair pub has cut-away barrel seats among the bay trees under its front awning – unusually peaceful for London. Inside, the little L-shaped bar has a relaxed and civilised atmosphere, with small winged settles on the partly carpeted scrubbed floorboards, and old photographs and London prints below the high shelf of china on its dark-panelled walls. Good food is served by a man in a butcher's boater and apron and includes ploughman's, generous rare beef sandwiches, salads and specials such as dressed crab or salmon. Children are allowed in the restaurant. Unusually for the area, food is served morning and evening seven days a week, and in winter includes hot dishes. A good choice of real ale includes well-kept Combes (Watneys' London brew), Manns IPA, Ruddles County, Watneys Stag and Websters Yorkshire on handpump. It can get crowded at lunchtimes.

Open 11 to 3, 5.30 to 11 **Underground** Green Park

Reeds, Austin Reed Map 4

103 Regent Street, W1 *Telephone* 01-734 6789   £

An ideal place for a quick lunch or as a break from shopping. There is a cold buffet of dishes such as smoked chicken with gooseberry sauce, roast forerib of beef, and asparagus quiche; and hot dishes such as lasagne and steak and kidney

NORTH KENSINGTON

pie. The open sandwiches are fresh, and come with a good side salad, and there are cheeses and puddings too. Three decent coffees. Licensed.

Open 9.30 to 5 (6 Thur) **Closed** Sun; most public hols; Christmas Day and Boxing Day **Underground** Oxford Circus

Saga Map 4

43 South Molton Street, W1 *Telephone* 01-629 3931   ££–££££

Downstairs is a black lacquered Samurai tent as well as a small sushi bar. Upstairs is a tappenaki bar, on which are fried such things as piles of garlic which are rolled into thin slices of fillet beef. If you sit at the tappenaki bar then you must eat at it, which is both plain and expensive, but at the tables it is possible to eat tappenaki and any other style. Dishes are a visual delight. Sashimi is arranged on a dark maroon plate shaped as a segment from a circle with a shaped bonzai bee made from daikon. Other dishes worth following are the exquisite soups; grilled brill with salt; salmon roes on dashi; the lightly battered tempura. To end, the oranges and pineapple are ornately carved. The unpriced items may prove costly. Music; air-conditioning; wheelchair access. Children are welcome.

Open Mon to Sat **Meals** 12 to 2.30, 6.30 to 10 **Cards** Access, Amex, Diners, Visa **Service** 15% **Underground** Bond Street

Wolfe's Map 4

34 Park Lane, W1 *Telephone* 01-499 6897   £–££

Claims to be London's only luxury hamburger restaurant (along with its brother in Knightsbridge). It's certainly comfortable and serves a wide range of decent burgers with various toppings. Stick to those, and you needn't exceed the minimum charge of £5 by much.

Open 11.30 to midnight **Closed** Christmas Day and Boxing Day **Underground** Hyde Park Corner

NORTH KENSINGTON

Chez Moi Map 1

1 Addison Avenue, W11 *Telephone* 01-603 8267   ££££

In the last couple of years competition among restaurants in W11 has got pretty fierce. Chez Moi, after twenty years one of the long-standing entries in *The Good Food Guide*, still holds its own. Its food and the calm of the dining-room are no longer by any means fashionable, but the quality – of the ingredients, the cooking and the service – is high. Among recommendations this year are a translucent mussel soup, the chicken liver pâté with prunes, and quenelles – of turbot with a lobster sauce and of salmon with a dill. Main courses feature lamb prominently, but there has also been a pot au feu of chicken and sweetbreads with vegetables. To finish there is white and dark chocolate mousse, and also

LONDON

well-textured sorbets. The wine list is strong on 1979 clarets, if rather loftily priced. House French is £6. No children under ten; no pipes in the dining-room. Air-conditioning; wheelchair access.

Open Mon to Sat, D only **Closed** 2 weeks Aug, 2 weeks at Christmas, public hols **Meals** 7 to 11.30 **Cards** Access, Amex, Diners, Visa **Underground** Holland Park

Frog and Firkin Map 2

41 Tavistock Crescent, W11   £

One of David Bruce's 'Firkin' pubs (a firkin is a small barrel). See the Ferret and Firkin in the Fulham section for further information if you're a fan of this flourishing formula. This version has a pianist and an unusual hat collection.

Open 11 to 3, 5.30 to 11 **Underground** Westbourne Park

Hilton International Kensington Map 1

179 Holland Park Avenue, W11 *Telephone* 01-603 3355   ££

Very up-to-date amenities are one of the attractions of this member of the Hilton group (see also the Hilton in the Mayfair section). Bedrooms are comfortable and air-conditioned, bathrooms well equipped. A carvery is one of the focuses of the hotel's Market Restaurant (£12.50 per head). Amenities offered include a beauty and hairdressing salon, 24-hour lounge service, and, possibly important to visitors planning trips out of London, ample parking.

Open (Restaurant) 12 to 3, 6 to 11 **Cards** Access, Amex, Diners, Visa **Accommodations** 606 rooms (all with bath/shower). B&B £40.50 to £85 **Underground** Shepherd's Bush

Julie's Champagne Bar Map 1

135 Portland Road, W11 *Telephone* 01-229 8331   ££

Canapés, Cole Porter and glasses of Lanson Rosé Brut make up the social cocktail in this small comfortable bar attached to a more expensive restaurant. Bucks Fizz and Pimms Royale are served with Stilton and walnut mousse, or there's eggs and prawns in aspic or smoked salmon sandwiches.

Open 12.30 to 2.30 (2.15 Sun), 7.15 to 11.15 (10.15 Sun) **Closed** Christmas Eve to 27 Dec; 4 days from Good Fri; Aug bank hol Mon **Underground** Holland Park

Monsieur Thompsons Map 2

29 Kensington Park Road, W11 *Telephone* 01-727 9957   ££–£££

Monsieur Thompson was in fact a cat. For the last few years this restaurant has been going through an identity crisis, unsure whether it is a serious modern French restaurant or a bistro *au coin*. The decor upstairs is boudoir-like and busy, and downstairs more of a country restaurant in scrubbed woods. The menu has the same crisis – the move to veal knuckle country-style on the one hand and excellent bitter chocolate slice with a hazelnut sauce on the other. It

NORTH KENSINGTON

works best when it is one thing or the other. The simpler dishes win out – for instance, the scallops with mussel sauce or the salad of baby vegetables with a coriander dressing. Wines come from ten different countries, unusual for a French restaurant, providing a commendable challenge, and are mostly under £10 at that. Children are welcome. No smoking during meals. Access for wheelchairs.

Open Mon to Sat **Closed** 1 week at Christmas **Meals** 12.30 to 2.30, 7.30 to 10.45 **Cards** Access, Amex, Diners, Visa **Underground** Ladbroke Grove/Notting Hill Gate

192 Map 2

192 Kensington Park Road, W11 *Telephone* 01-229 0482   £££

The matchbox-sized, red and black dining-room under the wine bar gets as full as a Hoover bag that needs changing. The menu alters almost daily and is a good example of new British cooking – cockle soup with lime leaves, scallops with red peppers, and fine pigeon in red wine sauce; there's always a vegetarian choice. The white and dark chocolate bavarois is first-class. Children's helpings; air-conditioning; music; wheelchair access. The wine bar offers some excellent wines from a list of about 50 (also available downstairs), many French, but a couple of interesting Australians, too.

Open All week, exc Sun D **Closed** 25 Dec, most public hols **Meals** 12.30 to 2.30, 7.30 to 11.30 **Cards** Access, Amex, Visa **Underground** Ladbroke Grove/Notting Hill Gate

Portobello Hotel Map 2

22 Stanley Gardens, W11 *Telephone* 01-727 2777   £££

'Undeniably slapdash and amateurish in terms of service, but charming if you don't expect too much, and very good value for money.' 'Nothing changes here (fortunately). They are perfectly happy for you to check in at weird hours. The place is relaxed, discreet; I remain a total fan!' 'Next time you say the service is "haphazard" and the establishment "laid back", we'll know you mean "bad". The service was sometimes downright contrary. It was the worst value of the many recommendations we patronised.'

This six-floor Victorian terraced house, within strolling distance of the Portobello Road Market and a little further to Kensington Gardens, has always been contentious. It is one of the few hotels in London with distinctive decor and life-style. Some of the rooms, called cabins, are pokey, even if they have essential elements of life-support like colour TV, tiny fridge and micro-bathroom. But there are also, as you work downwards, normal-sized rooms and ritzy suites. Some people can't take its easy-going approach to hospitality at all; others find its charms pall. But it has never lacked for ardent champions.

Open 2 Jan to 24 Dec **Cards** Access, Amex, Diners, Visa **Accommodations** 25 rooms, 4 with bath and shower, 21 with shower only. B&B £28.75 to £55 **Underground** Notting Hill Gate

---

If you are planning a trip to Scotland and the Lake District, there is another Guide in this series to those areas.

LONDON

PIMLICO

Le Mazarin Map 2 ✕

30 Winchester Street, SW1 *Telephone* 01-828 3366   £££

After a false start last summer, René Bajard has, with some help from his mentors Albert and Michel Roux, got this basement moving in top gear. The strange Mexican-style box-like entrance no longer leads to a grim olive room, but instead to a pink, pastelled and mirrored catacomb where bevies of young staff buzz around. The improvement is dramatic. Two things need underlining. The price is barely more than the cost of a meal at the Roux Brothers' vacuum-pack-supplied city restaurants; it is in fact the same price as the Gavvers (see Belgravia) and rather more individual. Second is Bajard's exceptional eye for the visual. He is able to make many well-known dishes look remarkably appetising. The choice is between the £15.50 menu of four to six items per course, or a set, no-choice gastronomic six courses for £22 which includes quite a few glimpses of Le Gavroche (see Mayfair), where he was previously head chef. Successes have been foie gras mousse, venison with cabbage, and lamb with a mousse of carrot and spinach. His training shows, especially with some exceptional fish, as in the suprême de bar de ligne vapeur au trois poivrons – served skin side up on a pond of three kinds of peppers, firm, well-cooked fish, vegetables not served separately but the plate dotted with scoops of carrot, courgette, turnip and potato – or, again, with salmon and sorrel. The sweets could be sold to the Tate Gallery (see below) and the cheeses to an anosmic. Petits fours come with the coffee and repeat the artistry. Other points are Gavrochean – tiny little canapés of tomato concassé, smoked salmon, whipped cream, and cream cheese with a quail's egg; wonderful tube-like long rolls, small balls of good butter. Service is enthusiastic, Gallic and young. The recommended wines are sensible and not overpriced, considering – £7.50 for Muscadet or Brouilly. Vegetarian meals; children's helpings. Music; air-conditioning; wheelchair access.

Open Mon to Sat, D only **Closed** 1 week at Christmas, public hols **Meals** 7 to 11.30 **Cards** Access, Amex, Diners **Service** Inc **Underground** Victoria

Orange Brewery Map 3 🍺

37 Pimlico Road, SW1   £

Friendly and attractive, this Victorian-style local brews beer on the premises (though tied to Clifton Inns, part of Watneys) which includes SW1, a stronger

---

It is usually advisable to book a restaurant table in advance.

✕ = *restaurant*
🏨 = *hotel*
🍺 = *pub*
🍷 = *wine bar*
☕ = *tea shop*

RICHMOND

SW2, and Pimlico Light – and they usually have a couple of guest beers on handpump as well. The bar servery has solid armed seats and armchairs around its high ochre walls, which are decorated with some Victorian plates, sepia photographs, and a stuffed fox above a nicely tiled fireplace. It leads through to the cheery Pie Shop, with lots more sepia photographs on the dark stained plank-panelling, plain wooden tables and chairs on pretty black and white tiles, and a shelf full of old flagons and jugs above the counter where they serve sandwiches, ploughman's or pâté, salads and daily hot dishes such as lasagne, steak and kidney pie, chilli con carne and chicken chasseur. Fruit machine, maybe piped music. There are seats outside facing a little concreted-over green beyond the quite busy street.

Open 11 to 3, 5.30 to 11 **Closed** 25 and 26 Dec **Underground** Sloane Square

Tate Gallery Map 2

Millbank, SW1 *Telephone* 01-834 6754   £££

Not, as the saying goes, what it used to be – the palette loses its colour from poor service and erratic cooking. And yet there are super wines at knock-down prices, and on good days there may be properly grilled liver, roast lamb full of flavour, summer fruit and meringue pie. It follows Escoffier's dictum of 'faites simple'. You can drink exquisitely – Ch Nenin 1955, Ch Gruaud-Larose 1950 by the magnum – and nothing, not even the magnums, over £50. Wine lovers will appreciate the no-smoking area as well as the air-conditioning. Access for wheelchairs. Children's helpings; vegetarian meals.

Open Mon to Sat, L only **Closed** Most public hols **Meals** 12 to 3 **Cards** None accepted **Underground** Pimlico

RICHMOND

Crowthers Map 1

481 Upper Richmond Road West, East Sheen, SW14   £££–££££
Telephone 01-876 6372

Philip and Shirley Crowther continue to maintain high standards in their upper-class restaurant: there are good reports of everything from the brown rolls to the petits fours. The pattern remains the same – a set evening menu (£17.50) with five or six choices at each stage – but a light vein now runs through many of the dishes, from poached scallops with leeks and vermouth, to a fruit terrine with mango and passion-fruit sauce that has echoes of Raymond Blanc (see Manoir aux Quat' Saisons in the Oxford section). Wild mushrooms appear with fashionable regularity, as a soup with chervil, with spinach in a roulade, with Boursin cheese as a stuffing for tiny brioches. Sweets come in for special praise, from hazelnut meringue and chocolate marquise with white chocolate sauce, to crème brûlée. Lunch is a set meal, too (£12). Interesting aperitifs, well-chosen wines. Wheelchair access; music; air-conditioning.

Open Tue to Sat, exc Sat L **Meals** 12 to 2, 7 to 11 **Cards** Access, Amex **BR station** Mortlake

LONDON

Mr Fish Map 1 ✖

393 Upper Richmond Road, SW15 *Telephone* 01-876 3083 £–££

The boast of this upper-crust fish and chip shop is that the fish is always fresh. It is fried in ground-nut oil or grilled. The menu may be restricted according to the market, but it also aspires to scampi to go with Chablis and has candlelit alcoves to complete the effect. There is a take-away next door. Children's helpings. Music; wheelchair access; no cigars or pipes in the dining-room.

Open Mon to Sat, exc Mon L **Meals** 12 to 2, 6 to 11 (11.30 Thur, Fri and Sat) **Cards** Access, Amex, Diners, Visa **Service** Inc (set meal); 10% (à la carte) **BR station** Barnes

Mrs Beeton's Map 1 ✖ ☕

58 Hill Rise, Richmond *Telephone* 01-940 9561 £–££

A delightful restaurant run as a cooks' co-operative and based on the idea of local housewives taking charge of the cooking for one session each week. Now the place boasts a whole posse of ladies from Poland, Italy and France as well as England. The emphasis is on home cooking and prices are kept as low as possible. Because the daytime cook finishes at 5pm and the evening lady arrives an hour later with her own menu, there are always surprises. One cook might offer bouillabaisse, kidneys Stroganoff and aubergine duxelles, another might put on chicken breast stuffed with mushrooms or veal with cream and vermouth sauce. Cakes and sweets are always good. Unlicensed; bring your own.

Open 10 to 5, 7 to 11 **Closed** Mon D and Tue D **BR station/Underground** Richmond

Newens & Sons Map 1 ☕

288 Kew Road, Kew *Telephone* 01-940 2752 £

Large gilt letters over the door proclaim that this is the home of the original Maids of Honour Cake. The Newens family have been baking them for 180 years, and serving them to locals and visitors to Kew Gardens. Other pastries are served on blue and white china by kindly waitresses. The chocolates are also home made.

Open 10 to 5.30 (9.30 to 1 Mon) **Closed** Sun; public hols **Underground** Richmond

Orange Tree Map 1 🍺

45 Kew Road, Kew *Telephone* 01-940 0944 £

Some interesting features in this spacious, open-plan and friendly pub include the unusual fruit and foliage pattern of the embossed ceiling, the big coaching and Dickens prints, and the courtly paintings of the seven ages of man by Henry Stacy Marks, presented to the Green Room theatre club here in 1921; there's still a fringe theatre upstairs carrying on the tradition. There are comfortable seats on the carpet that spreads around the efficient central servery. At lunchtime there's a full range of sandwiches, ploughman's and so forth upstairs;

RICHMOND

good food is also served in a wine-bar-like basement (lunchtime and evening, Mondays to Saturdays) which has soft lighting, simple tables on a tiled floor and old stripped brickwork walls: steak and kidney pie, beef salad, pheasant; good-value Sunday roast lunches. Children are welcome in the downstairs restaurant. Well-kept Youngs Bitter and Special on handpump, relatively reasonably priced for London; fruit machine, piped music.

Open 11 to 3, 5.30 to 11 **Underground** Richmond

Pissarro's Map 1

1, 3 & 5 Kew Green, Kew *Telephone* 01-940 3987   £

A beamed wine bar that is packed by 8 o'clock. Salmon trout mousse and duck pâté come with excellent French bread, and more substantial offerings, ranging from lamb curry and liver with sage to monkfish provençale, are served with plenty of vegetables. Pissarro lived and painted here.

Open 11.30 to 3, 5.30 to 11 (noon to 2, 7 to 10 Sun) **Closed** Easter Sun; Christmas Eve to Boxing Day **BR station** Kew Bridge **Underground** Kew Gardens

---

Le Provence Map 1

Kew Station Approach, Kew *Telephone* 01-940 6777   ££

Jean-Marie Raphel and Claude Leport's French café offers plain fare, from liver and bacon with onions to roast chicken, and specialities such as sautéed pork with rosemary or omelette with spinach and prawns. The tables have red and white checked cloths and the only bottles on the premises are those which have candles in them. This bring-your-own-wine-no-corkage policy is the main reason given by the proprietors for their success with locals, who tend to become regulars – so booking becomes important, especially at weekends.

Open Noon to 2 (Sat L only), 6 to 9.15 **Closed** Sun and Mon; Aug to Sept; Christmas **Underground** Kew Gardens

---

Refectory Map 1

6 Church Walk, Richmond *Telephone* 01-948 6264   £

Mary and Roger Kingsley have handed over the reins to their daughter and son-in-law, but the style of this sedate restaurant remains the same. Lunch is cheaper than dinner, and consists of well-executed dishes of jugged beef, steak and kidney pie, Shropshire fidget pie, lamb and basil casserole, pork and apple crumble, braised veal with lemon, and the like. There are more usual dishes too: flans, salads, soups and quiches. Good puddings are date and orange sponge tart, 'Eton mess', Boodles orange fool and apricot crumble cake.

Open 10 to 2.15, 7.30 to 8.45 **Closed** D Sun to Wed; Mon; Christmas, New Year and Easter **Underground** Richmond

---

If you cannot honour a restaurant booking, always telephone to cancel.

LONDON

Richmond Harvest Map 1

5 Dome Buildings, The Quadrant, Richmond *Telephone* 01-940 1138   £

A convivial vegetarian bistro with a good choice for vegans. The menu has enterprising salads, as well as main courses such as celery, mushroom and potato pie, black-eyed bean and mushroom moussaka, and parsnip and cashew-nut casserole. Carob cake or hot fruit crumble to finish. Attentive service, a cosy basement atmosphere and convenient opening times make it a favourite with locals. Good house red and a wide range of other drinks.

Open 11.30 to 11 (10.30pm Sun) **Closed** Christmas Day to 2 Jan **Underground** Richmond

White Swan Map 1

Old Palace Lane   £

The open-plan bar in this popular little pub is almost S-shaped, so doesn't give the feeling of one big room, and the atmosphere is more like that of a country local than a busy London pub. Copper pots hang from the dark beamed ceiling, there are old prints of London on the walls, along with one wall of old china plates, and captain's chairs, dark wood tables and red velveteen banquettes are set on the red patterned carpet and around the open brick fireplace. Bar food includes sandwiches, quiche and salad, chilli con carne or steak and kidney pie and four hot daily specials (meals served at lunchtimes only, Mondays to Saturdays). Well-kept Courage Best and Directors on handpump; fruit machine. Outside there is a paved garden with climbing plants, flowering tubs, flower-beds and wooden tables and benches. Summer evening barbecues include sausage and onion in a roll, spare ribs and eight-ounce rump steak. Best to get there by 9pm if you want a table.

Open 11 to 3, 5.30 to 11 **Underground** Richmond

ST JAMES'S

Athenaeum Hotel Map 4

116 Piccadilly, W1   £££–££££
Telephone 01-499 3464 (or from USA) (800) 223 5560

The Athenaeum is the flagship hotel of the Rank chain. It has an enviable position overlooking Green Park (jogging maps and suits available for the energetic), and all the trimmings that one would expect from a *de luxe* West End hotel – 24-hour service, excellent restaurant, hyper-elegant decor and furnishings. Ron Jones, the genial former manager, has departed to Claridge's but his successor, Nicholas Rettie, and the staff all continue to give dedicated service. 'Totally satisfactory for the most spoiled or pampered guest. They care.'

Open All year **Cards** Access, Amex, Diners, Visa **Accommodations** 112 rooms, all with bath and shower. B&B £70 to £125 + breakfast (£5.75 to £8) **Underground** Hyde Park Corner

ST JAMES'S

Le Caprice Map 4

Arlington House, Arlington Street, SW1 *Telephone* 01-629 2239   £££

Well named. In many ways it is, 'perfect for every occasion: business lunches, after-theatre dinners, children's birthdays and so on. The food is at its best when simple – salmon cru au citron vert, followed by calf's liver'. The menu is genuinely capricious, flirting with tabouleh, bang-bang chicken and saucisse de Toulouse. The monochromatic decor, the courteous service and the Sunday brunch are all pluses. The wine list has good bottles, including a rarely found, extensive collection of ten rosés. Wheelchair access; air-conditioning. A pianist plays.

Open All week, exc Sat L **Meals** 12 to 2.30 (3 Sun), 6 (7 Sat, Sun) to 12 **Cards** Access, Amex, Diners, Visa **Underground** Green Park

Crowns Map 4

3–4 Crown Passage, Pall Mall, SW1 *Telephone* 01-839 3960   ££

There are excellent cheeses in this wine bar, which is open throughout the day. All the food is cooked daily in the kitchen and varies from chilled melon soup to steaks to raised pies. There is also a carry-out sandwich service. House French is £4.75. Access for wheelchairs; music. Children are welcome.

Open Mon to Fri **Meals** 9.30 to 8 **Cards** Access, Amex, Visa **Underground** Green Park

Dukes Hotel Map 4

St James's Place, SW1 *Telephone* 01-491 4840   £££–££££

Dukes Hotel was built in 1895 as chambers for the nobility; it became a hotel in 1908. It still retains the gas-lit front courtyard and a gentleman's club atmosphere in the bar, with rich red leather upholstery and paintings of various dukes. The dining-room is small and exclusive, which gives it a potential that other London hotel dining-rooms do not have. Tables are set simply, and the menu, the dishes cooked by Tony Marshall, who came here via the Dorchester and the Savoy, is a well-balanced mix of the English and the French, the simple and the complex. Fish can be had sauced or plainly grilled with the offer of some béarnaise on the side. Chicken liver mousse is cooked to order. Sauces have brio – walnut with lamb, Pommery with grilled veal kidneys and fresh peaches. Potatoes have their own place on the menu – braised in cream with thyme and garlic, and flavoured with saffron. The set lunches (£16.50) are verging on

---

Theatre tips: most theatres begin at around 7.30 pm. You'll have to plan an early dinner, or a later one after the show. Some theatres have buffets, so you can get a drink and snack between the acts. If you arrive late, you will not be seated until the next interval (intermission). The levels of a British theatre tend to be called (from ground level upwards): the stalls, the circle or dress circle, the upper circle and the balcony.

LONDON

modern British cooking, while the sweets trolley will also contain bread-and-butter pudding and trifle. Service is of the old school, but personal. There are cheaper places in London to drink the better wines on a comprehensive list, but Hermitage, de la Sizeranne 1980 from Chapoutier at £18 is not over-priced. House claret is £7.50. Vegetarians can be catered for, and those in wheelchairs accommodated. It's not really a place for children, though the management claims they are welcome.

Open All week **Meals** 12.30 to 2.30, 6 (7 Sun) to 10 **Cards** Access, Amex, Diners, Visa **Accommodations** 52 rooms, all with bath/shower. Rooms for disabled. B&B £110 to £145. Deposit: 1 night's stay. Baby facilities **Underground** Green Park

Fortnum & Mason Map 4

181 Piccadilly, W1 *Telephone* 01-734 8040   £–£££

The Fountain, on the ground floor by some of the most famous grocery shelves in the world, stays open late for after-theatre custom. The post-shop hours entrance is at the side of the building. Breakfast is good value at £4.25 for the full English works, or there is a cold buffet of ham, beef, tongue or chicken. The full menu offers everything from consommé with cheese straws to prune and nut ring salad. Elegant teas, of course, and over 30 variations on the ice-cream soda/milkshake theme. A restrained grill menu operates in the evening. Good snacks are also available in the mezzanine patio bar and more expensive lunches in the fourth-floor restaurant. Licensed.

Open 9.30am to 11.30pm **Closed** Sun; public hols **Underground** Piccadilly Circus/Green Park

Green's Map 4

36 Duke Street, St James's, SW1 *Telephone* 01-930 4566 and 1376   £££–££££

'The best oysters I've ever had – and my mother comes from the Ile d'Oléron – Marennes area. These were £8 a half-dozen, very large, round, chewy, not blubbery, and had just the right amount of "iode" flavour. The house champagne, Floquet (£2.75 a glass), is light and correct.' Peter Manzi, who opens the oysters, regained his trophy at the oyster opening championships in Galway last year. In the air-conditioned dining-room behind the panelled bar the food is unmucked-about-with English – fish-cakes, shepherd's pie, steak and kidney pudding, good dressed crab. Cold roast meats and, when available, lobsters are laid out on display on the counter. The latter start at £17. Sweets are traditional – fritters, fools or Duke of Cambridge tart. Vin de table is £5, Dom Pérignon 1978 is £60, or you could opt for Pauillac, Réserve de la Comtesse 1980 (the second wine of Ch Pichon-Longueville Lalande), at £12.50. (Other good places in London for oysters and champagne are: Sweetings, 39 Queen Victoria Street, EC4 (01-248 3062) and Rudland and Stubbs, 35–37 Greenhill Rents, off Cowcross Street, EC1 (01-253 0148), both in the City, and Scott's, 20 Mount Street, W1 (01-629 5248) in Mayfair.)

Open Mon to Fri **Meals** 11.30 to 3, 5.30 to 10.45 **Cards** Access, Amex, Diners, Visa **Underground** Bond Street/Green Park

ST JAMES'S

The Ritz Map 4

Piccadilly, W1 *Telephone* 01-493 8181   £££–££££

That this is the most beautiful dining-room in London is not in dispute. The orange hues of the massive corridor give way to pinks and golds; the ceiling, garlanded with chandeliers, is reflected in a wall of mirrors; a mural of an English summer sky – blue, with clouds – echoes the reality outside, glimpsed through towering windows, and all this pillared romance held by the solidity of the bronze, larger-than-life-size statue of a reclining Neptune, who reappears on the front of the menu. The room has its own presence and even the waiters are aware of this, moving like characters in a film, waiting for their one line to come round. The way the woman cashier in her booth of mirrors busies herself adds to this effect. The waiters, carrying at shoulder-height trays of dead crockery discreetly hidden under pink napkins, filter off to the far bottom corner of the room and disappear, though there is no door to be seen. It is said that the Ritz has lost some of its class, but as you stand in the corridor someone takes your coat and you have to wait at the door to the restaurant to give your name as if you are about to enter a different country – which you are. The Ritz lives in the international world – Venice is next door, so is Fort Worth, both are just a telephone call and a plane-hop away. The cabaret, which the management are so keen on, reinforces this internationalism – songs of Harlem are sung at the tea-dance in the dining-room on Sundays. As well as all this there is the food. David Miller, whom *The Good Food Guide* discovered before anyone else, when he was cooking at the Sheraton Park Tower, has steered the menu back in time rather than forward. There is innovation rather than complexity, but what catches the eye more is the sheer common sense of the menu, which takes into account all the problems of this glorious dining-room. Here is a kitchen prepared to produce the perfect skate, pan-fried with capers, lemon and nut-brown butter. Here is a kitchen not afraid to offer avocado with prawns on its daily menu, but done properly and, this being the Ritz, including a bit of lobster for good measure. Even more outrageous in one sense is a lunch-menu starter that is tantamount to breakfast revisited – two eggs oven-baked with chipolatas, diced lamb's kidneys and a Madeira sauce. The ingredients are, of course, first-class, which means the plainer dishes, such as roast beef or calf's liver with back bacon or the Chewton Mendip Cheddar speak for themselves. But there is *cuisine* too, as in potted breast of duck in a port and wine jelly. The wine list is not quite the most expensive in London. Bordeaux is its major theme, running from 1981 to 1961 (price, £18.75 to £450), but at least there is plenty under £20. The house wine is Alsace or Cabernet at £9.50. Bedrooms are as opulent as the rest, with over 20 new luxury ones featuring marble fireplaces from French châteaux, and silk curtains. Afternoon teas are in this style.

Open All week **Meals** 12.30 to 2.30, 6.30 to 11 **Cards** Access, Amex, Diners, Visa **Service** Inc **Accommodations** 128 rooms. B&B £120 to £180 **Underground** Green Park

---

£ = *meal can be had for about £5*
££ = *meal can be had for about £12*
£££ = *meal can be had for about £20*
££££ = *meal can be had for about £30*

LONDON

Suntory Map 4   ✘

72 St James's Street, SW1 *Telephone* 01-409 0201   ££££

Among the Japanese community the Suntory is regarded as the most expensive and therefore the best restaurant in London. No expense has been spared – enormous spacious rooms in this regal part of town, very high ceilings of dark wood, white walls and paper shoji windows, hand-crafted pottery. The waitresses dress in fine kimonos and speak in hushed tones. The atmosphere is formal and correct. In the Japanese style, the menu tends to detail the manner of cooking of dishes, rather than the ingredients. Mr Miura, who took over the kitchen in October 1985, is the only Japanese chef in London to be doing anything approaching kaiseki. Tempura, sashimi, soups, grilled fish, dishes of the day written in English are all fairly accessible in price, though the set meals (£17 to £25) are more so. Lobster is plainly grilled, chopped into bite-sized pieces and put back into the shell. Drink saké or whisky.

Open Mon to Sat **Meals** 12 to 2.30, 7 to 9.45 **Cards** Access, Amex, Diners, Visa **Service** 15% **Underground** Green Park

Wiltons Map 4   ✘

55 Jermyn Street, SW1 *Telephone* 01-629 9955   ££££

Of all the old-school London restaurants Wiltons is the most impressive. It is so like a club it is almost one anyway. Unknowns, we wager, have to sit at the tables in the corridor. It is expensive: Ogen melon is £5.25. There is no prize for guessing why it has not been included in *The Good Food Guide* for years. Peas were frozen when Sainsbury was selling fresh. Yet this is the place to eat un-mucked-about food *par excellence* – oysters, lobster, grouse, asparagus and Dover sole, though langoustines, for example, may be less well handled. The cooking errs to the rather well-done and other faults are old-school too – slightly watery spinach, slightly stewed coffee. The bar is weighed down with buckets of champagne and the day's shopping. The waitresses in white tunics behave like nannies or, as the *London Standard* put it, like matrons in Cracow civic hospital. The wine list specialises in the finest white Burgundies. House claret is £8.50. Air-conditioning; wheelchair access.

Open Mon to Sat, exc Sat L **Closed** 3 weeks July to Aug **Meals** 12.30 to 2.30, 6.30 to 10.30 **Cards** Access, Amex, Diners, Visa **Service** Inc **Underground** Green Park

ST JOHN'S WOOD

Au Bois St Jean Map 2   ✘

122 St John's Wood High Street, NW8 *Telephone* 01-722 0400   ££–£££

The pun on the name is carried through with some dense, woody decorations, but essentially this is a small, dark French restaurant which plays Edith Piaf tapes, has a set menu (lunch from £9.50, dinner from £12) with a wide choice, and serves its soupe de poissons with rouille, croûtons and cheese. It is

ST JOHN'S WOOD

marginally cheaper than its sister, Porte de la Cité (see Holborn), and has been more consistent. Plenty of thought goes into main dishes, such as duck with a sauce of almonds and chocolate, chicken with oysters, and lamb with chive and saffron. The menu has become increasingly seasonal which is a good step, and fish is usually featured as a special of the day. The wines are imported direct but tend to be in the £20-plus category. House wine is £5.75.

Open All week, exc Sat L **Meals** 12 to 2.30, 7 to 11.30 **Cards** Access, Visa **Service** Inc **Underground** St John's Wood

Clifton Map 2

96 Clifton Hill, NW8 £

Voted the *London Standard* Pub of the Year in 1985, this pub – with it's relaxed and countrified atmosphere – seems rather like a private house, though it's been a pub for a long time; Edward VII and Lily Langtry used to come here, and there are quite a few prints of both of them (one signed by the King and his son – who became George V). It's a spacious place but keeps the idea of small rooms by careful placing of wooden balustrades and one or two steps from one level to another. There are high ceilings, attractively stripped doors, bare-boarded floors, panelling and other woodwork, Edwardian and Victorian engravings and 1920s comic prints on its elegant wallpaper, unusual art nouveau wall lamps, cast-iron tables and fine brass and glass ceiling lights. Good bar food includes tomato and vegetable soup, pâté, a selection of meats with crunchy salad, Norfolk turkey and cranberry bake, spicy chicken Marengo, steak and Guinness pie, Atlantic prawn thermidor, puddings such as orchard fruits crumble and some wrapped sandwiches; daily lunchtime specials include two starters and four main dishes. Children allowed in eating area. Well-kept Taylor-Walker and Ind Coope Burton on handpump; cribbage, fruit machine. As we went to press, there was news of a glass conservatory being built in the back courtyard, mainly for lunchtime diners; there are other attractive marble-topped tables on a very leafy front terrace (one is in a roofed porch).

Open 11 to 3, 5.30 to 11 **Underground** St John's Wood/Maida Vale

Holiday Inn (Swiss Cottage) Map 2

128 King Henry's Road, NW3 *Telephone* 01-722 7711 £££

One of the four Holiday Inns in London, this one is slightly out of the centre, but lacks none of the comforts or opulence that the chain is known for. Quite apart from various luxuries in the bedrooms – trousers presses, individual heating control, underfloor heating in the bathroom – the hotel has a sauna, indoor swimming-pool, a hairdressing salon and everything else you would expect. The coffee shop is open from 10 until 10. The restaurant offers a set meal at £13.75 as well as a *carte*.

Open (Restaurant) 12.30 to 2.30, 6.30 to 10 **Cards** Access, Amex, Diners, Visa
Accommodations 291 rooms, all with bath and shower. B&B £46 to £80 + breakfast (£5.25 to £7.10) **Underground** Swiss Cottage

LONDON

Ladbroke Westmoreland Hotel Map 2

Lodge Road, NW8 *Telephone* 01-722 7722   ££–£££

This modern Hotel would be the choice for cricket fans since it overlooks Lords cricket ground and several of the public rooms take the game and its famous as their theme. Regent's Park is no distance and access to central London is easy. Public rooms are relaxing, bedrooms and bathrooms very well equipped. Amenities include a coffee shop (open 10am to 1 in the morning), and a laundry service. Meals in the Carvery are £10 at lunchtime, £10.50 in the evening.

Open (Carvery) 12.30 to 2.30, 6 to 10 **Cards** Access, Amex, Diners, Visa **Accommodations** 347 rooms, all with bath/shower. B&B £45 to £80 **Underground** St John's Wood/Maida Vale

Ordnance Arms Map 2

29 Ordnance Hill, NW8   £

This friendly little local next door to the barracks is included for its Friday and Saturday night special – real fish and chips done in a way a Yorkshireman would be proud of. The fish is collected each Friday morning from Billingsgate – twelve- or fourteen-ounce cod or haddock fillets. Other bar food, simple stuff, includes sandwiches, toasties, three-egg omelette, basket meals, beef and onion pie and three daily specials such as lasagne or hot-pots, roast lamb or pork, home-cooked gammon with salad or roast beef and Yorkshire pudding; no snacks are served on Saturday evenings or on Sundays; very well-kept Bass and Charrington IPA; fruit machine, piped music and television. Rather a Raj-style decor, with a ceiling fan, high-backed bentwood chairs, stools and some leather Chesterfields on the smart brown patterned carpet; some little walls with bamboo-patterned panels and plants on top divide several booths off from the main part of the bar, and there are Art Deco-style painted glass wall lamps and ceiling lights, and lots of military paintings, diagrams of guns and cannons and even part of a heavy machine gun on the wall; witticisms of the day are chalked up on a board. Live entertainment is provided every second Tuesday. Up three steps is a quieter area and a modern conservatory which doubles as a sitting area or darts room; children are welcome here. A patio area with a barbecue has white or black garden furniture, and there are picnic-table sets out in front by the road.

Open 11 to 3, 5.30 to 11 **Closed** 25 Dec pm **Underground** St John's Wood

SOHO

Alastair Little Map 5

49 Frith Street, W1 *Telephone* 01-734 5183   £££

'Quite simply the best meal I have ever had in the West End. Exhilarating combination of the virtues of *nouvelle cuisine*, first-class fresh ingredients, low fat, good design, with the robustness, simplicity and portions of French country cooking.' These sentences could also describe the thrust of modern British cooking. Alastair Little changes the menu twice a day, which means the dishes lack some of the exactness of his French counterparts, but this is amply compensated for by the vibrance of cooking with the best produce – John Dory, salmon, scallops, brill, sea-bass, and monkfish all draw enthusiastic nominations, as if people have been taken aback to taste such freshness. You could walk past the building without noticing it: the micro blinds in the windows make it look like an office equipment supplier. Inside is bare: plank floors, shiny white walls, a deep Chinese-red lacquer-coloured ceiling reflected in the peppermills on the black tables. The kitchen is visible through a short corridor. The menu is surprisingly long for the style of operation. It draws on all corners of Europe – hard cheeses from England, espresso coffee, pumpernickel bread, foie gras terrine, osso buco with saffron rice. The main courses have the kind of vivid contrasts of flavours so typical of the new cooking – veal is roasted and served cold with a sauce that is just tuna and oil liquidised, and the plate seasoned with anchovies and given fragrance from capers. Other examples of the same principle are grilled salmon served with its roe, cucumber and sea-weed, roast leg of lamb with a confit of garlic and thyme, and boiled fillet of beef with mustard. The raspberry tart is more noticeable for what is not there than for what is – tart berries on thick cream in a nut-brown shortcrust base, but no glaze and no crème pâtissière, as would be found in a good French restaurant, and there is no particular need for them either. Sweets, particularly other tarts of lemon, chocolate, pear and almond, and apricot and almond, draw much praise for this step back into the larder. The chocolate truffle cake, though, 'took up where the foie gras left off'. Twenty-five wines offer a sensible choice from £6.50 to £20, relying almost exclusively on the less-established and better-value regions.

Open Mon to Fri **Closed** Public hols, 3 weeks Aug **Meals** 12.30 to 2.30, 7.30 to 11.15 **Card** Visa **Underground** Leicester Square

---

La Bastide Map 5	✕
50 Greek Street, W1 *Telephone* 01-734 3300	£££

Nicolas Blacklock and Susan Warwick were formerly at D'Artagnan in Blandford Street, which was small and cramped. The new version, air-conditioned, is in a restored Georgian building and sumptuous in peaches and pinks with ruffled, tied-back curtains. There are fixed-price regional French menus (from £12.50), a *carte* and a Soho menu: sometimes there have been more dishes than customers here. The cooking style is sturdy and owes little or nothing to *nouvelle*. Main courses have been good – an intriguing magret of duck in a walnut and lemon sauce the colour of chocolate, a rabbit casserole with prunes with a beautifully intense sauce, and cassoulet. Vegetables are

---

If a service charge is mentioned prominently on a menu or list of accommodations charges, you must pay it if service was satisfactory. If service was really bad you are legally entitled to refuse to pay some or all of the service charge as compensation for not getting the services you might reasonably have expected.

LONDON

top-class, cooked simply, and there are half a dozen French cheeses from Philippe Olivier in Boulogne. Mature clarets avoid the pitfall of all being first-growth, Burgundies are respectable, and, like the menu, the list explores other regions. The south-west is well represented by Jurançon, Cahors and Madiran. No children under eleven.

Open Mon to Sat, exc Sat L **Closed** Public hols **Meals** 12.30 to 2.30, 6 to 11.30 **Cards** Access, Amex, Diners, Visa **Underground** Tottenham Court Road

---

Beotys Map 5

79 St Martin's Lane, WC2 *Telephone* 01-836 8768 £££

A reliable, largely Greek restaurant, often 'better than many places in Greece'. It has become something of a haven of old-fashioned standards in the restaurant scene around Leicester Square. The service is attentive but not fussy, and can produce a pre-theatre meal in an hour without being rushed. The cover charge (80p) is still there, but the napery and table furnishing are good. Rolls, Melba toast and radishes are available. The menu includes continental dishes as well as those found in tavernas. Partridge has featured as a special alongside more familiar dishes such as taramosalata, moussaka, fried kalamarakia (yes, that is baby squid), and excellent whitebait. The quality of the ingredients, from the melon to the liver, gives the cooking a sharp edge. The Greek and Cypriot wines are probably the best value, though house claret is £6.80. Access for wheelchairs. No children under eight.

Open Mon to Sat **Closed** Public hols **Meals** 12 to 2.30, 5.30 to 11.30 **Cards** None accepted **Service** 12½% **Underground** Leicester Square

---

Brewer Street Buttery Map 4

56 Brewer Street, W1 *Telephone* 01-437 7695 £

Spotlessly clean, smart and functional café where the service is exceptionally warm and friendly, and the food as good as Soho can offer at these amazingly low prices. Most daily specials are excellent: roast sausage with vegetables, chicken, rich veal rissoles served with good mashed potatoes and fat peas; the piroshki are enjoyed less. Freshly squeezed juices and Gaggia coffee to drink. Fine pastries to finish.

Open 9 to 6 **Closed** Sat; Sun; public hols **Underground** Piccadilly Circus

---

Café Crêperie Map 5

27 Wardour Street, W1 *Telephone* 01-434 2820 £

There's a good range of sweet and savoury crêpes at this cool eaterie-cum-wine bar. The neat packages are well stuffed with everything from cheese and ham, egg and bacon, or spicy chicken, to rum and banana, chocolate, or pears and ice-cream. Generous side salads. Modern music from the charts.

Open 10am to 1.30am **Underground** Leicester Square

SOHO

Chiang Mai Map 5

48 Frith Street, W1 *Telephone* 01-437 7444   ££

Frith Street is rapidly becoming one of the best streets in London for eating out. As *The Good Food Guide* went to press, a second branch of the Bahn Thai (see Earl's Court) was opening directly opposite this Thai restaurant. Ingredients are authentic, flavours can be elemental: very hot, very sour, very sweet, and not much in between. Thai noodles are reliably good, and so is the soup of chicken, coconut and galanga. The ferocious hot-and-sour bamboo-shoot salad is mollified by crisp iceberg lettuce leaves, and there is spicy beef with Kaffir lime leaves, which have a fragrance not unlike lemon balm or geranium. To finish there are exotic fruits. Note that the cost (£13.95) is based on a meal for two people. Thai beer is a pricey but good match for the food. Music. Children are welcome.

Open All week **Meals** 12 to 3, 6 to 11.30 **Cards** Access, Amex, Diners, Visa **Underground** Leicester Square

Chuen Cheng Ku Map 5

17 Wardour Street, W1 *Telephone* 01-437 1398   £–£££

Dim-sum are served throughout the day until 6 o'clock. The choice is as varied and the dishes as competently cooked as anywhere in London – dumplings, cold roast meats, and copious rice dishes, some stuffed with hot meats. The noodle soups with either roast duck or pork comprise some of the cheapest lunches to be had in the capital. Lobster is also a bargain. The carp with ginger is sold according to weight, richly flavoured with coriander leaves, the sauce viscous, sticky and uncommonly good. More has been spent on the decor outside than in (the lease is running out), and there is a curious taste in muzak which sometimes resembles Shanghai versions of country and western. The place is related to the New World (see below, still in the Soho section). Access for wheelchairs. Children are welcome, of course. The restaurant is licensed, but they don't mind if you bring your own wine (corkage charge £1).

Open All week **Meals** 11 to 11.30 (11.45 Sat, 11 Sun) **Cards** Access, Amex, Diners, Visa **Service** Inc **Underground** Leicester Square

Cork and Bottle Map 5

44–46 Cranbourn Street, WC2 *Telephone* 01-734 7807   ££

Don Hewitson's crowded basement off Leicester Square, especially now that two more smoke-extractors/air-purifiers have been installed, is many people's ideal wine bar. About 150 wines are listed, never the same for long because the list follows the seasons – and the owner's enthusiasms. Quality is high, prices low, and you can try 20 or 30 wines by the quarter-bottle glass (starting with the house AC wines, Sichel's Bel Air Claret and Sauvignon Blanc, £5.75/£1.50). Special loves include Beaujolais, Alsace and Champagne, but New World wines feature too, as well as interesting bottles from Spain, Italy, Germany, the Loire

LONDON

and, of course, Bordeaux and Burgundy. Don't miss the Australian liqueur Muscats either. Imaginative and delicious food: the raised ham and cheese pie is reliably good, and salads remarkable. See also Shampers (below) and Methuselah's (Westminster), owned by the same proprietor.

Open All week **Meals** 11 to 2.45, 5.30 to 10 (12 to 2, 7 to 10.30 Sun) **Closed** Chr Day, Boxing Day, New Year's Day **Cards** Amex, Diners, Visa **Underground** Leicester Square

Cranks Map 4

8 Marshall Street, W1 *Telephone* 01-437 9431   £–££

The name that pioneered London's vegetarian health-food restaurants in Carnaby Street in 1961 now looks set in agar-agar. The ethic that food should be good for you rather than just plain good was fine as far as it went, but we are now conscious that both are possible on the same plate – light, exciting, fresh-tasting ways of cooking that put the well-intentioned steaming wholemeal crumble and cheese-sauce-topped vegetable bake to shame. Even so, the chain cooks fresh every day, takes creditable trouble with its ingredients and offers plenty of variety, both in savoury dishes and in its cakes, breads and puddings. (Branches can also be found in the Covent Garden and Tottenham Court Road sections.)

Open 10 to 11 (8.30pm Mon) **Closed** Sun; public hols **Underground** Oxford Circus

Desaru Map 5

60–62 Old Compton Street, W1 *Telephone* 01-734 4379   ££–£££

Enthusiastic reports have come in thick and fast about this lively restaurant – in fact the only negative comment in over forty is a reference to a stained tablecloth. The place is pleasantly young at heart: the waiters in flashy suits and shirtsleeves greet you almost before you have opened the door. Inside there are two long aisles of tables with turquoise cloths, the walls have mirrors, and the music is Talking Heads and Tina Turner. At one end there's a bamboo beach-hut that serves as the bar; at the other there are views of the kitchen. The menu spans Malaysia and Indonesia with a strong showing of fish and vegetables. Satay – especially the chicken version – is among the best in London: hefty chunks of meat are marinated with restraint to transform rather than overwhelm their natural flavour, then they are grilled so that the pieces are just flecked with charring. Among many dishes enjoyed have been kalio sotong, freshly butchered whirls and coils of squid in a creamy, pale beige coconut sauce, and sambal goreng terong, fried aubergines in a sambal sauce topped with plenty of tiny dried fish. Chillies are used with a free hand in some items, such as French beans with salted yellow beans, which is a neat idea but blisteringly hot. Rice is served on the plate. For a one-dish meal, try nasi ramas, a combination of rice with fried chicken, fish cutlet and various accompaniments. Tiger beer is £1.20; house wine £4.90 a bottle. No under-tens.

Open All week **Meals** 12 to 3, 6 to 11.45 **Cards** Access, Amex, Diners, Visa **Service** 10% **Underground** Leicester Square

SOHO

The Diamond Map 5

23 Lisle Street, WC2 *Telephone* 01-437 2517   £–£££

Despite the excellence of the competition, the Diamond remains a solid, old-fashioned, Chinatown-style Cantonese restaurant, still favoured by many for its value and lack of pretensions. Steamed large prawns in garlic are particularly good, spare ribs have plenty of meat on them, and soups are hot and made with fresh ingredients. Tea is free and oranges come with the bill. No children under five.

Open All week **Meals** 1pm to 2am (noon to 11.30pm Sun) **Cards** None accepted **Service** 10% **Underground** Leicester Square

Dragon Gate Map 5

7 Gerrard Street, W1 *Telephone* 01-734 5154   £££

The musical chairs ownership of this, the first and still the only proper Szechuan restaurant in London, has come full circle. The original owners, who have been running another restaurant, have returned. The dining-room is plainly decorated, with beige walls, framed porcelain pictures and carved Chinese characters denoting longevity, felicity and so on. The menu remains the same with over a hundred dishes, ranging from a cold platter of paper-thin cut pork with chilli sauce to sesame beef, shredded chicken with sesame paste, smoked fish and fiery hot-and-sour soup. The tea-smoked duck, the tripe dishes and the aubergine dishes are reliably excellent. Chang Ta-jian chicken is named after a Chinese painter who emigrated to Brazil after 1949, and authentically should be pieces of chicken with bone and skin still attached, stir fried, but here only the breast is used, which makes it ordinary. Licensed. Music and air-conditioning. Children are welcome.

Open All week **Meals** 12 to 2.15, 5.15 to 11.15 **Cards** Amex, Diners **Service** 10% **Underground** Leicester Square

Equatorial Map 5

37 Old Compton Street, W1 *Telephone* 01-437 6112 and 6093   ££

There are views of the action on Old Compton Street from the ground floor of this simple restaurant that has three floors connected by a red spiral staircase. It is less sleek than Desaru (above) and less of a cafe than the Melati (below), but the style is agreeable. The menu concentrates on Singapore and the Chinese influence is more obvious than in other, similar places. Satay is par for the course and comes with a rich, dark peanut sauce. Noodle dishes, such as meehoon goreng, are reliably good, as are the beef rendang, laksa soup and ayam tempra – sliced chicken breast in a soy-based sauce with onions and chillies. Vegetables are often lightly stir-fried, for example squeakily al dente French beans in a mild shrimp paste sauce. Achar – sweet-pickled vegetables sprinkled with sesame seeds – is a good side dish and, as an alternative to red chilli sauce, the kitchen may provide a dip of finely chopped fresh green chillies

135

LONDON

in soy sauce on request. Excellent rice is served in bowls, not on the plate. Drink Chinese tea or Tiger beer. The set lunch is good value (£4.60). Music; access for wheelchairs.

Open All week **Meals** 12 to 2.45, 6 to 11.15 (noon to 11.30 Sat and Sun) **Cards** Access, Amex, Diners, Visa **Service** 10% **Underground** Leicester Square

---

Frith's Map 5

14 Frith Street, W1 *Telephone* 01-439 3370   £££

The hero of Anthony Burgess's *Earthly Powers* takes his teenage sister to a Soho restaurant called Frith's on the night she discovers his homosexuality via a spare tin leg next to the bed. They ate 'very fair game pie into whose contents it was imprudent to enquire too particularly . . . a tinselly dessert which was really no more than a cleverly disguised bread pudding . . . a bottle of something eeley and alumey and North American with a Pommard label.' Today the decor is all reds for the woodwork, ceiling and blinds, softened by plants, white cloths and a propeller-driven fan. The menu is termed New British Cuisine and is characterised, as one reporter puts it, as 'a lot of unusual taste combinations . . . raw lamb, melon and sour cream . . . baked salmon trout with orange, the little bombs of orange flavour exploded with each mouthful of fish . . . I had cheeses different from anything I'd had before and delicious.' The dexterity of the menu takes in other innovations, for instance this testimony from another report: 'The beautifully presented starter was a warm, baked hollowed-out and skinned cucumber containing an olive and caper filling decorated with strips of radicchio and set on a faintly mustardy cream sauce – we were afraid that, as good as it was, we had strayed into another *nouvelle cuisine* establishment and would go home hungry. But not a bit of it.' Some of the techniques, notably on pastry, let the rest down, but there is no quarrelling with the list of successes – for instance, duck comes as a casserole with Seville oranges or with honey and ginger, and mallard is roasted with cranberries. Vegetables are separately plated and have featured notable carrots in all guises, from mousse to soufflé to sliced. Continuing the style of new British cooking, the set menus (£14 upwards) end with traditional sweets such as apple and rhubarb pudding or double burnt cream, one with chocolate, one without. Cheeses are farmhouse, either English or the finest French from Androuët in Paris. A glass of wine is included in the set price pre-theatre menu; otherwise there is a short list with some rather young clarets and Burgundies. Children's helpings; music; wheelchair access.

Open Mon to Sat, exc Sat L **Meals** 12 to 2.30, 6 to 11.30 **Cards** Access, Amex, Diners, Visa **Underground** Tottenham Court Road

---

Fuji Map 5

36–40 Brewer Street, W1 *Telephone* 01-734 0957   £££

This is the Japan of jeans, bobby socks and videos; short on ceremony if not courtesy – hot towels to wash hands and face arrive before meals, and a glass of plum wine with the fruit salad to finish. The decor is a functional mixture of slats and huge paintings of sloping mountains. The set meals (lunch from £13,

SOHO

dinner from £20) lean towards modern dishes, such as fillet steak of a quality usually found only in top French restaurants. The menu descriptions do not reflect the precision of the kichen as tiny bowl follows tiny bowl brought by waitresses in kimonos. Soups are typically picturesque, the chicken teriyaki succulent, and the arrangements of sushi and shashimi appetising. To drink there is Japanese beer, Carlsberg or saké. Wheelchair access. No children under five.

Open All week, exc Sat L and Sun L **Meals** 12.30 to 2.30, 6 to 10.45 (10.15 Sat and Sun) **Cards** Access, Amex, Diners, Visa **Service** Inc **Underground** Piccadilly Circus

---

Fung Shing Map 5

15 Lisle Street, WC2 *Telephone* 01-437 1539   ££–£££

The Fung Shing was one of the first restaurants in Chinatown to make a concession to Western ideas of eating out by spending money on the dining-room. But the concession has not run to compromising the food, which remains solidly, irrevocably Cantonese, for that is where its heart lies. It may look like a French restaurant, but it is not, and when the place is busy the waiters may ask for your table if other people are waiting. Also it is a place to eat the kind of dishes usually found only where the Chinese eat themselves – eel with coriander, aubergine with prawn, bean curd and scallop soup, winter melon soup. But other dishes are models of what they should be – the soups are magical, from hot-and-sour to beef west lake. A thickly sauced lemon chicken impressed one night, beef with ginger and spring onion another. Fish is reliably excellent. House French is £5.95. Music and air-conditioning. Children are welcome.

Open All week **Meals** Noon to 11.45 **Cards** Access, Amex, Diners, Visa **Service** 10% **Underground** Leicester Square

---

Gay Hussar Map 5

2 Greek Street, W1 *Telephone* 01-437 0973   £££

The Hussar rides on despite Victor Sassie's taking more of a back seat. The food is first-class and survives the decades from the heyday of Hungarian cuisine – excellent fish soup, fish salad, duck with red cabbage, carp quenelles with a rich dill sauce. Zander, baked in a vertical crescent shape, is impressive, as is jellied borshch and – brave, brave kitchen – grilled coley with boiled potatoes. The generosity and the sense of sharing the wonders of a cuisine mark the Hussar as

---

See the back of the Guide for ideas for day trips out of London: Brighton, Cambridge, Canterbury, Oxford, and Windsor and Eton.

The London subway, called the underground or tube, is the best in the world – clean, fast, efficiently laid out and exceptionally well signposted. A ticket may be purchased at a ticket office at tube stations or, if you have the correct change, at a machine in the station. Hold on to your ticket until the end of your journey, when it will be collected at the exit. You won't be bored waiting for your train – the platform advertisements are usually many, varied, literate and fun to read.

137

LONDON

one of the great London restaurants of the post-war era. Where else in London is it possible to have properly cooked grouse at lunch for £10, including starters and sweet? The bread is fresh, and there is no skimping with the enormous wedges brought to the table for the cheese course with a jug full of fresh celery, radishes, and spring onions. Coffee is strong and aromatic. Reports of Mr Sassie's retirement appear to have been rather premature: he is at the restaurant most days, at least in the mornings. Unflurried pre-theatre meals start as early as 5.30pm. Set dinners cost from £15. The Hungarian wines provide the major interest, but there are also vintage clarets at reasonable prices. Air-conditioning; access for wheelchairs. Children's helpings at lunch.

Open Mon to Sat **Meals** 12.30 to 2, 5.30 to 10.30 **Cards** None accepted **Underground** Tottenham Court Road

Govinda's Map 5

9 Soho Street, W1 *Telephone* 01-437 3662   £

The Krishna Consciousness Society runs this largely wholefood restaurant next door to their temple in sight of Oxford Street. The food is served canteen-style and is cheap – £5 goes a long way. The range of dishes changes regularly and conforms to international ideas of vegetarian food: couscous and vegetables, and Moroccan hot-pot, for example. Desserts come with plenty of cream and sugar. Main dishes tend to be reliable, though salads can be tired and savouries inclined to stodge. Herb teas; unlicensed. Children's helpings. Access for wheelchairs; air-conditioning; music; no smoking.

Open All week **Closed** Christmas, Easter **Meals** 11.30 to 8 (9 Fri, noon to 9 Sat, noon to 3.30 Sun) **Cards** None accepted **Underground** Tottenham Court Road

Grahame's Seafare Map 4

38 Poland Street, W1 *Telephone* 01-437 3788 and 0975   ££

The fish for this Jewish restaurant is delivered from Billingsgate daily and is then usually fried. The smoked salmon is a famous speciality, too. Service is friendly and efficient. Perhaps the best-value bolt-hole in the vicinity of Oxford Circus. House Frascati is £5.20. Vegetarian meals; children's helpings. Access for wheelchairs; air-conditioning.

Open Mon to Sat, exc Mon D **Meals** 12 to 2.45, 5.30 to 8.45 (7.45 Fri) **Cards** Amex, Visa **Underground** Oxford Circus

Han Kuk Hoe Kwan Map 4

2 Lowndes Court, Carnaby Street, W1 *Telephone* 01-437 3313   £

There is a £3 lunch at this Korean restaurant which is both good value and an interesting introduction to the cooking. Otherwise, choose carefully from the long menu and it is possible to eat well but inexpensively on dishes such as spinach soup with bean curd, and fried vegetables with beef, shrimps and fish-cake. Rice is served in a stainless steel lidded dish, and bulgogi – Korea's most famous dish of sliced beef – is cooked at the table on a flat ribbed pan. The waitresses instruct in wrapping meats with rice and sauce in a lettuce leaf. Some things are fiery hot, notably the pickled cabbage condiment.

Open Noon to 2.30 (3 Sun), 6 to 11 **Underground** Oxford Circus

Hokkai Map 4

59–61 Brewer Street, W1 *Telephone* 01-734 5826   ££–£££

Brewer Street has become a little Japan in recent years. There are now three restaurants as well as the Japan Services Travel Centre. This is like a Japanese country restaurant. What is unusual about it is that as well as the competently handled *carte* there is also a daily menu that is, quite exceptionally, available to non-Japanese-speaking customers (lunch ranges from £6.50 to £14.50, dinner from £13.50 to £17.50). Featured are a range of innovative dishes using Western ingredients in a Japanese way – for example, avocado is scooped out of its shell, chopped, mixed with wasabi, vinegar, mayonnaise, and sesame oil, put back, and topped with two heaps of roes, one red, one black. The atmosphere is relaxed, and most Japanese eat here for pleasure rather than for business. Wheelchair access; air-conditioning; music. Children's helpings.

Open Mon to Sat **Closed** Public hols **Meals** 12.30 to 2.30, 6 to 10.30 **Cards** Access, Amex, Diners, Visa **Service** 10% **Underground** Piccadilly Circus

Joy King Lau Map 5

3 Leicester Street, WC2 *Telephone* 01-437 1132   ££–£££

A successful mixture of East and West. Mirrors on the walls confuse as to quite which bits are which, but the overall effect is one of sharpness. It is smart enough for customers to wear suits, though it is not necessary. The menu is impressively extensive, with sub-divisions for noodles and bean-curd dishes as well as the more obvious beef and chicken ones. Dim-sum have to be ordered from the menu but they are freshly steamed and there is no holding back with the spicing. A short list also of Chinese dishes frustratingly in Chinese characters has included fine braised eel with garlic, black mushrooms and roast belly-pork served in a clay pot. The quality of the meats, for instance in Cantonese-style steak, is high. Sea-bass has been reliably good, but Dover sole, though neatly filleted, tends to be overpowered by black-bean sauce and has also been overcooked. House wine is £4.50. Music; wheelchair access. Children are welcome.

Open All week **Meals** 11 to 11.20 (10.30 to 10.20 Sun) **Cards** Amex, Carte Blanche, Diners **Service** 12½% **Underground** Leicester Square

Kettners Map 5

29 Romilly Street, W1 *Telephone* 01-437 6437 and 734 6112   ££

For around £5 a head it is just possible to drink Champagne and eat in one of London's great dining-rooms – luxury on a shoestring, in fact. In thirty years

LONDON

Kettners' dining-room has not changed. There is no muzak; but there is sometimes a pianist in the bar. The restaurant is still spacious, old-fashioned and only the food has changed: it is part of the excellent Pizza Express chain. The decor comes out only slightly more expensive than at other branches. The pizzas are Italian in style, freshly baked and liberally covered with a permutation of better-than-usual ingredients. There are steaks and hamburgers too, while the champagne bar stocks no fewer than twenty-five kinds of bubbly. Wheelchair access. Children welcome.

Open All week **Closed** Christmas Day **Meals** 11 to midnight **Cards** Access, Amex, Diners, Visa **Underground** Leicester Square

Last Days of the Raj Map 5

42–43 Dean Street, W1 *Telephone* 01-439 0972 ££

The original Last Days of the Raj, in Drury Lane, seemed to be on its last legs in 1985 but Amin Ali's empire is striking back, and his latest venture in Dean Street promises a great deal. The style is lavish and dramatic, backed up by service that tries very hard to be helpful. Much of the cooking is in the Lal Qila mould (see Tottenham Court Road), with good early reports of the subtly spiced rogan josh and chicken makhain, sag, and tandoori chicken. Fried Basmati rice has been as expertly cooked as any in London. Vegetarian dishes; children's helpings. Music; wheelchair access; air-conditioning.

Open All week **Closed** 25, 26 Dec **Meals** 12 to 3, 6 to 11.30 **Cards** Access, Amex, Diners, Visa **Service** 15% **Underground** Leicester Square

Man Fu Kung Map 4

Leicester Square, WC2 *Telephone* 01-839 4146 £

Emporium-style Chinese restaurant where the inexpensive lunchtime dim-sum snacks are wheeled in a procession of trolleys round the room. Outside is a helpful illustrated menu in colour. Sometimes a dim-sum stall is set up from which you can buy to eat in the street. From the main menu, a dish of pig's intestines rates highly with people who like such things. Much used by London Chinese.

Open 9am to 1am **Underground** Leicester Square

Mayflower Map 5

68–70 Shaftesbury Avenue, W1 *Telephone* 01-734 9207 ££–£££

The Mayflower has some of the best Cantonese food in Chinatown. It is usually necessary to wait for a table, even if you have booked, and sometimes the service is begrudging. The compensation is to be found in belly-pork with sweet plums, the speciality of deep-fried duck with yams, and triumphant lemon chicken. Fish is as excellent as might be expected in a restaurant of this calibre – steamed scallops, fried squid, seafood soup. There are also subtly flavoured bean curd dishes, such as fried spinach with fermented bean curd, which illustrates the

SOHO

point that this is still very much a restaurant that puts Chinese customers first. House French is a pricey £6.80. Music and air-conditioning.

Open All week **Closed** 25 and 26 Dec **Meals** Noon to 3.30am **Cards** Access, Amex, Diners, Visa **Service** 10% **Underground** Piccadilly Circus

Melati Map 5

21 Great Windmill Street, W1 *Telephone* 01-437 2745   ££–£££

A popular Malay café serving dishes that to the uninitiated will sometimes appear quite bizarre, for instance es kacang, a pudding of red beans, mixed fruit and jelly-like syrup, or the chef's special of fish head curry. The standard Malay dishes are there, too – an excellent sup Santan (coconut soup with chicken), satay, nasigoreng, and Singapore laksa, a meal in itself. The waiters are always ready to help and offer suggestions. Vegetarian dishes are starred on the menu, and as well as cocktails they offer Tiger beer and fruit juices, often a better choice with the highly spiced food. Music. Children are welcome.

Open All week **Meals** Noon to 11.30pm (1am Fri and Sat) **Cards** Access, Amex, Diners, Visa **Underground** Piccadilly Circus

Ming Map 5

35–36 Greek Street, W1 *Telephone* 01-734 2721   ££–£££

Until summer 1986 this was the Kaliwah; now the name means 'bright' or 'enlightened'. The light from the windows on two sides certainly makes the dining-room airy. The chef is from Shantung and it is to be hoped that he will bring more and more northern Chinese dishes into the repertoire. At the time of opening the menu was split between Canton and Peking. The starters, such as cold platter of sliced beef, jellyfish with shredded duck, and smoked fish, tend to the north, but an interesting new dish of sizzling veal with the bones still attached is an idea imported from a Hong Kong restaurant. Outstanding are the bean-curd skin rolls (bean-curd skin is one of the most sought-after ingredients, even in Hong Kong, as each sheet has to come off a simmering cauldron of soy-bean milk) filled with bean sprouts, Chinese mushrooms and shrimps. To finish there has been another northern dish – pancakes stuffed with red-bean paste. House wine is £5.50. Access for wheelchairs; air-conditioning; music.

Open All week **Meals** Noon to midnight **Cards** Access, Amex, Diners, Visa **Underground** Leicester Square

Safety tip: the British drive on the left-hand side of the road, so be very careful crossing busy streets. Look first to your right before stepping off the kerb.

Taxi tips: London taxi drivers are famous for their wide knowledge of their city and for their courtesy. But note that they can refuse to take you to your destination if it is after midnight, your destination is more than seven miles from the centre of London, you have more luggage than they deem necessary, or if you are not in a fit state to travel. If you wish, you can ask your hotel to ring one up for you.

LONDON

Mr Kong Map 5

21 Lisle Street, WC2 *Telephone* 01-437 7341   ££

Mr Kong is virtually a carbon copy of the Fung Shing a few doors up. The decor is shipshape, the menu Cantonese with some flamboyant touches, such as fine casseroles and potato nests for shellfish. Fish is a strong point. Meals end with oranges or slices of water-melon. House French is £4.50. Vegetarian dishes. Music.

Open All week **Closed** Christmas **Meals** Noon to 1.45am **Cards** Access, Amex, Diners, Visa **Service** 10% **Underground** Leicester Square

Mr Tang Map 5

61–63 Shaftesbury Avenue, W1 *Telephone* 01-734 4488 and 5001   ££–£££

One school of thought regards this upstairs restaurant overlooking Shaftesbury Avenue as among the best in Chinatown. It is of the old style, with dim decor and a long, authentic menu, and is essentially somewhere to explore Cantonese cooking. The soups, such as wun-tun and hot-and-sour, are potent. Also good are beef in a pot, lemon chicken baked with honey, and minced quail wrapped in lettuce. Dim-sum are ordered from the menu rather than chosen from trolleys. When the Chinese oil legation held a banquet at the Dorchester it was Bill Tang who supplied. There are good wines, if you have a mind to stray from tea or the house wine at £5.70. Vegetarian meals; children's helpings. Air-conditioning; music.

Open All week **Meals** Noon to midnight **Cards** Access, Amex, Diners, Visa **Service** 10% **Underground** Piccadilly Circus

Nam Long Map 5

40 Frith Street, W1 *Telephone* 01-439 1835 and 434 3772   ££

The board outside says the restaurant is Vietnamese, but in fact the cooking is south-east Asian taking in Thai, Vietnamese, Cambodian, and Chinese – very much in the modern fashion, in fact, including American and European influences. This is an interesting little restaurant in any language. The decor, with expensive washed wallpaper, a tiled floor, intriguing deep-coloured food prints and classical music, is affluent. On each table sit chopstick rests in the shape of white china oxen or other animals. Sizzling dishes, served in ornate grid-irons set in varnished wood are beautifully arranged – for instance, chunks of very good quality beef in garlic and chilli are surrounded by large red slices of giant tomato. Viet spring rolls arrive with leaves of lettuce and mint to roll up and dip in chilli oil. On the same principle is sliced pork with garlic and shredded peanuts and chilli for rolling in rice paper with noodles and cucumber. Rice and noodle dishes are both good. Service is first-class. House Blanc de Blancs is £4.95. No children under seven.

Open Mon to Sat **Meals** 12 to 2.30, 6 to 11 **Cards** Access, Visa **Service** 10% **Underground** Leicester Square

SOHO

National Gallery Map 4

Trafalgar Square, WC2 *Telephone* 01-930 5210   £

A light, airy restaurant making a creditable attempt to offer real food at modest prices in cheerful, spotless surroundings. Good choices from the blackboard menu have included spinach roulade, moussaka, coronation chicken, and salads such as kidney bean and celery, bean sprout, or cauliflower. Justin de Blank has now settled in as the caterer here, so his famous sausages are available too. Finish with fine fridge cake, rich chocolate and cream cake or lemon mousse. Fresh fruit juices, mineral water, wine or beer to drink.

Open 10 (2 Sun) to 5 **Closed** Christmas Eve to Boxing Day; 1 Jan; public hols **Underground** Charing Cross/Leicester Square

New World Map 5

Gerrard Place, W1 *Telephone* 01-734 0677   £–££

The dim-sum trolleys are wheeled around this cavernous, canteen-like emporium on three floors throughout the day. There is seating for 550, so the queues are not long even on a Sunday when the Chinese arrive in force. The trolleys work in convoys – the first two with steamed dumplings, one with the emphasis on Western tastes with pork, shrimp, and shark's fin dumplings (spare ribs in dim-sum are knuckles steamed with black beans, not the whole rib with a sweet-and-sour sauce), the second on Eastern tastes for ducks' webs, and winkles with chilli. The steamed pieces of chicken wrapped in bean curd are excellent. After these two come other trolleys, one with noodle soups and barbecued meats, another with a more porridge-like gruel. Cheung-fun gets its own trolley; the steamed rice-flour rolls are filled either with pork, beef or shrimp, while a different trolley will fry them along with stuffed peppers. For rice, which is not crucial to dim-sum, there are little covered pots topped with spare ribs or else fat squares of lotus leaves filled with rice and glutinous and assorted meats. On the cold trolley are fried wun-tuns, which are served with a dollop of sweet-and-sour sauce, or woo-kok, deep-fried taro vegetable puffs with a texture akin to Shredded Wheat. Best of all, perhaps, are the plates of cold roast meats – lacquered duck (usually with the bones, which are an important component of the cuisine), suckling pig with excellent crackling, or a smooth, cream-white chicken. The custard tarts are sublime, though some of the other desserts are an acquired taste. Each basket is around £1 and you just point to the ones you fancy. Tea is free, which can make it an amazingly inexpensive feast. Apart from dim-sum, there is also a long Cantonese menu, which is less exceptional than at some of the excellent Chinese restaurants in this area, although it is notable for doing very inexpensive lobster dishes. Access for wheelchairs. Children are welcome.

Open All week **Meals** 11 to 11.45 (11 Sun) **Cards** Access, Amex, Diners, Visa **Service** Inc **Underground** Leicester Square

---

As well as picking out tea shops in their own right, the tea shop symbol denotes that afternoon tea is available to non-residents in hotels.

143

LONDON

Old Budapest Map 5 �

6 Greek Street, W1 *Telephone* 01-437 2006 ££–£££

As the proprietor says: 'There is a chronic shortage of Hungarian chefs in London.' There aren't that many Hungarian restaurants either. Two are here in Greek Street. The chef, Mr Tyak, is doing a good job promoting his national cuisine, just a few doors away from his old home, the Gay Hussar (see above). The decor is folksy and rustic, and the cuisine tends towards hearty regional fare: thick bean soups, pancakes stuffed with goulash, and pressed boar's head with horseradish. Cold cherry soup, matyas herring with apple-cream sauce, or cucumber salad are lighter and worth trying. The grilled meats tend to be tough. The sweet cheese and the walnut pancakes are delicious. There is a good selection of Hungarian wines. Vegetarian meals. No children under ten. Music; air-conditioning; access for wheelchairs.

Open Mon to Sat **Meals** 12 to 3, 6 to 11 **Cards** Access, Amex, Visa **Underground** Tottenham Court Road

Olive Tree Map 5 �

11 Wardour Street, W1 *Telephone* 01-734 0808 £

Middle Eastern restaurant near Leicester Square with a complete vegetarian menu as well as meat dishes such as kebabs. It is possible to eat quite a lot for under £5: a heaped plate of mixed salads comes to around £1.70, pasta and Greek-style dishes also feature, and there are a few specialities from further east.

Open 11 to 11.30 (10 Sun and public hols) **Closed** Christmas Day D **Underground** Leicester Square

Il Passetto Map 4 �

230 Shaftesbury Avenue, WC2 *Telephone* 01-836 9391 £££

Behind the Shaftesbury Theatre, near an umbrella shop, this trattoria seems to be nothing out of the ordinary – and yet it is probably now the best of all the West End Italian restaurants. The food is carefully prepared and imaginative – an array of cold starters includes stuffed mushrooms and tomato and Mozzarella salad, and eight or nine other dishes are generously spread out on large trays. Artichokes have been served hot, filled with an anchovy and garlic stuffing. Pasta dishes have been excellent, notably the tagliatellini, the cannelloni, and also the risotto. Fish is consistently well reported. Sweets are conventional but, like everything else, freshly done, and there is plenty of coffee. House Soave or Valpolicella is £4.95. Access for wheelchairs; air-conditioning. Children are welcome.

Open Mon to Sat, exc Sat L **Meals** 12 to 3, 6 to 11.30 **Cards** Access, Amex, Diners, Visa **Underground** Tottenham Court Road

If you are planning a trip to Scotland and the Lake District, there is another Guide in this series to those areas.

SOHO

Poons Map 5

4 Leicester Street, WC2 *Telephone* 01-437 1528 £–££

Of the many great restaurants in Chinatown, Poons distinguished itself as the place to eat wind-dried meats. Sausages and whole ducks hang in the window and are perhaps the finest to be had in the country. The decor is monochromatic and shiny, the service efficiently bullish and the long menu contains the full range of Cantonese cooking. Booking does not always guarantee a table on the dot. If the queue is long the alternative is to go to the old premises in Lisle Street. There is no decor whatsoever there, but the food is cheap. House wine is £4. Children are welcome. Air-conditioning.

Open Mon to Sat **Closed** 25 Dec **Meals** Noon to 11.30 **Cards** None accepted **Underground** Leicester Square

Red Fort Map 5

77 Dean Street, W1 *Telephone* 01-437 2525, 2410 and 2115 ££–£££

Perfume hangs in the air and the pace never quickens at this elegantly laid out ground-floor Indian dining-room with a feeling of light and space. The kitchen works best when it is in familiar territory; both the gently spiced chicken makhani and chicken korahi – pointed up with strips of fresh ginger and coriander – have been excellent. Tarka dhal tastes more strongly of lentils than most versions, and new potatoes are cooked in their skins with fenugreek. The short menu has a few recent additions, with masha (an onion stuffed with spicy beans) and momo (Indian-style dumplings). Alas, the cocktails are rather better than the bread. Music; air-conditioning. Children's helpings only at weekends.

Open All week **Closed** 25 and 26 Dec **Meals** 12 to 2.30, 6 to 11.30 **Cards** Access, Amex, Diners, Visa **Service** 15% **Underground** Tottenham Court Road

Rendezvous Snack Bar, Swiss Centre Map 5

Leicester Square, W1 *Telephone* 01-734 1291 £–££

This massive trade centre has four eating places inside. The Rendezvous is the snack bar; Swiss misses lead you, and the murals when you get there are Swiss-style, Yellow Submarine-ish renderings of cows and yodellers. Main courses are the likes of frankfurters and potato salad, rösti potatoes covered with Emmenthal, ham and egg, or burgers including one with spinach and cheese. A good place to take children. Drinks are pricey. The cowbells outside that ring at noon, 4 and 8 o'clock are good fun.

Open Noon to midnight **Closed** Christmas Eve and Christmas Day **Underground** Leicester Square

---

The bathroom is not a 'john' in Britain, nor is it necessarily a bathroom. Ask for the lavatory, toilet or loo in private homes, or a cloakroom or ladies or gents in a restaurant or theatre.

LONDON

Rodos Map 4   ✕

59 St Giles High Street, WC2 *Telephone* 01-836 3177   ££

Loucas Savvides and his family have been running this West End Greek restaurant for more than 15 years. Meze (£10.45 per head) is a spectacular array of up to 15 dishes, from hummus and grilled haloumi to quail in butter with wine and lemon, and red mullet. Hot pitta bread is replenished throughout the meal and to round things off there's yoghurt, fresh dates, or Turkish delight.

Open Noon to 2.30, 5.30 to 11.30 **Closed** Sat L; Sun **Underground** Tottenham Court Road

Royal Trafalgar Thistle Hotel Map 4   🏨 ✕

Whitcomb Street, WC2 *Telephone* 01-930 4477   £–£££

This modern hotel is two minutes' walk from the National Gallery, the National Portrait Gallery (which has a really good stock of postcards) and Trafalgar Square in one direction, and the cinemas of Leicester Square and the theatres of Shaftesbury Avenue in the other. Yet it is a quiet place, with comfortable half-bedrooms-half-sitting-rooms, highly modern bathrooms and sophisticated public rooms, with 24-hour lounge service.

Open (Restaurant) 12 to 11.30 **Cards** Access, Amex, Diners, Visa **Accommodations** 108 rooms, all with bath/shower. B&B £42.50 to £75 **Underground** Piccadilly Circus

Saigon Map 5   ✕

45 Frith Street, W1 *Telephone* 01-437 7109   ££–£££

In the space of less than thirty yards, two restaurants claim to offer Vietnamese food. The other, the Nam Long, is written up above, but this one specialises exclusively in the cuisine. A black handwritten name-plate is on the wall by the entrance steps. Inside there is a feeling of space, whereas in reality there is little – like a nightclub, in fact, with a little hut of a bar, bamboo pillars, fans, black cane chairs, wooden floors . . . The menu is a long strip of paper stuck to a wooden board. The waitresses are unnerving, remembering orders without writing anything down, and quick to help with dishes such as Vietnamese duck, a variation on Peking duck using instead of pancakes rice paper which needs soaking in hot water to make it flexible enough for rolling up the meat with slices of cucumber, mint and coriander. The cooking is set apart from Chinese by unexpected combinations of tastes and textures, and also different ingredients. Herbs are used much more in the European way – peppermint with

---

The British railway system is exceptionally good, with modern, clean and fast trains. For long trips, first class is preferable to second class for privacy and comfort. If you do not buy your tickets in advance, allow at least 30 minutes to get them at the station. London has many termini serving different parts of the United Kingdom – Charing Cross, Paddington, St Pancras, Liverpool Street, King's Cross, Euston, Waterloo, Victoria, Marylebone and others – so make sure you know where your train leaves from.

SOHO

sliced fish, lemon grass with lamb. Intriguing starters are the deep-fried squid-cakes with iceberg lettuce for wrapping them up with more coriander and a dip of chilli, lemon and garlic, or the mashed prawn kebabs on a stick of sugar cane. Of the specialities, barbecued beef makes a fine centrepiece for two. Rice is boiled. The wine list is elementary or there is Tiger beer at a steep £1.50. Tea is Chinese and served in unglazed earthenware pots with matching cups. Children are welcome. Music.

Open Mon to Sat **Closed** Public hols **Meals** Noon to 11.30 **Cards** Access, Amex, Diners, Visa **Service** 10% **Underground** Leicester Square

Satay and Wine Map 5

10 Old Compton Street, W1 *Telephone* 01-437 3950   £

Malay restaurant-cum-wine bar specialising in satay; varieties include liver, heart, gizzard, scallop, and squid. The accompanying peanut or black sauces can also be taken away to use at home. Other dishes include smoked clams on toast, soft-shell crabs, and Assam ribs. The set meal for two people is £16.

Open Noon to 11.30 **Closed** Sun **Underground** Leicester Square/Tottenham Court Road

Shampers Map 4

4 Kingly Street, W1 *Telephone* 01-437 1692   ££

A cheerful relative of the Cork & Bottle (see above) wih the endearing family trait of boundless enthusiasm and the same varied and interesting wine list at reasonable prices. Watch out for the special offers and events throughout the year. Imaginative buffet, including some vegetarian items, still well stocked late in the evening. Stick to the ground floor rather than the self-service basement if you are unsure of foot.

Open Mon to Sat **Closed** Sat evening, Sun, Easter, Chr Day, Boxing Day **Meals** 11 to 3, 5.30 to 11 (Sat 11 to 3) **Cards** All accepted **Underground** Oxford Circus/Piccadilly Circus

Soho Brasserie Map 5

23–25 Old Compton Street, W1 *Telephone* 01-439 9301   £££

The discouraging outside gives way to the sound of a genuine brasserie – the hiss of the espresso coffee machine, the babble of voices, the chink of glass on glass, crockery on tile, the electrical whir of the cash register, the clunk of cutlery hitting other cutlery in a tray somewhere. The front bar with tables, where it is possible to get a snack, is separated by large engraved-glass partitions from the restaurant proper. Both sides seem to benefit from this, the restaurant getting the bar's informality. The staff wear white shirts, black ties and have short haircuts. Food is true to the brasserie-style too: warm salad of cabbage with bacon and an oil/herb vinaigrette with some good French bread and lactic butter and a couple of *pression* beers for £3.50. Smashing. There are lamb sausages with horseradish sauce, and good fish – nicely undercooked turbot in a creamy leek sauce, monkfish with fennel sauce, and fat juicy mussels. Vegetables may be

147

LONDON

no more complicated than green beans, turnip cubes and crunchy carrots, and puddings as plain as apricot tart or fromage blanc with fruit purée, but the quality of the cooking always surprises. One of the wine list's most pleasing wines is Sauvignon du Haut-Poitou 1984, £7.45. Vegetarian meals. Music; wheelchair access; air-conditioning. Children are welcome.

Open Mon to Sat **Meals** 10am to 11.30pm **Cards** Access, Amex, Diners, Visa **Underground** Leicester Square

---

Star Map 5

22 Great Chapel Street, W1 *Telephone* 01-437 8778   £

Indeed a star, in that it serves some of the best breakfasts and cheap non-ethnic food in central London. The wood panelling, bistro trappings, decor of old metal signs for Robin cigarettes and Gold Flake, and the wry charm of the ladies serving, add up to a very special atmosphere. Lunch might be a roast with fine accompanying vegetables, or pasta packed with chunks of seafood, and rhubarb crumble like Mother used to make. There is a wide range of sandwiches and snacks too. The palm tree on this island is the low cost.

Open 7am to 5pm **Closed** Sat and Sun; public hols **Underground** Tottenham Court Road

---

Taffgood's Map 5

128 Wardour Street, W1 *Telephone* 01-437 3286   £

Delicatessen and sandwich bar specialising in smoked salmon and home-cooked fresh meats. The brown, wholewheat or rye bread sandwiches run from salt beef to Torbay crab. There are baps of ripe Brie and salad, veal cutlet with cheese and salad, bagels with chopped liver, and lox with cream cheese.

Open 8.30am to 5pm **Closed** Sat and Sun; public hols **Underground** Piccadilly Circus

---

Wong Kei Map 5

41–43 Wardour Street, W1 *Telephone* 01-437 3071 and 6833   £

Once a wig-maker's, as the handsome clock outside reveals, but now a Cantonese emporium, and among all of them in Chinatown this one's claim for inclusion here is that it is probably the cheapest. Set lunch starts at £1.10. The four floors have even less decor than its rivals, but on the ground floor, by the window, chefs are surrounded by wind-dried foods, ducks, and freshly made noodles. The long menu includes inexpensive soups and noodle dishes. Children are welcome.

Open All week **Meals** Noon to 11.30 **Cards** None accepted **Service** Inc **Underground** Piccadilly Circus

---

You are unlikely to be able to pay by credit card for bar snacks at pubs or at the cheaper places in this Guide. Credit cards are usually accepted in restaurants including those in pubs which serve more formal meals.

SOUTH BANK

Woodlands Map 4

37 Panton Street, SW1 *Telephone* 01-839 7258   ££

The menus here and at the Marylebone branch (and at the one in Wembley – not included in this *Guide*) are the same and the standards are almost on a par with the other main Gujerati places in London. The southern Indian vegetarian repertoire takes in dosas, iddlies, samosas, bhajis and vadors, which are subtly and distinctively spiced. Breads and rice are first-rate and there are three good-value thalis (from £6), including a cut-price express version for a quick snack. Lassi comes salt or sweet. Service is keen and polite. Music; air-conditioning.

Open All week **Meals** 12 to 3, 6 to 10.30 **Cards** Access, Amex, Diners, Visa **Service** 12½% **Underground** Piccadilly Circus

Yung's Map 5

23 Wardour Street, W1 *Telephone* 01-734 4566   ££–£££

The decor is dark green and bamboo. The cooking is Cantonese and therefore seafood is a strongpoint – steamed scallops in a ginger and soy sauce, and squid in black-bean and chilli sauce. Of other dishes that impress has been beef in a clay pot. Braised duck with greens is not to be recommended. Orange segments arrive unprompted. Wheelchair access. Children are welcome.

Open All week **Meals** Noon to 4am **Cards** Access, Amex, Diners, Visa **Service** 10% **Underground** Piccadilly Circus

SOUTH BANK

Archduke Map 2

Concert Hall Approach (off Belvedere Road), SE1   ££
Telephone 01-928 9370

Tucked under the railway arches is this high-tech, multi-level wine bar and restaurant offering some fine drinking and a choice of four sorts of sausage in the evening – perhaps Justin de Blank's award-winning banger, Cumberland, smoked Bavarian, and Italian with fennel. The Archduke Trio slaps one each of three of these on to your plate with potatoes and salad. Reasonable wines. The place is extremely well placed for the South Bank arts complex, and there is live jazz at night, and an outdoor terrace. Tables are close together and you may have to share.

Open 11 to 3, 5.30 to 11 **Closed** Sat L; Sun; public hols **Underground** Waterloo

---

Driving advice: when you approach a roundabout (a circular traffic hub), always give priority to the driver coming from the right. 'Give way' in Britain means 'yield', and 'Have you paid and displayed?' signs indicate that you should get a parking ticket from a nearby machine and display it prominently on your windscreen (windshield). If you don't, you may be fined.

LONDON

Cooke's Eel and Pie Shop Map 2

84 The Cut, SE1 *Telephone* 01-928 5931   £

Busy little place a few minutes' walk from Waterloo Station. There are white tiles on the walls, plain bench seats and an area at the back of the shop where the eels are kept in metal drawers. Most people seem to come for the minced beef pies, but the eels are the attraction for connoisseurs. The fish is fresh and succulent, the mash good and the liquor well flavoured with parsley and not too glutinous. Jellied eels are also available. It is the custom to put your empty plate or bowl on the counter as you leave. Because the food is cheap and nourishing and the shop is unlicensed, it's a popular family eating place. Take-aways.

Open 10.30 to 3 (3.30 Fri and Sat) **Closed** Public hols; 2 weeks July **Underground** Waterloo

Hole in the Wall Map 2

Mepham Street, SE1   £

Every so often things really do shake in the main bar here as a train rumbles over: the dark brown brick ceiling is in fact a railway arch virtually underneath Waterloo Suburban Station. The well-kept real ales on handpump include Adnams, Brakspears SB, Burke's Best, Chudleys, Godsons Black Horse, King and Barnes, Ruddles Best and County and Youngs Ordinary and Special, reasonably priced for the area. They also keep Murphys as well as Guinness stout. A good range of amusements includes a juke box, two fruit machines and two space games, and the furnishings are very basic. Bar food includes filled baps, ploughman's, chilli con carne and steak and kidney pie.

Open 11 to 3, 5.30 to 11 **Closed** 25 Dec **Underground** Waterloo

Ovations Map 2

National Theatre, South Bank, SE1 *Telephone* 01-928 2033   ££

Restaurants in theatre complexes should be about quick service, acceptable food and reasonable prices. The meal, after all, is not the main event of the evening. This place – with views over the Thames at one end and the bustle of the Lyttleton foyer at the other – entirely fits the bill. A small à la carte menu is supplemented by a three-course supper for £7.95. The menu is advertised as 'changing with the repertoire'.

Open 12.15 to 3, 5.30 to 12.30 **Closed** Sun **Underground** Waterloo

Royal Festival Hall Map 2

South Bank, SE1 *Telephone* 01-928 3246   £

At this cultural centre there are coffee and pastries, a reasonable salad bar with smoked chicken and quiche, but most notable of all the Salt Beef Bar, the beef carved in front of you, placed on rye bread with mustard and gherkin and

SOUTH KENSINGTON

garnished with tomato and lettuce. The pasta stall is popular but hot meals in the big café downstairs on the ground floor have been disappointing. What with the wine bar, free foyer recitals, shops and so on, there is hardly any reason to leave.

Open Noon to 8 **Closed** 6pm Christmas Eve to 6pm Boxing Day **Underground** Waterloo

RSJ Map 2

13A Coin Street, SE1 *Telephone* 01-928 4554   £££

Apart from being the only long-standing restaurant to survive in the hinterland of the South Bank, RSJ, named after its reinforced steel joist, is also one of the more popular restaurants with *Good Food Guide* readers. The value is good. The starkness of the decor is relieved by wall hangings and fresh flowers. The menu has ten or so choices at each course. Lamb is a surgical tour de force, boned and carved into a fleur de lys served with the kidney carved in a similar shape. Fish is well handled in ambitious dishes, such as sea-bass with a lettuce mousseline. Vegetables are served on a separate plate and sweets are a decorous assemblage of French-style mousses, pralines and parfaits. There is no pressure on you to leave, even if you eat late, say, after the theatre. The wine list concentrates on excellent-value Loire wines and is worth exploring. House wine is £6.45. Wheelchair access; air-conditioning. Children's helpings.

Open Mon to Sat, exc Sat L **Closed** 3 days at Christmas **Meals** 12 to 2, 6 to 11 **Cards** Access, Amex, Visa **Service** 10% **Underground** Waterloo

SOUTH KENSINGTON

Anglesea Arms Map 3

15 Selwood Terrace, SW7   £

With Adnams, Boddingtons, Brakspears, Fullers London Pride, Greene King Abbot and Youngs well-kept on handpump, this popular and spacious pub gets very busy in the evenings and at weekends – when even the outside terrace (which has seats and tables) tends to overflow into the quiet side street. The main bar has faded Turkey carpets on the bare wood-strip floor, big central elbow tables, and leather Chesterfields against wood panelling at one end and under the big windows – which have attractive swagged curtains. Several partly glazed screens make booths for cushioned pews and spindleback chairs at the other end. It's decorated with big brass chandeliers and wall lights with green or red lampshades, prints of London, some heavy portraits, a big station clock, and bits of brass and pottery. The atmosphere is relaxed and cheery; down some steps there's a small carpeted room with captain's chairs, high stools and a Victorian fireplace. Food, from a glass cabinet, includes sandwiches, steak and kidney pie, cannelloni or roast leg of English lamb. Meals are served at lunchtimes only; snacks are available Monday to Saturday, lunchtime and evening. Children are welcome in the eating area.

Open 11 to 3, 5.30 to 11.30 **Underground** South Kensington

LONDON

Bombay Brasserie Map 3

Bailey's Hotel, Courtfield Close, SW7 *Telephone* 01-370 4040 ££–£££

The Bombay Brasserie looks and feels like no other Indian restaurant in Britain, with its air of magical opulence, tent-like awnings and airy conservatory. It also serves some of the most subtle and wide-ranging Indian food in the country. The food often defies expectations. People hoping for huge platefuls of red-hot chicken Madras are likely to be disappointed. Instead, the menu is a tour of the regions of the subcontinent, taking in roadside snacks from Bombay, fish curries from Goa and exotic Parsi specialities. From Hyderabad there is marinated lamb with spicy pickle and fresh green chillies, while the western Konkan coast is represented by lobster with steamed rice. There are very good reports of the chicken tikka, chicken shakuti – a dry, fierce curry flavoured with coconut and rare spices – and the boneless quail stuffed with lamb pilau and pistachio nuts. Masala poppadums come sprinkled with grated coconut, paprika and fresh coriander, and Basmati rice is very good, as is the lacha paratha. At lunch there is a renowned buffet (£8.50) and the thali dinners are worth trying. As well as a short wine list, there are cocktails, fruit juices and Kingfisher beer. Access for wheelchairs. A pianist plays.

Open All week **Meals** 12.30 to 2.30, 7.30 to 12 **Cards** Access, Amex, Diners, Visa **Service** 12½% **Underground** South Kensington

Daquise Map 3

20 Thurloe Street, SW7 *Telephone* 01-589 6117 £–££

The dependability of this little Polish café, in an area where there is very little that is not expensive, is a big plus. Typical dishes are cold chlodnik with ham and egg, stuffed cabbage, and excellent sauerkraut – just about everything Polish is reliable, non-Polish dishes less so. There are seven vodkas to choose from, as well as Polish beer. Children's helpings. Access for wheelchairs.

Open All week **Closed** 25 and 26 Dec **Meals** 12 to 3, 6 to 11.20 **Cards** None accepted **Underground** South Kensington

Golden Chopsticks Map 3

1 Harrington Road, SW7 *Telephone* 01-584 0855 ££–£££

This smart incarnation of a mainly Cantonese restaurant borders on the expensive, but at the same time has regularly provided dishes cooked with an

---

Prices for accommodations normally include cooked English or Scottish breakfast, Value Added Tax (currently 15%) and any inclusive service charge that we know of.

Don't forget: if you use a face flannel (washcloth), bring your own, since British hotels and B&Bs seldom provide one. It's a good idea to pack some plastic bags for the flannel and other items. Bring your own prescription medicines and, even if it's high summer, a warm sweater or jacket.

SOUTH KENSINGTON

exactness not often found outside Chinatown or even Hong Kong. Peking duck is consistently well reported, and the Cantonese equivalent of deep-fried crispy duck is also a highlight. Regular items such as spare ribs, stir-fried crispy beef, rice in lotus leaves, scallops with spicy onions and chilli, the tofu dishes, and apple and banana fritters have all been excellent. Service is helpful to the point of suggesting dishes that are not on the regular menu. House white is £5.80. Children's helpings; vegetarian meals. Access for wheelchairs; air-conditioning; music.

Open All week **Meals** 12 to 2.30, 6 to 11.30 (11 Sun) **Cards** Access, Amex, Diners, Visa **Service** 15% **Underground** South Kensington

Hilaire   Map 3

68 Old Brompton Road, SW7 *Telephone* 01-584 8993   £££–££££

The small shop front does not suggest any fireworks, but Simon Hopkinson's set menus are well balanced and inventive. His text is France, both bistro and bravura – to start, a baked potato, halved and scooped out, filled with sour cream and topped with caviare. The set-price dinner menu (from £21) with a minimum of four choices at each course, even for the cheaper, more limited lunch (from £12.50), changes from day to day according to the market. Of the many dishes – no fewer than eighty-one specific recommendations are on file – the range encompasses excellent gravlax, equally good home-cured herring with mustard sauce, boudin blanc before roast veal in a rich creamy garlic sauce, pork in madeira, and sweetbreads with wild mushrooms and cream. His sauces can be vibrant, as in a classic Nantua with quenelles of sole. Vegetables are varied to complement the meal – for example, when the fish sauce included lemon, the braised endive, which was flavoured with lemon, was replaced by spinach. Cheeses have come out of the fridge, which is a pity, but the sweets, like rhubarb ice-cream, parfaits and mousses, are competent. The wine list is seductive but not that cheap – Hermitages from Chapoutier; 1979 clarets from £15 upwards; house white from Duboeuf at £7. Music; air-conditioning. Smaller helpings for children over five.

Open Mon to Sat, exc Sat L **Meals** 12.30 to 2.30, 7.30 to 11 **Cards** Access, Amex, Diners, Visa **Underground** South Kensington

Number Sixteen   Map 3

16 Sumner Place, SW7 *Telephone* 01-589 5232

'I have found this hotel in your book. It is very good and so friendly. It is like house to house! Every room has flowers and many more in the reception . . . It is better than Holland! I am sending friends there every time.' A particularly gracious tribute from a Dutch reader for the four adjoining Victorian terraced houses in South Kensington which for several years past have provided an attractive individually designed bed-and-breakfast base for visitors to the metropolis. Most correspondents share the above favourable view, but there have been occasional complaints of cool reception. There is an attractive patio garden extending across the breadth of the terrace, and an enclosed Winter

LONDON

Garden is promised. Some of the rooms, those on the top floors, are inevitably on the small size, and don't expect big-hotel service, like theatre bookings. But the prices aren't big-hotel ones either. No restaurant.

Open All year **Cards** Access, Amex, Diners, Visa **Accommodations** 32 rooms, 18 with bath, 12 with shower. B&B £26 to £42 **Underground** South Kensington

Ponte Nuovo Map 3

126 Fulham Road, SW3 *Telephone* 01-370 6656   £££

The mood of Fulham Road changes more than once as it stretches due west towards Putney. At its source, near Knightsbridge, it is Belgravian suave; by the ABC cinema it has become cosmopolitan; further down, towards the football ground, it is immigrant; by Fulham Broadway station on a Saturday night at pub chucking out time, it is not a place to be. Amid all this – perhaps two miles of it – are myriad restaurants, many of them Italian. The Ponte is in the immigrant area, a sort of no-man's-land between Chelsea and South Kensington. It is chic, somewhat cramped, extremely well run, and the food makes some attempt to break away from the mundane clichés of Italian restaurant cooking which devil the competition. The menu is in sections. The pasta section always has some fresh, and the fish section is reliably excellent. Many dishes involve the waiters, which adds an element of cinema – linguine with seafood and tomato in a paper bag; red mullet cooked in foil; Dover sole taken off the bone. Chicken is spatchcocked, grilled and served in a viciously hot sauce of garlic, rosemary and chilli. Oils for the salad dressings are of good quality. The sweets trolley is adequate without being notable. Thirty-odd Italian wines start at £6.50 and most stay under £10. Children's helpings. Air-conditioning and access for wheelchairs.

Open All week **Meals** 12.30 to 3, 7 to 12 **Cards** Access, Amex, Diners, Visa **Underground** South Kensington

St Quentin Map 3

243 Brompton Road, SW3 *Telephone* 01-589 8005 and 5131   £££

This brasserie does simple things well. It is something of a production-line operation, with pleasant surroundings, attentive service, interesting fellow diners who form part of the decor, unelaborate fashionable French dishes, such as lamb with thyme, turbot with hollandaise, or entrecôte café de Paris. Although it has dropped the word brasserie from its name, it has not from its image. Cheeses are from Philippe Olivier in Boulogne. Lunch is good value (£9.50). House Burgundy is £6.60, and the serious collection of good French wines also includes the excellent Ch Millet 1978 at £7.40 a half-bottle. Wheelchair access; air-conditioning; children's helpings. Often the place is full and the new Grill, a hundred yards across the road, does excellent steak frites, though other dishes, such as confit and cassoulet, are out of a can.

Open All week **Meals** 12 to 3 (4 Sat), 7 to 12 (11.30 Sun) **Cards** Access, Amex, Diners, Visa **Service** 12½% **Underground** South Kensington

SOUTH KENSINGTON

San Frediano Map 3

62 Fulham Road, SW3 *Telephone* 01-584 8375   ££–£££

As standards in other Italian restaurants sink like waterlogged gondolas, so the estimation of this old favourite rises and rises. There is no doubting it is a very good restaurant all round, and has been for years. It seems to get better. The effusive Italian waiters in T-shirts with 'San Fred's' plastered across the front work up a carnival atmosphere. The long Italian menu is always supplemented with a wide choice of daily specials. These, if you can decipher the handwriting, often contain some surprisingly sophisticated dishes – marinated herrings with beans, roast duck in strawberry vinegar with redcurrants – as well as the expected fresh asparagus or cannelloni. Fish is excellent, as are the two veal dishes. Children are greeted with open arms at Saturday lunchtime. You do need to book though usually it is possible to get a table after ten on the same day. The wine list is predominantly Italian in the £6 region, but there are also several Champagnes plus the Italian dessert wine Moscato d'Asti, Fontanafredda, at £6.95. Air-conditioning; wheelchair access.

Open Mon to Sat **Meals** 12.30 to 2.30, 7.15 to 11.15 **Cards** Access, Amex, Carte Blanche, Diners, Visa **Service** 12½% **Underground** South Kensington

Tui Map 3

19 Exhibition Road, SW7 *Telephone* 01-584 8359   £££

Opposite the Ismaili centre and overshadowed by the Victoria and Albert Museum is this corner Thai restaurant. The decor is all blacks and whites broken only by the angularity of the downstairs dining-room and a long Buddhist scroll on gold-painted palm leaves. The menu is accessibly short and can be fiery with chilli-heat, and it is worth ensuring that a bowl of rice is on the table. A speciality is the rice baked with crab claws. The chicken with galingale, Chinese mushrooms and coconut milk is superb, and as a centrepiece both the two whole fish dishes are good too. The pick of the starters has been the dumplings. To finish, there is a Thai sweet which is three ways with coconut in any other language. There is a short, good list of wines, and also Singha Thai beer at twice the price of the Carlsberg – well, it has travelled more than twice as far. Music; wheelchair access. Children are welcome, but not cigar-smokers.

Open All week **Meals** 12 to 2.30, 6.30 to 11 (12.30 to 3, 7 to 10.30 Sun) **Cards** Access, Amex, Diners, Visa **Service** 12½% **Underground** South Kensington

We give details of service charges where we know what these are; otherwise, you should expect to add 10–15% to the total of your bill unless the menu or bill states that service is included.

London buses are big and red, have top decks, and are a great way to get to know the city. The conductor collects fares as he comes through the bus; prices are according to your destination.

LONDON

Victoria and Albert Museum Map 3

Cromwell Road, Sw7 *Telephone* 01-589 2159 £

Fine self-service restaurant in elegant brick, stone, glass and tile surroundings. There are buffet counters for snacks, salads and full hot meals with wine. The cooking is fresh and from good seasonal ingredients; the salads interesting and imaginative. In the morning they put on traditional breakfast. (The museum is worth a visit, too . . .)

Open 10 (2.30 Sun) to 5 **Closed** Public hols **Underground** South Kensington

SOUTHWARK

Anchor Map 2

Bankside, SE1 (Southwark Bridge end) *Telephone* 01-407 1577 £–£££

The present building, carefully restored in the 1960s, dates from about 1750, when it was rebuilt to replace the earlier tavern. It was probably here that Pepys came during the Great Fire of 1666: 'all over the Thames with one's face in the wind, you were almost burned with a shower of fire drops. This is very true; so as houses were burned by these drops and flakes of fire. When we could endure no more upon the water, we to a little ale-house on the Bankside and there staid till it was dark almost, and saw the fire grow.' The pub can still be an atmospheric place, with its several black-panelled little rooms, up and down stairs, creaky boards and beams, and old-fashioned high-backed settles as well as sturdy leatherette chairs. Bar food includes ploughman's with a good choice of cheeses, pies and cold meats with salads, plus lunchtime hot dishes such as casseroles, curries, lasagne, cottage pie and steak and kidney pie. There is also a separate restaurant. Children may go into the restaurant and eating area. Well-kept Courage Best and Directors on handpump, reasonably priced for the area; fruit machine and space game. A terrace has been built overlooking the river.

Open 11.30 to 3, 5.30 to 11 **Underground** London Bridge

Dining Room Map 2

1 Cathedral Street, SE1 *Telephone* 01-407 0337 ££

William English and Sandra Cross choose raw materials carefully in their basement vegetarian restaurant by Borough Market. Ninety per cent of their ingredients are organically grown, and that includes some of the wines; they use only wholewheat flour, brown rice, and cold-pressed oils, and avoid sugar completely. The menu is imaginative and eclectic, ranging from bean curd with

---

Pubs described in this Guide are pleasant places to have a drink, and many offer the added bonus of good bar snacks. Some pubs also have a separate restaurant which we may not have described.

SOUTHWARK

spicy peanut sauce to wholewheat pancakes with apricot purée and fresh lychees. Mushroom risotto is correctly made, and pipérade is served on a bed of lentil purée with a garlicky steamed lettuce salad. To drink, there are real fruit juices and herb teas as well as elderflower wine. Children's helpings. Music.

Open Tue to Fri **Meals** 12.30 to 2.30, 7 to 10 **Cards** None accepted **Service** 10% **Underground** London Bridge

Founders Arms Map 2

Bankside, SE1 (through new housing at end of Hopton Street) £
Telephone 01-928 1899

The main reason for coming to this modern riverside pub is its superb position; it has a fine view across to St Paul's Cathedral through its almost unobstructed glass walls facing the Thames. The pale green plush banquettes and free-standing elbowrest screens are cunningly placed to allow for the best view and still divide the spacious carpeted bar into friendly sized areas. Bar food includes large filled baps, pâtés, quiche or mackerel with a choice of ten salads, and a dish of the day; meals are not available at Saturday lunchtimes or on Sunday evenings; children may go into the separate restaurant. Well-kept Youngs Bitter and Special on handpump; dominoes and cribbage. A spacious terrace with white tables on herringbone brick looks out on the water and leads into the attractively planted new Bankside river walks.

Open 11 to 3, 5.30 to 11 **Underground** Blackfriars

George Map 2

Off 77 Borough High Street, SE1 *Telephone* 01-407 2056 £–£££

This is the only galleried coaching-inn left in London. The row of ground-floor rooms and bars all have square-latticed windows looking out to the cobbled yard (no cars allowed), with black beams, bare floorboards, some panelling, plain oak or elm tables, old-fashioned built-in settles, a 1797 'Act of Parliament' clock, dimpled glass lantern-lamps and so forth – perhaps the bar closest to the main road is the most natural and pub-like. Well-kept Fremlins, Flowers Original, Greene King Abbot and Wethereds are served from an ancient beer engine that looks like a cash register; bar food is served at the far end of this bar and includes ploughman's, sausage and beans and home-made steak and mushroom pie. A splendid central staircase goes up to a series of dining-rooms and to a gaslit balcony. Children are welcome here. When the pub was rebuilt in 1676 after the fire that destroyed most of Southwark (stopped only by the massive new building of St Thomas's Hospital), the building went round three sides of the courtyard. It was bought in the early nineteenth century, and well protected, by the trustees of neighbouring Guy's Hospital, but eventually sold to a predecessor of London and North Eastern Railways, who, in the words of E V Lucas, 'mercilessly reduced' it in 1889 to build railway sheds. Eventually LNER gave the surviving structure to the National Trust, who have kept it well and simply and very much on the lines of the inns where jugglers, acrobats, conjurers, animal-trainers, musicians and even Shakespeare's strolling players

157

LONDON

would have performed when Southwark was London's entertainment centre – as Thomas Decker said: 'a continuous ale-house, not a shop to be seen between red-lattice and red-lattice: no workers, but all drinkers.' There will be morris dancers (summer) and they hope to restart the tradition of Shakespeare plays.

Open 11 to 3, 5.30 to 11 **Underground** London Bridge

Market Porter Map 2

9 Stoney Street, SE1 *Telephone* 01-407 2495   £–£££

The main part of the long U-shaped bar in this lively and popular pub, which brews its own beer, has rough wooden ceiling beams with beer barrels balanced on them, a heavy wooden bar counter with a beamed gantry, red-cushioned bar stools, an open fire with stuffed animals in glass cabinets on the mantelpiece and several mounted stags' heads and 1920s-style wall lamps. Red-cushioned captain's chairs sit on the patterned dark red carpet and at one end there is a glass cabinet for food, which includes sandwiches, pasty and beans or chicken curry, liver and bacon or roast beef, pork or chicken or pork stuffed with Stilton. Snacks are only available at lunchtimes. Children may go into the restaurant. Besides its well-kept own brew Market Bitter, there are Boddingtons, Greene King IPA and Abbot, Sam Smiths OBB, Wadworths 6X and Youngs on handpump; darts, fruit machine, space game and piped music. A small partly panelled room has leaded glass windows and a couple of tables.

Open 10.30 to 3, 5.30 to 11 **Underground** London Bridge

TOTTENHAM COURT ROAD

Auntie's Map 4

126 Cleveland Street, W1 *Telephone* 01-387 3226   £££

Auntie's was famous as a tea-room through the 1960s and 1970s but has now become a dynamic new English restaurant. It is smart, small and offers set menus concentrating exclusively on English dishes, many out of Dorothy Hartley's book. The scope ranges from bangers and mash to spiced and buttered crab on toast. Especially good have been home-cured mackerel with horseradish sauce, Barnsley chop, and the apple pie. The fish of the day is usually cooked and served in a paper bag. There are fine unpasteurised cheeses as well as English wines, and of course a few clarets. Music; wheelchair access. Children are welcome.

Open Mon to Sat, exc Sat L **Closed** 2 weeks Aug **Meals** 12 to 2.45, 6 to 10.45 **Cards** Access, Amex, Diners, Visa **Service** 12½% **Underground** Great Portland Street/Warren Street

---

£ = *meal can be had for about £5*
££ = *meal can be had for about £12*
£££ = *meal can be had for about £20*
££££ = *meal can be had for about £30*

TOTTENHAM COURT ROAD

Chez Gerard Map 4

8 Charlotte Street, W1 *Telephone* 01-636 4975   £££

The service is diabolical, but there is very little wrong with the food in this quasi-French chain (see also the Mayfair and Holborn sections). The formula is entrecôte et frites with cold starters and sweets – and good cheeses. Extras put the bill up. House Rhône is £5.50, but Beaujolais is the most considered section of the list. Music. Children's helpings.

Open All week, exc Sat L **Meals** 12.30 to 2.30, 6.30 to 11 **Cards** Access, Visa **Service** 10% **Underground** Goodge Street/Tottenham Court Road

Cranks Map 4

9–11 Tottenham Street, W1 *Telephone* 01-631 3912   £–££

See the Regent Street section for the main Cranks entry.

Open 8 to 8 **Closed** Sun; public hols **Underground** Goodge Street

Efes Kebab House Map 4

80 Great Titchfield Street, W1 *Telephone* 01-636 1953   ££

The quality of the meats distinguishes this Turkish kebab house. Nineteen variations, from liver with aubergine sauce to doner, make up the selection of kebabs. Equally varied is the choice of starters, which can be brought together into a meze. The sweets are of the Middle Eastern school of baklava, kataif and börek. Coffee is pungent and the Turkish wines worth exploring. Vegetarian meals. Children are welcome. Music.

Open Mon to Sat **Meals** Noon to 11.30 **Cards** Access, Amex, Visa **Underground** Oxford Circus

Ikkyu Map 4

67 Tottenham Court Road, W1 *Telephone* 01-636 9280   ££–£££

The down-at-heel entrance just up from Goodge Street Tube station gives very little inkling to what happens in this basement. A tumble down some steep stairs and hello Tokyo: a big kitchen and preparation area is hemmed in by an eating bar, and tables stretch far out underneath Tottenham Court Road. The decor is minimal – a carved wooden fish, some saké warmers, and some chopsticks in a packet complete with instructions on how to use them. The clientele is nearly exclusively Japanese, but the staff have excellent English and also a good enough understanding of the menu to act as guides. It is the usual amalgam of different kinds of cooking to cater for homesick exiles. The pot dishes arrive with their own cooker at the table. The bean curd is arranged outside for dipping. There is an accent on yakitori. Various meats can be ordered, including such tiny delicacies as chicken hearts. Seaweeds come in three colours, and there is an unusual dish of a fish stuffed with roe and sealed up again and grilled. The

LONDON

potatoes and meat dish, though, is just that, and aubergine is cut thick, the middle taken out, chunked, put back and topped with bonito flakes. The place gets hot and café-like, but is a good inexpensive point of departure for eating less usually found dishes. Saké is £2 for a small bottle. Green tea is free. Children are welcome. Music.

Open All week, exc Sat L and Sun L **Meals** 12.30 to 2.30, 6 to 11 **Cards** Access, Amex, Diners, Visa **Service** 10% **Underground** Goodge Street

---

Lal Qila Map 4	✖
117 Tottenham Court Road, W1 *Telephone* 01-387 4570	££–£££

The food at Lal Qila is a shade more reliable and impressive than at its stablemate, the Red Fort (see Soho). The kitchen continues to deliver some of the finest tikkas in London. Sheesh kebabs are rolled in fresh coriander leaves before cooking. Sag is the real thing – perfectly blended and softened – and there is also a rich, potent mutter paneer. Murgh makhani has a sauce enriched with yoghurt and almonds, while curry-house die-hards will not be disappointed with the fiery chicken Madras. Service seems to have improved considerably in recent months, mainly because the waiters in Amin Ali's team are transferred more regularly than most first-division footballers. Some of the old surliness has gone, but their style is still as distinctive as the cooking. There are cocktails to match the plush decor, as well as Kingfisher beer and house wine at £4.95. Children's helpings. Music; air-conditioning.

Open All week **Closed** 25, 26 Dec **Meals** 12 to 2.45, 6 to 11.30 **Cards** Access, Amex, Diners, Visa **Service** 12½% **Underground** Warren Street

---

Mandeer Map 4	✖
21 Hanway Place, W1 *Telephone* 01-323 0660	£–££

Tucked away in an alley just half a minute's walk from Tottenham Court Road, this Indian vegetarian restaurant is authentic and offers good value. The dining-room must be one of the darkest in the country, the only light coming from hanging lamps ringed with Christmas-tree fairy lights. The menu has a wholefood slant with the choice of unpolished brown rice or Basmati, and tofu specialities, in addition to samosas, pari puri, chana masala and pahir mattar. Sweets include Loseley Park Farm ice-creams as well as carrot halva and wild Himalayan apricots in Jaipur rosewater. Thalis are good and there are bargain self-service lunches (from £2.65) in the light, airy Ravi Shankar Hall (though waiter service is also available). Licensed. No-smoking area. Children's helpings. Music.

Open Mon to Sat **Closed** Public hols **Meals** 12 to 2.30, 6 to 10.15 (10.30 Fri and Sat) **Cards** Access, Amex, Diners, Visa **Service** 10% **Underground** Tottenham Court Road

---

Bangers and mash, anyone? Gammon? Now and again, the typical British menu may be a bit of a puzzler to Americans. Please consult the Glossary on page 218 for an alphabetical listing of unusual food items.

TOTTENHAM COURT ROAD

Ragam Map 4

57 Cleveland Street, W1 *Telephone* 01-636 9098   £–££

The big scoring point about this unpretentious southern Indian restaurant is that it serves classic Keralan dishes that are reckoned to be as good as those eaten on the subcontinent. As well as kaallan – a curry made with yoghurt, coconut, mango and spices – there is avial – vegetables flavoured with coconut and curry leaves. Most of the specialities are vegetarian and the list takes in iddly – a steamed cake of rice and black lentils – and uppama, as well as many variations on the pancake theme. Crisp vegetable masala dosai comes with creamy coconut chutney and a savoury sambar that goes to the limits of chilli tolerance. The menu also has a full quota of meat, poultry and seafood dishes including good chicken biriani and colourful keema curry with lots of green and red peppers. Peach or mango lassi is a pleasant alternative to the usual salty version. Licensed, or you can bring your own bottle (corkage 50p). Children's helpings. Music; access for wheelchairs.

Open All week **Meals** 12 to 3, 6 to 12 **Cards** Access, Amex, Diners, Visa **Service** 10% **Underground** Great Portland Street

Rue St Jacques Map 4

5 Charlotte Street, W1 *Telephone* 01-637 0222   £££–££££

The tables are closely packed together in Gunther Schlender's attractive, futuristic restaurant. The food is extravagantly lavish, beautifully presented, French by inclination, international by persuasion: crab mousse with cream and lobster sauce; calf's liver in sweet-and-sour sauce; quail salad; scallops in red butter; fresh eel stuffed with fish mousse; lamb with almonds. The dozen main courses are more extravagant than the starters, of which half are likely to feature foie gras, caviare, Champagne, and lobster. The service is still awkward and has upset otherwise fine, albeit expensive meals. Areas of excellence over the past year have been the fish – typical would be steamed monkfish with a red wine and beetroot sauce – and the desserts, such as marron glacé bombe or pears with chocolate sauce. The set lunch costs virtually the same as a single main course at dinner (£15). The wine list is breathtakingly expensive, but with anomalies that a shrewd scouting should reveal. The balance is around £30 to £40 a bottle. House wine is £9. Children are welcome. Music; air conditioning; access for wheelchairs. Jacket and tie to be worn at dinner.

Open Mon to Sat, exc Sat L **Closed** Christmas, Easter, public hols **Meals** 12.30 to 2.30, 7.30 to 11.15 **Cards** Access, Amex, Diners, Visa **Service** 15% **Underground** Goodge Street/Tottenham Court Road

Tower Grill Map 4

86 Cleveland Street, W1 *Telephone* 01-387 2375   ££

A smaller and quieter alternative to Efes Kebab House (see above), this modest room with its homely decor and tables outside on the pavement in the summer

161

LONDON

provides a fine menu of meze and kebabs. The meal starts with a dish of radishes, plump olives and salt-pickled chillies. Imam bayildi (cold aubergine in olive oil), broad beans with mint and garlic, small koftas, and fried cheesy filo parcels are all good to start. Follow with a hot grilled minced-meat kebab from the south of Turkey, or one with yoghurt and tomato sauce on a bed of pitta bread from the north. Raki (like ouzo) and Turkish wines to drink. Children's helpings. Music; wheelchair access.

Open All week **Meals** 12 to 3, 6 to 11.30 **Cards** Access, Amex, Diners, Visa **Underground** Great Portland Street/Warren Street

White Tower Map 4

1 Percy Street, W1 *Telephone* 01-636 8141   £££

The White Tower was so popular in the 1950s and early 1960s that bookings were taken weeks in advance. It is less fashionable now, but whether there has been any deterioration in service, cuisine or ambience is debatable. In the context of London Greek restaurants, it shines. There is a lot of atmosphere, which does not come just from the upstairs mural of dancing girls. The evocative menu is one of the finest pieces of gastronomic literature – which is perhaps why no one dares to change it, apart from the two dishes of the day. The restaurant has its faults – the bread, the waiters who lean across diners, the tinned peas, a tendency for late lunchers to find the specials a bit dry. But on the other hand, the fish salad is exemplary and the duck is . . . well, the White Tower ducks have almost the same reputation as those of the Tour d'Argent in Paris. As the menu says: 'These aristocrats of the poultry world, specially reared for the White Tower, are prepared for the table before they are eight weeks old. (After that they grow their "second feathers" which means they are not ducklings any more!) Broad as they are long, they weigh between 5½ and 6½ lbs . . . just right for two hungry people. Stuffed with the famous bougourie of Cyprus, chopped almonds and ducks' livers . . .' A proper beef Stroganoff is also on the menu; otherwise, heavy use of the charcoal grill provides the majority of centrepieces. Sweets tend to be strictly Greek, and there is a marinated fruit salad. The wine list is not for poor men. The 1979 clarets come in to their own at around £15-plus. Other mark-ups are close on double what they are at other restaurants. In this company Othello, from Cyprus, at £6 is a welcome sight.

Open Mon to Fri **Closed** 1 week at Christmas, 3 weeks Aug **Meals** 12.30 to 2.30, 6.30 to 10.30 **Cards** Access, Amex, Diners, Visa **Underground** Tottenham Court Road

WANDSWORTH

Green Man Map 1

Wildcroft Road, SW15   £

This friendly old pub on the edge of Putney Heath used to be a haunt of ruthless young highwaymen like Jerry Avershawe, hanged at Kennington in 1795, as well as the rather pitiful footpads (the old equivalent of muggers) like Will Brown and Joseph Whitlock who were hanged after they'd stolen a baker's

WANDSWORTH

boy's silver buckle and a ha'penny: now it's altogether more cheerful, with a cosy green-carpeted main bar opening into a quiet sitting-room. Bar food includes rolls and sandwiches, steak sandwiches, lasagne, chilli con carne or moussaka, steak and daily specials; good-value barbecues, weather permitting, with burgers, kebabs ribs, one pound of Cumberland sausages, trout, steak and whole poussin. Well-kept Youngs Bitter and Special on handpump, reasonably priced for London; ring the bull, dominoes and cribbage as well as sensibly placed darts and a fruit machine. Outside, there are lots of seats and a swing, slide and see-saw among the flowering shrubs and trees on the good-sized lawn behind, and there are also tables outside on sheltered colonnaded side terraces.

Open 11 to 3, 5.30 to 11 **Underground** East Putney (quite a walk)

Hoults Map 1

20 Bellevue Road, SW17 *Telephone* 01-767 1858   ££–£££

The decor of this vivacious wine and food bar is scrubbed wood, mirrors, a piano, and a view of Wandsworth Common and the other customers: it is nearly always packed. Behind the bar is stacked a respectable selection of wines including good-value Riojas, while the blackboard menu reaches into avenues more often found in restaurants – salmon hollandaise, grilled fish, and roast lamb with a sauce of port wine. Soups and pies are reliable, too. Vegetarian options; children's helpings. Music; access for wheelchairs.

Open All week **Closed** Christmas **Meals** 12 to 2.30, 7 to 10.30 **Cards** Access, Amex, Visa **Service** 12½% **BR station** Wandsworth Common **Underground** Balham

---

Ship Map 1

41 Jews Row, SW18   £

The main reason for coming to this rather plain house is to sit at the good, sturdy – and well spaced – tables on the big riverside terrace; partly cobbled and partly concrete with pretty tubs of flowers in summer, it spreads over a wide area and is divided into sections by low planted walls – one part even has a bower of runner bean plants. In the evenings, and at weekend lunchtimes, a substantial charcoal barbecue counter out here does good home-made hamburgers and three sausages, whole leg of lamb for four or five and split-roast beef, all imaginatively garnished (only meals are available at Sunday lunchtimes). Other bar food includes fresh tomato, basil and mint soup, baked potatoes, club sandwich, seafood lasagne, and beef in Guinness. The pub is well away from traffic. Inside, there's a comfortably relaxed atmosphere, and the bar opening on to the terrace (there are no river views from the pub itself) has easy chairs, sofas and a harmonium; the public bar has sensibly placed darts, shove-ha'penny, a fruit machine, juke box and pinball table. Well-kept Youngs Bitter and Special on handpump. A Thames barge is moored alongside and can be used for private parties, although she sails along the East and South Coasts during the summer months.

Open 11 to 3, 5.30 to 11 **BR station** Wandsworth Town

LONDON

WESTMINSTER

L'Amico Map 2   ✗

44 Horseferry Road, SW1 *Telephone* 01-222 4680   £££

There are a few private areas behind sliding partitions for meetings at this professionally run Italian restaurant within earshot of Parliament's division bell. The menu is conservative in the extreme, but the standard of cooking is reliable – minestrone, chicken with mushrooms, and tortellini have all been excellent. Spaghetti Gorbachev – so named because Neil Kinnock brought the Russian leader here – comes with caviare, tomato concassé and smoked salmon. House Valpolicella is £5.30. Children are said to be welcome. Music; air-conditioning.

Open Mon to Fri **Closed** Aug **Meals** 12 to 2.30, 6.15 to 11 **Cards** Access, Amex, Diners, Visa **Service** 12½% **Underground** St James's Park/Westminster

Auberge de Provence Map 2   ✗ 🏠 🍽

St James's Court Hotel, Buckingham Gate, SW1   £££–££££
Telephone 01-834 6655

The magnificent building is owned and being lavishly restored by Taj International Hotels, among whose credits is the immensely popular Bombay Brasserie (see under South Kensington). The only thing that needs to be stressed is that here is an auberge as might be found in a town in France, not a pompous hotel dining-room in the British manner. The price reflects this. The flavours are loud Punch and Judy material – fish soup, red mullet mousse, charlotte of lamb with aubergines, or else lamb with a garlic infusion, or beef, for two people, with baby onions. The charming waiters and waitresses wheel trolleys filled with explosive sorbets; the sweets trolley is so pungent that it needs its lid. The wines are on the young side for drinking, but the house Côtes du Ventoux and the Duboeuf white Burgundy at £6.50 suit the food. Vegetarian meals; children's helpings. Air-conditioning. The hotel has a sauna. Afternoon teas.

Open All week **Meals** 12.30 to 2.30, 7.30 to 11 **Cards** Access, Amex, Diners, Visa **Accommodations** 400 rooms, 90 apartments, all with bath/shower. Rooms for disabled. Lift. B&B £100 to £115. Deposit: £100. Baby facilities **Underground** Victoria/St James's Park

Methuselah's Map 2   ♀ ✗

29 Victoria Street, SW1 *Telephone* 01-222 0424   ££–£££

Don Hewitson, one of London's most successful wine bar proprietors (see also the Cork and Bottle and Shampers in Soho), lists wonderful wines from around the world: 1983 Alsace, 1985 Beaujolais, under-rated 1980 claret, a selection of champagnes, Torres wines from Spain, Tiefenbrunner from South Tyrol, and others from the New World. There are salads and simple hot dishes at the bar, and more eleborate dishes in the Brasserie and Burgundy Room, à la carte and fixed price respectively: chicken tandoori 'French-style', lamb tagine, and a casserole, fish or vegetarian dish of the day. Children's helpings. Wheelchair

WIMBLEDON

access; music; air-conditioning. It's more peaceful in the evening than at lunchtime.

Open Mon to Fri **Closed** 25 and 26 Dec, 1 Jan, Easter **Meals** 9am to 11pm **Cards** Access, Amex, Diners, Visa **Service** 15% **Underground** St James's Park

WIMBLEDON

Mai Thai Map 1

75 The Broadway, SW19 *Telephone* 01-542 8834   ££–£££

The opening of new Thai restaurants is mostly greeted with enormous enthusiasm. This is no exception. The Broadway has a number of restaurants, including a Chinese one confusingly called Mai's Kitchen, but this one is between the loud awnings of Alfred Marks and Pizzaland. The staff help with a menu that is not intimidating. A centrepiece of snub-nosed pomfret – looking not unlike a plaice, but in fact flown in from Thailand – is served fried and covered with a sauce of minced pork and ginger, and hot-and-sour prawn salad with herbs has impressed. Unlike in Chinese restaurants, ends of meals take intriguing turns in the shape of hot bananas in coconut-milk or Thai custard. House wine is £5.25. Children's helpings. Music; wheelchair access.

Open All week, exc Sun L **Meals** 12 to 3, 6 to 11 **Cards** Access, Amex, Diners, Visa **Service** 10% **Underground** Wimbledon

Oh Boy Map 1

843 Garratt Lane, SW17 *Telephone* 01-947 9760   £££

This quasi-Thai restaurant, easily missed in a row of shops, has one of the more romantic dining-rooms south of the river. Ceiling spotlights pick out the stained dark wood panelling. The floral wallpaper matches the tablecloths and napkins. On the walls are traditional Thai prints and pictures of the king and queen of Thailand. The menu, like the napkins, is fashioned in the shape of a concertina. It is an entertainment, taking in Thai, Franglais, and even Wimbledon, with Wimbledon soup, which is 'bean vermicelli with minced pork, fish ball, fungus and vegetables'. Three Siam Grill'Ee are prawns served with a trio of sauces: a) oily and chilli, b) sweet and vinegared chopped green chilli, and c) excellent fresh coriander and garlic. The waiters enjoy flambé-ing at the table and perform it with great solemnity. Worth seeking out are volcano chicken and the satay. Deep-fried dishes can be less effective. House white is £4.45. Children are welcome. Music.

Open Mon to Sat, D only **Closed** 2 weeks Aug **Meals** 7 to 10.30 (10.45 Fri and Sat) **Cards** Access, Amex, Diners, Visa **Service** Inc (set dinner); 12½% à la carte **Underground** Tooting Broadway

---

Restaurant hints: sweets are candy and a sweet is dessert (often a pudding unless otherwise specified). If you want your drink straight up, ask for it neat. Out of London ask for ice if you want a drink on the rocks (but you won't always get it). At the end of the meal, ask for the bill, not the check.

LONDON

Rose & Crown Map 1

55 High Street, SW19   £

The rambling main bar in this comfortably modernised ex-coaching-inn used to be the poet Swinburne's local. It has a full set of Hogarth's proverb engravings above the open fire, comfortable green plush seats in friendly carpeted alcoves, and a relaxed background babble of conversation. A snack bar, opening off this room, has sandwiches, Scotch eggs, baked potatoes, ploughman's or chilli con carne, home-made pies, burgers, gammon steak, scampi, steak and daily specials; well-kept Youngs Bitter and Special on handpump; dominoes, cribbage. Children may go into the snack bar. There are lots of tables outside in the long courtyard with a trellis of roses and honeysuckle along one side, and a little verandah at the far end; close to Wimbledon Common.

Open 11 to 3, 5.30 to 11 Underground South Wimbledon

Sree Krishna Map 1

194 Tooting High Street, SW17 *Telephone* 01-672 4250   ££

The seating has been increased to accommodate 120, which has considerably reduced the waiting time for a table. For a South Indian establishment there is a lot of meat, but for any restaurant it is very cheap: chicken, beef, prawn, and lamb in varying strengths of curry are mostly £2.50 or less. But vegetable dishes are still good: pancakes filled with potatoes and fried onions (masala dosai) or lentils (adai), or lentil 'donuts' (vadai), or a mixture of vegetables cooked with coconut, yoghurt and curry leaves. Lassi to drink. Children are welcome. Wheelchair access; music.

Open All week Meals 12 to 2.45, 6 to 10.45 (11.45 Fri and Sat) Cards None accepted Service 10% Underground Tooting Broadway

Village Restaurant Map 1

8 High Street, SW19 *Telephone* 01-947 6477   £££

Nestling behind a smart white fascia at the end of the High Street is this large, rectangular dining-room loudly decorated in burnt orange and with a vast collection of modern paintings and drawings. The set menu offers a fashionable choice – starters of poached eggs with mushrooms and madeira, a warm duck salad with honey vinaigrette, or vegetable gratin. Fish is elegantly cooked – monkfish is sautéed in garlic butter, fresh salmon is steamed with a julienne of vegetables. Meat dishes fit the style of modern British cooking – loin of lamb sautéed with spring onions and mint, rabbit stew with peppery mustard sauce. Cheeses and puddings can be disappointing, though the grilled glazed fruit have been delicious. Downstairs is a bistro with a more conservative but commendably inexpensive menu. Two dozen wines. Vegetarian meals. Children's helpings at Sunday lunch. Wheelchair access; air-conditioning.

Open All week, exc Mon L, Sat L and Sun D Closed 2 weeks Aug Meals 12 to 2.30, 7 to 11.30 Cards Access, Amex, Visa Service Inc Underground Wimbledon

Trips out of London

Brighton

The South Coast town of Brighton owes much of its fame to two men, neither of whom was born there. The first was Dr Richard Russell from nearby Lewes, who in 1754 began prescribing sea water and bathing as a cure for many and various ills. The second was the Prince Regent, later George IV (1820–1830), who visited the town in 1783 on the advice of his physician to take the cure for a swollen neck.

The Prince Regent's liking for the place rapidly made it fashionable among high society and it became a thriving resort. Most of its important buildings date from around this time, but the settlement had already been in existence for many years. The fishing village of Bristelms-tune is mentioned in the Domesday Book of 1086, and its 'twittens' (narrow lanes and alleyways) formed the pattern for eighteenth-century Brighthelmstone, as it was known in George's time.

There was a second rise in popularity with the coming of the railway, and the town today has a fascinating mixture of Regency and Victorian styles, elements of the traditional British seaside, and a racy, slightly raffish charm all of its own.

The station, built in 1841, is a convenient starting point for any exploration of the town. More than 3500 men were needed to build it and the small terraced houses around it, which were originally for the railway employees. In 1880 a wrought-iron canopy was added to the front to protect travellers from inclement weather, rather spoiling the original Italian design.

From the station, head straight towards the sea down Queens Road and turn right up Church Street. At the top of the hill is St Nicholas Church, built in the fourteenth century and originally isolated on this hill overlooking the village of Brighthelmstone, and a convenient beacon and landmark for fishermen in the English Channel. Substantially altered in the nineteenth century, the church has an interesting graveyard with two famous residents. Martha Gunn was one of the original and best known of the 'dippers', or bathing attendants, an occupation that sprang up after Dr Russell's therapeutic discoveries. The other is Phoebe Hessel, who when her soldier sweetheart was posted abroad disguised herself as a man in order to be near him. She remained undiscovered until he was injured and about to be shipped home, when she revealed who she was to her surprised commanding officer. She died at the age of 108.

Still at the top of the town, adjacent to the graveyard, is Clifton Terrace, a fine example of a mid-nineteenth-century terrace, south-facing with good views of the sea and a communal garden on the other side of the original carriageway. Note how numbers 12–14 in the middle of the row have been emphasised by being taller and slightly forward of the others. The neighbouring street walls incorporate beach pebbles and squared-off flints in their facing, showing the use of local materials at a time of poor transport.

From Church Street, walk down Dyke Road towards the sea. On the left, just before the junction of Western Road and the modern Churchill Square shopping precinct, is Wykeham Terrace. This is a neat row of Regency Gothic houses built in the 1820s, when Brighton's popularity with the gentry led to a property boom.

BRIGHTON

Turning left at the bottom of the hill, Brighton's Clock Tower comes into view. Erected by James Willing in 1888 to commemorate Queen Victoria's Golden Jubilee, it is a stunning combination of architectural styles. The top is baroque, complete with a gilt time ball that used to move up and down on the hour but was stopped after complaints about the noise it made. The tower itself is Renaissance in style, with inlaid pictures of Victoria, the Prince Consort, and the Prince and Princess of Wales. The base is Classical, with Grecian-style pediments. To complete an already crowded picture, the whole thing is situated above a public convenience!

Turn right into North Street and then left into Duke Street, which has some of Brighton's more exclusive clothes shops and leads into the Lanes, the heart of the Old Town. These narrow twisting streets and alleyways criss-cross a small area and seem to have a surprise around each corner. The Lanes are best explored by simply wandering. Some of the highlights are the Deryk Carver in Black Lion Street, a building reconstructed in 1974 which was originally a brewery and home of the eponymous first Protestant martyr to be burned at Lewes in 1555; the Webbs Mechanical Music Shop in Prince Albert Street, with its collection of musical boxes and old gramophones; and 43 Meeting House Lane, reputed to be the oldest house in Brighton.

Emerging from the Lanes via Market Street, cross North Road and enter the gardens of the Royal Pavilion. Undoubtedly the grandest building in Brighton, this has been described as an Indian palace in an English garden. The original building was commissioned in 1786 from Henry Holland by the Prince Regent and had sumptuous Chinese-style interiors. In 1815 John Nash, of Regent's Park fame, was employed to redesign the exterior. Seven years and half a million pounds later the Prince Regent was proud possessor of one of the most exotic buildings in Europe, with its external cupolas and minarets and its retained Chinese interiors.

Nash, unfortunately, appears to have been a better artist than artisan. The bulk of the Pavilion is currently covered in blue plastic sheeting while massive restoration, scheduled to finish in 1988, takes place. Nash used iron cores and clamps which have rusted and expanded, splitting the stone they were designed to support, and his attempt to hide external drainpipes by placing them inside walls has led to many damp patches as these too have rusted. Add to this the climatic erosion caused by the salt-laden sea air on the Bath stone, and it is clear that a massive effort had to be made to save this unique structure.

On the other side of the garden and originally used for stabling is the Dome. Modelled on the Halle de Blé in Paris, the 85 feet high 65 feet in diameter building was redesigned in 1935 and is now used as a concert hall. Beyond the Dome in Church Street are the Library, Art Gallery, Museum and Corn Exchange. These have a continuous frontage with ornate stonework that echoes the design of the Pavilion. Turn right from the bottom of Church Street, pass the statue of George IV and walk past the front of the building into the Old Steine. Once a marshy river area but drained in 1793, it is dominated by a central fountain built by Amon Henry Wilds in 1846. The fountain is supported by three entwined dolphins. Facing the fountain, and now the YMCA, is the former residence of Mrs Maria Fitzherbert, another reason for the Prince Regent's affection for Brighton. This twice-widowed lady was secretly married to George in 1785 – a marriage technically invalid under the terms of the Royal Marriage

BRIGHTON

BRIGHTON
1. Allan Johns
2. Billabong
3. Café Royale
4. Clarence Wine Bar
5. Cripes
6. Al Duomo
7. Food for Friends
8. Al Forno
9. French Cellar
10. Latin in the Lane
11. Melrose
12. Mock Turtle
13. Muang Thai
14. Pizza Express
15. Shades of Green
16. Topps Hotel
17. Twenty One

BRIGHTON

Act – and was installed in a handily placed villa close to the Prince's first residence in the town. Their relationship lasted a number of years but ended before he came to the throne.

Walk through the Steine to the seafront and the Palace Pier – built in 1901 and a good example of this peculiarly British phenomenon. Also here is the Volks Railway, Britain's first electric railway, constructed in 1883; it now offers train rides along the beach to Brighton's newest attraction, the Marina, the largest in Europe.

Retrace your steps through the Steine, past Church Street, take any of the turnings left up the hill towards the station and discover row upon row of neat terraced cottages in narrow streets in the North Laine area. The layout is based on the early agricultural pattern of fields or tenantry laines in the area before the building boom at the start of the nineteenth century. As well as housing there are shops and markets and an atmosphere of residency missing from the more touristy parts of the town. The route through this area will eventually lead you back to the station.

BRIGHTON

Allan Johns ✕

8 Church Street *Telephone* (0273) 683087 £

Shellfish bar in the old tradition with take-away and a few tables. Jellied eels, crab, prawns, sandwiches cut fresh to order, and a few hot dishes too. Lobster on high days. Some things may be from the freezer.

Open 10 (10.30 Sun) to 5.30 (3 Sun) **Closed** Public hols

Billabong ✕

34 Hampton Place *Telephone* (0273) 774386 £

Strictly functional café specialising in croissants with all kinds of fillings. The menu makes interesting reading, with some unusual combinations such as artichokes with Gruyère, spicy spinach laced with chilli, aubergines with garlic, or smoked ham. Alternatives to croissants include ratatouille, bacon and beans on toast, or pasta with French bread; there are also the usual cheesecakes and ice-creams for dessert. The decor is of strong colours and angles, and there's rock and jazz on tape.

Open 10.30 to 6 (6.30 Sat & Sun) **Closed** Mon (exc public hols, when closed Tue)

Going out to dinner? Hotel and restaurant dining, especially outside London, is usually conducted at a pleasantly civilised pace. Upon entering the restaurant, you and your party are invited to sit in the lounge and order drinks while you study the menu. Your food order is then taken and, after a suitable interval, you are ushered to your table. Coffee (and tea) after the meal can also be taken in the lounge. This dining ritual lends a leisurely touch to eating out and is especially pleasant if you have several in your party.

BRIGHTON

Café Royale

50 Preston Street *Telephone* (0273) 202603

Immaculate and stylish café serving modest food in far-from-modest surroundings. Jacket potatoes with various fillings are the mainstay of the menu, and there are assorted sundaes and ice-cream concoctions to finish. Excellent Gaggia coffee. Unlicensed.

Open 10 to 6 **Closed** Sun; Christmas Eve; 2 weeks Jan

Clarence Wine Bar

Clarence Yard, Meeting House Lane, The Lanes
Telephone (0273) 720597

On a sunny Sunday morning it's pleasant to sit in the courtyard, drink a glass of wine and read the papers. Inside, the lights are dim and the music is loud. The menu takes in French onion soup, Parma ham with green figs, grilled sardines with tarragon, and baked potatoes with various fillings. The steak and kidney pies look spectacular, with pastry puffed so high that they resemble loaves of bread. Helpings are substantial.

Open 11 to 11 (10.30pm Sun)

Cripes

7 Victoria Road *Telephone* (0273) 27878

A good crêperie. Savoury buckwheat versions are filled with mixtures such as tuna fish, cauliflower and cheese, or salami, Mozzarella and asparagus, while sweet ones come with anything from lemon and honey to rum and chocolate. To drink there's dry Normandy cider as well as wine and good strong coffee.

Open Noon to 3, 6 to 11.30 **Closed** Christmas Day and Boxing Day

Al Duomo

7 Pavilion Buildings *Telephone* (0273) 26741

Authentically Italian restaurant close to the Royal Pavilion and very good value for money. Giant pizzas come with a score of different toppings and there's also a good choice of pasta dishes for cheap eaters: the tagliatelle with pesto sauce is excellent. The minestrone is a fine gutsy brown and salads are well dressed. Vegetarians do well. Related to Al Forno (see below).

Open Noon to 2.30, 6.30 to 11.30 **Closed** Sun

£ = *meal can be had for about £5*
££ = *meal can be had for about £12*
£££ = *meal can be had for about £20*
££££ = *meal can be had for about £30*

BRIGHTON

Al Forno
36 East Street *Telephone* (0273) 24905

Long-established, authentically Italian restaurant on two floors. Most of the action takes place downstairs where the style is 1970s Habitat and the room is dominated by a pizza oven and a battery of coffee-making equipment. Pizzas come with a dozen different toppings and there are also half a dozen pasta dishes, plus salads. Puddings are large and good – especially the profiteroles. Related to Al Duomo (see above).

Open Noon to 2.30, 6.30 to 11.30 **Closed** Sun L; Mon

Food for Friends
17A–18 Prince Albert Street, The Lanes *Telephone* (0273) 202310

Cheap, chaotic and liberally vegetarian – and the queues for this cramped self-service café do not get any shorter. 'The whole food and nothing but the food' is the philosophy, and although the emphasis is on big tastes and big helpings, there are inventive touches. Savoury pizzas are the stuff of which student parties are made, and the stir-fried vegetables are fine when they emerge fresh from the kitchen. Robust soups are eaten from stoneware bowls and specialities range from leeks and sweetcorn au gratin in ginger sauce to Mexican pancakes with peanut and chilli relish. Salads are made with all kinds of ingredients, and quiches and cakes are in abundance. To drink there's apple juice, cidre bouché, or house wine at £3.75 a bottle. Children's helpings; wheelchair access; music; take-away service.

Open All week **Meals** 9am (11.30am Sun) to 10pm

French Cellar
37 New England Road *Telephone* (0273) 603643

The best way to eat cheaply in this Gallic restaurant is to head for the informal groundfloor brasserie with its bare floor, red-and-white-checked tablecloths and colourful prints on the walls. Have a cup of coffee, a plate of snails or a full meal from the menu, which ranges from sardines provençale and shark steak créole to rump steak or pork fillet in sherry and mushroom sauce. Excellent Pavlova to finish. Better-than-average coffee. Lunch is cheaper than dinner.

Open Noon to 2.30, 7 to 10 (10.30 Sat) **Closed** Sun; Mon L

Latin in the Lane
10 Kings Road *Telephone* (0273) 28672

Just off the seafront, behind the Queen's Hotel, this is the sort of neighbourhood Italian restaurant that would give the breed a better name. Home-made pasta is cooked al dente and there are plenty of variations: spaghetti with pesto, with fresh mussels, and a la vongole are all good. Plainly cooked fish is the best bet

BRIGHTON

for main course – for example grilled Dover sole or grey mullet. Vitello tonnato is sometimes a special of the day.

Open Noon to 2.30, 6 to 11

Melrose

132 Kings Road *Telephone* (0273) 26520

Cypriot café by the West Pier specialising in gigantic fresh sole and plaice, large sirloins, and lunches of roast beef and Yorkshire pudding for £2.40. The mixed grill at £4.90 includes lamb chop, 3oz steak, liver, sausage, bacon, tomato and mushrooms. Some Greek/Cypriot dishes too.

Open Noon to 11 **Closed** End Dec to early Feb

Mock Turtle

4 Poole Valley (off East Street) *Telephone* (0273) 27380

This is one of the last of a dying breed – a genuine old-style tea-room with a window full of home-made cakes and a dresser loaded up with jams, lemon curd, fruit cakes and gingerbread. It is tiny and crowded. At lunchtime there are real home-made sausages and bacon, or a fish dish, while light snacks are served all day. The scones are two inches high and come stuffed with cream and home-made jam. The owners have their tea blended to their own specifications, available in small packets to take away.

Open 10 to 6 **Closed** Sun & Mon

Muang Thai

77 St James's Street *Telephone* (0273) 605223

The name means the Thai nation. The food is authentically prepared at this attractive, split-level restaurant on a corner. The bare wooden tables and pictures of Thai dancers add to the effect. Whole fish with chilli, hot-and-sour soup, and noodles have all been excellent. Poy Sien is a mixture of meats and vegetables with seven different flavours. Depending on deliveries, fresh fruit and Thai beer are available. Otherwise drink whisky, which is more suitable than wine. Vegetarian meals; children's helpings; wheelchair access; music.

Open All week, D only **Meals** 6 to 12.30 **Cards** Access, Amex, Diners, Visa **Service** 10%

Pizza Express

22 Prince Albert Street, The Lanes

This is one of the 31 branches of by far and away the best of the pizza chains in the UK. Though each branch is individually decorated, one uniform thing is the smell – a fresh, yeasty, herby aroma hangs in all the dining areas. The staff know what the kitchen is serving, and although informal are efficient. What

175

BRIGHTON

distinguishes the pizzas: (*a*) the bases are made with properly kneaded yeast dough and are pushed out on to the pan/platter just before cooking, and (*b*) the toppings are the genuine article rather than cheap imitations – good-quality Mozzarella cheese, capers, sausage and so on are used. The choice includes seven pizzas for vegetarians. Licensed. No reservations.

Open Noon to midnight **Closed** Christmas

Shades of Green

13 Boyces Street *Telephone* (0273) 25195 £

Refreshingly normal wholefood and vegetarian restaurant. The name describes the decor. Short, straightforward list of dishes from moussaka to stir-fried vegetables with brown rice. A pot of herbal tea goes well with a fudge brownie or an oat and date slice. Unlicensed, but bring your own (no corkage).

Open 10.30 to 7

Topps Hotel

17 Regency Square *Telephone* (0273) 729334 ££

This conversion of two terraced Regency houses in a sea-front square is owned and run by Paul and Pauline Collins, who say their aim is to provide complete rest and relaxation in a friendly casual atmosphere: 'We do not appeal to people who like big hotels.' In the basement is a small restaurant called Bottoms, offering unpretentious home-cooked English dishes on a set dinner menu (£9.95). 'I believe Topps must be unique in Brighton. Unlike other period hotels in the area, it has been modernised from top to bottom. The double rooms are enormous: more suites than rooms. The bedroom boasts a settee, two armchairs, a coffee-table, a desk, very comfortable beds, remote-control colour TV, radio, telephone, mini-fridge, trouser press, also flowers and plants. The bathroom has a walk-in cupboard, two basins, bidet and hair dryer, plus lots of extras. Good-night chocolates are put out at night. Single rooms are much smaller, but nevertheless most comfortable. Paul and Pauline Collins are available from early to late as counsellors, tourist guides and friends to all their guests ... The food is home cooked by Mrs Collins on the premises, even including the bread rolls at breakfast. All the food is extremely "moreish". Prices are extremely reasonable ... A gem.'

Open 21 Jan to 31 Dec. Restaurant closed Sun and Wed **Cards** Access, Amex, Diners, Visa **Accommodations** 12 rooms, all with bath. B&B £22.50 to £39.50

The Twenty One

21 Charlotte Street *Telephone* (0273) 686450 £££

Simon Ward and Stuart Farquharson's early Victorian town house in Brighton's fashionable Kemp Town (warning: no lifts and lots of stairs to the top floor), offers a sophisticated personally caring place to stay as an alternative to large impersonal hotels and mediocre look-alike guest-houses. A bonus for 21's guests is that the owners serve ambitious gastronomic dinners in the French country cooking style. These no-choice five-course *menus dégustation* (£18) are said to be on the generous side of *nouvelle cuisine*, so you should go easy on Sussex cream teas. Typical offerings might be soup of carrot and coriander, salad of bacon and salsify dressed in walnut oil, and a main dish of fillet of beef coated with ground hazelnuts, sautéed and served with three kinds of mushrooms and a red wine sauce. Smaller appetites and special diets can be catered for with advance notice. 'Not a hotel of great luxury. You get the door key and there are often times when the owners are out shopping or whatever. They operate with the minimum of outside staff, so you have the odd feeling at times that it is like home when all the family are out. But it *is* comfortable and has style, which comes from personal involvement of the owners, and it doesn't take long to fall into the easy rhythm of the place. Take plenty of exercise before dinner: the menu tells only half the story!' One room has a four-poster bed. No children under 12, and no cigars or pipes in the dining-room.

Open 26 Jan to 21 Dec. Restaurant closed Sun; also lunchtime first 2 weeks Aug **Cards** Access, Amex, Diners, Visa **Service** (Restaurant) 12½% **Accommodations** 6 rooms, 4 with shower and WC. B&B £15 to £28.

Cambridge

At the time of the English Civil War in 1642–6, Cambridge was very much at the heart of anti-Royalist land, the leader of the Parliamentary troops, Oliver Cromwell, having been born a few miles away in St Ives. Oxford was equally staunchly on the side of King Charles I. There are those who maintain that the Puritanism of the Roundheads can still be perceived in Cambridge attitudes and the easy luxury, even decadence, of the Royalists in those of Oxford. But for a new visitor to Cambridge the first main focus is the river.

Many of Cambridge's oldest Colleges are on the river, and one of the nicest ways to spend a morning or afternoon would be to weave through them, crossing and re-crossing the Cam. Start at Magdalene College, particularly if Pepys' famous library is open, then wind your way through the back of St John's College, with its Bridge of Sighs, less menacing than Venice's version, and proceed to the majestic Trinity, with its vast first court and its Chapel, where statues of Trinity men such as Sir Isaac Newton and Alfred, Lord Tennyson welcome the visitor. This was Prince Charles's College. Trinity Hall, a totally separate College, is much more intimate, and is currently notable for spawning many British High Court judges and bishops.

One of the best views of the river is from the next College's bridge – Clare – a favourite spot to watch the punts drifting or zigzagging along under the willow trees. If your answer to the riddle 'How many balls are there on Clare bridge?' is fourteen, try feeling round the other side of them. The next College boasts Cambridge's most famous landmark, King's Chapel, whose choir broadcasts to the world every Christmas Eve. Even if you haven't time for the river walk, a visit to King's is essential, particularly if you can attend a service (the choir is on holiday in July and August). Rubens' painting of the Adoration of the Magi and the spectacular fan vaulting are just two of the Chapel's glories, but there are plenty wherever you look.

On to Queens', with its more higgledy-piggledy feel. Undergraduate plays are often held in the summer term in its Tudor court, but if your timing is wrong you can still walk over Sir Isaac Newton's Mathematical Bridge, allegedly designed to stand up without recourse to nuts and bolts (although these are in place out of deference to the nervous, and perhaps to the winds that blow off the fens). The dining halls of most colleges tend to be kept locked, but if you are able to peek into that of Queens' you will see one of the best and most colourful examples of Tudor halls in existence. (Note that you will have to pay an admission charge to enter the College grounds.)

On a beautiful day in the Easter Term (April to June), an even more romantic way to see these Colleges would be to hire a punt, either from Magdalene Bridge or Queens' Bridge, and settle down in the cushions to watch the best of Cambridge's architecture glide past. Your punter/guide in boater and cricket flannels and punting from the flat end will probably be earning a few pounds in between revising for the Tripos or Finals exams, and the picnic will seem twice as good for being partaken afloat. The punt option may well be the only one in the early summer when many of the Colleges reluctantly close their gates to visitors so that study can be uninterrupted.

CAMBRIDGE

There are plenty more Colleges for those smitten – any guidebook to the University will propose the attractions. But a one-day or weekend visitor may also want to wander in the town where fast bicycles rule the narrow streets. On foot, and again starting at Magdalene Bridge, you could drift in and out of some of Cambridge's most attractive shops: the silversmith's by the bridge itself and the Scottish Wool Shop further along opposite St John's. Turn right at the Round Church (also worth a visit): Trinity Street holds several traditional tailors and men's outfitters, two famous bookshops, Heffers and the former Bowes & Bowes (now Sherratt & Hughes), a branch of Laura Ashley, with its nostalgic and very British fashions, Liberty's, with its delectable fabrics and clothes, and old print shops and more besides. You could either carry on to the end of Trinity Street, passing into King's Parade, or else turn left off into Rose Crescent which leads past more gorgeous shops into the colourful open market.

If you're in a car and have the urge to eat outside Cambridge, the quiet village of Grantchester to the south-west of the city is famously beautiful. World War I poet Rupert Brooke lived here while he was at Cambridge – his are the lines 'Stands the Church clock at ten to three? And is there honey still for tea?' (Also his are the lines that run 'For Cambridge people rarely smile, Being urban, squat and packed with guile' . . .) The best of the village pubs, the Green Man, is low-beamed and dimly lit, with an open fire and wood-burning stove, and might be a cosy place to go if the weather is grey.

Slightly further afield is the village of Madingley, with its imposing Jacobean mansion (not open to the public) and, for many American visitors, an opportunity to pay homage to family and friends killed in World War II and commemorated at the American Cemetery. The Three Horseshoes in the middle of the village is a smart, thatched, white pub that comes into its own in summer when it's nice to sit out on the lawn, surrounded by flowering shrubs, roses and trees. The summer cold buffet includes meats, pâté, trout, prawns, crab and salmon, and you can choose from up to 14 fresh fish for the chef to charcoal-grill, such as herring, plaice, lemon or Dover sole.

A village that gives a taste of the fens, of which Cambridge is on the edge, is Horningsea. Its pub, the Plough and Fleece, is starred for its home-cooked food, which often uses imaginatively recast antique recipes, including Elizabethan rabbit (with apples, grapes, raisins and orange), honey-roast guinea-fowl, Suffolk ham hot-pot; Norfolk treacle tart and home-made ginger and brandy ice-cream too; Greene King beers. The pub has black beams in the red ceiling, butter-yellow walls, high-back settles, plain wooden tables – including the regulars' favourite, an enormously long slab of elm (with an equally long pew to match it) – and a stuffed parrot on the black fireplace.

As a final choice, the zany charm of the Tickell Arms at Whittlesford, south of the city, appeals to many. It is unique as much for the larger-than-life personality of its vivid owner as for its theatrical decor and atmosphere. The landlord will not serve you if you are in a collarless shirt or a T-shirt or wearing braces or a waistcoat without a jacket, or if you are a man with earrings or a 'long-haired leftie'. Shadowy and gothic, the no-smoking main room has good opera or ballet music. A big conservatory with pews on its flagstone floor opens on to a very neat garden with flower-filled stone urns and a long formal lily pool with a fountain. From quite a wide choice of food, we'd recommend

CAMBRIDGE

the unusually locally smoked meats such as quail or pike, cheese or pâté with good bread, and game casseroles and pies. There is good punch and in winter mulled wine (they also have Adnams and Greene King Abbot on handpump).

CAMBRIDGE

Auntie's

St Mary's Passage *Telephone* (0223) 315641   £

This is just the sort of tea shop you might expect if this were a cathedral city: the walls are apple-green, there are lacy cloths on the table, and the waitresses wear ruffled aprons over black dresses. The excellent scones, pies and cakes are all either made on the premises or by one of auntie's friends; the Black Forest gateau, chocolate fudge cake, and carrot and cream cheesecake are particularly good. Savoury snacks include a range of sandwiches and salads. The establishment's success is clearly shown by the queues.

Open 10 (noon Sun) to 6 **Closed** Christmas Day, Boxing Day, 31 Dec from 2pm

Cambridge Arms

King Street   £

The menu in this popular city-centre pub is split into sections – starters (which can be treated as a light snack) such as home-made soup, egg mayonnaise, two sorts of pâté, and avocado with prawns; hot main meals cooked to order from trout in almonds, escalope of chicken cooked in cider, and steak chasseur; cold buffet dishes such as home-made quiche and topside of beef; hot and tasty curries, chillies or goulash; and specialities such as savoury stuffed pancakes and moules marinière; also sandwiches (to order) and ploughman's. Well-kept Greene King IPA and Abbot on handpump. The comfortable and airy back lounge bar is a fairly recent conversion of what until 1925 was the Scales Brewery; an expanse of plummy carpet winds through arches of bare brick and up and down steps: you can look up through what used to be the opening housing the great mash tun to the old brewing floor, and big windows show tables out in a neat and sheltered brick-floored yard. Piped music. The friendly and simple public bar has bar billiards, darts, shove-ha'penny, cribbage and a fruit machine. Children are allowed in the eating area of the bar. Live jazz on Sundays, Mondays and Tuesdays.

Open 10.30 to 2.30, 6 to 11

Copper Kettle

4 King's Parade *Telephone* (0223) 65068   £

Framed prints of the colleges set the tone in this spacious beamed café across the road from King's College Chapel. Morning coffee comes with croissants; afternoon tea with gateaux and sandwiches. Lunches have a traditional flavour:

CAMBRIDGE

CAMBRIDGE

1 Auntie's	8 Free Press	16 Roof Garden
2 Cambridge Arms	9 Greenhouse	17 Salisbury Arms
3 Copper Kettle	10 Hobb's Pavilion	18 Shao Tao
4 Eagle	11 Martin's	19 Sweeney Todd's
5 Fitzbillies	12 May View Guest House	20 Twenty Two
6 Fitzwilliam Museum Coffee Shop	13 Nettles	21 University Arms
7 Fort St George	14 Pentagon	22 Upstairs
	15 Pizza Express	23 Waffles

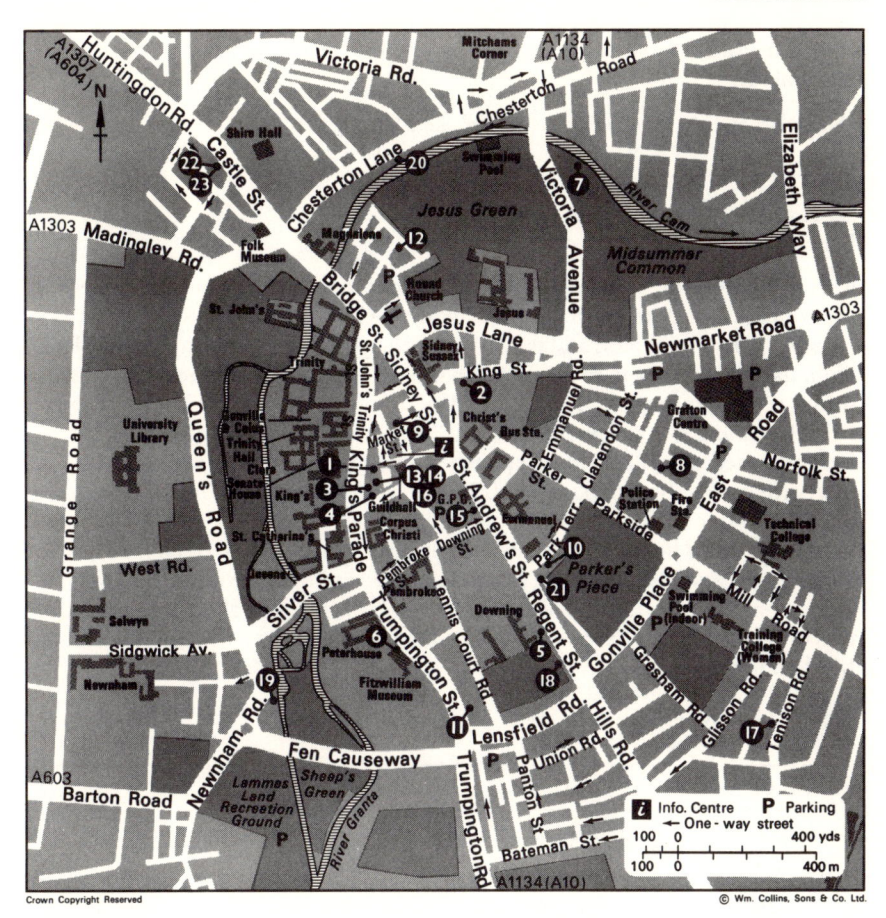

181

CAMBRIDGE

roast beef and Yorkshire pudding; steak and kidney pie; honey-roast ham with salad.

Open 9 (10 sun) to 5.30 **Closed** 25 & 26 Dec and 1 Jan

Eagle

Bene't Street £

This lively, central, 16th-century inn is a popular place all year – in summer for the cobbled and galleried coachyard, hidden behind a sturdy gate, with heavy wooden seats and tables, and in winter for the very warm little inglenook. The high, dark red ceiling in the main bar has been left unpainted since the war to preserve the signatures of British and American airmen worked in with 'Zippo' lighters, candle smoke and lipstick. The smaller Smoke Room has more old-fashioned sturdy furniture, and there is a separate family-room set with tables for eating. Bar food (at lunchtime, and between 6 and 8 in the evening – not Sundays) includes a choice of ploughman's, good-value salads and a choice of home-cooked hot daily specials such as Lancashire hot-pot or chilli, steak and kidney pie, casserole of pork in paprika, minted lamb casserole, or beef in orange Suffolk ale; traditional Sunday lunch (£2.45). They also serve afternoon teas between June and September. Well-kept Greene King Abbot, IPA and XX Mild on handpump.

Open 11 to 2.30, 6 to 11

Fitzbillies

50 Regent Street *Telephone* (0223) 64451 £

A tea room selling the same fine quality bread, cakes and pastries to eat in, as the shop, a famous Cambridge institution, does to take away. Chelsea buns are the most renowned speciality, and there are savouries too – such as pork and apple pie – especially popular at lunchtimes. The chocolates are worth the relatively high prices. Plans are afoot to open a tea room at the original branch – set up in the 1920s and little changed since – sometime during 1987: 52 Trumpington Street (0223) 352500.

Open 9 to 5 (6 Fri & Sat) **Closed** Sun

Fitzwilliam Museum Coffee Shop

Trumpington Street *Telephone* (0223) 69501 £

There's nothing fussy about the food in this friendly little coffee shop attached to the museum. Home-made soup and vegetable lasagne supplement the simple choice of fresh salads, wholemeal mushroom quiche and Cornish pasties. Scones are served with home-made jam and there are cakes to go with a cup of coffee or a pot of tea. Licensed.

Open 10.30 to 4 **Closed** Sun and Mon; Sun before Christmas to 2 Jan

CAMBRIDGE

Fort St George

Midsummer Common *Telephone* (0223) 354327   £

On fine days, the riverside terrace is the best spot for a drink at this 16th-century pub. To go with a pint there are home-made Scotch eggs; pâtés and cheeses with hunks of bread and bowls of soup. More substantial offerings might include broccoli bake.

Open Noon to 2, 6 to 9.30 **Closed** Sun D; Christmas Day

Free Press

7 Prospect Row *Telephone* (0223) 68337   £

Well off the beaten track, this welcoming and unspoilt pub used to be the city's smallest until it was extended into the house next door – without losing any of its cosy and friendly atmosphere. One room is served from a hatch, and furnishings are traditional throughout. There's a no-smoking area (unusually for a pub). Children are allowed in the snug. Popular bar food (lunchtime only) includes soup, cold dishes with three salads such as cheese, pâté, Scotch egg or quiche, meat pies, smoked ham and smoked mackerel; hot dishes such as Cornish pasties, African pork, chicken à la king or moussaka and vegetarian curry. Sweets are home made, too. Well-kept Greene King IPA and Abbot on handpump; dominoes and cribbage. Though many pubs in Cambridge sport oars and rowing photographs, this has the perfect right to them, as it's the only one here – or indeed anywhere – which is registered as a boat club.

Open 12 to 2.30, 6 to 11.30

Greenhouse

Eaden Lilley's (Department Store), Market Street   £
Telephone (0223) 358822

The self-service restaurant is on the second floor of this department store, behind the soft furnishings. Freshly prepared salads are the mainstay of the menu, and mayonnaise is made on the premises. There's also an array of fruit flans, trifles, cheesecakes, gateaux and pastries. The place is licensed too. On the first floor of the store is a coffee shop noted for its ice-cream sundaes.

Open 9.30 to 5 **Closed** Sun; public hols

Hobb's Pavilion

Park Terrace *Telephone* (0223) 67480   £

Filled pancakes are the theme here, and the choice is wide. On the savoury side there might be anything from pastrami with horseradish to smoked haddock with egg, plus vegetarian specials such as mushrooms with garlic. Sweet types

183

CAMBRIDGE

have included a straightforward Shrove Tuesday version with lemon and sugar and an unlikely combination of sliced Mars Bars with whipped cream. Greene King IPA, Aspall cider and a short wine list.

Open Noon to 2.30, 7 (8.30 Thur) to 10.30 **Closed** Sun and Mon

Martin's

4 Trumpington Street *Telephone* (0223) 61757   £

This little place is highly rated by locals and students from the nearby architectural school for its excellent Gaggia coffee, cheese scones, apple strudel and chocolate cake. It also serves traditional breakfast, as well as salads, pâté, omelettes, spaghetti and jacket potatoes. Very cheerful, very friendly. A handy stop before or after visiting the Fitzwilliam Museum.

Open 8.30 (9 Sat, 10 Sun) to 7.30 (5.30 Sat & Sun) **Closed** 25 & 26 Dec, 1 Jan, Good Fri

May View Guest House

12 Park Parade *Telephone* (0223) 66018

A great raft of compliments have arrived for this pretty Victorian B&B establishment in a quiet position overlooking Jesus Green and the river Cam, and only a few minutes' walk from the town centre and the colleges. It shows how rare and much needed such 'finds' are. Bedrooms are attractively decorated, likewise the breakfast room. There is an attractive courtyard/garden. The house has been in Roger Stock's family for more than half a century. He tells us that as there is no space for a guests' lounge, he has made a point of giving rooms antique furniture and paintings so as to make visitors feel they are in their own home. 'A little gem.' 'Extraordinarily reasonable charges.' No children under 7. There is no restaurant.

Open All year except 20 Dec to 2 Jan **Cards** None accepted **Accommodations** B&B (double room) £24 to £28

Nettles

6 St Edward's Passage *Telephone* (0223) 350983   £

Nettles is so tiny – it seats barely a dozen – that the person clearing the crockery has to go out the back way and come in through the front armed with a plastic bowl. The food is vegetarian: hot dishes like macaroni cheese, couscous or lentil roast are cooked each day and there are savoury flans, 100 per cent wholemeal rolls and bowls of salad, as well as a great dish of apple crumble with a nut and oat topping. Breakfast is real muesli with unpeeled garden apples and fresh cold milk. St Edward's churchyard is a peaceful retreat for anyone who wants to eat outside.

Open 9 to 3.30 **Closed** Sun

CAMBRIDGE

Pentagon

Arts Theatre, 6 St Edward's Passage
Telephone (0223) 359302

A wine bar and restaurant on the first floor of the Theatre complex, run separately from the Roof Garden listed below. There is a cold buffet of cold meats and fish and a selection of salads, as well as a choice of hot dishes, such as carbonnade of beef, fried skate, turkey and vegetable pie and escalope of veal chasseur. There are some decent half-bottles on the wine list, and the coffee is strong.

Open Noon to 2, 6 to 10.30 **Closed** Sun; some public hols; Christmas Day

Pizza Express

28 St Andrew's Street

This is one of the 31 branches of by far and away the best of the pizza chains in the UK. Though each branch is individually decorated, one uniform thing is the smell – a fresh, yeasty, herby aroma hangs in all the dining-areas. The staff know what the kitchen is serving, and although informal are efficient. What distinguishes the pizzas: (*a*) the bases are made with properly kneaded yeast dough and are pushed out on to the pan/platter just before cooking, and (*b*) the toppings are the genuine article rather than cheap imitations – good-quality Mozzarella cheese, capers, sausage and so on are used. The choice includes seven pizzas for vegetarians. Licensed. No reservations.

Open Noon to midnight **Closed** Christmas

Roof Garden

Arts Theatre, 6 St Edward's Passage
Telephone (0223) 355246

There are views of the city centre from the terraced garden of the self-service restaurant, which is open right through the day. The menu of salads and hot dishes changes daily. Hot quiche is the favourite with regulars, or there are local sausages, fried fish, a roast, omelettes and perhaps a curry or ragoût. Ploughman's lunch comes with a pint of beer or a glass of wine. There is usually a long queue for the lunch buffet when it opens at noon.

Open 9.30 to 8 **Closed** Sun; some public hols, Christmas Day

Salisbury Arms

Tenison Road

A dozen or so different real ales are on sale at a time in this big back-street pub, which obviously attracts crowds of customers to the large high-ceilinged back-lounge; even so, you can usually find a seat in the calmer side areas, which

185

CAMBRIDGE

are decorated with reproductions of old posters relating to beers and brewing. The much smaller front-bar is sometimes a haven of relative quiet. Bar food (lunchtime only) includes ploughman's with granary bread and a choice of cheeses or pâté, a hot dish such as chilli con carne, and a cold table; darts, dominoes, ring the bull, a pin-table and a fruit machine; they also keep farmhouse cider.

Open 11 to 2.30, 6 to 11

Shao Tao

72 Regent Street *Telephone* (0223) 353942   ££

The first reports of Mr Tao, who, the menu assures us, is very famous in London, say his is the best food in the city. Regent Street, Cambridge, though, is not Regent Street, London, and rates only a lower-second, but inside there are deep pink tablecloths in the two informal but pleasant air-conditioned dining-rooms. The menu shuns Canton in favour of Peking, Szechuan and Hunan with set meals (from £8.50) for initiates. Other stopping-off points are the duck dishes, such as Peking or Yu-Lung, a variation on it in which the duck arrives at the table already mixed in an aromatic sauce, crispy fried beef with chilli and carrots and spicy aubergine with garlic sauce. Lobster when it is available is £9. Sweets concentrate on toffee bananas and toffee apples. Tea is jasmine. The house wine from France is £5. Children's helpings. Music.

Open All week **Meals** 12 to 2.30, 6 to 11 (11.30 Fri and Sat) **Cards** Access, Amex, Diners, Visa **Service** 10%

Sweeney Todd's

The Watermill, Newnham *Telephone* (0223) 67507   £

A converted watermill on the Newnham Road is the setting for this East Anglian link in a stylish chain of five pizzerias. Customers can look through the glass-topped tables to see the millstream racing below. The pizzas are enjoyable and the hamburgers okay. If the place is full go next door to J Miller's cocktail bar: Sweeney's will call you when a table is free. Licensed.

Open Noon to midnight **Closed** 25 & 26 Dec, 1 Jan

Twenty Two

22 Chesterton Road *Telephone* (0223) 351880   £££

Twenty Two is a small restaurant near Jesus Green and fashionably decorated in greys and pinks. The menu (£13.50) offers at least four choices at each stage, displaying the trademarks of modern British cooking – the changing menu; the heavy showing of vegetable soups, such as carrot and orange, parsnip and

---

If you have to cancel a reservation for a bedroom or table, please telephone to warn the proprietor. A small place will suffer if you don't.

CAMBRIDGE

coriander; the three-dimensional main courses, such as a fine dish of skate with dry cider, apples, tomato, and cream; and pigeon, mussel, and steak pie; vegetarian options, too. The salads are from Joy Larkcom and are an education in varieties. The sweets are multi-flavoured, for instance pineapple with coconut ice-cream and mango purée, or apple, calvados, and walnut cake. The wine list has a little of something from everywhere, mostly cleverly chosen without being too expensive. Children welcome; music.

Open Tue to Sat, D only **Closed** Christmas to New Year, 1 week Mar, 3 weeks Sept **Meals** 7.30 to 10 **Cards** Not accepted

University Arms

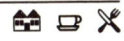

Regent Street *Telephone* (0223) 351241 £

The most stylish place for a leisurely snack in the city is under the great glass dome of the Octagon lounge. The furnishings are grand, the coffee is good, the sandwiches excellent and the sweets trolley has an impressive array of creamy confections alongside Swiss roll, fruit cake and Battenberg cake. Afternoon tea here is as good value as anywhere else in Cambridge. Hobson's Bar by the hotel entrance serves baked potatoes and pizzas; the more spacious Parker's Bar, overlooking the green sweep of Parker's Piece, offers sandwiches and salads. Bedrooms are comfortable, some traditional, some modern, and all with bathroom.

Open 7am to 9.45pm **Closed** Christmas Day **Cards** Access, Amex, Diners, Visa **Accommodations** 115 rooms (all with bath) B&B £23.50 to £33

Upstairs

71 Castle Street *Telephone* (0223) 312569 ££

Cambridge, for so long Oxford's poor relation in terms of interesting restaurants, seems suddenly to have come to life, and new enterprises such as this mean that there are now alternatives to eating in College which won't break the bank. The cosy L-shaped dining-room above Waffles (see below) has Persian rugs on the tiled floor, Arabic latticed screens, and a beautiful metal bird-cage with a candle in it. To match this, the food is North African and Middle Eastern without compromises, which means earthy forthright flavours and generous helpings. There are no prizes for guessing where chef Hywel Evans was born, but he was taught by a Moroccan and has learned his lessons well. His couscous is leg of lamb cooked with ginger and vegetables and the couscous grain itself, topped with a rich sauce of chickpeas, onions, and raisins, and served in an earthenware tajine. To start there is hearty harira (a Moroccan beef broth with lentils and chickpeas), healthy tabouleh, or amram (minced lamb and bulghur patties). To finish, try haytaliah, a refreshing fruit salad with limes. Coffee is a complex brew flavoured with cardamoms and orange water, and it comes with soft, freshly made cubes of halva. House wine is Bulgarian at £4.25 a bottle. They prefer you to dress not too casually. Children's helpings. Music.

Open Tue to Sun **Meals** 6.30 to 10.30 (9.30 Sun) **Cards** Access, Visa **Service** Inc

CAMBRIDGE

Waffles

71 Castle Street *Telephone* (0223) 312569

The mood here is very 'Upstairs, Downstairs', from the Victorian decor, old cash register and sparkling urn to the menu which is priced in 'old' money (pounds, shillings and pence). Crisp savoury waffles ('from one guinea'), come topped with anything from asparagus and egg sauce or ratatouille, to tuna supreme. Sweet versions ('from eighteen shillings'), might have butter and maple syrup; brandied raisins or spiced apple. On Sundays there is also an excellent breakfast. Fruit juices and buttermilk as well as a tea and coffee; also beers and wines.

Open Tue to Fri 6.30 to 11, Sat 6 to 12, Sun 9.30 to 2, 6 to 11 **Closed** Mon; 25 & 26 Dec

Canterbury

Canterbury, ringed by its Norman walls, has been the focus of the English Church for almost 1400 years. At its core is the Cathedral, which dominates the city and lies at the heart of English Christianity. Canterbury's history, however, goes back long before St Augustine established an abbey here in AD 597, bringing the Christian faith to the Saxon king, Ethelbert. Even the Roman invaders of 43 BC arrived to find a settlement on the banks of the Stour. But it was the Normans who have left the greatest legacy, and despite the ravages of war, including Hitler's bombing raids of 1942 (the Cathedral survived relatively unscathed), the city retains a significant number of its fine buildings.

Approximately half the city's walls remain intact, tracing the foundations of the Roman wall built in the third century AD. The ancient streets within the walls have largely shunned the onslaught of cars, making the city an ideal place in which to wander. But like the pilgrims of Chaucer's *Canterbury Tales*, the Cathedral forms the centre of any visit.

The Cathedral replaced the Saxon church burnt down after the Norman Conquest. The present Cathedral was started in 1070 by Archbishop Lanfranc, but it was added to over the next few centuries, giving it a mixture of both Norman and Perpendicular styles. It is not the largest of England's cathedrals, but it is one of the most beautiful and has some of the finest stained-glass windows in the country. Christ Church Gate is the main entrance, an imposing sixteenth-century stone gatehouse opening on to a spectacular view of the Cathedral and its three towers. The largest of these towers houses the enormous old 'Bell Harry', which is still rung each evening to signify an ancient curfew.

Probably the most significant single event to occur in the Cathedral was the murder of Thomas à Becket in 1170. As Archbishop, Becket defied King Henry II in favour of the Church and was consequently slain by four of the King's knights in the north-west transept. A small slab of stone on the floor denotes the spot where he fell. A shrine was built for the remains of St Thomas (he was canonised two years after his death) in Trinity Chapel. It was to here that the pilgrims came for the next 350 years to pay tribute, the mosaic floors worn from the passage of so many feet. It is here too that the tomb of the Black Prince lies; at the base of the Pilgrims' Steps a glass case contains his original armour and helmet.

From the cloisters it is possible to make your way into King's School, which was founded by King Henry VIII but which claims a heritage back to the time of Ethelbert at the beginning of the seventh century. More recently it was the school of Somerset Maugham, whose ashes are buried beneath a rose bush outside the library, to which he gave his collection of books. One of Maugham's most famous works, *Of Human Bondage*, is set in King's School and is based on his own early experiences. Opposite the library is an impressive Norman staircase.

Outside the school, on the corner of Palace Street, stands one of Canterbury's more curious Tudor buildings, The King's School Shop, with its slanting door. Both Palace Street and The Borough, which adjoins, are good haunts for those interested in antiques. From The Borough it is possible to follow the line of the

CANTERBURY

old walls alongside the Stour towards the Westgate, a formidable structure. It is the only one of the original seven gates to have survived. Though long used as the city's jail, Westgate is now a museum.

Across the Stour is one of Canterbury's most famous inns, the Falstaff. Built at the beginning of the fifteenth century and now a hotel, it was commonly used by pilgrims arriving too late to enter the city. Further along St Dunstan's stands St Dunstan's Church, which dates from the eleventh century. In the church is St Nicholas' Chapel, established by the Roper family, and buried within the chapel vault is the head of Sir Thomas More, which was brought from his execution at the Tower of London by his daughter, Margaret Roper.

On the other side of the bridge is Canterbury's main street, its name changing from St Peter's to High Street, Parade, and finally St George's Place. Among the many fine medieval buildings, the Weavers' House is perhaps the most picturesque. The sixteenth-century half-timbered building is close to the waters of the Stour, along which barges delivered the fleeces for the Flemish and Huguenot weavers who had come to Canterbury to seek religious refuge. Demonstrations of hand-weaving are given, and brass rubbings can be made in the same building.

In the streets leading off the High Street is a wealth of interesting buildings, many with historical and literary associations. Charles Dickens stayed at the Sun Inn (*David Copperfield* is set in Canterbury). Chaucer owned a house here near The Borough. Christopher Marlowe was born in Canterbury, and a memorial to him stands near the city's walls in Dane John Gardens. Joseph Conrad spent his last years here and is buried in the Canterbury Cemetery.

If you want a diversion from history, Canterbury has some interesting shops to explore. Laura Ashley's shop at Buttermarket and Liberty's nearby in Burgate are both in interesting old buildings. For a good choice of gifts the Cathedral has its own gift shop near the Christ Church Gate. For some very English gifts, try the National Trust gift shop in Burgate; it sells scented soaps, home-made jams, pot-pourri, and so on. In St Margaret's Street, Culpeper The Herbalist is full of English garden scents. And for the bookworm The Chaucer Bookshop on Beer Cart Lane has two floors of books and prints.

Canterbury has still more to offer with a walk along the remaining eastern walls of the city or seeing the remains of the Roman pavement. For the dedicated who have a taste for history, outside the walls to the east of the Cathedral lie the ruins of St Augustine's Abbey and College where King Ethelbert is buried. Nearby is St Martin's Church, believed to be the oldest church in England.

CANTERBURY

Cogan House ✗ ⌸

53 St Peter's Street *Telephone* (0227) 472986 ££

Ian and Jane McAndrew of Restaurant Seventy Four (see below) have opened this all-day bistro in Canterbury's oldest private residence, which dates from 1170. Peter Chapman uses fine local ingredients and cooks the set meals (£6) with gusto. Pork, chicken and walnut terrine with orange and redcurrant sauce is a highlight among the starters, and soups are skilfully made. Main courses can

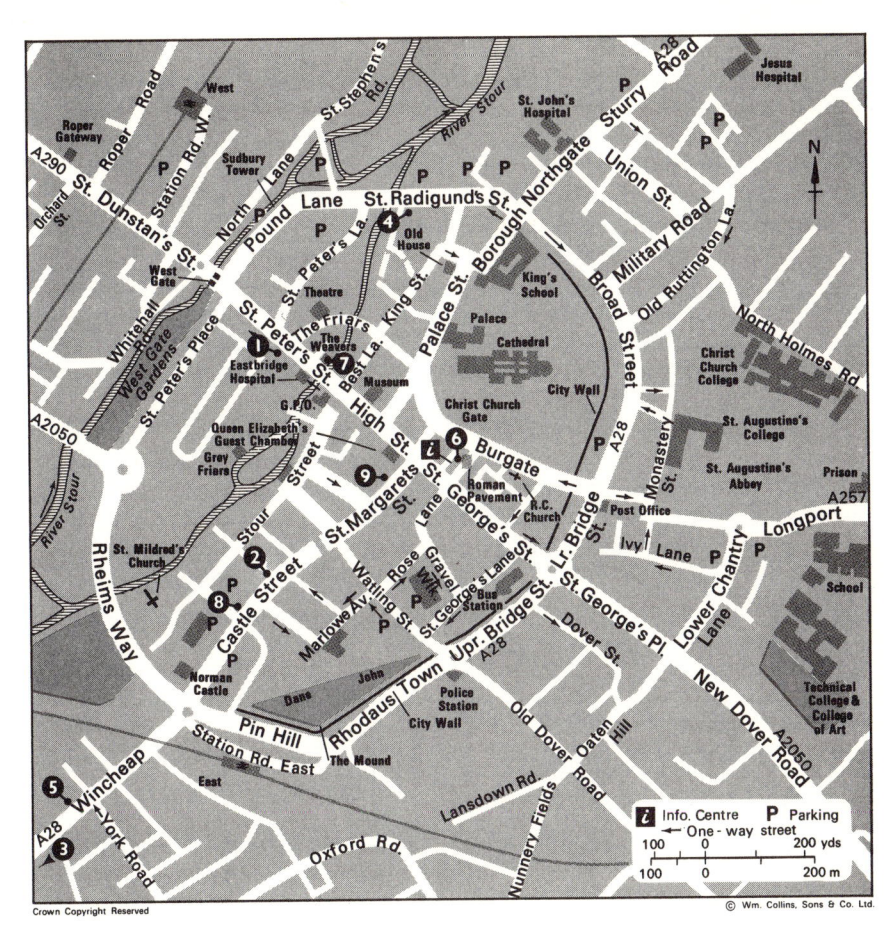

CANTERBURY

CANTERBURY
1 Cogan House
2 George's Brasserie
3 Howfield Manor
4 Millers Arms
5 Restaurant Seventy Four
6 Sweeney Todd's
7 Sweet Heart of Canterbury
8 Tascolls Wine Bar
9 Il Vaticano

CANTERBURY

range from lamb with tomato and herb sauce to fillets of plaice fried in butter with sliced banana and fennel. Vegetables are crisp and buttered and vegetarian main dishes are easily come by. To finish there are good sweets and a whole table of excellent English farmhouse cheeses. The bistro offers morning coffee, light snacks, afternoon teas and suppers as well as full meals, but alcoholic drinks are only available during licensing hours. House wine is £4.50 a bottle. Children are welcome. There is a no-smoking area.

Open Tue to Sun **Closed** Mid-Feb to early Mar **Meals** 10.30 (noon Sun) to 10.30 **Cards** Access, Visa

George's Brasserie

71–72 Castle Street *Telephone* (0227) 65658 £–££

A request for kippers, three boiled eggs, couscous and mussels raised no eyebrows in this all-day brasserie with bare white walls and views of the immaculate kitchen. Pink roast rack of lamb comes with apricot sauce, salmon is cooked with ginger and spring onions, and there is chorizo sausage with peperonata. Watch the prices charged for vegetables and potatoes. Open late for theatre-goers.

Open 10 to 10 (to 10.30 Fri and Sat) **Closed** Sun

Howfield Manor

On A28 2m SW of Canterbury at Chartham Hatch £££
Telephone (0227) 738294 and 738495

Howfield Manor is owned and run by the Lawrences, Clark (who is American) and his wife Janet (English). It may be used as a staging post for those *en route* to the Channel ports, but it also makes a luxurious centre for touring the area: Canterbury, of course, is just two miles up the road, Leeds and Bodiam castles and many other tourist attractions are within easy driving distance. 'Amazingly beautiful... Manor is the right word for it – gabled red-brick, parts dating from the twelfth century, a monk's well, the outline of a Gothic chapel window, beams and enormous inglenook fireplaces, candlelight glimmering on antique furniture, the unaffectedly friendly welcome of the owners – all this contributes to the most notable feature of this hotel, its atmosphere. The bedroom accommodation is luxurious. The cooking is straightforward in its style, relying on good ingredients.' It is a relaxed, friendly sort of place. Guests sit family-style in the beamed dining-room and pour their own drinks in the bar. Meals – their four-course set menu (£14) is warmly recommended – can be taken out of doors in fine weather. The Manor has a five-acre garden with a croquet lawn. No children under 12.

Open Mid-Jan to mid-Dec **Cards** Access, Amex, Visa **Accommodations** 5 double rooms (all with bath). B&B £21.50 to £38

If you are planning a trip to Scotland and the Lake District, there is another Guide in this series to those areas.

CANTERBURY

Millers Arms

Mill Lane, St Radigunds *Telephone* (0227) 452675 £

A pub-lover's pub across the road from the Stour, offering well-kept beer, including ale from the landlord's own Canterbury Brewery – and a short blackboard list of bar lunches (no food in the evenings). A typical day might offer chilli, lamb stew, hot Kentish smokey, and chicken in a wine sauce served with mushrooms and courgettes and a salad of peppers and celery. There are no starters or desserts, and service is take-it-or-leave-it.

Open 12.30pm to 2pm, evenings

Restaurant Seventy Four

74 Wincheap *Telephone* (0227) 67411 ££–££££

Ian McAndrew has quietly developed his own style at this big house with panelled rooms. He experiments with jellies – a crab-flavoured aspic around a fish mousse, a cucumber jelly sent out before the meal starts, a fruit salad set in a mould of Muscat de Beaumes de Venise. His cooking straddles both classic and modern, French and English. One element of the new British cooking evident in the main courses is the use of a third ingredient – beef in port wine with bone-marrow, tomatoes and herbs, or veal fillet in madeira butter sauce with shiitake mushrooms. Outstanding have been bright yellow saffron soup fragrant with thin slices of scallops and the tiniest diced vegetables; spinach soufflé in spinach sauce; halibut with a mousse of scallops and spinach, half pink, half green, surrounded by a pool of butter and cream sauce and garnished with one scallop coral; and lamb with scallops, perfect pink circles of lamb and circles of scallop with a terracotta-coloured tarragon-flavoured sauce. Bread is either round and brown or long and white poppyseed, served with curls of fresh butter. Sweets are far from traditional – brioche filled with hot raspberries and served on a glaze. Lunch and dinner are set meals (from £9.50 and from £20 respectively). The wine list has some expensive bottles but not to the exclusion of house wine at £6.20 nor to a good-value Loire section. Children's helpings for over-fives. No smoking area; wheelchair access.

Open Mon to Sat, exc Sat L **Closed** Public hols, 2 weeks summer, 1 week Easter **Meals** 12.30 to 2, 7.30 to 9.30 **Cards** Access, Amex, Diners, Visa

Sweeney Todd's

8 Butchery Lane *Telephone* (0227) 453148 £

The Kent branch of this stylish chain of pizzerias is in the cellar of a fifteenth-century building. From the zany menu, pizzas are reasonable, burgers okay. Licensed.

Open Noon to midnight (11am to midnight Sat) **Closed** 24, 25, 27 & 31 Dec

---

You can expect to pay about £5 for a good snack or pub meal.

CANTERBURY

Sweet Heart of Canterbury 🍵

Old Weavers House, 2–3 Kings Bridge *Telephone* (0227) 458626   £

German-Swiss-style café transplanted into the garden of England. English tea-time specialities are supplemented by savoury dishes including quiche, bacon croissants and bratwurst; ice-cream is home made without artificial flavourings or colourings; there's a range of confectionery. At Easter and Christmas seasonal items such as Stollen and Lebkuchen are on offer. But the real forte is the selection of deliciously light cakes and pastries from Diplomat torte (chocolate sponge, rum, glacé cherries and almond marzipan coating) and Canterbury cake (which is iced with an edible map of the city) to Kent apple pie, blackberry tartlets and red plum flan. Good coffee and ten varieties of tea.

Open 9 to 6 **Closed** 2 weeks early Jan

Tascolls Wine Bar

49 Castle Street *Telephone* (0227) 60381   £

A wooden wine bar off the beaten track with a liking for Henri Rousseau-style murals (painted by local art students to match the cloth parrot in the window) loud classical music, and garlic in the avocado sauce as well as the machine-made pasta. Mince is laced with chilli – otherwise, the menu ranges from beef bourguignonne to croque-monsieur. As a change from wine, try clear, still Biddenden cider or apple juice from Heronsgate Fruit Farm, Stourmouth.

Open 10.30am to 12.30am (midnight Sat) **Closed** Sun; public hols

Il Vaticano ✕

35 St Margaret Street *Telephone* (0227) 65333   £

This old building has been given a new lease of life as one of the new breed of pasta bars. The brightly painted chairs, bare wooden floors and fresh flowers on the stone-topped tables lend an air of polished functionality. The menu is printed on the place-mats: fresh pasta (shells, spirals, tubes, noodles), sauces (mushroom, clams, pesto, vegetables, chicken), a few starters such as gazpacho, tuna and bean salad, plus garlic bread. For pudding there's sometimes chocolate pasta. Licensed.

Open 11 to 11 (noon to 10 Sun) **Closed** Christmas Day and Boxing Day

---

As well as picking out tea shops in their own right, the tea shop symbol denotes that afternoon tea is available to non-residents in hotels.

✕ = *restaurant*
🏨 = *hotel*
🍺 = *pub*
🍷 = *wine bar*
🍵 = *tea shop*

Oxford

With a population of some 120,000 Oxford is quite a sizeable city, but the Colleges are in a relatively confined area and are ideal for exploring on foot. The restricted parking and exasperating one-way system manage to deter drivers, too, and many of the university's 12,000 students either walk or cycle – the hundreds of bicycles everywhere testify to their popularity.

Perhaps the best point at which to begin exploring Oxford is from the ancient crossroads known as Carfax. Two of the streets that lead off Carfax, Cornmarket and Queen Street, are popular shopping precincts. To the east lies the sweeping arc of the High Street ('The High'), and leading off to the south is St Aldate's with two important Colleges.

Christ Church, referred to as simply 'The House', is the largest of Oxford's colleges and has the largest quadrangle – in keeping with the grand aspirations of its founder, Cardinal Wolsey. The gatehouse entrance, crowned with Wren's later addition of a domed tower, houses the enormous bell, 'Great Tom'. Each night at 9.05 the bell is rung 101 times, representing the original number of students, to announce the shutting of the gates. The College's chapel is also Oxford's Cathedral; it dates from the beginning of the thirteenth century and is the smallest cathedral in Britain.

Among its alumni Christ Church has spawned 18 of England's Prime Ministers, but one of its dons (academics), Charles Lutwidge Dodgson who, under his pen name, Lewis Carroll, is perhaps better remembered. *Alice in Wonderland* was inspired by the daughter of the Dean of Christ Church, Alice Liddell. Near to the College, at 83 St Aldate's, is the shop from Carroll's *Through the Looking Glass*.

Opposite Christ Church is Pembroke College, where Samuel Johnson studied until poverty caused him to leave before he could complete his degree. The College now has a portrait of him by Sir Joshua Reynolds and that most important of an Englishman's accoutrements, his teapot.

From Pembroke, return to Carfax and into The High, and admire the splendour of the Cotswold stone buildings with their golden glow. Among them are Brasenose and All Souls Colleges, the latter unique in that it consists solely of fellows (senior members), distinguishing it from the other colleges. Queen's College nearby is one of the oldest in the University.

Opposite, a lane leads to Merton Street, Oxford's only surviving cobbled street. Merton College was the first of Oxford's Colleges and dates from 1264. Also in Merton Street is the college of Corpus Christi, with its famous sundial in the quadrangle. In a narrow street leading back to The High stands Oriel College, where in the early part of the nineteenth century, was centred the Oxford Movement, which opposed rationalism and liberalism within the Church of England.

On the other side of The High, two alleys lead into the Covered Market, something of a temple to food, with inviting displays of produce and small cafés noted for their breakfast fare. For that favourite English breakfast preserve, Frank Cooper's Shop on The High is the home of fine marmalades.

Further north towards St Giles is the Ashmolean Museum. Architecturally it

OXFORD

is a glorious example of the Classical style, but it is also outstanding for its varied collections, which include such curiosities as Guy Fawkes' lantern as well as a wealth of paintings.

From the Ashmolean, aim for one of Oxford's most interesting streets, Broad Street. It is the setting for Balliol and Trinity Colleges as well as the Sheldonian Theatre. Christopher Wren's first building, the Sheldonian, is based on a Roman theatre, the entrance guarded by a curious row of monumental busts. For the hearty it is worth climbing to the theatre's cupola, where you get excellent views of the dreaming spires and of the Bodleian Library. The University's main library, the Bodleian, comprises several buildings around Radcliffe Square. The Library's massive collection numbers over four million volumes, and it receives a copy of every book published in the UK. The beautiful Venetian-styled Radcliffe Camera now serves as a reading room for the Bodleian.

For those with a love of books, Broad Street has still more to offer with the old bookshop Thornton's remaining relatively unchanged over the years. In a basement under Trinity College, Blackwell's Norrington Room houses the world's largest display of books for sale. Oxford also has a fine tradition of tailoring, which is maintained at such shops as Hine's in the High Street, Castell's in Broad Street, and Walter's of The Turl.

A final stroll through the Colleges should include Hertford College, with its Bridge of Sighs. More recent than its Cambridge counterpart, it is nevertheless a more faithful reproduction of the Venetian original. Nearby is New College, the first of Oxford's Colleges to be constructed on the quadrangle format. Further east along the High Street is Magdalen College. At 6.00 am on May Day each year the choir sings from the top of Magdalen Tower.

Lying beside Magdalen College is the River Cherwell (pronounced Charwell), and it is from here that you can take a leisurely punt along its waters lined with graceful weeping willows. But remember to punt from the sloping end . . .

As well as the pubs and restaurants within the city listed below you might like to visit a couple just outside. To get to the **Perch** at Binsey you need to keep your eyes skinned for Binsey Lane on the right as you leave Oxford on the A420 (the turning is just before Bishop's Furniture Depository). At the end of the long lane this spacious thatched pub rambles about comfortably, with some flagstoned areas, wooden dividers between stone pillars, high-backed settles, high shelves of plates, and a couple of log fires in winter. The bare stone walls have quite a few pictures (especially of perches – including the US Submarine *Perch* sunk in 1942). Bar food includes curried beef, Somerset pork or Kentish beef, trout or harvest pie and a help-yourself salad bar; they also do afternoon teas at weekends. The garden leads down to the riverside meadows.

The **Bear and Ragged Staff** at Cumnor, further out of the city but also off the A420, is popular for meals, with quite elaborate bar food including a fine cold table in summer with lots of salads, pâté, hot dishes such as ham and asparagus quiche or spicy sausage flan, grilled salmon with caper butter, breaded sweetbreads with tartare sauce, or beef and apricot pie. There's a good log fire in winter, guarded by a three-feet model of the Warwick heraldic bear from which the pub gets its name. The bar area is a spreading, comfortable one, with sofas as well as more orthodox cushioned seats, soft lighting, polished black sixteenth-century flagstones in one part and Turkey carpet elsewhere.

Wytham (pronounced White-ham) to the north-west of the city (signposted from the A34 ring road) holds the **White Hart**. The main room of this tall, creeper-covered, seventeenth-century stone pub has flagstones, wheelback chairs and high-backed black settles built almost the whole way around its cream walls, with a shelf of blue and white plates above them, and a fine relief of a hart on the iron fireback. The big self-service cold table neatly laid out in one room (not winter lunchtimes) – with some fourteen salads and a good choice of cold meats and home-made pies – is particularly good value. At lunchtime in winter there is home-made soup and one hot dish such as a casserole or hot pie. In the evenings there are hot dishes too. Well-kept Halls Harvest and Ind Coope Burton on handpump, and a good choice of malt whiskies; the atmosphere is cosy and relaxed but get there early if you want a table. More seats in the garden.

Finally, not far from Oxford is **Le Manoir aux Quat' Saisons**. We print here the entries from both *The Good Hotel Guide* and *The Good Food Guide* since both acknowledge it, with the occasional reservation, as one of the foremost hotel-restaurants in the country.

Le Manoir aux Quat' Saisons

Church Road, Great Milton *Telephone* (084 46) 8881   ££££

Raymond and Jenny Blanc's triumphant realisation of the platonic idea of a country house hotel incarnate in a serene country manor amid 27 acres of gardens and parkland, a mile off the M40, eight miles south-east of Oxford, continues to garner compliments of the most unstinting kind: 'Exquisite. Expensive but worth every penny.' 'Probably the best food in England.' 'Expensive, but no hidden charges and they do everything possible to make guests feel pampered. Fresh flowers *everywhere*. Fruit bowl in room refilled twice a day. Special dietary needs attended to with utmost seriousness. All the staff pleasant and competent. Perfection!' 'The set dinner was superb: it finally converted me to the view that Blanc is a genius. Our multi-course meal was notable for its multiplicity of clear flavours and for its lightness – no question of over-richness or surfeit here. Service was both accomplished and informal. Breakfasts were faultless too.' There have been, however, a few niggles on the hotel side. Two readers have commented on snootiness at reception, and several readers found blemishes in their room which they felt the management should have picked up. As usual, when prices are high, guests expect perfection, which the two-rosetted restaurant appears to be able to deliver every time and the hotel side with slightly less dependability. (*The Good Hotel Guide*)

It is testimony to Raymond Blanc's cooking that despite the expense of eating here, the *Guide* has sixty-two recommendations for different dishes that reporters have eaten at Le Manoir in the past year. Coffee with petits fours at an astonishing £3 claims seven specific endorsements. Even the French guidebook *Gault/Millau* has finally rumbled what we have known since the late 1970s – that Blanc's is no ordinary talent. The restaurant's main weakness at present is that it lacks some consistency: occasionally, dishes are not of the level of the rest of the repertoire. But these are exceptions in what has become an extraordinary procession of creativity, passion, subtlety, indeed genius, which comes out of the electrically operated kitchen doors. Eating at Le Manoir is like eating in the

OXFORD

future. Take, for example, new season's lamb with a mild curry and basil sauce. Or partridge and duck with a veal sauce. Or salmon and turbot steamed in cabbage leaves. Or grain-fed Norfolk pigeon baked in salt. All this is served with grace and good humour in the elegant pink dining-room of the aristocratic house, which has equally elegant grounds and garden. The emphasis is on dramatic presentation; the now often-plagiarised salmon tartare – the opening trademark of the move from Oxford to this old village – wrapped up in cucumber and crowned with caviare, is one end of a spectrum that extends right through to a virtually *bourgeois* and very rich amalgam of fried foie gras with pigs' trotters stuffed with veal sweetbreads and lambs' tongues. Fish draws thunderous applause – the red mullet fillets pan-fried with pistou and the sauce of veal stock with more basil. Among the many sweets commended are coconut soufflé, apple mille-feuille, and peach in Sauternes. There is more, much more. One meal may be a temptation to return for another, but, alas, the wine list assists in making this more financially difficult. (As it is, the set lunch cost upwards of £19.50, dinner upwards of £25.) Three figures for Drouhin's Musigny may be justified because it is a 1949, but credibility is stretched as much as the pocket with a £118 tag for Bonneau du Martray's undoubtedly first-rate 1978 Corton Charlemagne. Both négociants and growers provide the Burgundies, and the vintage spread of clarets is impressive with all the big names here; but Ch La Cardonne 1978 is one of the few under £20. Côtes de Buzet 1982 Cuvée Napoléon is a relatively inexpensive alternative to red Bordeaux at £11.65. Sweet teeth are indulged with good Barsac, and Jaboulet dominates the Rhône. No smoking in the dining-room; wheelchair access. No children under seven. (*The Good Food Guide*)

Open (Restaurant) Tue to Sun, exc Tue L and Sun D **Closed** 4 weeks from 24 Dec **Meals** 12.15 to 2.30, 7.15 to 10.30 **Cards** Access, Amex, Visa **Service** Inc **Accommodations** 10 rooms (all with bath and shower, 2 with four-poster bed). B&B (double room) £95 to £180. Deposit £50.

OXFORD

Bear

Alfred Street £

The special feature at this pub is the unrivalled collection of club ties, all neatly arranged behind glass – beware of wearing a really uncommon one, as scissors are still ready to chop off a new specimen. The four low-ceilinged and partly panelled rooms have a genuinely old-fashioned feeling, with their traditional built-in benches and plain tables, and parts of the building date back over seven hundred years. Even the handpumps – serving well-kept Halls Harvest and Ind Coope Burton – are over a century old. The home-made bar food including sandwiches or filled rolls, ploughman's, home-made pâté, quiche, and chicken or pies served generously with chips and beans, goes down well in term-time with a throng of students from Christ Church and Oriel Colleges. There are tables on a side terrace.

Open 10.30 to 2.30, 5.30 to 11

OXFORD

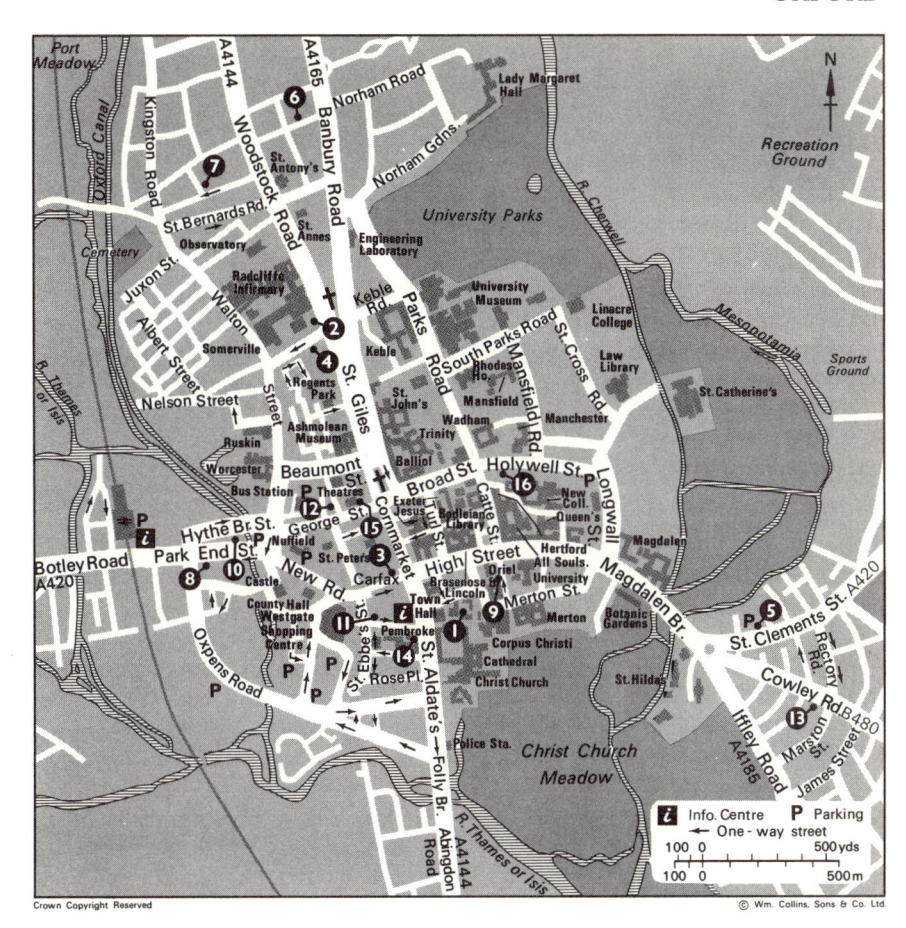

OXFORD

1. Bear
2. Browns
3. The Crypt
4. Fasta Pasta
5. Fellows Brasserie
6. 15 North Parade
7. Gardeners Arms
8. Go Dutch
9. Health Food Shop
10. Munchy Munchy
11. Museum of Modern Art
12. Oxford Bakery and Brewhouse
13. Pak Fook
14. St Aldate's Coffee House
15. Sweeney Todd's
16. Turf

OXFORD

Browns ✕

5–9 Woodstock Road *Telephone* (0865) 511995 ££

Oxford is a city of institutions: Browns is its most light-hearted. Cocktails, imported beers, music, papers to read – all the touches that so many places self-consciously try to imitate come naturally here. The decor is staccato: cream colours, mirrors, potted plants à l'Astoria, hanging baskets à la Babylon, fans, parquet flooring, polished deep brown circular wooden tables, some big (for eight or so), but mostly smaller, for twos and fours. Under the skylight in the centre, with its hanging baskets, is a good place to sit when the sunlight streams through. Sometimes there are long waits: twenty minutes outside can mean half an hour inside before getting a table. There is no booking. Some dishes are very good, some a bit misconceived, but the standard is reliable and unfluctuating. Ruben's sandwiches are excellent if you like corned beef and Sauerkraut. Vegetarian salads are enormous. Browns' leg of lamb grilled with rosemary and served with Oxford sauce of redcurrants, orange zest and wine claims many good reports, as do desserts such as banana cream pie. Steak and Guinness pie is another favourite. The house wine is £4.45. Children's helpings; wheelchair access; air-conditioning.

Open All week **Closed** 24 to 28 Dec **Meals** 11 (12 Sun) to 11.30

The Crypt ♀

Frewin Court, off Cornmarket *Telephone* (0865) 251000 £

These 'wine and steak vaults' follow John Davy's attractive formula (see under Davys in the City of London section): Victorian atmosphere, sawdust floors, wine paraphernalia. The wine list is the standard reliable three dozen, sensibly chosen and priced, from French 'Ordinary' red or white (£4.50/75p) to Ch Haut-Batailley 1974 (£11.75). Look out for blackboard special offers, and don't neglect the excellent port, sherry and Madeira from the wood. The food formula is less attractive, but adequate.

Open Mon to Sat 11.30 to 2.30, 6 to 10.30 (Fri 6 to 11, Sat 7 to 11) **Closed** Sun, public holidays **Cards** Access, Amex, Diners, Visa

Fasta Pasta ✕

3 Little Clarendon Street *Telephone* (0865) 57349 £

This dark green and white pasta shop with its pot plants and wall-paintings of rural Italy sells fresh pasta and sauces to take out and eat in at little garden tables. Apart from a usual run of sauces – pesto, alfredo, bolognese – there is a sauce of the day (the spinach and cream is good), and a dish of the day – perhaps ravioli with cream and tomato, or an excellent cannelloni. Good sorbets to follow. Licensed.

Open 10 to 11 (1 to 10.30 Sun) **Closed** Christmas Day, Boxing Day and 1 Jan

OXFORD

Fellows Brasserie ✕ ◻

37 St Clements *Telephone* (0865) 241431 £

Fellows has pine tables, a maple floor, well-placed plants and newspapers in a rack near the coffee machine. It also has some of the slickest waiters in the business – they carry bleepers in their back-pockets. The all-day menu is eclectic: vegetable terrine with mixed bean salad; lamb satay; salmon brioche; breast of chicken with ginger and lime. Morning coffee and afternoon tea come with croissants, Danish pastries or German apple cake. Cocktails, Beck's beer, wines.

Open 12 to 2.30, 7 to 10.30 (12.30 to 3 Sun)

15 North Parade ✕

15 North Parade *Telephone* (0865) 513773 ££–£££

Light, airy restaurant with a menu of stylish, popular, modern cooking. After initial teething problems the kitchen has now found its pace and offers a real alternative to the city's culinary high-flyers. The long room is a big plus, with plants, low wall lights and wicker chairs. Accomplished starters have been warm scallop salad and a tartlet of quail eggs on spinach with a smooth hollandaise; good main courses have included salmon cooked *à point* with watercress sauce, and sticky duck breast stuffed with prunes. Vegetarian options. To finish there is a fine version of cranachan (raspberries, oatmeal, whisky, cream). The set lunch is £7.50. House French is £5.50. Children's helpings. Wheelchair access.

Open Tue to Sun **Meals** 12 to 2, 7 to 10.30 **Cards** Access, Amex, Diners, Visa

Gardeners Arms ◻

39 Plantation Road; first left turn into a narrow one-way street £
after Horse & Jockey, heading out from centre up Woodstock Road

Honest, unpretentious and quiet pub. There are no frills; but the room on the right off the entry corridor has nice David Hobbs rustic prints above the panelled dado, and the bar (which is in here) keeps quite a few malt whiskies including the Macallan, three Madeiras, an interesting wine of the month, and Westons scrumpy, as well as well-kept Morlands Mild and Bitter on handpump. As in the second room on the left, there are simple chairs and built-in wall seats around the solid low tables, and a relaxed and chatty atmosphere – close in

---

Food can be obtained at nearly all the pubs listed in the Guide but may not be available throughout opening hours, especially in the evening.

You are unlikely to be able to pay by credit card for bar snacks at pubs or at the cheaper places in this Guide. Credit cards are usually accepted in restaurants including those in pubs which serve more formal meals.

OXFORD

spirit to the Free Press in Cambridge. A back garden dining bar serves sandwiches, about five freshly cooked changing hot dishes, or salads in summer, and a number of vegetarian dishes (food available at lunchtime only), and past this there are tables on a terrace and in a walled garden with old fruit trees. Friendly service; fruit machine. Children are allowed in the garden room.

Open 11 to 2.30, 6 to 11 **Closed** 25 and 26 Dec

Go Dutch

18 Park End Street *Telephone* (0865) 240686 (evenings only) £

Across the road from the railway station, this pancake house offers alternative travellers' fare. The big old wooden tables, pendant lights, stripped-wood dresser, Delft tiles and split-cane blinds give a relaxed and convincingly Dutch feel. The selection of pancakes runs through combinations of ingredients such as peppers, salami, sweetcorn, sausage, mushrooms and cheese. Try the Dutch practice of spooning sweet syrup from the pots on the table over your savoury pancake (especially if you've chosen bacon as one of the ingredients). Good coffee. Licensed.

Open 6pm (noon Sat, Sun and public hol Mons) to 11 **Closed** Christmas to New Year; Easter Sun

Health Food Shop

3 King Edward Street *Telephone* (0865) 243407 £

A pine-furnished basement below the Holland and Barrett health food store serving generous helpings of wholefood dishes at knock-down prices. The hot dishes of the day are as good a bet as the salads, and there are always filled baked potatoes. Juices, herb teas, decaffeinated coffee and strawberry soya milk to drink. No smoking.

Open 9.30 to 4.30 **Closed** Sun; public hols

Munchy Munchy

6 Park End Street *Telephone* (0865) 245710 £–££

Ethel Ow's small restaurant dining-room might claim to serve the finest South-East Asian food in the Midlands. The competition may not be very stiff, but that should not detract. She cooks at a counter-bar virtually spontaneously to a short blackboard menu that changes daily according to market. The freshness of tastes and their often myriad complexities can be a delight – for instance, scallops are sautéed with ginger, ground Macadamia nuts, and fresh lime leaves and juice, and are served with mange-tout and cherry tomatoes. King prawns come with coriander. Generally the choice is of lamb, chicken, beef and vegetable dishes, with king prawns in two ways, and sometimes satay. The same dish never seems to taste the same on different days – the spices and the manner of cooking change. Good ice-creams and tropical fruits to finish. Service is usually attentive, especially in keeping the teapot full, but can be brusque with those who hang around too long after they have finished eating, when a queue will have formed outside, as often happens in term-time. Some hold that the cooking has an aphrodisiac quality. There are half a dozen varieties of good tea; there is no licence, but no corkage is charged. No children under six on Friday and Saturday nights. No cigars or pipes in the dining-room.

Open Tue to Sat **Meals** 12 to 2.10, 5.30 to 9.40

Museum of Modern Art

30 Pembroke Street *Telephone* (0865) 722733   £

An article in the *Tatler* last year gave this white basement as *the venue* for Oxford's café society. Readers may have been disappointed, unless teenagers in second-hand coats, and mums resting their feet from shopping across the street in Fenwicks, now count as the demi-monde. The food is good – from freshly made, innovative salads, and excellent home-made soups such as pea and lettuce; to substantial wedges of fine cakes, and home-made gooseberry ice-creams. The art gallery upstairs generally has the most exciting touring exhibitions of modern art to be doing the rounds, and there is a good shop selling catalogues, art books, and cards. Unlicensed.

Open 10 to 4 (2.30 to 4.30 Sun) **Closed** Mon; public hols

Oxford Bakery and Brewhouse

14 Gloucester Street, Gloucester Green   £
Telephone (0865) 727265

This enterprising pub, in the building that was for years the Red Lion, brews its own beer, supplies a range of other people's real ale, and has a list of bar food second to none in the city. The fine pizzas, which come on a wooden board, are available only in the evenings; but at lunchtime there are snacks highlighting products from the bakery; hummus comes on sourdough rye bread with Mexican bean salad; French onion soup is served with caraway bread; beef in beer is accompanied by dark brown bread. There are also hefty hot salt beef sandwiches with dill pickles and horseradish sauce. Good cheeses and charcuterie. Picnic tables in the small courtyard under a tall ash tree are about the only quiet spot when one of the good jazz bands is playing on a Wednesday evening (not in August). Children are allowed in the upper levels, which are furnished with lots of interesting junk. Note that food is not available on Saturday or Sunday evenings.

Open 10.30 to 2.30, 5.30 to 11 **Closed** Christmas Day and Boxing Day

Pak Fook

100 Cowley Road *Telephone* (0865) 427958   £

The best-value Chinese restaurant in town is this charmingly weird little place opposite the Penultimate Picture Palace. The dining-room is dark, part-panelled

OXFORD

with a brightly lit counter at the back, giving the effect of a modest, traditional, English-cathedral-city tea room tacked on to the front of local Chinese take-away. The steps up to the back room add a touch of guest-house hallway to the arrangements. Of course, there are ups and downs on the longish menu, but some dishes compare favourably with food at any other Chinese restaurant in the city. The chef's specials are particularly good, for example hot-and-sour soup and the vegetables and oyster sauce. Sweets are only for the brave.

Open Noon to 2 (2.30 Fri to Sun and public hols), 5.30 (6 Sun & public hols) to 11.30 (midnight Fri & Sat) **Closed** Christmas Day and Boxing Day

St Aldate's Coffee House

94 St Aldate's *Telephone* (0865) 245952

Owned by St Aldate's Church and run in conjunction with the church bookshop. The atmosphere is more town than gown, with dark polished tables and panelling on the walls. Home-baked cakes and scones are served all day with tea and coffee, while at lunchtime there are filled rolls, jacket potatoes, salads and dishes such as chicken curry, lamb, fruit and nut risotto or vegetarian cottage pie. No smoking.

Open 10 to 5 **Closed** Sun, public hols

Sweeney Todd's

6–12 George Street *Telephone* (0865) 723421

It's relatively rare for a fast food joint to have genuine style, but this small chain certainly does – in plenty. This branch – after a disastrous fire several years ago – is in fine fettle. There is a downstairs cocktail bar, and a big two-tiered space upstairs with a central spiral staircase, convincing artificial plants, smooth lighting, cool sounds and arty black and white photographs of the backs of cars, and so on. Pizzas are either the thin crisp ones or the deep cakey ones. Burgers, salad, ribs and filled baked potatoes too.

Open Noon to 11 **Closed** Christmas Day, Boxing Day and 1 Jan

Turf

Bath Place; via St Helen's Passage, between Holywell Street and New College Lane *Telephone* (0865) 243235

The pub has a timeless appeal; surrounded by flagstoned or gravel courtyards, it's quite secluded from the modern bustle of the city by the high stone walls of some of its oldest buildings, including part of the ancient city wall. Inside, it's still much as described by Thomas Hardy in *Jude the Obscure* – a low-ceilinged tavern up a court, with dark beams and low ceilings. It buzzes with life in term-time and is always fun (except for a while in the height of the summer, when they may have recourse to cardboard plates and plastic cutlery to cope with the influx, and the normal friendliness is less conspicuous). Even in winter

OXFORD

(thanks to the warmth of a brazier) crowds can overflow into the courtyard. The extensive cold buffet (out of doors in summer) has cold meats priced by the thick slice, quiche, pasties and salads priced by the spoon. There's a baked potato bar, and other hot dishes include chilli con carne, shepherd's pie and other pies such as fish with mussels and prawns or venison with blackcurrants. Hook Norton Best and Old Hookey, Wethereds SPA and Youngs Special on handpump, with a guest beer such as Adnams changing every ten days or so; they bring in mulled wine or a hot rum punch in winter, and have a Pimms fruit punch in summer, besides a range of country wines and farm cider. Fruit machine. Evening folk music at weekends.

Open 10.30 to 2.30, 5.30 to 11 **Closed** 25 Dec **Accommodations** (In separate cottages) B&B £9 to £14

Windsor and Eton

Eton is famous for its College just as Windsor is for its Castle. These two bastions of Britain's establishment face each other across the Thames. From one has come a long line of British Prime Ministers and statesmen; from the other every English monarch since William the Conqueror.

In 1066, after the surrender of London, William the Conqueror set about securing his position. He built seven fortifications around London, one of which was Windsor Castle. In a commanding defensive position on this chalk cliff overlooking the Thames, William began the Castle in timber. Although subsequently strengthened in stone, reconstructed and added to by later monarchs, the Castle has been occupied continually as a royal residence since that date. The town grew up around it as the needs of the court and garrison demanded services and accommodation. Queen Victoria spent her honeymoon here. It is reputed to have been her favourite residence, too, and from the 1840s until the death of Prince Albert in 1861 it was the social centre of the country. If there were any doubt as to its continuing royal connection, its role was assured when in 1917 George V declared that his family would henceforward take the surname Windsor.

Arrival by train takes you straight into Victorian England, with Madame Tussaud's Royalty and Empire Exhibition. This is housed in the original royal waiting-room and the large Jubilee glass canopy built for the present station in 1897 by the Great Western Railway Company to celebrate Queen Victoria's Diamond Jubilee. The Exhibition is an impressive re-creation of the arrival of the Queen at Windsor station in her Jubilee year, with life-size models and accompanying sound effects.

You emerge from the station mews opposite the Castle; the entrance to the Castle precincts is clearly signposted, as are the sights within. St George's Chapel faces you across the Lower Ward. Begun in the late fifteenth century, it is one of the finest examples of the late Perpendicular style of Gothic architecture. Still used as a chapel, it also serves as a royal mausoleum, although Albert and Victoria were buried in the mausoleum at Frogmore House in Windsor Great Park.

The Albert Memorial Chapel, the Round Tower, the State Apartments, Queen Mary's Dolls' House and Exhibition of Drawings are only some of the other sights well worth seeing at Windsor Castle. Don't miss the views over Eton and the Thames Valley from the terrace behind the Horseshoe Cloisters. It is worth trying to time your visit to include the Changing of the Guard, which takes place daily in the Castle precincts at around 11am, often accompanied by the regimental band.

A bronze statue of Queen Victoria commemorating her Golden Jubilee stands at the crossroads at the foot of Castle Hill. Just up from here, almost opposite the entrance to the Castle, is Windsor's original town centre – a small network of narrow cobbled streets dating from the Middle Ages. Here you will find some of the earliest town houses: look out for Ye Olde King's Head (1525) in Church Street, with its plaque depicting the warrant for the execution of Charles I in 1649; Nell Gwyn's house, built in 1640, and the Engine House (1803), where

WINDSOR AND ETON

the town fire engine was kept. Many other old buildings are now gift and clothes shops, tea and coffee places and a few are pubs.

Passing Market Cross House, an unsupported building which leans rather alarmingly on its timber frame, you emerge on the High Street by the Guildhall. Begun by Fitch in 1689, it was completed by Sir Christopher Wren. Carefully examine the pillars at the centre of the building: Wren was instructed to add them by nervous townspeople, who considered the outer pillars too flimsy to support the upper chamber. He obliged, but made them fractionally shorter than the others so they remain ornamental and proof of the infallibility of his original design.

Continue down the High Street, and when the road bears to the right go straight on into Park Street, which is lined with fine Georgian houses. A walk to the end is rewarded by a view through the gates down the Long Walk, a three-mile processional avenue stretching through the Great Park to Westmacott's equestrian statue of King George III at the far end. Retracing your steps past the Guildhall and down Thames Street you pass the Theatre Royal. Rebuilt in 1910, it is a thriving theatre, and if you are staying overnight try to take in a production.

Directly opposite the end of Thames Street, Eton beckons across Windsor Bridge. On the way you have to pass Wren's Old House Hotel. This was reputedly designed and lived in by Wren and is now run as a hotel. Note the Eton boathouses on your left as you cross the river to Eton High Street, a long narrow street crammed with pretty old houses and shops. If time is short, it is probably best to make your way straight to the College and then walk back down the High Street to take in the buildings and shops.

You approach the boundaries of Eton College at the end of the High Street, crossing Barnes Pool Bridge, which dates from the fifteenth century (the present structure was erected in 1884). Until 1860 the High Street was out of bounds to the College boys: to overcome this it was customary for boys to dart into a shop if a master or sixth-former appeared; this was known as 'shirking' and was tacitly permitted.

The College was founded in 1440 by Henry VI, who was only twenty years old. The College was largely modelled on Winchester College and was to consist of a provost, 10 'sad priests', 4 clerks, 6 chorister boys, 25 poor and indigent scholars and 25 poor men; this was altered a few years later to provide schooling for 70 poor scholars and '13 poor infirm men'. Further revisions of the statute enabled it to admit fee-paying pupils, and in the seventeenth century it became fashionable as a school for the sons of the nobility. There are still 70 scholars, as originally provided for, but the Oppidans (as the fee-paying pupils are known) now number over 1200 and with a staff of over 100 masters Eton is now the largest public school in the country. The distinctive uniform of pin stripes, tail coats and wing collars never fails to surprise and is still the daily dress requirement.

The College buildings around a central quadrangle known as School Yard are approached through the archway almost opposite Keate's Lane, named after the longest-serving headmaster (1809–34). It is worth a detour down this lane to see a plaque marking the proposed end of what was to have been the nave of Eton College Chapel, which was originally conceived to be of cathedral size but built in more modest dimensions. Tours of the College buildings are available

WINDSOR AND ETON

daily and can be as short or as detailed as required. The main buildings to see are the Lower School (1443), one of the oldest schoolrooms in the country still in use, the Upper School, built in the seventeenth century, and the fifteenth-century College Chapel, another example of Perpendicular Gothic and similar to King's College Chapel, Cambridge: note the unusual 13-feet-high base, a precaution against Thames Valley floods. The recently opened Museum of Eton Life, a history of Eton from its conception to the present day, is worth a visit.

The passage under Lupton's Tower at the east of School Yard leads to the Cloisters and the renowned playing fields beyond. It may be a relief to historians that there is no record of the Duke of Wellington, one of Eton's famous pupils, saying 'The Battle of Waterloo was won on the playing fields of Eton'. The playing fields stretch around the outskirts of the College, but it is in this partially walled area that the Eton Wall Game is played once a year – incomprehensible to anyone outside the College.

Emerging from the College buildings, you will notice a cast-iron lamppost prominently set at the junction of Common Lane and Slough Road. Made in 1864, it has rather obscurely become a famous Eton landmark, gaining the name 'the burning bush' due to its extravagant design.

Returning towards Windsor along the High Street, you pass a variety of attractive buildings: some date from the fifteenth century, but the majority are Georgian. For the keen collector, Eton High Street is a haven of antique shops both in their contents and in their history. Turks Head Antiques, built in 1500, was a tavern until 1950; the carved demons flanking the archway are thought to have been imported from the Continent. A clutch of banks, bookshops, tailors and tuckshops for the boys remind you of the town's purpose. At the Cock Pit restaurant, Eton's oldest house, built in 1420, cock-fighting took place here in the seventeenth century and was reputedly patronised by Charles II; the pit itself is still visible at the back.

This brings you almost back at Windsor Bridge. Return as you came, perhaps taking in a short river boat trip, time and season permitting; you can either drive your own or take a captain, and either way is a pleasant and relaxing experience.

Note: beware of the many rather poor eating places, particularly in Windsor. We are sad to be able to recommend only the following collection, and you might do better to arm yourself with a picnic. However, if you are in a car and want to explore Henley, good food can be had at the **Three Tuns** in the Market Place; unusually they serve food all afternoon in the buttery (but no alcohol, of course). The **Ship** at Marlow (West Street) has an interesting collection of warship photographs and very low prices for good, simple food. Marlow's **Two Brewers**, just a few steps from the Thames, also offers food that's worth seeking out.

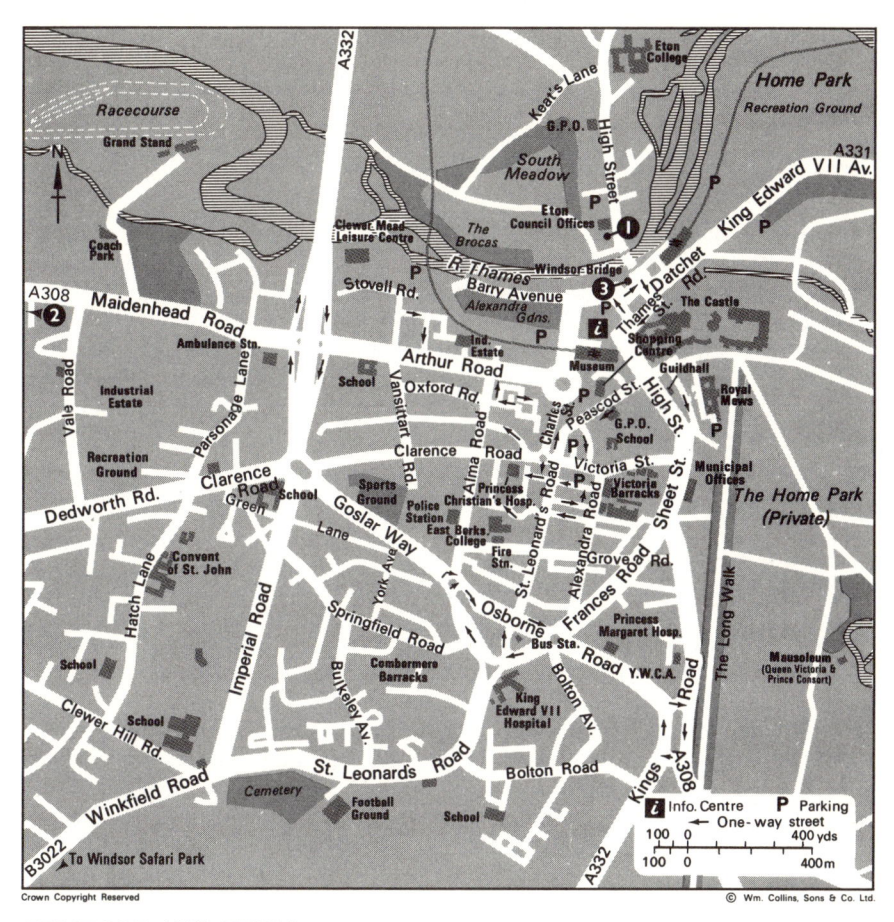

WINDSOR AND ETON

WINDSOR AND ETON

1 Eton Wine Bar   2 Oakley Court Hotel   3 Punter

WINDSOR AND ETON

WINDSOR AND ETON

Eton Wine Bar   ♀

82–83 High Street, Eton *Telephone* (0753) 854921/855182   ££

The stripped-pine tables and church pews fill up quickly in this exemplary wine bar run by two couples, all of them Honourables. The menu moves with the markets, taking in some deliciously adventurous fare as well as sugar-baked ham, quiche Lorraine, and farmhouse chicken. Puddings are a strong point, too: the chocolate and date one is a favourite. The wines are equally stimulating and diverse, though the pricing is more restaurant than wine bar. Service is first-class. The wine bar would be a more than useful place for a meal before a show at Windsor Theatre across the bridge. Five tables in the garden; access for wheelchairs. Music. Children are welcome.

Open All week **Closed** Easter Sun and 3 days at Christmas **Meals** 12 to 2.30, 6 (7 Sun) to 10.30 **Cards** Access, Visa **Service** 10%

Oakley Court Hotel

Windsor Road, Windsor *Telephone* (0628) 74141   £££–££££

No charming little country hideaway, but a real show-place mansion, built in 1859, half French château, half romantic Gothic, full of turrets, towers, castellations and crenellations, used as a set for many Hammer horror films, notably the *Dracula* series – and achieving its present incarnation as a grand hotel in 1981 after a £5 million conversion. There are 90 rooms, including 18 suites, as well as a library and billiard room, and 30 acres of grounds (terrace, croquet lawn) leading down to the Thames, on which the hotel has a quarter of a mile of fishing rights. Furnishing tends towards the ornate which admirably suits the style of the house, though there is also a modern annexe. The restaurant is in the hands of Murdo McSween, a Master Chef of Great Britain, who has introduced a Gourmet Menu in addition to the regular set dinner menu. Large expensive hotels, close to capital cities (London 28 miles) and to airports (Heathrow 15 minutes), are often much of a muchness, inevitably catering for conferences and banquets and passengers in transit. But Oakley Court, though it has international hotel characteristics, also has individuality and class: most correspondents, though not all, speak warmly of the welcoming staff and the quality of the cooking. No babies in the dining-room but under-12s can eat half-portions for half-price. (The hotel is three miles from Windsor: leave the M4 at junction 6, then take the A355 to Windsor roundabout; follow the A308 to Maidenhead for two miles.)

Open All year **Cards** Access, Amex, Diners, Visa **Accommodations** 90 rooms, all with bath and shower. B&B £41 to £70

Prices for accommodations normally include cooked English or Scottish breakfast, Value Added Tax (currently 15%) and any inclusive service charge that we know of.

WINDSOR AND ETON

Punter

Thames Street, Windsor *Telephone* (0753) 865565 £

Good traditional English cooking is the attraction here. Half-pints of prawns, and thick vegetable soup, come before pies – such as pork and apple or steak and oyster – in individual dishes. There is also roast duck, and proper fresh fruit salad. Licensed.

Open 12 to 3, 6 to 11; 12 to 3, 7 to 10.30 Sun **Closed** 25 & 26 Dec

General Section

Time, gentlemen, please

Almost the first thing people from abroad notice about English pubs is that they're closed. By law, they are allowed to open only for three or four hours around lunchtime, then again for a few hours in the evening. The law dates from the introduction of strict controls on the sale of alcohol, to improve industrial performance during the 1914–18 World War. Until then, London pubs were open for 19½ hours out of the 24; during wartime, the hours were cut to 5½. Though there has been some relaxation since, the hours are still kept to a strict total of 9 hours a day (9½, if evening closing is at 11 rather than 10.30).

In London, they are normally fixed at 11–3 for the lunchtime session, 5.30–11 for the evening. A handful of pubs near wholesale markets keep special early morning hours for the market workers. On Saturdays many London pubs near rowdy football grounds aren't allowed to open before 7pm, when the crowds have gone home (or been locked up). In other parts of the country weekday times are set annually for each area by some 350 panels of local magistrates, with wide variations – lunchtime opening varies between 10 and 12, closing between 2 and 4, and evening hours can vary as widely. On Sundays (throughout the country) the times are 12–2 and 7–10.30.

A pub may be allowed to serve drinks in a separate restaurant for an extra hour, in the evenings and/or with Sunday lunch. If you plan a late leisurely meal, it's worth checking in advance whether it has this extra 'supper licence'.

'Drinking-up time' is a subject of great confusion to pub-goers. The licensee has to stop selling alcohol at the end of the 'permitted hours', but the law allows his customers an extra ten minutes after that to finish their drinks. Going on drinking for yet another quarter-hour after that is, technically, breaking the law. But it's virtually unknown for customers to be charged with an offence if they are very slow to finish their drinks. And the licensee himself isn't even breaking the law (by 'aiding, abetting, counselling or procuring' his customers' illegal late drinking) if he and his staff are at least trying to clear the pub of drinkers.

There are three ways in which pubs can give their customers more time. The law allows half-an-hour's drinking-up time if you are eating a table meal (even in the bar), or if you bought the drinks in conjunction with a meal. If you are staying overnight at an inn or hotel, you can be served an alcoholic drink at any time. And there is nothing to prevent a pub staying open all day, serving anything other than alcohol outside the permitted hours.

Real ale

You can't spend long in English pubs without getting involved in the 'real ale' controversy. People who like real ale – also called traditional ale, or cask-conditioned ale – dismiss the big-selling brands of pressurised 'keg' beer as worthless; and to them lager is a dirty word.

The great advantage of keg beer or lager over real ale is that it needs little or no special skill to look after. At the brewery, the natural yeasts which have fermented the sugars in the malted barley into alcohol are killed off by filtration or pasteurisation, and the beer, sealed in sterile metal kegs, undergoes no further change. At the pub, it's given its fizz by compressed carbon dioxide, and may go through a flash cooler to chill it. Quite inert, it's as unlikely to 'go off' as any can of vegetable soup from a supermarket shelf. The publican's skill is confined simply to selling the stuff.

By contrast, real ale continues its development after its first fermentation at the brewery; the natural yeasts are never killed off, and their continued activity in a secondary fermentation gives the beer its slight natural sparkle. To reach the drinker in peak condition, the ale needs as much loving care as any living thing. When it reaches the pub, the beer needs a week or so to settle, then a day in which the excess gas that's built up in the secondary fermentation is carefully released. The beer should be kept in a scrupulously clean, cool cellar, and the apparatus used to serve it needs frequent careful cleaning. Well kept by a conscientious landlord, real ale develops a depth of flavour which is impossible to beat.

Sadly, the boom in its popularity means that some pubs stock real ale without the necessary care. Also, some stock too wide a range of different real ales: it has quite a short life, so if trade isn't brisk the casks, hanging around for weeks, slowly die. Only a masochist would prefer badly kept real ale to ordinary keg or lager.

A well-kept real ale should be cool but not cold (55°F is ideal for the life of the yeasts and the fullness of its taste); clear, showing its colour well; with a white 'head' of foam that leaves a lacy tracery down the sides of the glass as you drink it (a natural head is usually rather uneven – a very even head, and a pronounced fizz on the tongue, is a sign of artificial carbonation). Complain if the beer is cloudy, flat or too cold, if it has little fluffy lumps or flecks floating in or on it, if it smells of soggy cardboard or has any other dead smell, or if it tastes dirty, like stale vegetables, or of bleach or metal.

Pub games

In many of the pub entries in the *Guide* you may spot references to certain games played on the premises. Here we give brief explanations of some of the more common ones.

Darts is the most popular pub game. Each turn, you throw three darts at a round target with 20 numbered segments, trying for the highest score; the outer rim counts double, the inner ring treble, and the central bull's eye 25 (outer) or 50 (inner). Generally, you start at 201 (and must get a double to start counting your score) and count down to zero. To finish, you have to get the exact score you need to reach zero, often with a double (rules vary locally).

with white dots, usually from one to six. Each player in turn puts down a domino or 'bone', matching the number of dots on one half against a domino at an end of the row already down on the table with the same number, or against a double in mid-row showing that number on both halves (doubles are put down to cross a T, singles put down end to end). Though it sounds complicated on paper, it's easy in practice – and local players are almost always keen to show you the ropes.

In *shove-ha'penny*, a coin is slid along a polished board or slate. Usually, you put the coin overlapping the end of the board and hit it with the edge of your hand, so that it slides into the score 'beds' marked on the board.

Cribbage or crib is the most popular pub card game – too complicated to describe briefly here, but again a game (for two players) that locals are pleased to explain. The cribbage score block, with pins or matchsticks in its rows of holes, is used in many other pub games too.

Ring the Bull is an ancient game: you swing a metal ring (originally from a bull's nose) on a line usually hanging from the ceiling, to land it on a hook or bull's horn on the wall.

Skittles is rarer around London than, say, in the West Country: you bowl a ball down a long indoor alley to knock down nine skittles or 'pins' (it may be called 'Nine-pins' – one or two London pubs still play an even noisier forerunner called Old English skittles). In a table-top indoor variation, *Devil Among The Tailors*, you swing a ball on a string to knock the pins down. In and around the Chilterns, *Aunt Sally*, played outside, involves throwing half-a-dozen clubs to knock down a single pin. North of London *hood skittles*, where a wooden or composition disc is hurled to clatter among skittles on a screened table, is quickly getting more popular.

The best Kentish summer pub game – very popular around Canterbury – is *Bat-and-Trap*. The trap flicks a ball up for the batsman to hit towards a target; a fielder throws it back and if it hits the trap the batsman is 'out'. And in remoter places you may come across really odd games like Nurdling – when you've tried Dwyle Flunking you'll be ready for anything!

Glossary

Arbroath smokie	whole salted smoked haddock, served hot with butter
aubergine	eggplant
bangers and mash	sausages with mashed potato
bap	flat soft bread roll
beef olives	thin slices of beef rolled round a stuffing of onion, breadcrumbs, lemon, herbs and egg yolks, then baked in stock
black pudding	large black sausage made of a mixture of pig's blood, milk, onion, suet, oatmeal and herbs; usually sliced and fried or grilled with eggs and bacon for breakfast
bream	yellowish freshwater fish
brill	European flatfish a bit like turbot
bubble and squeak	fried leftover potato and cabbage
buckling	smoked herring
buck's fizz	champagne with orange juice
buttery	small dining-hall
ceps	type of mushroom
chip butty	sandwich with a filling of French fries
coley	a tasty, firm-fleshed fish, nevertheless usually considered to be at the bottom of the gastronomic scale
courgettes	zucchini
elvers	baby eels
flummery	cold dessert made from lemons, egg yolks, wine or sherry, sugar and gelatine
fruit machine	one-armed bandit
gammon	ham slice
kedgeree	originally a breakfast dish but now served at other times, too, consisting of cooked fish, such as smoked haddock, stirred into rice with hard-boiled eggs, butter, cream and parsley
kippers	smoked fish, especially herring
laverbread	edible seaweed
Marmite toast	toast spread with a brand of yeast extract
mash and beans	mashed potato and baked beans
meze	Greek hors d'oeuvre consisting of a variety of tasting dishes
muesli	Swiss version of granola cereal, now widespread in the UK
offal	variety meats
pasty	small beef turnover, often with diced root vegetables (usually known as a Cornish pasty)
ploughman's lunch	popular pub lunch consisting of cheese, bread, pickles and salad garnish
pomfret	type of seawater fish

GLOSSARY

raised pie	diced meat, often pork or veal, flavoured with onions and spicing, which is packed into a tall pastry casing made with a hot-water crust
savoury flan	quiche
Scotch egg	popular pub food of hard-boiled egg encased in sausagemeat, rolled in breadcrumbs and fried, usually served cold
shove ha'penny	pub game (see page 217)
snug	a cosy enclosed area in a pub
soused herring	herring pickled in vinegar and spices
spatchcocked chicken	a way of preparing chicken by splitting it in two before cooking
spotted dick	sweet suet pudding with raisins or currants
swede	rutabaga
toasties	toasted sandwiches
trotters	pigs' feet
zander	a type of freshwater fish sometimes known as a pike-perch

GAZETTEER of London hotels, restaurants and pubs

Ajimura 46
Akasaka 70
Alastair Little 130
Albertine 68
L'Amico 164
Anchor 156
Angel 58
Anglesea Arms 151
Anna's Place 80
Antelope 21
Archduke 149
Arch 9 40
The Ark 84
L'Arlequin 16
Athenaeum Hotel 124
L'Auberge 54
Auberge de Provence 164
Auntie's 158
L'Autre 104
L'Aventure 88
Aziz 69
Baalbek 56
Bahn Thai 56
Balls Brothers 35
Bambaya 71
Barnaby's 15
La Bastide 131
Bayleaf Tandoori 71
Bengal Lancer 27
Beotys 132
Berkeley Hotel 90
Bishop of Norwich 40
Bishop's Parlour 40
Le Bistroquet 27
Black Friar 36
Blake's Hotel 62
Bleeding Heart 36
Bloom's 58
Au Bois St Jean 128
Bombay Brasserie 152
Bombay Inn 69
Boos 99
Boot & Flogger 40
Bottlescrue 40
La Bouffe 16
La Bougie 27
Boulestin 46
Bow Wine Vaults 36
Brewer Street Buttery 132
Brown's Hotel 104
Bulls Head
 (Barnes) 15
Bulls Head
 (Chiswick) 34
Bunch of Grapes 105
Bung Hole 40
Burgundy Bens 40

Busabong 63
Butters 17
Café Crêperie 132
Café du Jardin 47
Café Pelican 47
Café Rouge 37
Café St Pierre 37
Calabash 47
Capital Hotel 91
Le Caprice 125
Il Cavaliere 72
Central Park 20
Champagne Charlie's 40
Champagne Exchange 105
Le Champenois 38
Chanterelle 63
Charing Cross Hotel 48
Le Chef 97
Chelsea Pasta Bar 63
Chez Gerard
 (Holborn) 78
Chez Gerard
 (Mayfair) 105
Chez Gerard
 (Tottenham Court
 Road) 40
Chez Moi 117
Chez Nico 17
Chiang Mai 133
Chopper Lump 40
Christian's 34
Chuen Cheng Ku 133
Ciboure 22
Cittie of York 79
City Boot 40
City Flogger 40
City FOB 40
City Pipe 40
City Vaults 40
Claridge's 106
Clarke's 84
Clifton 129
Colonel Jaspers
 (The City) 40
Colonel Jaspers
 (Greenwich) 40
Colonnade 89
Como Lario 22
Compton Arms 80
Connaught Hotel 106
F Cooke 59
Cooke's Eel and Pie
 Shop 150
The Cooperage 40
La Copita 69
La Corée 48
Cork and Bottle 133

Corney & Barrow
 (Cannon Street) 38
Corney & Barrow
 (Moorgate) 39
Corney & Barrow
 (Old Broad Street) 39
Country Life 106
Cranks
 (Covent Garden) 48
Cranks
 (Soho) 134
Cranks
 (Tottenham Court
 Road) 159
Crockers 89
La Croisette 63
Cross Keys 29
Crowders 67
Crowns 125
Crowthers 121
Crusting Pipe 40
Cumberland Hotel 97
Dalat 89
Daphne 28
Daquise 152
Davy's Wine Vaults 40
Desaru 134
Dewaniam 54
The Diamond 135
Diana's Diner 48
Dining Room 156
Al Diwan 97
Diwana Bhel Poori
 (Bayswater) 20
Diwana Bhel Poori
 (Euston, 2 restaurants) 61
Don Pepe 99
Dorchester Hotel 107
La Dordogne 35
Dove 69
Dragon Gate 135
Dukes Hotel 125
Durrants Hotel 99
Eatons 22
Ebury Court 23
Ebury Wine Bar 23
Efes Kebab House 159
Equatorial 135
L'Express 91
Ferret & Firkin 64
Fielding Hotel 49
Flask 72
Fleet Tandoori 72
Food for Thought 49
Fortnum & Mason 126
Founders Arms 157
Fox and Anchor 41

GAZETTEER

Frith's 136
Frog & Firkin 118
Front Page 30
Fuji 136
Fung Shing 137
Gastronome One 64
Le Gavroche 107
Gavvers 23
Gay Hussar 137
Geales Fish Restaurant 85
General Trading
  Company 91
George
  (Marylebone) 100
George
  (Southwark) 157
George IV 81
Ginnan 42
Golden Chopsticks 152
Good Friends 59
Gordon's 49
Goring Hotel 24
Govinda's 138
Grahame's Seafare 138
Grapes 59
Grape Shots 41
Green Cottage II 73
The Greenhouse
  (The City) 42
The Greenhouse
  (Mayfair) 108
Green Leaves 100
Green Man 162
Green's 126
Grenadier 92
Gyngle Boy 41
Habitat Café 30
Al Hamra 109
Hana Guruma 42
Han Kuk How Kwan 138
Hard Rock Café 109
Henry J Bean's 30
Hiders 65
Hilaire 153
Hilton Hotel 110
Hilton International
  Kensington 118
L'Hippocampe 65
Hodja Nasreddin 81
Ho-Ho 110
Hokkai 139
Hole in the Wall 150
Holiday Inn
  (Chelsea) 92
Holiday Inn
  (Marble Arch) 98
Holiday Inn
  (Mayfair) 111
Holiday Inn
  (Swiss Cottage) 129
Hollands 60
Holly Bush 73
L'Hôtel 92

Hoults 163
Hungry Horse 66
Hung Toa 21
Ikeda 111
Ikkyu 159
Inigo Jones 50
Inter-Continental Hotel 111
Island Queen 81
Jacques Wine Bar 82
Joe Allen 50
Joy King Lau 139
Julie's Champagne Bar 118
Justin de Blank 112
Just Williams 18
Kalamaras 21
Kettners 139
Kitchen Yakitori 112
Knightsbridge Hotel 93
Knightsbridge Green
  Hotel 93
Knoodles 98
Korea House 113
Ladbroke Curzon Hotel 113
Ladbroke
  Westmoreland 130
Lakorn Thai 82
Lal Qila 160
Lamb 26
Lamb & Flag 21
Langan's Bar & Grill 113
Langan's Bistro 100
Langan's Brasserie 114
The Lantern 90
Last Days of the Raj 140
Launceston Place 85
Laurent 73
Leek's Fish Bar 18
Lees Bag 41
London Tara Hotel 86
Lou Pescadou 57
Luigi's 55
Magno's Brasserie 51
Maharajah 21
Mai Thai 165
Malabar 86
Mandalay 67
Mandeer 160
Man Fu Kung 140
Marine Ices 74
Market Porter 158
Maroush 98
Maroush II 94
Masako 101
Mayflower
  (East End) 60
Mayflower
  (Soho) 140
Le Mazarin 120
Mediterranean
  Kebab House 74
Melati 141
Le Métro 94
Methuselah's 164

Michel 87
Mijanou 24
Ming 141
Minogues 83
Miyama 114
Molnars 74
Monkeys 31
Mon Plaisir 51
Monsieur Thompsons 118
Montcalm Hotel 98
Mother Bunch's 41
Mr Fish 122
Mr Kong 142
Mrs Beeton's 122
Mr Tang 142
M'sieur Frog 83
M'sieur Frog's Bistro 75
Le Muscadet 101
Museum of London 43
Museum Tavern 26
Mustoe Bistro 28
Nag's Head 94
Nam Long 142
Nanten Yakitori Bar 102
National Gallery 143
Neal Street Restaurant 52
Neal's Yard Bakery
  & Tea Room 52
Newens & Sons 122
New World 143
Ninety Park Lane,
  Grosvenor House 115
Nontas 28
North Sea 26
Number Sixteen 153
Oh Boy 165
Old Budapest 144
Olde Cheshire Cheese 43
Olde White Bear 75
Olde Windmill 18
Old Mitre 43
Old Wine Shades 44
Olive Tree 144
L'Olivier 66
192 119
One Two Three 116
Orange Brewery 120
Orange Tree 122
Ordnance Arms 130
Orso 53
Ovations 150
Le Papillon 67
Il Passetto 144
Pasta Connection 31
The Pavilion 44
Peachey's 75
Le Petit Prince 29
Phoenicia 87
Phoenix & Firkin 55
Pissarro's 123
Pollyanna's 19
Ponte Nuovo 154
Poons 145

221

GAZETTEER

Porte de la Cité 79
Portobello Hotel 119
Ports 95
Le Poulbot 45
La Preferita 19
Prince of Orange 60
Princess Louise 80
Le Provence 123
The Pulpit 41
Punch & Judy 53
Punters 45
Le Quai St Pierre 57
Quincy's 76
Ragam 161
Ravi Shankar 62
Rebato's 96
Red Fort 145
Red Lion 116
Red Sea 90
Reeds, Austin Reed 116
Refectory 123
Rendezvous Snack Bar 145
Reuben's 102
Reynier at Fleet Lane 45
Richmond Harvest 124
The Ritz 127
Rodos 146
Rose & Crown 166
Royal Festival Hall 150
Royal Trafalgar Thistle Hotel 146
RSJ 151
Rue St Jacques 161
Saga 117
Saigon 146

St George's Hotel 102
St Quentin 154
Salloos 95
Sandringham Hotel 76
San Frediano 155
San Lorenzo 96
Santini 25
Satay and Wine 147
Savoy Hotel 53
Seashell 103
Segar & Snuff Parlour 41
Shampers 147
Ship 163
Shireen Tandoori 70
Shish Mahal 83
Skinkers 41
Soho Brasserie 147
Sonny's 15
Spaniards 77
The Spittoon 41
Sree Krishna 166
Star 148
Steamboat Charley's 87
Suntory 128
Le Suquet 32
Swiss Cottage Hotel 77
Taffgood's 148
Tante Claire 32
Tappit-Hen 41
Tapster 41
Tate Gallery 121
Tea Time 20
Tiger Lee 57
Topkapi 103
Tower Grill 161

Tower Thistle Hotel 61
Treasure of China 68
Tui 155
209 88
Udder Place 41
Unicorn Café Bar 54
Upper Street Fish Shop 84
Victoria and Albert Museum 156
Villa Estense 66
Village Restaurant 166
The Vineyard 41
Wakaba 78
Waltons 33
White Swan 124
White Tower 162
Wilbraham Hotel 125
Wiltons 128
Windsor Castle 88
Wine Gallery 66
Wine Shop 41
Wolfe's (Knightsbridge) 96
Wolfe's (Mayfair) 117
Wong Kei 148
Woodlands (Marylebone) 103
Woodlands (Soho) 149
Yerakina 29
Yung's 149
Zaki's 78
Zen 33

KEY MAP

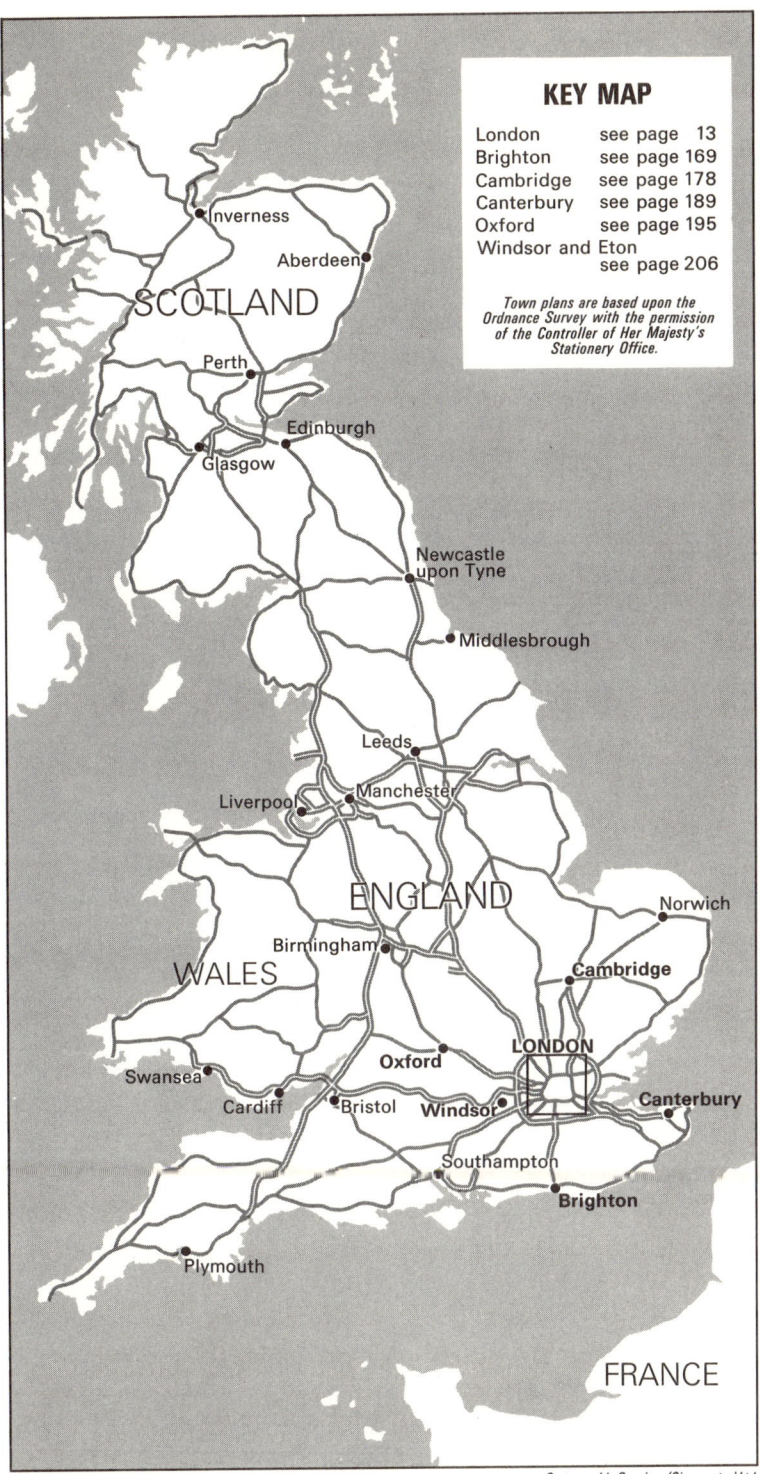

London	see page 13
Brighton	see page 169
Cambridge	see page 178
Canterbury	see page 189
Oxford	see page 195
Windsor and Eton	see page 206

Town plans are based upon the Ordnance Survey with the permission of the Controller of Her Majesty's Stationery Office.

Cartographic Services (Cirencester) Ltd.

Akasaka 70
Albertine 68
L'Arlequin 16
L'Auberge 54
Aziz 69
Bambaya 71
Barnaby's 15
Bayleaf Tandoori 71
Bombay Inn 69
La Bouffe 16
Bulls Head
 (Barnes) 15
Bulls Head
 (Chiswick) 34
Butters 17
Il Cavaliere 72
Chez Moi 117
Chez Nico 17
Christian's 34
Colonel Jaspers 40
La Copita 69
Crowders 67
Crowthers 121
Davy's Wine Vaults 40
Dewaniam 54
La Dordogne 35
Dove 69
Ferret & Firkin 64
Flask 72
Gastronome One 64
Good Friends 59
Grapes 59
Green Man 162
Hiders 65
Hilton International
 Kensington 118
L'Hippocampe 65
Hollands 60
Hoults 163

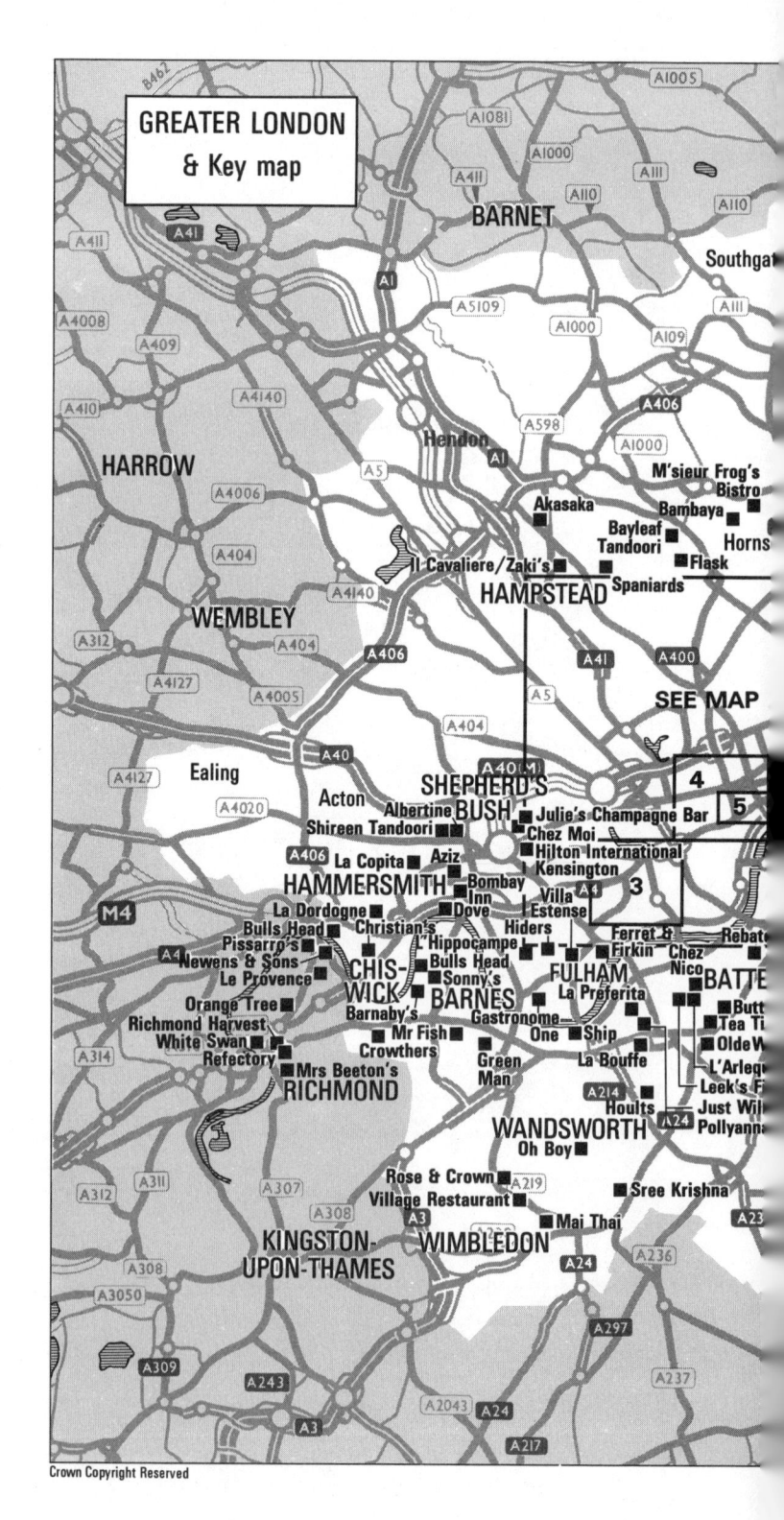

GREATER LONDON & Key map

Crown Copyright Reserved

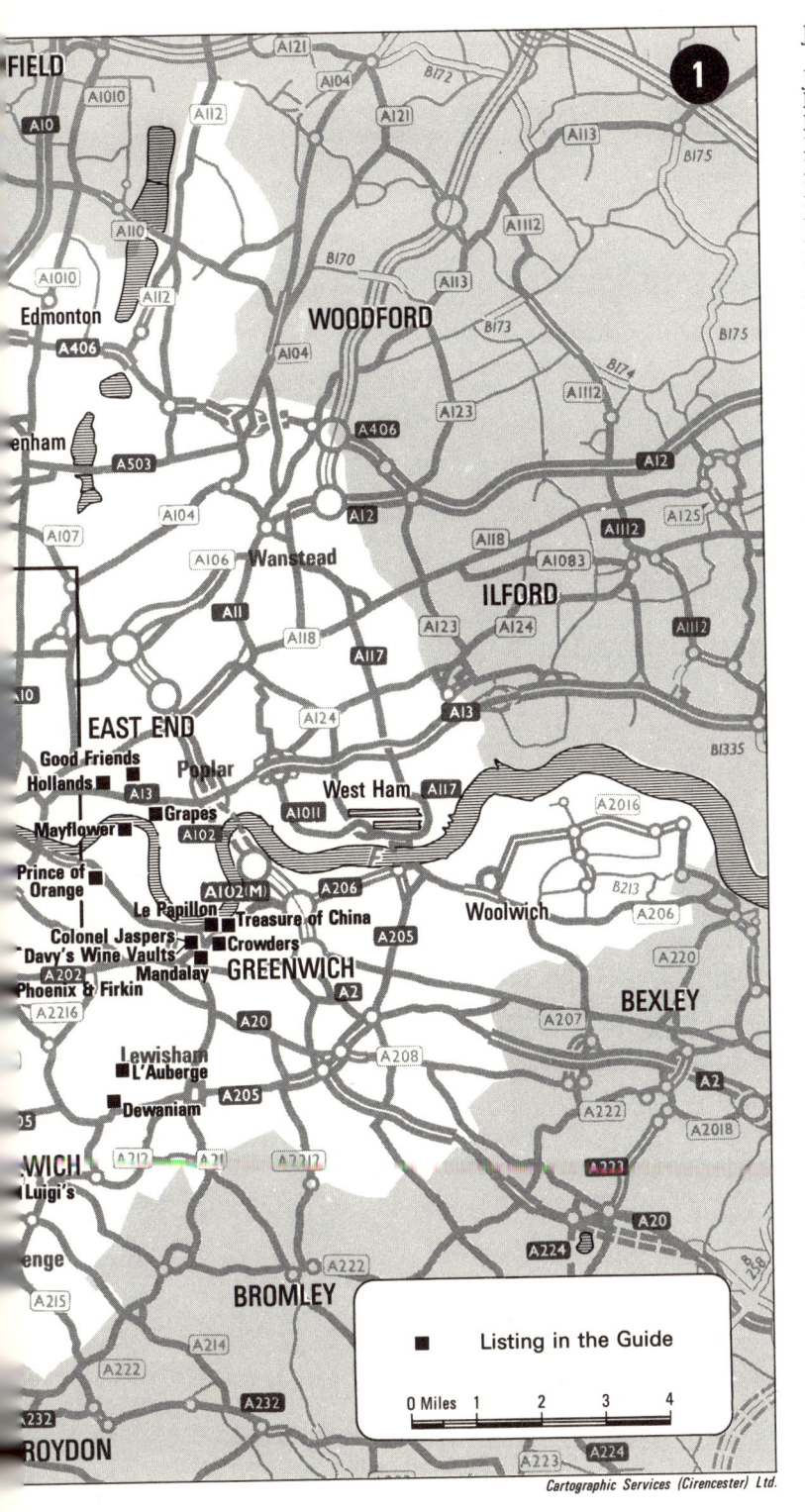

Julie's Champagne
  Bar 118
Just Williams 18
Leek's Fish Bar 18
Luigi's 55
Mai Thai 165
Mandalay 67
Mayflower 60
Mr Fish 122
Mrs Beeton's 122
M'sieur Frog's
  Bistro 75
Newens & Sons 122
Oh Boy 165
Olde Windmill 18
Orange Tree 122
Le Papillon 67
Phoenix & Firkin 55
Pissarro's 123
Pollyanna's 19
La Preferita 19
Prince of Orange 60
Le Provence 123
Rebato's 96
Refectory 123
Richmond Harvest
  124
Rose & Crown 166
Ship 163
Shireen Tandoori 70
Sonny's 15
Spaniards 77
Sree Krishna 166
Tea Time 20
Treasure of China 68
Villa Estense 66
Village Restaurant 166
White Swan 124
Zaki's 78

CENTRAL LONDON

L'Amico 164
Anchor 156
Angel 58
Anna's Place 80
Archduke 149
The Ark 84
Auberge de
 Provence 164
L'Aventure 88
Baalbek 56
Bahn Thai 56
Bengal Lancer 27
Le Bistroquet 27
Bloom's 58
Au Bois St Jean 128
Boos 99
Boot & Flogger 40
La Bougie 27
Burgundy Bens 40
Café Rouge 37
Café St Pierre 37
Central Park 20
Champagne Charlie's 40
Le Chef 97
Ciboure 22
Clarke's 84
Clifton 129
Colonel Jaspers 40
Colonnade 89
Compton Arms 80
F Cooke 59
Cooke's Eel and
 Pie Shop 150
Crockers 89
La Croisette 63
Cross Keys 29
Cumberland Hotel 97
Dalat 89
Daphne 28
Dining Room 156
Al Diwan 97
Diwana Bhel Poori
 (Bayswater) 20
Diwana Bhel Poori
 (Euston) 61
Don Pepe 99
Ebury Court 23
Fleet Tandoori 72
Founders Arms 157
Frog & Firkin 118
Geales 85
George 157
George IV 81
Goring Hotel 24
Green Cottage II 73
Green Leaves 100
Gyngle Boy 41
Hodja Nasreddin 81
Hole in the Wall 150
Holiday Inn
 (Marble Arch) 98
Holiday Inn
 (Swiss Cottage) 129
Holly Bush 73
Hung Toa 21

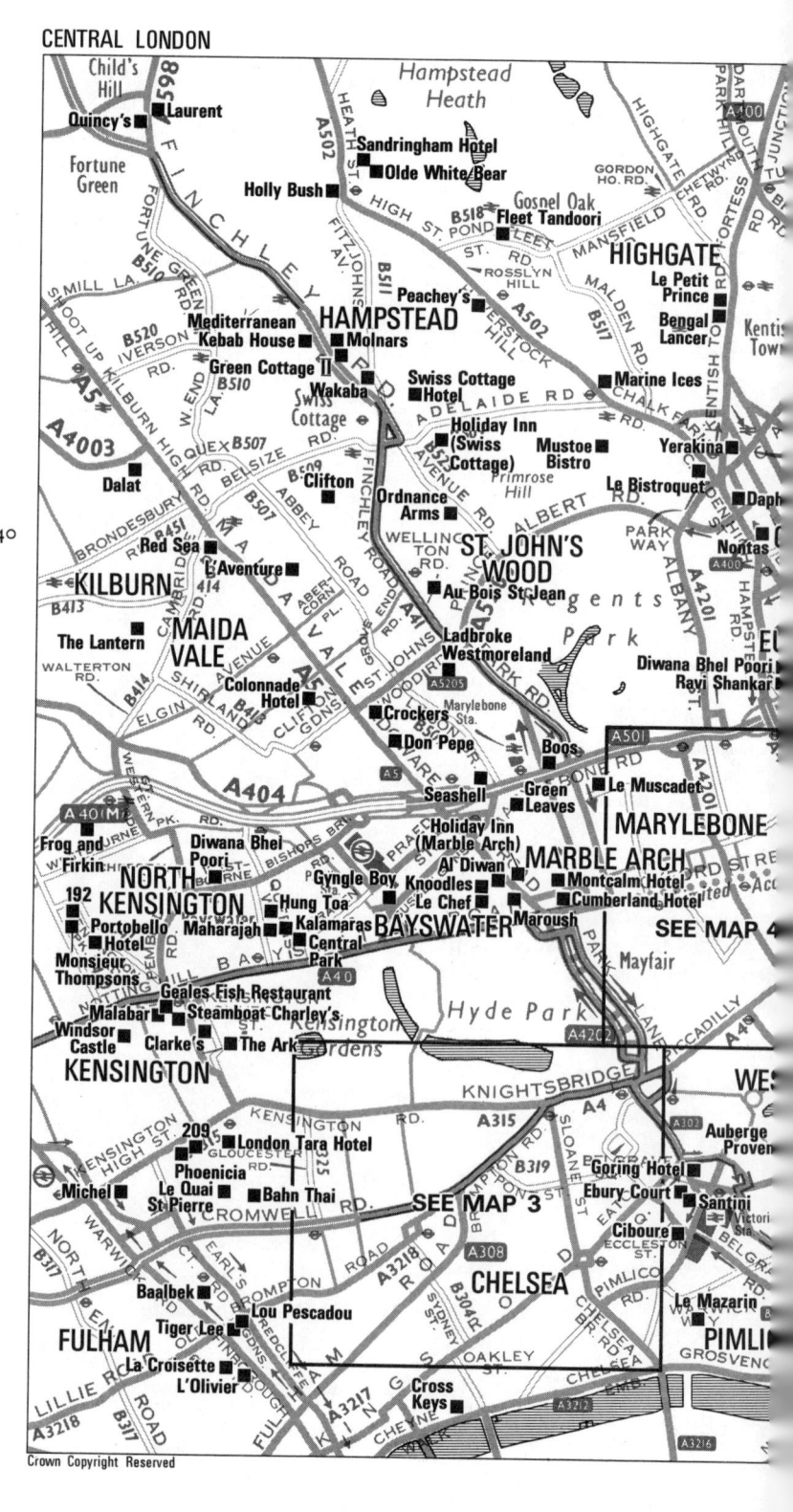

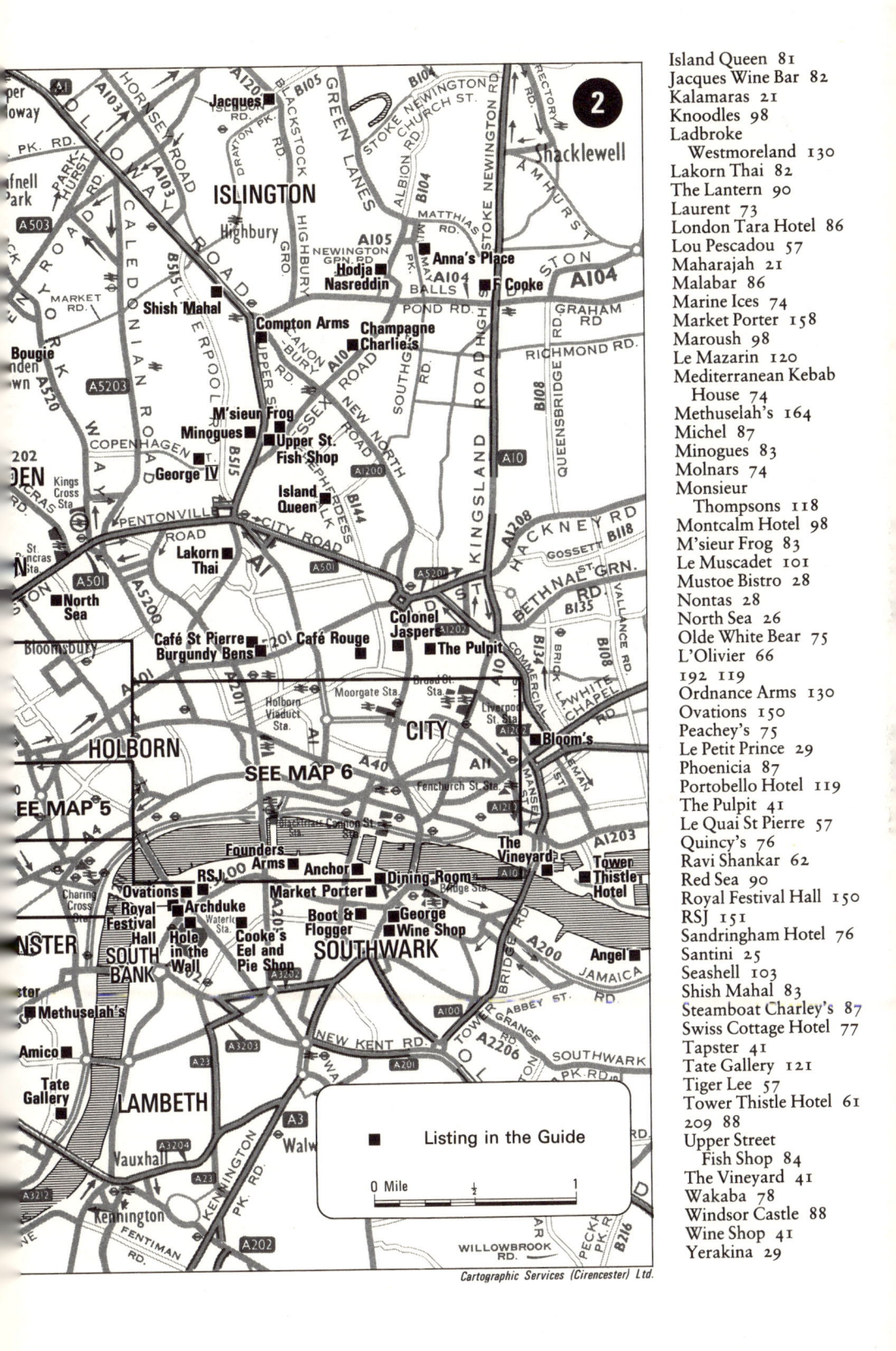

Island Queen 81
Jacques Wine Bar 82
Kalamaras 21
Knoodles 98
Ladbroke
  Westmoreland 130
Lakorn Thai 82
The Lantern 90
Laurent 73
London Tara Hotel 86
Lou Pescadou 57
Maharajah 21
Malabar 86
Marine Ices 74
Market Porter 158
Maroush 98
Le Mazarin 120
Mediterranean Kebab
  House 74
Methuselah's 164
Michel 87
Minogues 83
Molnars 74
Monsieur
  Thompsons 118
Montcalm Hotel 98
M'sieur Frog 83
Le Muscadet 101
Mustoe Bistro 28
Nontas 28
North Sea 26
Olde White Bear 75
L'Olivier 66
192 119
Ordnance Arms 130
Ovations 150
Peachey's 75
Le Petit Prince 29
Phoenicia 87
Portobello Hotel 119
The Pulpit 41
Le Quai St Pierre 57
Quincy's 76
Ravi Shankar 62
Red Sea 90
Royal Festival Hall 150
RSJ 151
Sandringham Hotel 76
Santini 25
Seashell 103
Shish Mahal 83
Steamboat Charley's 87
Swiss Cottage Hotel 77
Tapster 41
Tate Gallery 121
Tiger Lee 57
Tower Thistle Hotel 61
209 88
Upper Street
  Fish Shop 84
The Vineyard 41
Wakaba 78
Windsor Castle 88
Wine Shop 41
Yerakina 29

CENTRAL LONDON: South-West

Anglesea Arms 151
Antelope 21
Berkeley Hotel 90
Blakes Hotel 62
Bombay Brasserie 152
Busabong 63
Capital Hotel 91
Chanterelle 63
Chelsea Pasta Bar 63
Como Lario 22
Daquise 152
Eatons 22
Ebury Wine Bar 23
L'Express 91
Front Page 30
Gavvers 23
General Trading
  Company 91
Golden Chopsticks 152
Grenadier 92
Habitat Café 30
Henry J Bean's 30
Hilaire 153
Holiday Inn
  (Chelsea) 92
L'Hôtel 92
Hungry Horse 66
Inter-Continental 111

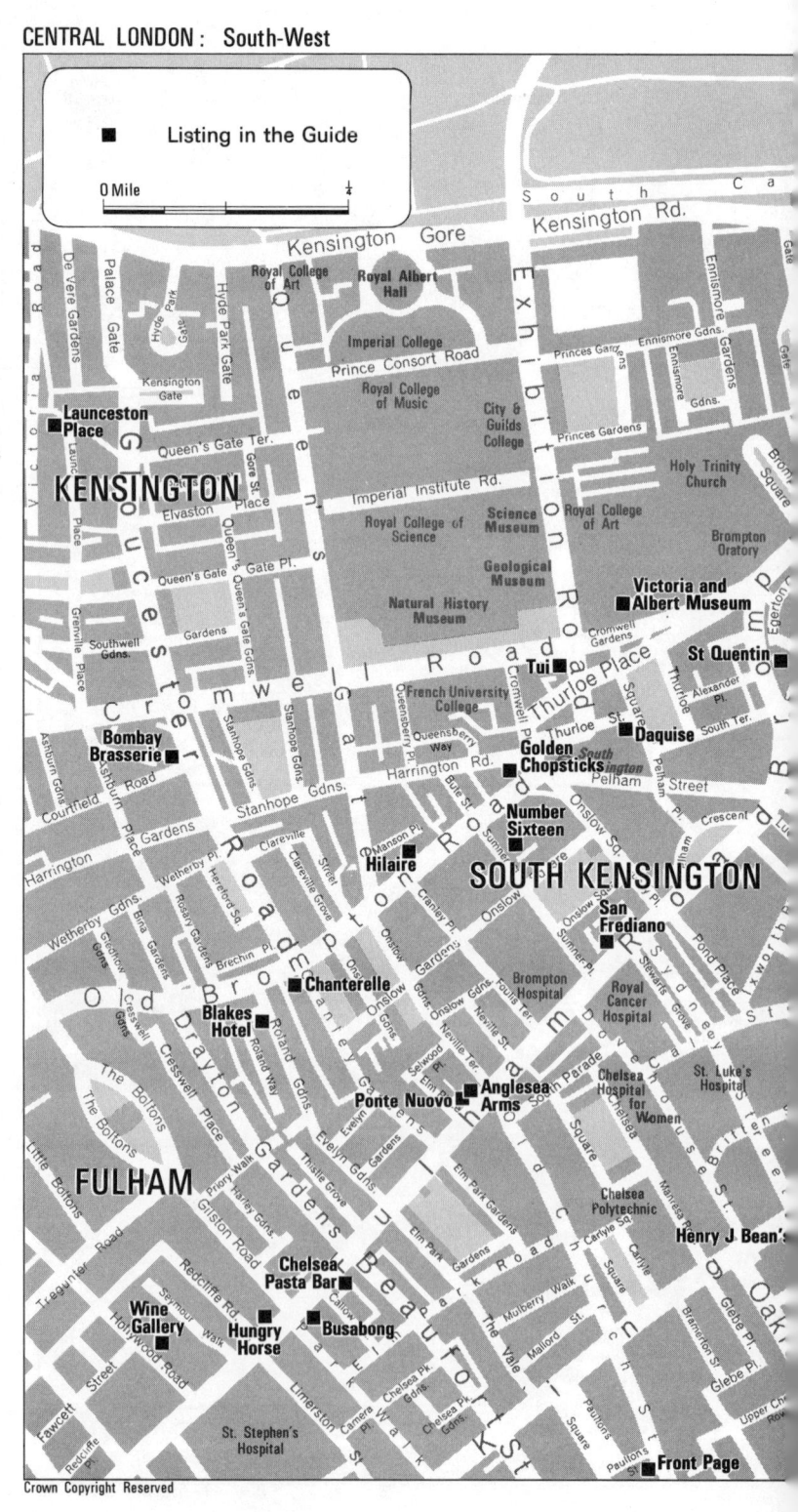

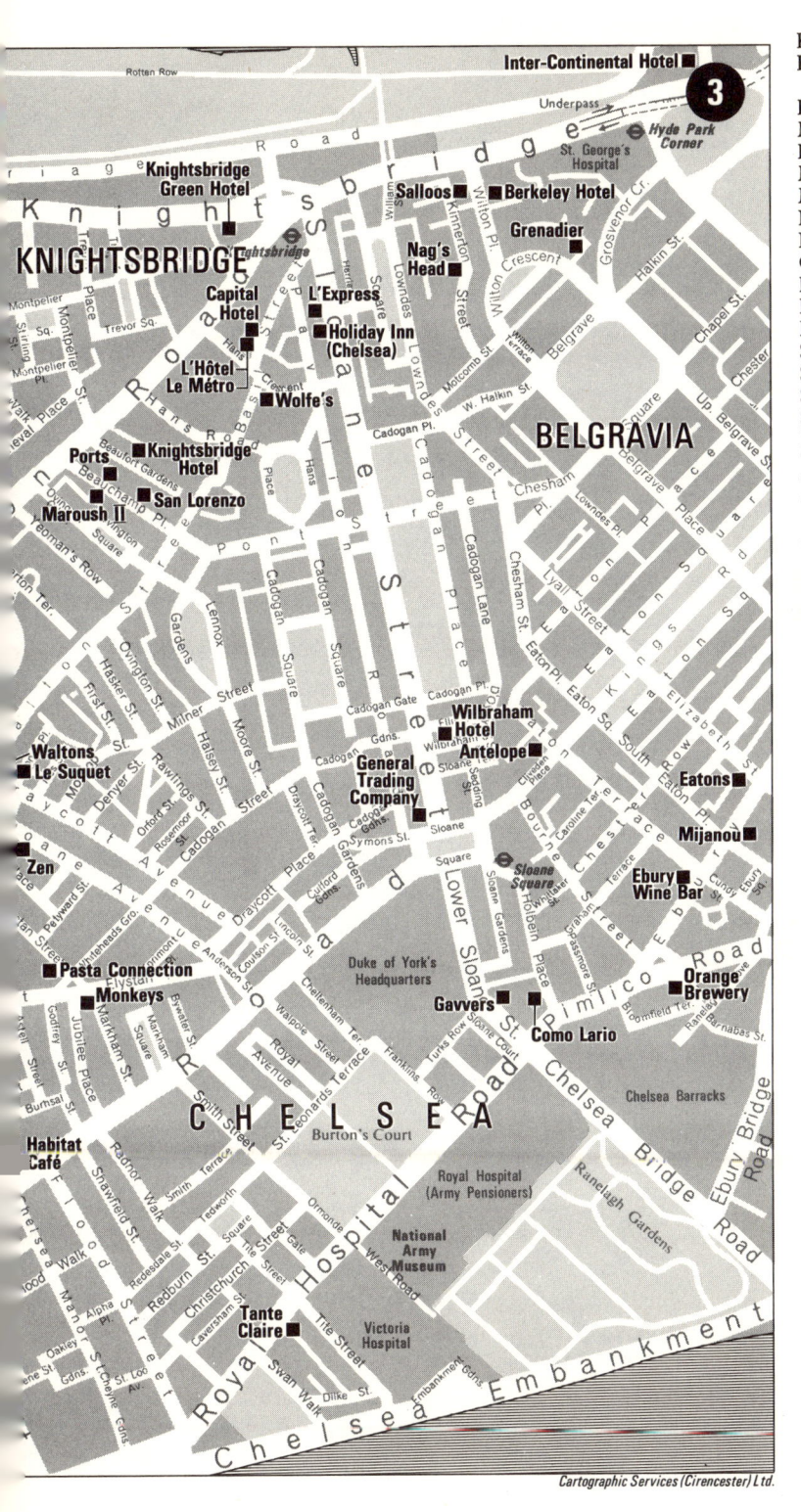

Knightsbridge Hotel 93
Knightsbridge Green
  Hotel 93
Launceston Place 85
Maroush II 94
Le Métro 94
Mijanou 24
Monkeys 31
Nag's Head 94
Number Sixteen 153
Orange Brewery 120
Pasta Connection 31
Ponte Nuovo 154
Ports 95
St Quentin 154
Salloos 95
San Frediano 155
San Lorenzo 96
Le Suquet 32
Tante Claire 32
Tui 155
Victoria and Albert
  Museum 156
Waltons 33
Wilbraham Hotel 25
Wine Gallery 66
Wolfe's 96
Zen 33

Cartographic Services (Cirencester) Ltd.

Athenaeum Hotel 124
Auntie's 158
L'Autre 104
Brewer Street
  Buttery 132
Brown's Hotel 104
Bunch of Grapes 105
Le Caprice 125
Champagne
  Exchange 105
Charing Cross
  Hotel 48
Chez Gerard
  (Mayfair) 105
Chez Gerard
  (Tottenham Court
  Road) 159
Chopper Lump 40
Claridge's 106
Connaught Hotel 106
La Corée 48
Country Life 106
Cranks (Soho) 134
Cranks (Tottenham
  Court Road) 159
Crowns 125
Dorchester Hotel 107
Dukes Hotel 125
Durrants Hotel 99
Efes Kebab House 159
Fortnum & Mason 126
Le Gavroche 107
George 100
Gordon's 49
Graham's Seafare 138
The Greenhouse 108
Green's 126
Al Hamra 109
Han Kuk Hoe
  Kwan 138
Hard Rock Café 109
Hilton Hotel 110
Ho-Ho 110
Hokkai 139
Holiday Inn
  (Mayfair) 111
Ikeda 111
Ikkyu 159
Justin de Blank 112

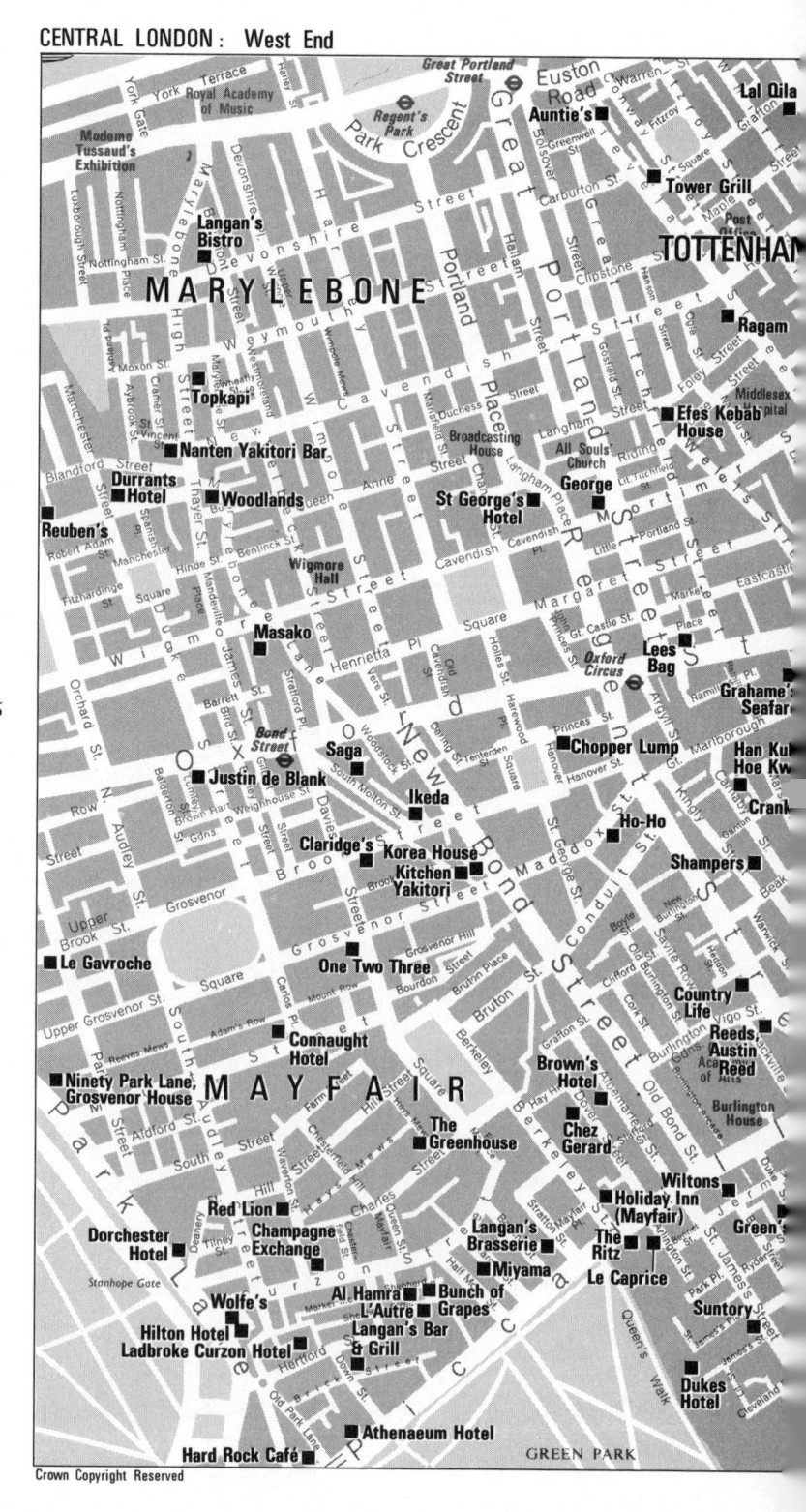

CENTRAL LONDON: West End

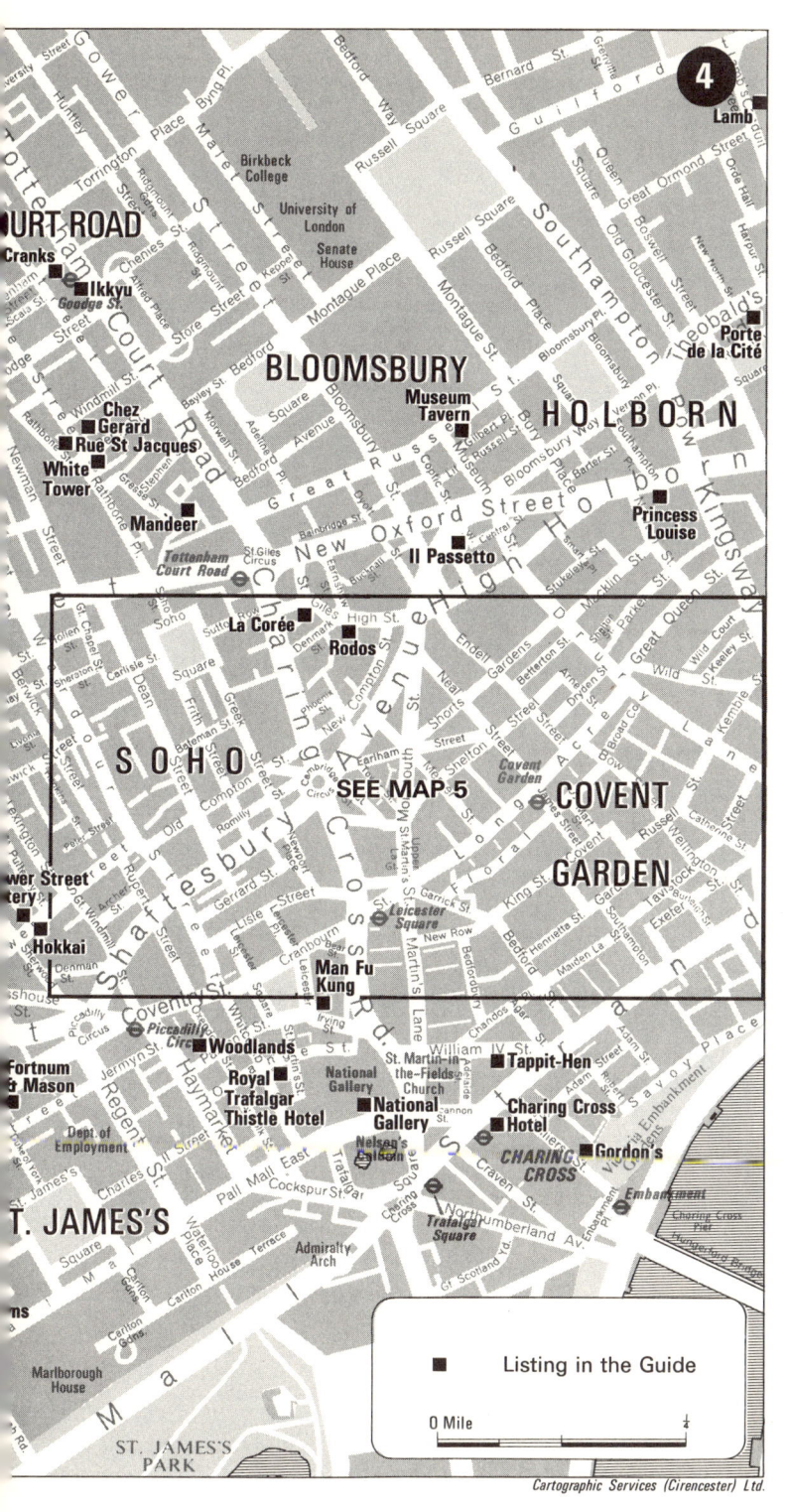

Kitchen Yakitori 112
Korea House 113
Ladbroke Curzon
　Hotel 113
Lal Qila 160
Lamb 26
Langan's Bar &
　Grill 113
Langan's Bistro 100
Langan's Brasserie 114
Lees Bag 41
Mandeer 160
Man Fu Kung 140
Masako 101
Miyama 114
Museum Tavern 26
Nanten Yakitori
　Bar 102
National Gallery 143
Ninety Park Lane,
　Grosvenor
　House 115
One Two Three 116
Il Passetto 144
Porte de la Cité 79
Princess Louise 80
Ragam 161
Red Lion 116
Reeds, Austin Reed 116
Reuben's 102
The Ritz 127
Rodos 146
Royal Trafalgar
　Thistle Hotel 146
Rue St Jacques 161
Saga 117
St George's Hotel 102
Shampers 147
Suntory 128
Tappit-Hen 41
Topkapi 103
Tower Grill 161
White Tower 162
Wiltons 128
Wolfe's 117
Woodlands
　(Marylebone) 103
Woodlands
　(Soho) 149

CENTRAL LONDON: Soho and Covent Garden

Ajimura 46
Alastair Little 130
La Bastide 131
Beotys 132
Boulestin 46
Café Crêperie 132
Le Café du Jardin 47
Café Pelican 47
Calabash 47
Chiang Mai 133
Chuen Cheng Ku 133
Cork and Bottle 133
Cranks 48
Crusting Pipe 40
Desaru 134
The Diamond 135
Diana's Diner 48
Dragon Gate 135
Equatorial 135
Fielding Hotel 49
Food for Thought 49
Frith's 136
Fuji 136
Fung Shing 137
Gay Hussar 137
Govinda's 138
Inigo Jones 50
Joe Allen 50
Joy King Lau 139
Kettners 139
Lamb & Flag 51
Last Days of
  the Raj 140
Magno's Brasserie 51
Mayflower 140
Melati 141
Ming 141
Mon Plaisir 51
Mr Kong 142
Mr Tang 142
Nam Long 142
Neal Street
  Restaurant 52
Neal's Yard Bakery
  & Tea Room 52
New World 143
Old Budapest 144
Olive Tree 144
Orso 53
Poons 145
Punch & Judy 53
Red Fort 145
Rendezvous
  Snack Bar 145
Saigon 146
Satay and Wine 147
Savoy Hotel 53
Segar & Snuff
  Parlour 41
Soho Brasserie 147
Star 148
Taffgood's 148
Unicorn Café Bar 54
Wong Kei 148
Yung's 149

CENTRAL LONDON : The City

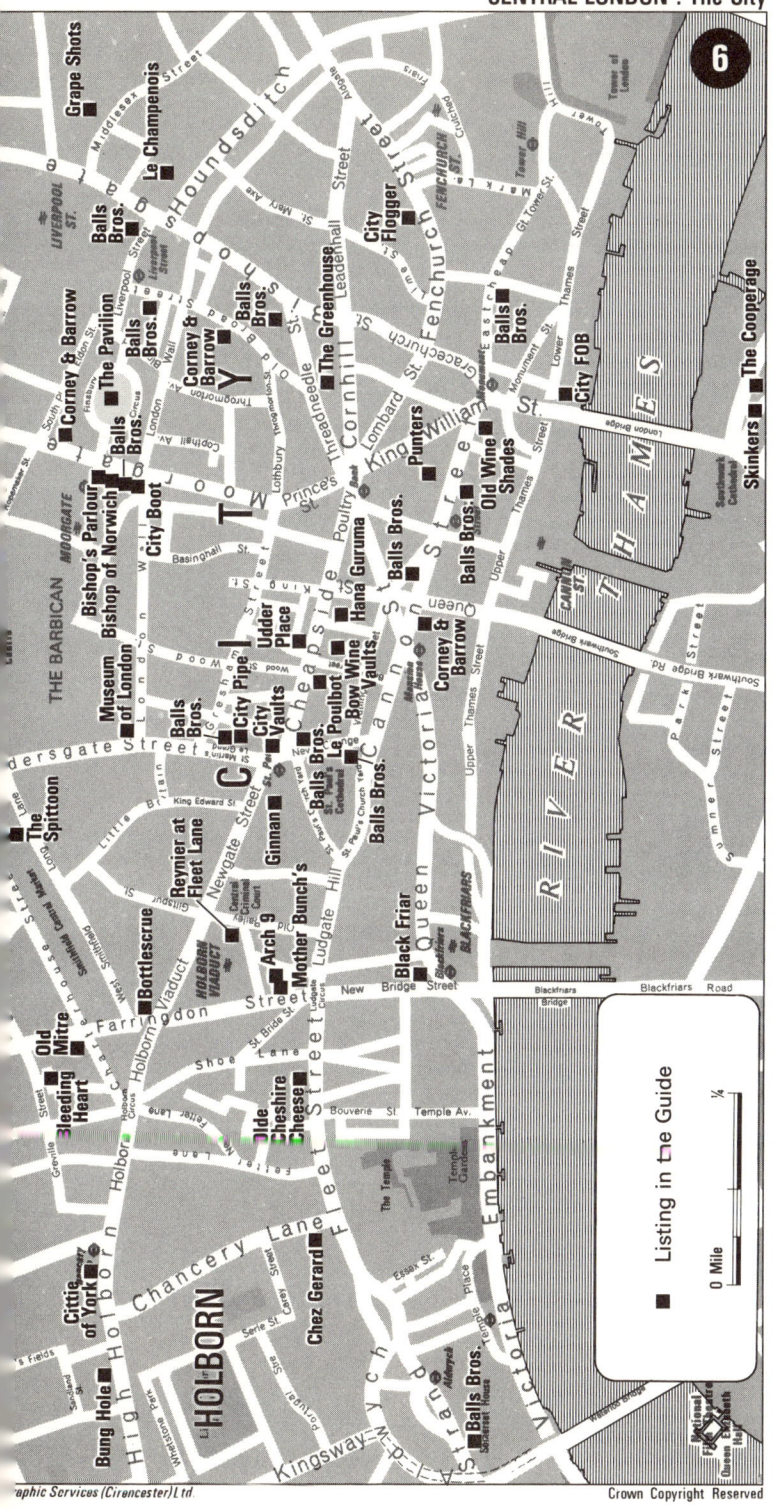

Arch 9　40
Balls Brothers
　(all branches)　35
Bishop of Norwich　40
Bishop's Parlour　40
Black Friar　36
Bleeding Heart　36
Bottlescrue　40
Bow Wine Vaults　36
Bung Hole　40
Le Champenois　38
Chez Gerard　78
Cittie of York　79
City Boot　40
City Flogger　40
City FOB　40
City Pipe　40
City Vaults　40
The Cooperage　40
Corney & Barrow
　(Cannon Street)　38
Corney & Barrow
　(Moorgate)　39
Corney & Barrow
　(Old Broad Street)　39
Fox and Anchor　41
Ginnan　42
Grape Shots　41
The Greenhouse　42
Hana Guruma　42
Mother Bunch's　41
Museum of London　43
Olde Cheshire
　Cheese　43
Old Mitre　43
Old Wine Shades　44
The Pavilion　44
Le Poulbot　45
Punters　45
Reynier at Fleet
　Lane　45
Skinkers　41
The Spittoon　41
Udder Place　41

Reports

As described in the Introduction, the Editors of all the Guides that have gone into making up this book rely on reports sent by members of the public; they particularly value the comments of overseas visitors, who are often better equipped to give an impartial commentary. If you would like to contribute to this venture, which will in turn benefit any future edition of this compilation, please send your reports to: Dept. SD, Consumers' Association Limited, 14 Buckingham Street, London WC2N 6DS, United Kingdom. Reports are welcome on places already in the Guide or ones that you have discovered on your travels that we may not know about. Feel free to write as lengthily or succinctly as you like. All reports or letters will be acknowledged.

Report form

To: Consumers' Association Limited, Dept. SD, 14 Buckingham Street, London WC2N 6DS, United Kingdom

Please forward this report to the Editor(s) of

☐ The Good Food Guide ☐ The Good Hotel Guide

☐ The Budget Good Food Guide ☐ The Good Pub Guide

Name of establishment

Address

(Please give directions for any remote place that you are nominating in order to help us find it.)

Date of visit

Report

(Please comment on atmosphere, food, drink, service, cost, anything else you think interesting or relevant.)

I am not connected directly or indirectly with the management or proprietors

Signed

Name and address (CAPITALS please)

Continue overleaf or use a separate sheet

Report form

To: Consumers' Association Limited, Dept. SD, 14 Buckingham Street, London WC2N 6DS, United Kingdom

Please forward this report to the Editor(s) of

☐ The Good Food Guide ☐ The Good Hotel Guide

☐ The Budget Good Food Guide ☐ The Good Pub Guide

Name of establishment

Address

(Please give directions for any remote place that you are nominating in order to help us find it.)

Date of visit

Report

(Please comment on atmosphere, food, drink, service, cost, anything else you think interesting or relevant.)

I am not connected directly or indirectly with the management or proprietors

Signed

Name and address (CAPITALS please)

Continue overleaf or use a separate sheet

Report form

To: Consumers' Association Limited, Dept. SD, 14 Buckingham Street, London WC2N 6DS, United Kingdom

Please forward this report to the Editor(s) of

☐ The Good Food Guide ☐ The Good Hotel Guide
☐ The Budget Good Food Guide ☐ The Good Pub Guide

Name of establishment

Address

(Please give directions for any remote place that you are nominating in order to help us find it.)

Date of visit

Report

(Please comment on atmosphere, food, drink, service, cost, anything else you think interesting or relevant.)

I am not connected directly or indirectly with the management or proprietors

Signed

Name and address (CAPITALS please)

Continue overleaf or use a separate sheet